Making Americans

Also by Desmond King

In the Name of Liberalism: Illiberal Social Policy in the United States and Britain (Oxford 1999)

Separate and Unequal: Black Americans and the US Federal Government (Oxford 1995)

Actively Seeking Work? The Politics of Unemployment and Welfare Policy in the US and Britain (Chicago 1995)

Making Americans

Immigration, Race, and the Origins of the Diverse Democracy

DESMOND KING

HARVARD UNIVERSITY PRESS
Cambridge, Massachusetts, and London, England

Third printing, 2002

First Harvard University Press paperback edition, 2002

Library of Congress Cataloging-in-Publication Data

King, Desmond S.
    Making Americans : immigration, race, and the origins of the diverse democracy /
Desmond King.
        p.   cm.
    Includes bibliographical references and index.
    ISBN 0-674-00088-9 (cloth)
    ISBN 0-674-00812-X (pbk.)
    1. United States—Emigration and immigration—Government policy—History.
    2. United States—Race relations—History.   I. Title.
JV6483.K54   2000
323.6'0973—dc21   99-087546

For my Father, with love and gratitude

Acknowledgments

For financial assistance to undertake the research necessary for this book, I am grateful to the Mellon Trust at Oxford University. I have received access to primary sources and courteous assistance from archivists at the National Archives and the Manuscript Division of the Library of Congress in Washington, D.C., and the Houghton Library at Harvard, as well as from Judith May-Sapko at the Truman State University's Pickler Memorial Library and from librarians at Rhodes House Library, Oxford. Part of the material presented in Chapter 6 appeared in *In the Name of Liberalism* published by Oxford University Press in 1999. Professor Noah Pickus, of Duke University, generously made available to me draft chapters from his important forthcoming study of U. S. citizenship, for which I am grateful.

I have received both encouragement for this project and a range of valuable comments and suggestions from colleagues, given informally and at seminars in Oxford, Rochester, and Paris, and at meetings of the American Political Science Association. I should like to acknowledge this support and to thank in particular Eric Bleich, Nigel Bowles, Alan Brinkley, Michael Burleigh, Dominic Byatt, Edward Carmines, Michael Comber, David Goldey, Randall Hansen, Frederick Harris, Victoria Hattam, James Hollifield, John Holmwood, Eric Kaufmann, Daniel Kryder, Robert Lieberman, Ian Haney López, Gerry Mackie, Paul Martin, Ernest May, Lois McNay, Michelle Mitchell, Serena

Olsaretti, Noah Pickus, Byron Shafer, Rogers Smith, Marc Stears, Julie Suk, Reed Ueda, Alan Ware, Patrick Weil, Margaret Weir, Mark Wickham-Jones, and Gavin Williams. None of them is responsible for the views expressed here.

At Harvard University Press, Jeff Kehoe has been an admirable model of support during the book's production. Jeff's commitment to the project has been invaluable. Carolyn Cowey has provided unstinting support at every stage of the book's research and writing, for which I am immensely grateful.

Contents

Tables

CHAPTER ONE

Introduction

Americans' toleration of diversity has always been easier in principle than in practice. A multiracial and multicultural society built on immigration, both involuntary and voluntary, the United States has nonetheless agonized at various stages about whom it should permit to enter, reside, and naturalize.[1] One of the most dramatic shifts in the history of the United States, between the nineteenth and twentieth centuries, occurred in policy toward immigrants. From broadly accepting all comers in the former century, in the twentieth century, U.S. immigration policy shifted in the 1920s to a finely filtered regime of selection. This restrictionist agenda developed from the 1880s, a good century after the founding of the republic. In this book[2] I use archival research to examine this policy's formulation and illustrate how the enacted restrictions, based on racial quotas and eugenic categories, contributed to the formation of the United States "multiple traditions."[3] Immigration policy proved to be a forum in which eugenists and eugenic arguments flourished. Eugenic priorities link the debates and arguments advanced by restrictionists and Americanizers in the years before 1930, coalescing political interests with a superficial scientific authenticity.[4] I argue that the debates and analyses about U. S. immigration and immigration policy conducted in the three decades prior to 1929 illuminate how different groups' values have always been present in the United States, a significant precursor to the recent multicultural and group rights politics. This debate was conceived in terms of desirable and undesirable immigrants—a discussion almost entirely confined to immigrants from European countries, since nonwhites were unwelcome and, in fact, Asians had been excluded—which not only cemented judgments about particular types of Europeans but also fed and reinforced prevailing views of groups already present in the United States. The most salient of these groups were African Americans, whose inferior status and second-class citizenship—enshrined in jim crow laws and assumed, if only en passant, in pseudoscientific arguments about racial and eugenic classifications to be unassimilable—appeared to be consolidated in these decades.[5] The immigration debate served, in the long run, to reinforce the racial inequality faced by African Americans in the U.S. polity.[6] Inferiority was imputed also to Native Americans and Chinese immigrants, according to Ronald Takaki, who writes that "what enabled businessmen to degrade the Chinese into a subservient laboring caste was the dominant ideology that defined America as a racially homogeneous society and Americans as white. The status of racial inferiority assigned to the Chinese had been prefigured in the black and Indian past."[7]

Detailed consideration of immigration policy and its consequences assumes intellectual interest because they illustrate a defining characteristic about the United States polity. A political system that celebrates, both rhetorically and institutionally, individualism and plurality of group identity and allegiance has historically subscribed to a unifying conception of Americanization: this is the only politically plausible means of overcoming a diversity that, left without such a unifying, ideological support, might become politically destructive. This conception is the only stabilizing political solution, though it is not necessarily stable. It is not surprising that the meaning of "American" has dogged and haunted the United States from de Crèvecoeur's (1782) seminal "melting pot" formulation to the recent (1997) U.S. Commission on Immigration Reform.[8] Is there a common set of values acquired through socialization or, for immigrants, Americanization, that constitutes de Crèvecoeur's famous "new man," or have these processes been the means through which a dominant image of "American-ness" has been artificially constructed to hold a fragile and centrifugal society intact? The resolution of this dilemma has occurred, I propose, by the promotion of a unifying framework or a set of ideas that have proved, over time, sufficiently broad to facilitate a multiplicity of views; however, as the ensuing chapters document, this resolution has often been achieved at the price of the short-term suppression or the neglect of some groups' or individuals' values, limitations that have left their mark on U.S. politics. This characteristic has encouraged the scholarly imperative to unearth, in Rogers Smith's phrase, the U.S.'s "multiple traditions."

I argue that the choices made about immigration policy in the 1920s—and the reasons for those decisions—played a fundamental role in shaping democracy and ideas about group rights in the United States. By establishing barriers to immigrants, the policy-makers privileged an Anglo-Saxon conception of U. S. identity, thereby rejecting the claims of other traditions in the nation. Immigration policy also helped solidify the second-class position of nonwhites, notably African Americans, already exposed to segregated race relations,[9] a judgment mirrored in Rogers Smith's observations about Progressives: "perhaps the most far-reaching consequence of the government's embrace of racial rationales for imperial rule and immigration and naturalization restrictions was the manner in which they strengthened political coalitions and ideological defenses supporting segregation."[10] Federal public policy in the 1920s presented a two-sided discrimination, externally toward certain types of immigrants and domestically in the system of segregation imposed on African Americans, complemented by the Americanization process that also disregarded black citizens. Structuring this discriminatory framework was a conception of American identity or nationality, that was biased toward the white Anglo-Saxon element of the U. S. population over others. By circumscribing the dominant image of American identity, the possibilities of U.S. citizenship were also affected in a number of ways. First, the common retrospective narrative of a gradually unfolding and expanding American citizenship is rendered problematic, since efforts systematically to prevent this broadening are so readily identifiable; a punctuated development path, at best, is more accurate. Second, the possibility of acknowledging a U.S. identity composed of "multiple traditions" was preempted by policy-makers' attempts to impose uniformity and to devalue diversity, a course explicitly endorsed in national policy in the 1920s toward resident aliens and potential immigrants. Third, since these processes were realized, in large part, through an active strategy of Americanization, this concept was rendered troublesome, more commonly associated with division than integration. As the historian Gary Gerstle tellingly observes, "any analysis of Americanization, past and present, must accord coercion a role in the making of Americans."[11] Yet the 1997 commission holds out for the "Americanization of new immigrants, that is the cultivation of a shared commitment to the American values of liberty, democracy and equal opportunity," and cites approvingly the late Texan congresswoman Barbara Jordan's effort to dissociate the term from its earlier, largely racialist, incarnation: "'that word [Americanization] earned a bad reputation when it was stolen by racists and xenophobes in the 1920s. But it is our word, and we are taking it back.'"[12]

The legacy of these debates and decisions undertaken in the 1920s was to create a set of fundamental questions about U.S. identity, membership, and citizenship in American political development. These issues include the rejection of cultural pluralism for a policy of assimilation in respect to immigrants; the linking of Americanization to a specific—and in some ways, exclusionary—conception of U.S. identity (for example, before the Second World War, as predominantly white); the importance of what Gerstle terms a "coercive" dynamic in the formation of U.S. identity, since ethnic and group loyalties or values did not evaporate but were simply marginalized;[13] and ultimately posing the question whether Americanization can be an autonomous and valuable process in a society with competing views about the content of such a process. When consideration of the position of African Americans, who were deprived by law of their full rights and equality of opportunity until the 1960s, is added to this context, some purchase on the way in which the boundaries of citizenship excluded both this group and immigrants from beyond western Europe is attained. The historical and political juncture of the 1920s reveals important roots of subsequent developments in the United States, especially the criteria for full membership of the U.S. polity and the relative rights of selected groups in the polity. These effects were both ideological and institutional. Ideologically, the political debate about who was appropriate to be admitted as members of the U.S. and who qualified under the Americanization process ineluctably defined some groups (for example, southern Europeans) as unsuitable and others (for example, African Americans) as irrelevant. Institutionally, these limitations and assumptions were effected in policy through the national origins quota system, enacted in the 1920s, which consolidated the existing exclusion of Asian immigrants by extending restrictions to finely drawn divisions within the potential European American immigrant population.

In this book I argue that the interaction of these ideological and institutional dynamics is most convincingly understood as a major part of the historical process through which U.S. citizenship was established in ways that created problems for policy-makers at a later period. Historically and politically, the interesting question becomes why, from the Progressive era to the 1930s, when a variety of possible future paths were available in terms of immigration and the contours of American citizenship, the narrow path was pursued.[14] As Gary Gerstle has argued, in his major interpretation of American liberalism from the Progressive Era to the 1960s, "the first demands for cultural pluralism—what we now call multiculturalism—date from this [Progressive] era."[15] The ethnically and racially restrictionist path was chosen, an option that narrowed, in the short term, the United States's conception of membership and citizenship. It is also necessary to consider these developments dynamically: although the immigration decisions taken in the 1920s combined with the prevailing discriminatory segregationist regime toward African Americans presented a polity insensitive or, indeed, hostile to diversity, thirty years later these restrictions were powerfully challenged and displaced, and a politics based on the demand for equal rights was initiated. Nonetheless, the decisions and policies of the 1920s constituted a powerful mobilization of the ascriptive strands in U.S. political culture, and their dissimulation was a prerequisite for the broadening of U.S. values and traditions represented by multiculturalism and the strengthening of ethnic group attachments. I therefore do not propose a static view of American political development but do contend that to understand aspects of contemporary debates about group membership and multiculturalism, it is valuable to consider how such debates resonate historically.

The immigration debates and decisions of the 1920s are germane to understanding the more general patterns of discrimination within the United States and their place in American political development. This period was one in which most African Americans labored under the segregationist regime. Prior to the 1920s, the restrictions imposed in immigration policy concerned potential Asian immigrants; however, the legislation enacted in the mid-1920s drew distinctions among European Americans, favoring northwestern over southern and eastern Europeans, partly for explicitly eugenic reasons. These decisions, which were undertaken in respect to white immigrants, acted to re-confirm the problematic place of nonwhites in the U.S. polity's conception of membership and definition of American identity, residents who were consequently perceived as located outside the Americanization drive of the 1910s and 1920s. Policy-makers were exercised about differences among white Europeans at a time when, in some states, Asians were prohibited from buying property and excluded from immigration and when most African Americans were denied civil and voting rights. This latter arrangement enabled policy-makers to make immigrant policy a way of contributing to American identity as principally white and Anglo-Saxon.[16] Although mostly not consciously racist, the eugenic-inspired policy-makers in Congress and their advisers nonetheless presumed a white identity for the dominant conception of U.S. citizenship, an inclination heightened by the character of the post-1918 Americanization movement. It is unremarkable that the dismantling of the discriminatory immigration regime in 1965 occurred concurrently with the passage of civil rights legislation for African Americans.

Establishing a direct link between the politics of the 1920s and those since 1960 is fruitless; it is not my intention to do so. Instead, the purpose of this book's detailed consideration of the formation of immigration policy in the 1920s is better historically to ground the analysis and understanding of the politics of contemporary multiculturalism and identity politics in the United States. The sociologist Nathan Glazer, among others, plainly recognizes the importance of such an exercise when he observes that "'multiculturalism' is a term that many of us who have studied immigration and ethnic diversity might have found perfectly satisfactory to cover our sense some decades ago that American history and social studies needed to incorporate a larger recognition of American diversity."[17] Without such a historical perspective, making sense of some of these modern political issues is immensely difficult. The United States is a political system constituted by diverse elements, and recognizing this diversity is a means to fortifying its democratic institutions.

Structure of the Book

Chapter 2 rehearses the crucial role of immigration in the development of U. S. society, identifying major trends before 1900. I identify the dominant "Anglo-Saxon" image of the United States in the nineteenth century and introduce the key terms with which immigration is discussed. Chapter 3 provides a detailed demographic profile of the "new immigrants" arriving from the 1880s, whose characteristics were meticulously examined by the Dillingham Commission that was set up in 1907. I then turn to the institutional means through which a conception of U.S. identity as Anglo-Saxon was fostered, examining in Chapter 4 the Americanization movement of the 1910s and 1920s. Chapter 5 documents how a view of the dominant U. S. nationality, or "race," in eugenic arguments, structured the perception of the new immigrants, and found them severely wanting. The chapter reviews the position of African Americans at the time of these debates: the discussion illustrates how this group was separated from the immigration debate because of its alleged unassimilability with the dominant nationality. The labor economist John Commons was one of several commentators to equate such issues, remarking in 1907 that "the race problem in the South is only one extreme of the same problem in the great cities of the North."[18] Chapter 6 explains how eugenists' research influenced the restrictionist movement of the 1920s, whose aims were enacted in the 1924 Johnson-Reed Act, the subject of Chapter 7.

Chapters 8 and 9 deal with the legacies and consequences of these earlier choices. The defense and eventual abrogation (in 1965) of the national origins system of immigration is detailed in Chapter 8. Chapter 9 considers the legacies of immigration choices in respect to the revival of ethnic politics and the diffusion of multiculturalism. Chapter 10 considers how the United States is building a national political culture that is respectful of diversity and the values of the different groups constitutive of its citizens. I emphasize the striking capacity of U. S. citizens to confront and resolve the country's uncomfortable historical legacies, and then I conclude that the new regard for diverse cultural and political traditions is a logical manifestation of this ability.

PART ONE

Immigrant America

CHAPTER TWO

Immigration and American Political Development

The formulation of immigration policy in the early twentieth century rapidly focused on the suitability and quantity of immigrants arriving at U.S. ports. A debate principally about European immigrants, it was fueled by alarm about southern and eastern European immigrants; they were considered less desirable than those migrants emanating from northwestern Europe, which was the dominant source of nineteenth-century immigration. Hostility to economic migrants became subsumed into a more general fear of alien groups and so-called racially "undesirable" immigrants. It was the unassimilability of new immigrants—in terms of several criteria such as race, mental competence, or criminality—that vexed policy-makers (an unassimilability often presumed in respect to Mexicans).[1] This anxiety prompted racial restrictions. As Robert Divine concludes, the restrictionist quota-based system that was formalized in the 1920s substituted "the traditional belief that the European who came across the Atlantic could be remade by the power of the American environment and the democratic system . . . with . . . racist theory."[2] The abandonment of the universal right of entry subverted the traditional faith in individual self-worth as a basis for selection, superseding it with racially informed notions of "group" and what later proved to be a problematic conception of the "American race."

Restrictionist legislation was effected in two stages: first, the allocation of quotas to European countries within an aggregate immigrant figure, a policy that advantaged northwestern over southeastern Europeans; and second, the refinement of this quota system into one based on the principle of "national origins," which distinguished Americans of direct "settler descent" from all other European groups, a distinction common in American culture and defended by the Anglo-Saxon elite. In Willa Cather's novel *Sapphira and the Slave Girl,* set in the 1850s, the author records that the main family, the Colberts, "were termed 'immigrants,'—as were all settlers who did not come from the British Isles."[3] Late-nineteenth-century legislation anticipated part of this new policy in its exclusion of epileptics, so-called "idiots," and lunatics from the right to immigrate and in the restriction of Chinese immigrants.

These restrictions reflected a particular conception of American national identity. A Tocquevillean view of U. S. identity as white and Anglo-Saxon[4] dominated the conception of an "American" in the decades before the 1950s; maintaining or strengthening this view structured the debates about immigration restriction from the 1880s, complementing the treatment of African Americans (and discernible in white supremacist doctrines such as Manifest Destiny).[5] This conception has two elements. First, the key makers of U. S. immigration policy traced American identity to the country's white English inheritance and wanted this emphasis enshrined in legislation to ensure that new immigrants were assimilable on these terms; plainly, African Americans already present in the United States were not considered assimilable. Thus, in his influential study of American democracy, Alexis de Tocqueville refers to the "English race in America" or "Anglo Americans" as terms synonymous with that of "American," and he reserves discussion of both African Americans and American Indians to a separate chapter; indeed, he sees these as two separate races distinct from the American race and reflects on the incompatibility of the "three races." De Tocqueville marshals a view of racial differences commonplace to the 1840s: "if we reason from what passes in the world, we should almost say that the European is to the other races of mankind what man himself is to the lower animals: he makes them subservient to his use, and when he cannot subdue he destroys them."[6] This subordinate position informs de Tocqueville's perception of what constituted the dominant American nationality, and it was a view promoted by those who were politically and intellectually powerful in the nineteenth century and who were resistant to a broader conception of American nationality.

Second, American policy-makers and politicians believed in the openness of U.S. society to immigrants and generously conceived of the opportunities available to them. For example, a speech in 1918 by Secretary of the Interior Franklin Lane, which was entitled "The Answer of the Foreign Born," is characterized by a romantic account of how opportunity was open to all in the United States:

> and we, the foreign born, are here now to do our part, our full part, in the making of America. All the thousands of years of upward struggle, the climb from serfdom up, has led to the Land of Equal Chance. We fled from The Man Above. Here we have no master but ourselves. Our hats come off to genius, not to rank. The great house on the hill is the home of one who once was a section hand. If Justice fails in this land ours is the fault. If the torch of liberty fades or fails, ours be the blame. If our flag falls all the eager and struggling ones in other lands will lose heart, all those who painted its starry field in hopeful blue and drew its stripes in courageous red will reproach us forever more.[7]

This statement not only ignored members of the U.S. polity whose forebears arrived involuntarily or been displaced but also conflicted with both American history and politics. These were common omissions. The presidential commission, established by President Truman, which vigorously criticized the immigration law, retained a version of U.S. history that privileged one group of immigrants over others: "[I]n a short period of human history the people of the United States built this country from a wilderness to one of the most powerful and prosperous nations in the world. The people who built America were 40 million immigrants who have come since the Mayflower, and their descendants. We are still a vigorous and growing nation, and the economic, social and other benefits available to us, the descendants of immigrant forebears, are constantly expanding."[8] Thus, even critics of discriminatory immigration laws subscribed to a sanguine view of U.S. history and failed to recognize that not all voices and traditions received equal representation in the prevailing conception of U. S. identity. In particular, the descendants of involuntary immigrants and the "new immigrants" of the late nineteenth century were consigned to a subordinate place.

I undertake several tasks in this chapter.[9] Principally, the chapter sets out the intellectual agenda against which immigration policy has come to assume significance and introduces the main concepts in which this discussion is pursued. The main thesis of the chapter is how debates about immigration in the 1920s galvanized three enduring issues in American political development that, when combined, constituted an Anglo-Saxon Americanism. These issues are the appropriate content and boundaries of any notion of Americanization for immigrants; the historic sources of multiculturalism; and the influence of immigration choices in determining—to employ current language—the "whiteness" of U.S. identity. These issues have proved enduring ones in part because of how the immigration debate of the 1920s unfolded and of how it influenced American political development.

Theoretically, this study engages with the efforts of those scholars seeking to develop a richer analysis of the traditions constitutive of American political culture and to find a compatibility between the competing claims of universal citizenship, group traditions, and diversity. This book contributes to that scholarship by examining the United States's selective policy in the 1920s, a policy that operated most forcefully externally toward prospective immigrants (when, in Margo Anderson's description, U.S. immigration policy was set in a "kind of racialist concrete"[10]) and that was complemented domestically in an intense Americanization campaign and in segregated race relations. The suspicion of diversity in the decades leading up to and including the 1920s stemmed from the political dominance of one group's conception of U. S. identity: that the identity was constituted by a white Anglo-American inheritance, the conception propagated in the Americanization movement. In this view, the melting pot assimilationist model implied first that those permitted to engage in assimilation should be largely preselected and second that the purpose of the process was to produce not the unpredictable outcome of a genuine melting-pot mixture but a citizenry consistent with a prior conception of American identity.

The Melting Pot and Americanization

The single most important issue about immigration in twentieth-century-America has been the assimilability of immigrants. Opponents of immigration have consistently alighted on the problem of immigrant suitability to become members of the U.S. polity, a suitability measured against an Anglo-American conception of American identity. How this process of "becoming American" has been conceived, therefore, assumes great significance. The dominant approach has been one that presumes that assimilation through the melting pot has functioned to Americanize immigrants.

The Melting Pot

From the late nineteenth century, a conception of American society as a hybrid melting pot that was derived from its mixture of immigrants quickly became the orthodoxy about how immigration shaped the political culture. This melting-pot process was famously described a hundred years earlier by the Frenchman St. Jean de Crèvecoeur:

> [W]hence came all these people? they are a mixture of English, Scotch, Irish, French, Dutch, Germans, and Swedes. From this promiscuous breed, that race now called American have arisen . . .
>
> What, then, is the American, this new man? He is either an European, or the descendant of an European; hence that strange mixture of blood, which you will find in no other country. I could point out to you a family whose grandfather was an Englishman, whose wife was Dutch, whose son married a French woman, and whose present four sons have now four wives of different nations. *He* is an American, who, leaving behind him all his ancient prejudices and manners, receives new ones from the new mode of life he has embraced, the new government he obeys, and the new rank he holds. Here individuals of all nations are melted into a new race of men, whose labours and posterity will one day cause great changes in the world.[11]

The term "melting pot," as a metaphor for American life, received a popularity boost in 1908 when Israel Zangwill's play of that title was performed to acclaim in New York. It included a eulogy to the new nation:

> [T]here she lives, the great Melting Pot. Listen! Can't you hear the roaring and bubbling? There gapes her mouth—the harbor where a thousand mammoth feeders come from the ends of the world to pour on their human freight. Ah, what a stirring and a seething! Celt and Latin, Slav and Teuton, Greek and Syrian—black and yellow. Yes, East and West, and North and South,—how the great Alchemist melts and fuses them with his purging flame! Here shall they all unite to build the Republic of Man and the kingdom of God. Ah, what is the glory of Rome

and Jerusalem where all nations and races come to worship and look back, compared with the glory of America, where all races come to labor and look forward.[12]

A literary version of this vision is presented in Saul Bellow's character Augie March, who begins his eponymous adventures with this famous declaration: "I am an American, Chicago born and go at things as I have taught myself, free-style and will make the record in my own way."[13]

Even at the time of Zangwill's play, the melting-pot idea was viewed with suspicion by some groups in the United States. One German author noted that "for us German-Americans the teaching of this play [*The Melting Pot*] is simply a mixture of insipid phrases and unhistorical thinking." Germans did not want to melt and quite happily combined being both German and American: "we did not come into this American nation as an expelled and persecuted race, seeking help and protection, but as a part of the nation, entitled to the same consideration as any other." Americanization was irrelevant, "for we are Americans in the political sense."[14]

That the melting pot was neither an open nor an inclusive process was first formally demonstrated in the Chinese Exclusion Act of 1882. By the end of the 1920s, the melting-pot norm was tarnished. The discriminatory system enacted in that decade, which was formalized in the national origins regulations, was designed to limit immigration to certain groups already assimilated into American identity. Immigrants were to be selected on the grounds of their cultural, racial, and eugenic compatibility with the dominant conception of U. S. political culture and its people, an Anglo-Saxon conception. More fundamentally, the melting pot historically and institutionally had no room for African Americans. For this reason, in his important book, *White Over Black,* Winthrop Jordan refutes the whole melting pot thesis, arguing instead that Americans were "modified Englishmen rather than products of a European amalgam" and therefore that American identity was not such a hybrid. This configuration had profound consequences for African Americans' position in the U. S. polity, as Jordan explains, writing about the post-Revolutionary decades: "Americans' conclusions about themselves, no matter how vague or inconsistent, virtually precluded their arriving at certain conclusions about Negroes. Because they viewed the architecture of their culture as modified-English rather than fused-English, most Americans were not led to ponder the dynamics of cultural amalgamation in America, much less the pronounced African element involved. In fact there was little consideration given to the possibility that Negro language and manners had contributed to American uniqueness."[15] This telling description retains its validity and urgency. Thus, the melting pot framework, despite its allegedly inclusionary character, in practice contributed to that view of U. S. nationality as a white one. For many of those active in the immigration debate, no thought at all was given to the experience of the African Americans among them, descendants of slaves. Thus, Woodrow Wilson's frequent panegyrics about the United States consciously excluded involuntary immigrants: he told one group of newly naturalized citizens in 1915 that "this country is constantly drinking strength out of new sources by *the voluntary association with it* of great bodies of strong men and forward-looking women of other lands."[16] I draw attention to this omission not especially to castigate Wilson but to underline the intellectual and political context within which the discussion about immigration was conducted.

The melting-pot metaphor had particular force in the 1900s because Americans could look back on the massive immigration of the nineteenth century, the first great wave of immigrants.[17] This latter population consisted principally of Irish Catholics and German Protestants, the former's religion immediately conflicting with the Protestantism that some Americans believed inherent to the United States (a conflict for German Catholics too). Protestantism was linked fundamentally to the "Englishness" of the original settlers, and it fostered immediate barriers and distinctions, as Dinnerstein et al summarize: "[T]he English, as did other peoples, regarded those who differed from them as inferior. Black Africans, because of their color and customs, were both feared and scorned. Toward Europeans from the continent, whose ways varied only slightly from their own, Englishmen felt a certain kinship, but they regarded their own practices as superior."[18] The hostility or indifference of the descendants of these first settlers extended in time to African Americans to the waves of European immigrants in the nineteenth century, including the Irish, and to American Indians. Thus, Francis Prucha discerns a profound Protestantism motivating the humanitarian "friends of the Indian" reformers of the late nineteenth century, a Protestantism that "merged almost imperceptibly into Americanism." He explains that "in a period when traditional values seemed threatened by hordes of immigrants coming to American shores—immigrants from eastern and southern Europe who seemed to fit only with difficulty into the accepted culture—the reformers insisted on the Americanization of all unfamiliar elements."[19] An equal concern about the unassimilability of the European groups—on grounds of religious, cultural, or ethnic differences—exercised the existing American population. The reason for these attitudes lies in the conception of "American-ness" dominant in the nineteenth century.

Such a view has been advanced by other scholars. Barbara Solomon examines the construction of an Anglo-Saxon identity among descendants of the first English settlers in New England: to many New Englanders of the 1870s and 1880s, "the American was already recognizable by definite traits. Citizens of Yankee stock were likely to attribute such traits to English roots and to believe that they were maintained from generation to generation, in a swiftly changing nation, by qualities derived from Anglo-Saxon forebears."[20] The historian Jack Pole comments that among the "undisclosed assumptions" about U. S. democracy held by political leaders, from reformist intellectuals to labor spokespeople, the "most basic" was that "of a pervasive homogeneity of national character."[21] Interchangeability and assimilability were deemed necessary conditions for citizenship. Citing a view attributable to both Woodrow Wilson and Theodore Roosevelt, Pole writes that "both these men believed that the character of American nationality was fixed in the period from 1776 to 1787." As a consequence, "all subsequent mingling was a process of continued assimilation into the original type," whose "basic qualities in such fundamentals as law, education, and religion" were immutable.[22] Any melting-pot process was not as random as the rhetoric might imply. Woodrow Wilson's fears about racial mixing and about the threat posed by immigrants were of a long-standing character, since he had expressed concern in the 1880s about southern and eastern European immigrants: he concluded that they possessed "neither skill nor energy nor any initiative of quick intelligence."[23] Wilson's history of the American people was assiduously cited by W. B. Griffith in the footnotes accompanying his movie *Birth of a Nation,* a racially biased narrative of the United States's history. Wilson's views were certainly not unique, not least among Progressives.

The melting pot is a term still widely used despite its partial description of historical practices. The populist Peter Salins eulogizes the "magic of assimilation" provided by such a framework, declaring biblically that "assimilation, American style . . . is nothing less than a miracle." He argues that the United States has achieved "an almost impossible feat: It has forged a culturally unified nation, hundreds of millions strong, spanning a continent, at peace with itself, out of people drawn, literally, from every corner of the world."[24] Salins endorses de Crèvecoeur's thesis that a "new race" was created through assimilation. He writes that "this concept of Americans constituting an entirely 'new race' distinct from any particular ethnic stock is the bedrock of assimilation because it so completely contradicts the ethnic particularism that is assimilationism's great enemy."[25] But this early view was a partial one in that not all groups were equally welcomed as potential members of the melting pot. This limitation seriously qualifies continuing advocacy of the melting pot as an inclusive doctrine. Furthermore, Salins's employment of the term "new race" to describe Americans demonstrates a curiously innocent use of this term: is it meant sociologically or biologically or in some other sense?[26] Inadequate and imprecise though the term "melting pot" may be, it is still regularly employed in discussions of immigration and U.S. politics.

Americanization

The presumption of a single national identity precluded diversity and devalued some ethnic or group traditions in comparison with others. Here the 1920s had a crucial effect, since legislation formalized this national Anglo-Saxon identity under the guise of a "melting-pot" ideology. Increasingly the narrowness of the assimilationist assumptions of the melting pot have stimulated a more critical appraisal of the Americanization implied by this hybrid elixir. But historically it was the proposition that new immigrants failed to be sufficiently American that enabled populist Americanization to flourish.

The construction of an Anglo-Saxon conception[27] of the desirable American was consolidated between the 1890s and the 1920s when restrictionist rhetoric and anti-immigrant sentiment peaked, as Barbara Solomon notes: "[I]n the process of solving American problems, the native conception of democratic society became somewhat Anglicized. The country which had received all the European nationalities, as well as the Chinese, Japanese, and Negroes, was offered another, higher image of the American: Anglo-Saxon in coloring, lineaments, and physique; Protestant in religion; masterly in nation-building." At this time, "the abstract ideal of homogeneity, so lacking in the concrete land of diverse Americans, dominated the thoughts of most native educated citizens."[28] That Americans in the nineteenth century held a particular conception of national identity, which excluded many groups, has gained increasing currency amongst scholars. Rogers Smith suggests that this narrow ethnic conception of American identity arose from what he terms an "ascriptive Americanism," rooted in a perception of Americans as white and Protestant.[29] Such a view favored a process of Americanization based on assimilation rather than on the celebration of diversity. But in doing so, this view lay the foundations for strong group loyalties, which were suppressed in the short run.

This implication was apparent to observers in the 1910s and 1920s when the "Americanization as assimilation" movement was at its zenith. Writing about Japanese immigrants in 1922, the sociologist Robert Park observed that "the isolation of the Japanese in America has the added effect of making them keenly self-conscious, as a race. This leads to analysis of the position of their group in the country" and to "point out danger signs,"[30] a tendency doubtless heightened by the Supreme Court's ruling in the 1922 *Ozawa* decision that Japanese were ineligible for citizenship because they were not white.[31] In a related point, Matthew Jacobson argues that Anglo-Saxon was "a racialist unit of meaning" that was exclusionary in two ways when articulated in the 1840s: "it separated racially 'pure' Americans from 'mongrelized' and 'degenerate' Mexicans on the one front; and it divided virtuous, self-governing Anglo-Saxon citizens from pathetic Celtic newcomers on the other."[32] The crucial point is how the notion of Anglo-Saxon, effected in Americanization, defined some groups in and others out of the dominant conception of U.S. national identity.

The hostility of restrictionists toward southern and eastern European immigrants echoed reactions toward a previous generation of immigrants. Thus, by the middle and late nineteenth century, American society had developed a strong nativist movement, whose members defined themselves as defenders of a genuine "Americanism." The Catholic Irish were the principal object of its hostility.[33] This movement further solidified a definition of an American. Germans, despite their foreign language (and in some cases Catholicism), were welcomed because of their "reputation for hard work, thrift, and determination." In contrast, the disembarking of three million Irish between the 1840s and 1850s stimulated hostility. They challenged the United States's religious composition: "their Catholicism, at the core of all their values, came into direct conflict with the Protestantism of old-stock Americans and most of the other European immigrants."[34] Irish laborers took more unskilled jobs than German immigrants who mostly occupied skilled positions. Both groups were disliked for their Catholicism, especially the Irish, while their politics were feared. The historian Ray Billington records that by the 1850s, the "solidarity of the foreign-born vote, whether cast for Whigs or Democrats, created the impression that the immigrants were all acting in accord with a general command and that that command came from the Catholic Church."[35]

The Know-Nothing (or American) Party—vigorously nativist in its tenets—flourished in this conflictual and tense environment, as new members of the U. S. polity vied with the established mores and customs of the old. The Know-Nothing movement was premised on a hostility to foreigners and non-Americans, a hostility crystallized by the movement's attitude to Catholicism, a "hatred" toward which "held members of the Know-Nothing party together."[36] It arose, according to Matthew Jacobson, because of the excessive inclusivity of the 1790 naturalization laws that permitted whites to acquire citizenship. He writes that "the period between the first massive Irish migration of the 1840s and the triumph of racially engineered immigration restriction in the 1920s was thus marked by a profound ideological tension between established codes of whiteness as inclusive of all Europeans, and new, racialist revisions."[37] Resentment of Catholicism extended especially to Irish immigrants; the Know-Nothing Party disseminated anti-Catholic propaganda. Meeting in secret, its members were initially unknown to each other; consequently, when questioned about their party, they answered, "I don't know," which supplied the movement's appellation. After local and state electoral successes, the party organized nationally in 1855. In its platform, adopted in Philadelphia, the party demanded restrictive naturalization laws, the disfranchisement of unnaturalized foreigners, and a repeal by Congress of acts making grants of land to unnaturalized foreigners. Its electoral support and congressional presence were, however, insufficiently large to accomplish these ends, though some of its proposals received wide support.

Religious conflict and division reflected deeper cultural and racial antagonism, which was resonant until the end of the nineteenth century. Irish immigrants could, however, conjoin the common disdain for African Americans and, in time, assert their superiority and citizenship rights.[38] The determination of immigrants to assimilate—the acceptance of the English language, for instance (though German was permitted in schools in several Midwestern states until the First World War)—ultimately won over the suspicion of American Protestants about the inherent "foreignness" of Catholicism, and that determination also encouraged Irish immigrants to embrace the prevailing attitudes toward African Americans. This grudging acceptance took some time, at least until the early twentieth century, since as Orlando Patterson remarks, "no 'white' person in his right mind considered the Irish 'white' up to as late as the 1920s,"[39] even though Irish immigrants were entitled under the naturalization law to acquire citizenship. Assimilation through public schools proved also to be partial, according to Dinnerstein et al: "whereas educators were eager to get the children of immigrants into the schools to 'Americanize' them, they were frequently indifferent to black youngsters."[40] By the end of the century, "Americanization" had become a major motif of American life, with industrialists such as Henry Ford providing English instruction and lessons in "American" values for their foreign employees.

Politically, Irish and German immigrants exploited the opportunities presented by trade unions—joining them—and thereby conspired in the treatment of African Americans, who were either excluded or relegated to segregated locals, especially in the Northeastern and Midwestern cities.[41] Assimilation or entry into the melting pot permitted European immigrants, despite the strictures of the Know-Nothings, gradually to become part of the dominant group, able in turn to look askance on new entrants and those already marginalized. This option—embraced by Catholic Irish immigrants in the early twentieth century who found themselves a surprise member of the "northwestern European" coalition, advocating restrictionist immigration policy that would favor their constitutive nationalities—was denied to the Chinese and the Japanese in the United States and inconceivable in respect to African Americans. Apparent here is the way in which the "whiteness" of American identity was constructed sociologically and historically, an issue I take up later. Preliminarily, the importance of such sociological distinctions is reported by Orlando Patterson: "those who were visibly or vaguely 'white' eagerly sought membership within the Caucasian chalk circle and were usually welcomed as long as they could prove no trace of African 'blood.'"[42] This strategy evoked some novel alliances, as Patterson comments ironically: "indeed, 'whiteness,' or rather non-'blackness,' became a powerful unifying force." Thus, "swarthy Sicilians and Arabs now found themselves one with blond Northern Europeans, Irish Catholics with English Protestants, formerly persecuted Jews with Gentiles—all were united in the great 'white republic' of America by virtue simply of not being tainted by one drop of the despised Afro-American blood."[43]

Asians were excluded from the dominant U.S. identity. Before the Exclusion Act of 1882, about a quarter of a million Chinese entered the United States, generally to work at low-paid manual jobs. Chinese immigrants "experienced discrimination and abuse. Most of them had come over as indentured or bond servants, having had their passage paid for in return for a promise to work for a stipulated period of time."[44] Such Chinese immigrants—like the Japanese—were viewed as fundamentally unassimilable.[45] For instance, in California both Chinese and Japanese immigrants were poorly treated, often by the white working class, as Tomás Almaguer has documented: "[T]he 'heathen Chinese,' and later the Japanese 'Yellow Peril' attracted intense opposition from segments of the white working class and self-employed, petit bourgeois commodity producers. White immigrants in these classes railed against the fundamental threat that these Asian immigrants posed to their rights and entitlements as 'free white persons' in the new state."[46] Almaguer argues that the racialized hostility toward Chinese immigrants arose from their location at the point of conflict between American capitalists—eager to employ Chinese labor—and white workers—who considered them a threat to the free laboring class. This dual pressure proved fatal to the political and economic position of the Chinese immigrants, since "white male laborers believed that Chinese workers threatened both their precarious class position and the underlying racial entitlements that white supremacy held out to them and to the white immigrants who followed them into the new class structure."[47] In Almaguer's view, it was the interests of working-class people in California, divided by race, that structured the disadvantaged position of Chinese immigrants. Thus, he writes that "white craftsmen and other skilled workers consistently sought to maintain their privileged racial status over the Chinese and, in the process, reaffirmed the centrality of race as the primary organizing principle of nineteenth-century Anglo California."[48] Chinese immigration, after the 1880s, gave way to Japanese, with over 120,000 people claiming Japanese ancestry who were living in the United States by the 1920s.[49] The same hostility and restrictions were extended a generation later to the Japanese immigrants. The ensuing tensions and limitations—Japanese Americans were often not allowed to buy or own property and were limited in the occupations open to them—are caught in David Guterson's novel *Snow Falling on Cedars,* which is set in Washington state. The internment of 110,000 Japanese-Americans during World War Two symbolized brutally the inferior position of these people in the United States.[50] Of the 120,000 persons imprisoned in this way, 70,000 were American citizens.[51]

The Naturalization Act of 1790 determined eligibility for citizenship, the first exercise in what Omi and Winant term the U. S. state's "racial policy," the main object of which has been, they claim, "repression and exclusion."[52] The police excluded nonwhites from that entitlement and set a two-year waiting period before white aliens were entitled to apply for citizenship in the United States.[53] The exclusion of nonwhites from the entitlement to naturalization sealed the fate not only of Asians resident in the United States but also of black immigrants. As Dinnerstein et al. remind their readers, no matter how abusive behavior was toward immigrants, African Americans fared worse, certainly in the decades after 1896: "despite widespread antipathy toward immigrants, the worst demonstrations focused on African Americans."[54] The shifting eligibility for naturalization illustrates the changing definitions of membership. This fluidity arises from the sociological and historical basis of "racial" delineations; as Tomás Almaguer remarks, "how and where racial lines are drawn is an open question and the possibility for contestation always exists,"[55] a proposition demonstrated in respect to legal judgments by Ian Haney López.[56]

The 1870s and the ensuing four decades witnessed another major wave of immigration to the United States, which acted as the stimulus to new restrictions, culminating in the Johnson-Reed Act of 1924. These European immigrants came from southern and eastern Europe, a contrast to the northwestern origin of earlier European arrivals. The disdain heaped on these new arrivals proved a propitious atmosphere for the promulgation of theories and arguments that were skeptical about the immigrants' values, commitment to U.S. institutions, and alleged inferiority. In his widely read book *Our Country,* Josiah Strong argues that "immigration is detrimental to popular morals." He adds that "it has a like influence upon popular intelligence, for the percentage of illiteracy among the foreign-born population is thirty-eight per cent greater than among the native-born whites. Thus immigration complicates our moral and political problems by swelling our dangerous classes." Anticipating a major concern of restrictionists in the early twentieth century, Strong worried that despite naturalization, "many American citizens are not Americanized. It is as unfortunate as it is natural, that foreigners in this country should cherish their own language and peculiar customs, and carry their nationality as a distinct factor, into our politics."[57] The cleavages opened up by this wave of immigration marked the accession of northwestern Europeans into the dominant Anglo-Saxon conception of U.S. identity.

The question of Americanization has recurred. Its modern advocates confront critics for whom this process unavoidably echoes the prejudices and exclusionary impulses of the 1920s. But the pressure to identify common values to which citizens can subscribe is a constant one politically. Thus, the political scientist Noah Pickus argues that a common sense of membership is a prerequisite to a successful polity: "we must . . . reaffirm the necessity of a shared sense of identity."[58] The 1997 Commission on Immigration Reform's members concluded that in order to succeed, Americanization must be a "two-way street." This notion of a "two-way street" is meant to break decisively with the assimilationist and exclusionary tendencies of earlier Americanization initiatives: "[I]mmigration presents mutual obligations. Immigrants must accept the obligations we impose—to obey our laws, to pay taxes, to respect other cultures and ethnic groups. At the same time, citizens incur obligations to provide an environment in which newcomers can become fully participating members of our society."[59] The purpose of this exercise does not seem especially novel, however: "[I]mmigration and immigrant policy . . . is about the meaning of American nationality and the foundation of national unity. It is about uniting persons from all over the world in a common civic culture."[60] Can these political ends be reconciled with a genuine "two-way" process of Americanization? Unquestionably, without such a reformulation, the less attractive features of Americanization will prevail.

The 1997 Commission on Immigration Reform identifies four "truths" as constitutive of American nationality and of the classic *e pluribus unum* maxim: the principles and values of the Constitution such as equal protection before the law; ethnic and religious diversity as the basis for national unity; a shared English language; and "lawfully admitted newcomers of any ancestral nationality—without regard to race, ethnicity, or religion—truly become Americans when they give allegiance to these principles and values."[61] The commission defined Americanization as the "process of integration by which immigrants become part of our communities and by which our communities and the nation learn from and adapt to their presence. Americanization means the civic incorporation of immigrants, that is the cultivation of a shared commitment to the American values of liberty, democracy and equal opportunity."[62] This is a fulsomely patriotic version of the process of "becoming American." In a workshop organized to coincide with the commission's deliberations, the subject of Americanization generated continuing disagreement: "[P]articipants applauded the Commission for characterizing Americanization as a two-way street. But what, they asked, does this metaphor actually mean?" Four alternative versions emerged: immigrants adapt; Americans adapt; America adapts; or "America is the wrong category."[63] Emerging from the workshop is a profound disagreement about the content of American identity and the apposite role of Americanization. The alternative positions are, for some, that to integrate and unite a disparate population, it is appropriate to take the values of the U.S. Constitution as a basis for a shared American identity, whereas others maintain that the United States's failure historically to realize those values is so severe that retaining a shared conception, attainable through Americanization, is unsustainable.

Rogers Smith provides additional concern about Americanization from his study of the failure of the courts to expand citizenship: "[T]he near-total failure of federal courts and Congress to expand either the content of national citizenship rights or the range of those entitled to claim them during the Progressive Era is significant. It indicates that, contrary to Hartzian expectations, the civic vision of the centrist progressives never defined national identity chiefly in terms of personal liberties." He spells out the implications for national U.S. values: "centrists sought to build both order and national loyalty through civic measures designed to bolster what they took to be traditional national traits, including the organic racial and ethnic character, of the U. S. citizenry."[64] Even more pointedly, Gary Gerstle documents just how extensive and consequential "cultural coercion" was in the 1920s: as American cities in the Northeast and Midwest were transformed by the predominance of "ethnic and racial minorities," so "attacks on minority cultures were issues of national import." He adds that during the 1920s, "millions of ethnics felt culturally beseiged . . . Prohibition, mandatory Americanization programs, and immigration restriction were coercive measures designed to strip immigrants of their foreign languages, customs, and politics."[65] Such cultural and ethnic tensions have endured, Gerstle argues: "our history suggests that building a national community depends on repression and exclusion, hardly a happy prospect for any architect of postethnic America to contemplate."[66]

From Cultural Pluralism to Multiculturalism

Melting-pot assimilation advantages unity over diversity. But there have always been advocates, however muted, of a pluralist conception of U.S. identity.

Cultural Pluralism

The melting-pot model implied that immigrants to the United States discarded their previous ethnic values and loyalties, diving into a pool of mixed groups and becoming part of the resultant heterogeneous potion. Such a casting off of previous ethnic loyalties and values to join a new single identity was the obverse of a community premised on cultural plurality and a multiplicity of ethnic allegiances. However, there were champions of a cultural pluralism in the 1920s, whose views proved to be precursors of multiculturalism.

The leading proponent of a "cultural pluralism" perspective was Horace Kallen, who introduced the term in two articles in *The Nation* in 1915.[67] Kallen shared many of the assumptions of a patrician American about class divisions and ethnic failings but nonetheless was fearful that advocates of Americanization, and of a dominant American identity, would seek unduly to suppress ethnic diversity by creating an artificial "American" nationality. Gary Gerstle notes that thinkers such as Kallen and, more especially, John Dewey were "immersed since youth in the culture of American Protestantism and republicanism," a background that made it difficult for them "to acknowledge an equivalent value in the very different heritages of immigrants, especially of those from Southern and Eastern Europe."[68] Doing so required breaking with prevailing sentiments and their own education. Kallen's worry was principally that attempts to create what he called an "Americanized unison" from diverse immigrant or ethnic groups would prove counterproductive and would dilute the very source of the United States's prosperity and political stability. Kallen argued that assimilation and economic progress for immigrant groups initially encouraged them to suppress their distinctive ethnic traits but that these subsequently reemerged:

> [O]nce the proletarian level of such independence is reached, the process of assimilation slows down and tends to come to a stop. The immigrant group is still a national group, modified, sometimes improved, by environmental influences, but otherwise a solitary spiritual unit, which is seeking to find its way out of its own social level. This search brings to light permanent group distinctions, and the immigrant, like the Anglo-Saxon American, is thrown back upon himself and his ancestry. Then a process of dissimilation begins. The arts, life, and ideals of the nationality become central and paramount; ethnic and national differences change in status from disadvantages to distinctions. All the while the immigrant has been using the English language and behaving like an American in matters economic and political, and continues to do so.[69]

In a memorable description, Kallen added, with a reference to the most intense efforts at assimilation, that "on the whole, Americanization has not repressed nationality. Americanization has liberated nationality."[70] Comparable claims would be advanced about the "new ethnic politics" from the 1970s. And recent research on immigrants' attitudes has increasingly unearthed a resistance to complete Americanization and even hostility to the submersion of ethnic traditions, as Gary Gerstle writes: "for the majority of immigrants stuck in the working class, Americanization meant only acquiescence in their oppression."[71]

Horace Kallen argued that critics of immigration fundamentally feared the *"difference"* posed by immigrants, despite the fact that American political institutions themselves made such diversity possible and, indeed, promoted it: "democratism and the Federal principle have worked together with economic greed and ethnic snobbishness to people the land with all the nationalities of Europe, and to convert the early American nation into the present American state."[72] Diversity presented a dilemma for the United States, in Kallen's view: a choice between an imposed "unison, singing the old Anglo-Saxon theme 'America,'" or a "harmony" constituted by the various ethnic groups of the United States. Kallen warned strenuously against attempts to create a homogenous identity: "[T]o achieve unison would be to violate . . . the basic law of America itself and the spirit of American institutions . . . Fundamentally it would require the complete nationalization of education, the abolition of every form of parochial and private school, the abolition of instruction in other tongues than English, and the concentration of the teaching of history and literature upon the English tradition."[73] A "unison" nation or "American race" would necessitate the "unison of ethnic types." Furthermore, "it must be, if it is to be at all, a unison of social and historic interests, established by the complete cutting-off of the ancestral, exclusive use of our populations, the enforced, exclusive use of the English language and English and American history in the schools and in the daily life."[74] Kallen counseled against such a model, proposing instead an openness to diversity and recognition of the value of ethnic traditions. It was an alternative vision to that of the homogenizing Americanization program, and one that found support initially with some employers, though much less so as Americanism and anticommunism intensified in the 1920s.[75]

Writing three decades later, Kallen remained an advocate of a cultural pluralism consisting of One World "but One World *in pluribus,* as a federal union of diversities, not a diversion of diversities into undifferentiated unity."[76] Without individuality and an acceptance of diversity, he argued, cultures become sclerotic. Kallen maintained that the conflict or tension between what he termed "an ancient authoritarian monism of culture" and a "free cultural pluralism intrinsic to the American Idea"[77] underpinned the United States's cultural richness and innovation.

The philosopher John Dewey also presented a more inclusive approach to U.S. identity. He castigated critics, including Woodrow Wilson and Theodore Roosevelt, of "hyphenated" Americans: "the fact is, the genuine American, the typical American, is himself a hyphenated character." Dewey argued that "he is not American plus Pole or German. But the American is himself Pole-German-English-French-Spanish-Italian-Greek-Irish-Scandinavian-Bohemiam-Jew—and so on. The point is to see to it that the hyphen connects instead of separates."[78]

However, this cultural pluralist approach to immigration policy and the accommodation of immigrant identities in the United States was racially limited, since its proponents assumed a white national identity. African Americans make no appearance in Dewey's inventory of the ingredients of the American, an omission that his formulation shares with de Crèvecoeur's melting pot. Dewey's comments are, a reminder of the historical overtones of the multiculturalist debate. Horace Kallen reproduced commonplace stereotypes about African Americans (at one point lumping them with "the degenerate farming stock of New England, the 'poor whites' of the South"[79]) even though there is no reason, in terms of his own argument, why they should not have had equal claim to be part of the United States. Kallen was writing on the eve of the Harlem Renaissance,[80] when New York also became the home to over a million African Americans migrating from the South.

The alternative views of an Americanized melting pot or a cultural pluralism were rendered salient by the divisions of the First World War and the intense Americanism stimulated by the U.S.'s entry to the European conflict. Anti-German feeling in particular was pronounced (with German excised as an acceptable language of instruction in schools), and patriotic tests were widely discussed as, for instance, in the opposition to hyphenated self-descriptions. In this climate, Gary Gerstle singles out the significance of John Dewey's quiet abandonment of the cultural pluralist agenda and his retreat to a focus on questions of labor. Gerstle writes that, in contrast to Dewey's prewar writings, "in the 1920s, this founding member of the NAACP grew silent on the still-vexing questions raised by America's racial and ethnic diversity, publishing dozens of essays, none of them focused on African Americans." In fact, "only once did he protest the racist character of the immigration restriction system put in place between 1921 and 1924, and his protest was motivated not by his concern that such a system betrayed liberal ideas but that it would influence militarist passions in Japan and thereby increase the likelihood of war."[81] He adds that Dewey "turned away from his personal involvement with immi-

grants."[82] A committed opponent of racism and anti-immigrant sentiment, Dewey emphasized class rather than ethnic or racial sources
of social conflict. As Gerstle concludes, former proponents of ethnic
diversity grew to doubt its plausibility in the United States: "even
the Progressives, like Dewey, who were most understanding of ethnic
needs and most committed to developing an inclusive American nationalism, had never felt entirely comfortable in the presence of strong
ethnic cultures."[83] This discomfort resurfaced in the postwar pessi-
mism. Horace Kallen also became disillusioned with diversity and
anxious about how it fostered intolerance (ignoring the paradox that
Americanization itself sacrificed tolerance for a unified identity), in
large part, Gerstle agues, because of his unpleasant experience among
Boston's Irish community in 1927 and 1928 (where he was almost arrested for portraying Jesus Christ as an anarchist). He had already
broken with Zionism, and by the end of the 1930s, Kallen had little
faith in cultural pluralism, though after 1945 he did return to this
position.

Kallen's arguments have had an influence on analyses of how
historically to conceptualize the attitudes of immigrants toward the
U.S. polity; this conceptualization has proved a shifting and elusive
question. The historiography of this topic has passed through several
phases, the content of which has been greatly influenced by changing
perceptions of immigrants in the U.S. polity. There are two broad
sweeps to this scholarly literature.[84] First, in terms of how immigrants
become full members of the polity, attention has moved from the
earlier assumption that a melting-pot assimilationist Americanization
process incorporated all comers to the recognition that this process
was in some ways partial (not everyone was included) and, furthermore, that the product of the process was not a random melting pot-
pourri but one biased toward certain interests already entrenched in
the United States. As the historian Russell Kazal observes, by the
1960s, scholars considered assimilation as a "process . . . occurring
within a society made up of groups clustered around an Anglo-American core,"[85] a core itself wrenched asunder by the so-called new ethnic
politics and the multiculturalism of the post-1960s decades. Consequently, the "concept of an unchanging, monolithic, Anglo-American
cultural core is dead."[86] The second development has been an evolv-
ing view of immigrants themselves and their attitudes toward Americanization and political incorporation: where scholars once described

a discarding of historical and ethnic ties, later commentators found these to be retained, prized, and cultivated. Thus, the view that assimilating into American society "emancipated" immigrants has been disputed, as Gerstle documents.[87] It is this second dynamic that facilitated the development of the "new ethnic politics" of the 1960s.

Multiculturalism

Multiculturalism is the explicit acknowledgment of competing and coequal sources of cultural and ethnic identity in a political system. Politically, these multiple identities have been integrated into public policy in a way purported to respect the inherent value of each tradition and not to privilege any one tradition over another. Multiculturalism has had considerable impact on education policy.[88] In this sphere, it refers to the revision of educational curricula in high schools and universities to include accounts of the historical experience of groups previously accorded a small role or no role at all in the standard narratives. It was an attack on the allegedly dominant "Western" conception of the United States's historical formation, or as David Goldberg states it: "multiculturalism is critical of and resistant to the necessarily reductive imperatives of monocultural assimilation."[89] Noting that there is no authoritative author or canonical text on multiculturalism, Melzer et al. propose the following "working" definition: "it is a movement that radicalizes and Nietzscheanizes the liberal ideal of tolerance—thus turning that ideal against liberalism—by tending to deny the possibility of universal truths as well as of nonsuppressive power and by seeking, through this very denial, a comprehensive redistribution, not so much of wealth as of self-esteem, and not so much to individuals as to various marginalized groups."[90]

Multiculturalist accounts of U.S. history include not only African Americans and Native Americans but also ethnic groups, whose representatives all laid claim to being depicted in the historical record. The decision by Congress, in 1972, to fund an ethnic heritage studies program proved both a signal about the revival of ethnic politics in the United States and a boost to multicultural-type education. Bilingual education curricula were introduced in some states in response to multicultural pressures, though these have recently induced fierce political divisions rather than unity.[91]

Multiculturalism, an attempt programmatically to address the consequences of a political system characterized by "multiple traditions," or as a modest exercise in cultural pluralism, is criticized precisely on the grounds that it dilutes the core values of U. S., or American, identity. The debate between assimilationists and cultural pluralists, articulated during the 1920s, has recurred in the 1980s and 1990s. In this sense, multiculturalism is a tendency that has been beneath the surface of U. S. politics for several decades, although recently its salience has plainly mounted. John Higham provides an appropriate historical perspective on the recent debates: "under the milder label of 'pluralism,' multicultural sensibilities had been quietly spreading at all levels of the American school system since the 1960s."[92] The same point is made in a recent essay by Nathan Glazer.[93]

Multiculturalists would mostly reject the assumption of a uniform American identity, which was held by nineteenth-century nativists and was common among policy-makers when immigration restrictions were enacted in the 1920s; and although there were voices in this latter decade wishing to conceive of a pluralist United States, they were marginalized in policy choices. Multiculturalists challenge the assumption of the United States as stated in its Constitution and inferred from its ideology: in essence, that there is a distinct American identity, formed through an assimilationist melting-pot process in which all ethnic groups and nationalities participate more or less equally, living in a *Mr. Smith Goes to Washington* Capraesque world.

Multiculturalists question the idea of a universalist identity in two ways. First, representatives of some groups argue that the formation, or assumption, of a dominant group necessarily reinforces the marginality already experienced by their members in the U. S. polity. This dominant identity is an Anglo-Saxon one: that is, it is one that prioritizes the traditions and values of the English settlers and their descendants in defining being American. Representatives of African Americans who wanted racial integration and the elimination of discriminatory segregation, such as the National Association for the Advancement of Colored People (NAACP), can make such a case with particular strength. For such proponents, multiculturalism—as defined in high school curricula, for instance—is presented as a means better to integrate all groups or nationalities resident in the United States into the dominant conception of the country's culture, including its political culture. It is about inclusion by broadening the country's core political ideology to acknowledge a variety of cultural traditions and values, though whether these latter can in fact be made complementary rather than conflictual is an unresolved question. Second, and more recently, representatives of some groups argue that they wish to *maintain* a separate identity and related customs or practices, and they reject a "melting" of their traditions and identity into a dominant national group. This form of multiculturalism implies separatism (a tendency with relatively few supporters in the United States).[94]

Multiculturalists reject the notion of a dominant and shared set of values and cultural motifs as the basis of citizenship and politics in the United States. This implication is identified by Nathan Glazer, who observes that "for most of those who advocate multiculturalism, it is a position-taking stance on the racial and ethnic diversity of the United States. It is a position that rejects assimilation and the 'melting pot' image as an imposition of the dominant culture, and instead prefers such metaphors as the 'salad bowl' or the 'glorious mosaic,' in which each ethnic and racial element in the population maintains its distinctiveness."[95] Preserving group distinctiveness and loyalty is the obverse of the assimilationist principle, assumed, until the last twenty-five years, to be the rational aim in all discussions of immigration and the rationale for Americanization. Striving for group identity is also a judgment about the dominant culture.

Historically, group differences have rarely been sought by those compelled to identify themselves in this way in a democratic polity: instead, they are assumed, often reluctantly, as a necessary means to achieve justice and the very equality of citizenship on which the democratic creed rests.[96] As Orlando Patterson notes, "Afro-Americans had no choice but to emphasize their Afro-Americanism in mobilizing against the inequities of a system that discriminated against them because they were Afro-American."[97] In the 1920s, both Europeans of certain nationalities and African Americans and Asian Americans were discussed in terms of their unsuitability for assimilation in the United States, a framework that privileged, often explicitly, "whiteness" as an element of U.S. identity. The groups and individuals described as unassimilable in public debates began to feel that they were unassimilable because members of the country's mainstream would not let them assimilate, that is, would discriminate against them even if they learned English and acted "American," an attitude that made them reluctant to try and that encouraged an emphasis on their own culture. Consequently, debates about assimilability were performative, that is, they facilitated the very unassimilability they criticized by insisting on its existence. An emphasis on cultural distinctness was part of a survival strategy, both economic and political. For instance, in the case of Chinese Americans, because they were excluded from the mainstream, they formed their own enclaves, places where they could shop and work and live without experiencing discrimination.[98] This strategy meant associating only with other members of their ethnic group, which led to an emphasis on their own culture, language, and traditions rather than on a pursuit of assimilation.[99]

The multiculturalist or group rights challenge has had wide political repercussions. Educationally, an intense debate has been generated by efforts to incorporate the writings and arguments representative of hitherto neglected groups into high school and university curricula. The occasional eccentricity of these modifications has been the subject of media and intellectual comment. Positively, it has forced genuine reflection on the viability of the assimilationist model, as well as a greater openness to and welcoming of diversity. But it has also exacerbated the pressure placed on a political system by multiple and competing interests: Berlinian "pluralism" is problematic to reconcile with national unity, since some values can never be respected in equal amounts concurrently. Finally, multiculturalism, as a debate about group rights, is linked with the divisions and tensions associated with affirmative action and other measures designed to rectify historic injustices.

In common with the revival of Americanization and the notion of whiteness, multiculturalism is a term with obvious historical resonance in the choices and debates of the 1920s. Cultural pluralism, of the sort promoted by Dewey and Kallen, anticipated in a limited form the politics of multiculturalism. The key difference is that cultural pluralists ignored African Americans' interests in the U.S. polity, a concern that has been at the forefront of multiculturalists' initiatives. The greater point of commonality between the two periods is apparent in the way in which both movements have been stimulated by the consequences of assuming a dominant national identity neglectful of some groups' values and traditions.

As an intellectual and educational agenda, multiculturalism has many critics as well as advocates. It is reviled as a source of intolerance instead of diversity. For political scientist James Ceaser, the multiculturalist turn is a sectarian and narrowing one. He writes that "the doctrinarism of multiculturalism stands in the way of examining the means by which various groups have been able to move in America from a marginalized status in the past to achieve a place of approximate equality today." Ceaser argues that the dichotomy between those central and those marginal in the political system underpinning multiculturalism precludes considered analysis of the "means by which various groups have been able to move" from positions of historic marginality to a "place of approximate equality today."[100] I return to these conflicting views in Chapter 9.

The United States's Multiple Traditions and "Whiteness"

The establishment of a discriminatory immigration regime, in place until the mid-1960s, which was aligned with, in practice, a limited melting-pot assumption, the rejection of a cultural pluralist approach to identity, and the disfranchisement of African Americans, meant that fundamental elements of U. S. political culture were suppressed in most general formulations or statements about its constitutive components. Both this aversion to diversity in the conception of national identity and the emphasis on an inflated commonality had several consequences once the civil rights movement unfolded in the 1960s and the national origins system reformed. Politically, African Americans became central to U. S. politics, and programs of affirmative action and multiculturalism were enacted to address past inequities in respect of them, though not exclusively so. As Orlando Patterson writes, "some recognition of 'race' had to inform policies aimed at alleviating centuries of racial ignorance."[101] Intellectually or theoretically to understand this historical process, some scholars formulated analyses of the formation of U.S. political culture or identity alert to its multiple elements, a rejection of the common monolithic perception of "Americanness." Two complementary intellectual developments, dealing with the notions of the United States's multiple traditions and its "whiteness," address these concerns.

Multiple Traditions

The political theorist Rogers Smith has compellingly articulated a view of the United States's political culture as constituted by "multiple traditions," within which some traditions or groups' values have been decidedly better placed than others and which over time have competed for dominance.[102] It is the multiple traditions framework that most fully attempts to incorporate the implications of recognizing the United States's diversity into its account of American political culture and development. Rogers Smith argues that through most of its history, "lawmakers pervasively and unapologetically structured U. S. citizenship in terms of illiberal and undemocratic racial, ethnic, and gender hierarchies, for reasons rooted in basic, enduring imperatives of political life."[103] From his study of U. S. citizenship laws, Smith concludes that "rather than stressing protection of individual rights for all in liberal fashion, or participation in common civic institutions in republican fashion, American law had long been shot through with forms of second-class citizenship."[104] The grounds for these restrictions conflicted with the values imputed to the United States's political culture, such as equality of opportunity or individualism; instead, the criteria "manifested passionate beliefs that America was by rights a white nation, a Protestant nation, a nation in which true Americans were native-born men with Anglo-Saxon ancestors."[105] Smith found inegalitarian ascriptive traditions to be far more entrenched in American political culture than was commonly appreciated, and certainly more salient than in conventional histories. To establish this argument, he provides a detailed analysis of two-and-a-half-thousand Supreme Court decisions concerning citizenship, which were taken between 1798 and 1912. Citizenship laws illustrate the competing pressures—"civic ideologies that blend liberal, democratic republican, and inegalitarian ascriptive elements"—constitutive of the multiple traditions framework. They are driven by political pressures that resulted in inequalities and hierarchies rather than in a Tocquevillean or Hartzian egalitarianism.[106] In fact, until the 1950s, ineligibility criteria based on "racial, ethnic, and gender restrictions" were "blatant, not latent"; and "for these people, citizenship rules gave no weight to how liberal, republican, or faithful to other American values their political beliefs might be."[107] Since political development is a dynamic process, Smith's analysis implies that illiberal arguments could well recur in U.S. national debates, and in subsequent work he identifies a range of alarming parallels between debates about race and equality now and at the end of the nineteenth century. Of eleven such parallels, he notes that one is the renewed agitation about immigration.[108]

The definitions of U.S. identity and whiteness have also changed over time.

Rogers Smith's argument is supported by studies of individual state's racial experiences. For example, from his study of California, Tomás Almaguer concludes that its "racial patterns were not monolithic but contained multiple racial histories that were unique in their own terms while also sharing elements with the racial formation process elsewhere in the United States."[109] "Racialization" in California was the work of proponents of a white supremacist framework who established an "Anglo California" social structure. This process unfolded in respect to Mexicans, Native Americans, Asians, and African Americans resident in the state. More generally, the United States's republican traditions have been dominated, in the view of some scholars, by a conception of citizens as being white.

In sum, the multiple traditions thesis holds that U. S. politics and history is littered with examples of members of the political elite attempting to define American identity as one rooted "in part on inegalitarian ascriptive themes. The history of U. S. citizenship policies demonstrates incontrovertibly that the legal prerogative of the majority of the domestic population through most of the nation's past have officially been defined in conformity with those ascriptive doctrines."[110] The latter offered a way of protecting the political order and resisting democratization initiatives. This is not a process unique to the United States, but its effects there are immense. Historically, it has resulted in two variants of democratic cultural pluralism (to recall Horace Kallen's term), according to Rogers Smith: universalist integrationists and separatist pluralists, differentiated by their approach to recognizing and protecting group differences in the polity. The danger of subgroup loyalties coming to subsume or outshine commitment to the national unified polity exercises Smith: "just as it is hard to see why national allegiances should often prevail, given democratic cultural pluralist views, it is also hard to see how these pluralist positions can be politically sustained if national obligations are minimized." He adds that "if citizens feel that their most profound commitments go to a racial, ethnic, religious, regional, national, or voluntary subgroup, then the broader society's leaders may find that their government lacks adequate popular support to perform some functions effectively."[111]

In Smith's view, therefore, although the multiple traditions constitutive of the United States's political culture must be fully acknowledged ("Americans should value the civic identity as something real with a rich and distinctive history, not as something valorized in ascriptive myths of national superiority");[112] and the danger of destroying any group's culture through an oppressive system of national assimilation assiduously guarded against, nonetheless some sort of "national political identity" has to be retained for political durability and functioning. Smith's concern echoes the classic problem of liberal democracy identified by Isaiah Berlin:[113] there are key values in liberal democracies, such as liberty, justice, or equality, that inherently clash and that can never be entirely reconciled. Such incommensurability is at the heart of liberal democracies and is a consistent source of political debate.

Such anxieties are entirely valid and sensible, but given historical attitudes to immigrants and African Americans, it is unsurprising that the issue of genuinely and usefully recognizing diversity—manifest, for instance, in the multiculturalist agenda—has been salient. Proposing that the problems of integration and diversity within political communities approximates that of political parties in a democracy, Smith urges reformulating liberal democratic conceptions of citizenship to "retain the historic strengths of egalitarian liberalism and respond to its greatest weaknesses, especially its failure to define compelling senses of national identity that can build support for living in accordance with liberal democratic principles within specific political societies."[114] He argues that such a conception should permit some "dissimilar treatment" for subgroups that are victims of "dissimilar situations"[115] such as African Americans. This political agenda needs also to be strengthened by historical studies of how and why some of the country's multiple traditions came to be marginalized and, in some cases, suppressed.

"Whiteness" and U.S. Politics

Because the debates in the 1920s about whom to restrict concerned solely white Americans, this set of legislation had implicit consequences for both nonwhites and calibrations within the white population. The "descendants of slave immigrants" were purposefully written out of the 1924 law. Although the recent literature on "whiteness" can seem somewhat rarefied, nonetheless given these intrawhite divisions, its importance to American political development is elemental, even when it is implicit.[116] Building on the widely agreed assumption that racial distinctions reflect sociological, legal, or political manipulations,[117] the scholar Matthew Jacobson, who has made whiteness the subject of his recent book, argues that it is necessary to examine how "racial categories themselves" arise from and express "the competing notions of history, peoplehood, and collective destiny by which power has been organized and contested on the American scene."[118] Ian Haney López makes a comparable point from his analysis of the legal construction of race: "Whiteness is simply a matter of what people believe. There is no core or essential White identity or White race. There are only popular conceptions of Whiteness. And this common knowledge, like all social beliefs, is unstable, highly contextual, and subject to change."[119]

The writer Toni Morrison argues that race has a key place in textual analysis: "In matters of race, silence and evasion have historically ruled literary discourse . . . the habit of ignoring race is understood to be a graceful, even generous, liberal gesture. To notice is to recognize an already discredited difference. To its invisibility through silence is to allow the black body a shadowless participation in the dominant cultural body."[120] Morrison provides numerous examples, many historical, of how the common narrative of the U.S. polity's formation and of American identity is peppered with assumptions about "whiteness." She remarks that "it is no accident and no mistake that immigrant populations (and much immigrant literature) understood their 'Americanness' as an opposition to the resident black population. Race, in fact, now functions as a metaphor so necessary to the construction of Americanness that it rivals the old pseudoscientific and class-informed racisms whose dynamics we are more used to deciphering." In her strongest statement, the Nobel laureate concludes that "American means white" and that "deep within the word 'American' is its association with race."[121] That the immigration debates of the 1920s were exclusively about categories among potential European immigrants underscores Morrison's point that immigrants "understood their 'Americanness' as an opposition to the resident black population." Involuntary immigrants and their descendants were forgotten.

The most important source of involuntary immigration to the United States consisted of those individuals brought as slaves or indentured servants; by 1808 an estimated 333,000 slaves had been imported into the United States.[122] As a consequence, African Americans have constituted a fundamental element in both the United States's population and its culture since English settlers first arrived. However, although the self-image of the United States as an immigrant nation has been an intensely powerful one among Americans, until comparatively recently this conception gave little explicit attention to the position of those citizens descendant from slaves.[123] That African American slaves were treated poorly in the centuries before emancipation and Reconstruction has been documented by numerous contemporary observers and scholars. Of the former, de Crèvecoeur's views are representative: African Americans were "obliged to devote their lives, their limbs, their will, and every vital exertion to swell the wealth of masters who look not upon them with half the kindness and affection with which they consider their dogs and horses."[124] These miseries were, in many respects, mirrored in the injustices and humiliations of the jim crow era of segregated race relations.[125] The enduring effects of this period are manifest in the new focus on whiteness, a point suggested by Patricia Williams's observation that "'whites pretend race is invisible. Yet for most blacks, race remains central.'"[126]

Morrison's proposition that "American means white" had considerable purchase in the 1920s. For nonwhites, citizenship was either partial or withheld, as Moorfield Storey, NAACP president, pointed out in 1921:

But are you citizens? And I speak now to the men and women of color.

When it is a question of rendering military service and risking life and limb on the plains of France your color disappears. When taxes are to be paid to state or nation your right to pay them is fully recognized. Whenever it is a question of bearing any burden or doing any duty of citizenship, no one doubts that are you are citizens. But when you seek a voice in choosing the men who govern you, when you ask the right when accused of crime to be tried by a jury and if found guilty to be punished according to law, when you ask for protection against the barbarous cruelty of the mob, your citizenship disappears, and you may be burned with every refinement of torture while governors, legislatures and all the officers of the state sit quietly by and do nothing to defend you or to punish your murderers. Yours is a curious citizenship which loads you with burdens but denies you the fundamental rights to which all men are entitled unless we repudiate the faith of our Fathers proclaimed in the great Declaration of Independence upon which our government rests.[127]

Three years later, the descendants of involuntary immigrants, with Native Americans, were deemed not to be part of the U.S. population used in calculating the country's "national origins."

Immigration debates, such as those of the 1920s, illustrate how the "whiteness" of American identity was constructed, a process observable in other aspects of U.S. society. As a member of the NAACP wrote in 1929, "race prejudice is not necessarily racial . . . If visibility is the criterion the white Negroes should of course be classed as white. The fact that they are not gives a highly sociological color to the concept. For it develops that it is not what races are, but what various men at times call races that racial antipathy is based upon."[128] The construction of a white American identity was complemented in a range of educational, cultural, and political institutions in the nineteenth century; in the law, as Jacobson notes, the "idea of citizenship had become thoroughly entwined with the idea of 'whiteness,'"[129] an interlinking confirmed in the *Dred Scott* decision and in judicial decisions about naturalization. As a speaker to the NAACP in 1922 explained, in *Dred Scott* the Supreme Court decided that "a Negro was not a citizen of this country and had no attributes of citizenship which any white man was bound to respect."[130] That the definition of white has proved elusive or that its content has varied over time does not diminish its political consequences;[131] in fact, this shifting content points to its artificiality and significance as an instrument of political interests.

One important popular source defining "whiteness" was minstrelsy entertainment, an institution that the political scientist Michael Rogin uses to decipher the centrality of notions of black and white in American identity. Studying the phenomenon of blackface— white actors donning minstrel colors—Rogin argues in a brilliant study that this practice became pivotal to how American identity was conceived, especially when immigration was of a scale to overturn existing identities: "[B]lackface provided the new country with a distinctive national identity in the age of slavery and presided over melting-pot culture in the period of mass European immigration . . . Minstrelsy claimed to speak for both races through the blackening up of one." Furthermore, "in the making of American national culture, whites in blackface acted out a racially exclusionary melting pot."[132] In Rogin's view, "blackface, the performance of the white man's African American, opens the door to the meanings of whiteness in the United States."[133] "Whiteness," in common with "race," is best seen as a sociological and historical process that enabled formerly reviled immigrants—for example, the Irish and Italians in the nineteenth century—to become part of the U.S. nation; consequently, "blackface minstrelsy founded the new nation culturally in racial wrong."[134] Conjoined with the frontier myth, "blackface enacted triumphs over peoples of color . . . Blackface and the frontier myth, bringing race and ethnicity together, created the distinctive feature of American multiculturalism: racial division and ethnic incorporation."[135]

The tenacity of this "distinctive feature" has been remarkable, and I argue that the 1920s were a key moment in its formation. The assimilationist pressures of this decade were partial: they addressed the circumstances of some groups of white Europeans only, relegating nonwhite (potential and real) Americans to the status of the unassimilable. Blackface fueled the division between whites and others, since it was the former who were blackening up; and Rogin accurately recognizes blackface as a source of American identity recognizable throughout the country: "[W]hatever challenge blackface had originally offered to genteel culture, it defined the United States for natives, immigrants, and foreigners, Europeans and African American alike, by the turn of the twentieth century . . . Normalized in its own self-understanding, minstrelsy was neither racially nor regionally nor class divided; it served instead as our unifying, national popular culture."[136] In this process, the national culture based in blackface successfully reified, as a basic element of the U.S. polity, the inequality of African Americans, a strategy cinematically conveyed in such movies as *Birth of a Nation* (in which racial conflict Americanized immigrants) and *Gone with the Wind*.[137] These filmic expressions were powerful. Speaking in 1929, Mary Ovington, a prominent African American activist and a member of the NAACP, memorably described the impact of *Birth of a Nation* when it was first shown: "[T]o my mind that was the worst propaganda there ever was against the Negro in this country. So many millions of people saw the picture and it was perfectly evident that the idea was to get over to the American people that the educated Negro was always striving for social equality and that the uneducated Negro was a brute unless he was a faithful old domestic servant. Those of you who went to see 'The Birth of the Nation' saw the audiences respond to all those terrible things." She concluded that "it was one of the greatest ordeals that I have had to sit as I did and see people aroused to this feeling against the Negro and then to know it was going all over the United States."[138]

Ethnicity, the badge of immigrant groups, gradually diminished as a basis for exclusion from citizenship until the middle of the twentieth century, whereas alleged racial differences were enforced: "[M]instrelsy accepted ethnic differences by insisting on racial divisions. It passed immigrants into Americans by differentiating them from the black Americans through whom they spoke, who were not permitted to speak for themselves." It is a fundamental process: "facing nativist pressure that would assign them to the dark side of the racial divide, immigrants Americanized themselves by crossing the racial line."[139]

The case of Irish immigrants, often enthusiastic blackface participants, is instructive: economically they eventually entered the labor market by exploiting whiteness as a source of power.[140] Culturally, as Rogin remarks, "blackface brought Irish immigrants into the white working class, freeing them from their guilt by black association,"[141] a change in status strengthened by the political need to incorporate Irish Americans in the restrictionist alliance forged from the 1890s. The historian Barbara Solomon summarizes this new position of the Irish: "[W]ith the arrival of southern European groups, stranger in appearance than the Irish, these English-speaking aliens were less disturbing; and, irrespective of private sentiments, they had a place in American society. Those who opposed a free immigration policy, had made an emotional transference to more vulnerable objects of distaste, the 'new' ethnic groups seeking admission to the United States."[142] Indeed, according to James Barrett's fascinating study, Irish immigrants "occupied vital positions as Americanizers of later groups,"[143] transmitting racist values to new arrivals. Jennifer Hochschild describes the same transformation for immigrants arriving in the 1920s: "[A]s late as the 1920s descendants of old-stock immigrants thought of southern and eastern European immigrants as a different race. But that language disappeared over the next few decades, in favor of an increasingly general category of 'white' or 'American.'"[144]

What Rogin observes culturally was reproduced in other areas of U.S. society. The use of racially restrictive covenants by the real estate industry (until they were declared illegal by the Supreme Court in 1948)[145] was a deliberate means of distinguishing citizens by color and an illustration of the sociological construction of "whiteness": real estate groups argued that mixed neighbors and the presence of so-called minorities both affected property value adversely. This strategy not only reinforced prejudices rooted in race but in many cases also fostered them, an outcome complemented by federal housing authorities.[146] The strategy gave a logic to the postwar homeowners' associations that dedicated themselves to resisting integrated housing;[147] more generally, it illustrates how important legal judgments were in defining whiteness.[148] Writing in 1911, Mary White Ovington contrasted the division in the British West Indies between "white, colored and black" with the more bald dichotomy in the United States where there were "but two groups, white and colored, or as the latter is now more frequently designated, Negro, the term thus losing its original meaning, and becoming a designation for a race."[149] This dichotomy has hardly receded over time, with the broadening of those counting as white sharpening its resonance.

Finding a place for "whiteness" in accounts of American political development may appear, on one reading, a regrettable concession to fashionable nomenclature, obscuring and complicating explanations instead of illuminating. Yet if, as most scholars and scientists now correctly accept, "race" is itself a sociological and ideological phenomenon, not an essentialist biological one,[150] then consideration should be extended to the notion of "whiteness" against which conceptions of race in the United States have been formulated. (In this connection, whiteness had been used empirically as a criterion for legislation in general and naturalization legislation in particular.)[151] Such a move has several merits. First, it quickly becomes apparent that the very concept and the definition of white have proved both highly fluid and have been manipulated to exploit social and political interests. Both these points are central to Ian Haney López's outstanding analysis of how whiteness has been construed in the courts, particularly in respect to eligibility to naturalize. Dissecting the language and logic behind a range of judicial decisions, Haney López finds that the use of "common sense" and so-called "scientific evidence" in demarcating white from nonwhite has fluctuated with judicial need. It was specifically in respect to determining plaintiffs' whiteness that this process operated: "the social construction of the White race is manifest in the [Supreme] Court's repudiation of science and its installation of common knowledge as the appropriate racial meter of Whiteness."[152] Haney López addresses the consequences of the constitutional restriction, operative from 1790 to 1952, that only white persons could acquire U.S. citizenship through naturalization. Thus, in *Ozawa v. United States,* the plaintiff was denied the right to naturalize because he was a member of the "yellow" race rather than the Caucasian race and therefore not white, whereas in *United States v. Thind,* the plaintiff, who was a Hindu and considered a Caucasian by ethnologists, was not white "in accordance with the understanding of the common man."[153] Judges used alleged scientific grounds or common sense, depending on their relative strengths. The tortuous and wearing contortions that were marshaled to define whiteness by the courts underscores powerfully not just how such categories are social constructs but also what are their political effects: "the legal reification of racial categories has made race an inescapable material reality in our society, one which at every turn seems to reinvigorate race with the appearance of reality."[154]

Second, the specification of acceptable and unacceptable immigrant populations changes over time, often within the apparently white population. Furthermore, nonwhite groups such as Asian Americans can acquire the attributes of whiteness in a way that, for example, the Irish did in the nineteenth century. This transformation is manifest in the Supreme Court's recognition of changes in the category of "white" between 1790 and the 1920s, whereby southern and eastern Europeans were included legally but sociologically were cast as eugenic inferiors to immigrants from northwestern Europe.[155]

Third, this approach permits a historical perspective to bear on multiculturalist debates both better to appreciate the arguments of those claiming to be excluded and to document how some groups succeeded in becoming robust members of the U.S. polity before others. Hochschild conveys well some of the lasting significance of these distinctions when she writes that "some African Americans interpret succeeding in accord with the tenets of the American dream as going over to the enemy; much of the history of the twentieth century suggests that some immigrants define success as demonstrating that they are not like blacks." She adds that "if 'some' is an understatement on both sides, the very incorporation of immigrants into the ideological terrain bounded by the American dream means the failure of blacks ever to be able to join."[156]

This last observation indicate two general points about the employment of "whiteness" in the analysis of American political development. First, there is a danger of downgrading the role of agency in these apparently socially and historically constructed categories. It is individuals and groups who ultimately create and dissolve these distinctions. However, the political significance of how these distinctions have been formulated and deployed in American political development is plain and elemental to analysis of immigration and its consequences. Second, the notion of whiteness may reinforce instead of challenge persisting racial divisions, by appearing to limit the potential inclusivity of U.S. society. Thus, its utility as an explanatory factor in the United States's political development, where it is undoubtedly valuable, may not extend to discussion of present circumstances,[157] though calls for whites to renounce their "privileged racial status" suggest otherwise.[158] As the quotations from Toni Morrison and others confirm, for many Americans the binary division encoded in black-white distinctions remains an overarching and consequential one.

Conclusion

These concepts—melting pot, Americanization, cultural pluralism, multiculturalism, multiple traditions, and whiteness—permit analysis of the historical consequences of the national origins regulation system that was introduced in the United States in the 1920s. They each contribute to understanding how diversity was undervalued in the U. S. until the 1960s and 1970s. The 1920s is a key decade in this process, shaping the relationship between immigration and American political development.[159] Despite the inconsistencies and inherently exclusionary character of the de Tocquevillean idea of Americanness, the fact that there is an identifiable and defensible universal notion of the American creed or the American idea remains a powerful aspect of the U. S.'s political culture regularly advanced by scholars and commentators. It embodies the traditional view of U. S. identity. Access to this "American common culture" has been uneven and unequal in several ways. First, the historical experience has been one of inequality because of how "race" or ethnicity or group membership has been delineated politically. Second, the recognition of distinct traditions in U.S. identity has been thwarted by efforts to impose a single conception. It is unsurprising that these limitations have had political consequences and have prompted extensive scholarly consideration.

The logic of decisions taken in the 1920s about who was an acceptable immigrant (measured by both their potential compatibility with a vision of the common American culture and their eugenic suitability) necessarily and ineluctably had negative implications for those groups considered unassimilable under this general model. That some of these groups were already present in the United States while these debates unfolded and were resolved, underscored their marginality and compelled them either to emphasize or at least to acknowledge being treated as "distinct" or "different" (whether an accidental linkage or an organically connected one). Emphasizing such separate cultural traditions was one response to this marginality, most fully developed in separatism; however, integrationists who sought equality within the existing system were also inclined to stress distinctness, for inevitable political reasons. Both the separatist and the integrationist strategies constituted a means of having choices for the affected groups. Once political mobilization and empowerment—although delayed for five decades—provided the opportunity for African Americans fully to participate in the political system, it is not surprising that a consequence of such participation was to underline the diversity of the U. S. polity's citizenry and the need for policies addressing past inequities. As Orlando Patterson notes, "the Afro-American identity movements and some form of affirmative action were the inevitable social fires that had to be ignited in the fight against the centuries-long holocaust of Euro-American racism."[160] An explanation for the neglect in the decades after 1930 is suggested by Gary Gerstle in his persuasive thesis that Progressive liberals found the ethnic conflicts of the 1920s, which were intimately associated with the new immigration policy, too intense and disturbing to address, and they therefore aligned themselves increasingly with the economic analyses and prognoses of New Dealers. This shift in the liberal intellectual agenda both ensured (unintentionally) the downgrading of ethnic and group diversity in the U.S. polity in the 1920s and encouraged a blind eye to be turned on the inequalities meted out to African Americans and some other citizens. The consequences of this neglect were elemental, however: in the 1960s, Gerstle concludes, liberals "were unprepared for the racial hatred that the advances of the civil rights movement unleashed among whites. Liberals could neither dissolve this hatred through social policy nor abandon their commitment to racial equality."[161]

These themes in American political development were greatly enhanced at the end of the nineteenth century. The thrust of immigration debates from the 1880s was for tighter restrictions based on categorizing potential immigrants. By the 1920s, there was little doubt that U. S. immigration policy was to be selective and exclusionary in terms of racial categories. Its discriminatory character was widely accepted. Senator David Reed, the cosponsor of the 1924 Johnson-Reed Act, told his colleagues: "I think most of us are reconciled to the idea of discrimination. I think the American people want us to discriminate; and I don't think discrimination in itself is unfair. *We have got to discriminate*. The only question that I think worries the committee is [which method] is the more plausible method of attaining that discrimination. Practically all of us are agreed that [racial discrimination] is an end that should be attained."[162] *The New York Times* declared in an editorial supporting the proposed (1924) law, that in respect of immigration, "the great test is assimilablity",[163] and this criterion plainly permitted differentiations between types of immigrants. These remarks crucially concerned divisions drawn between European immigrants, since both Chinese and Japanese immigrants were considered wholly ineligible for assimilation. Of the new European immigrants arriving in the 1920s, the historian Elliott Barkan remarks, "many Americans believed that the programs to Americanize immigrants and promote citizenship had failed and, in fact, these new people were not assimilable."[164] The stage was set for systematic restriction that would employ discriminatory criteria.

CHAPTER THREE

A Less Intelligent Class?

The Dillingham Commission and the New Immigrants

The political initiative systematically to restrict immigration into the United States began in the 1880s—quickly symbolized by the 1882 Chinese Exclusion Law and the specification of certain categories of excludables such as paupers and "idiots"—and culminated almost five decades later in the implementation of the national origins scheme in 1929. Between these dates, immigration policy was a salient issue in domestic American politics, as restrictionists mobilized support for new limits on immigration in terms of both overall numbers and "type" of immigrant. These restrictionist efforts included the promotion of a literacy test, stringent specifications of the eugenic or racial grounds for admission, and the establishment of quotas allocated to different nations. The period also included a highly detailed study of immigrants and immigration in the United States, undertaken by the Dillingham Commission, which is the focus of this chapter. Its conclusions and recommendations structured the subsequent debate about immigration policy and embodied the dominant assumption of the principal policy-makers.

Although the effects of immigrants on the composition of the U.S. population were apparent by the census of 1870,[1] it was the dramatic shift, between the 1880s and 1900s, in the sources of European immigration to the United States from northwestern countries to southeastern ones that excited sustained public debate and comment. In 1882, 648,186 European immigrants arrived in the United States, of whom 13.1 percent came from southern and eastern European countries, comprising Austria-Hungary, Greece, Italy, Montenegro, Poland, Portugal, Romania, Russia, Serbia, Spain, and Turkey. In 1907 these countries supplied 81 percent of a total of 1,207,619 European immigrants. In 1882 the principal sources for European immigrants were Belgium, Britain and Ireland, France, Germany, the Netherlands, Scandinavia, and Switzerland. For the period 1819 to 1910, 62.9 percent of European immigrants came from northern and western countries, 37.1 percent from southern and eastern Europe and Turkey in Asia.[2]

The restrictionist turn in American immigration policy rested on assumptions about the types of immigrants and their suitability for citizenship. It is not without irony that restrictionist politics often consisted of the most recently accepted immigrants mobilizing to delay a new generation (a point that President Grover Cleveland made especially in his statement in March 1897, when he vetoed the Lodge literacy bill: observing that the argument for restriction turned on the immigrants' "undesirability," he remarked that "the time is quite within recent memory when the same thing was said of immigrants who, with their descendants now are amongst our best citizens").[3] This phenomenon is most obviously illustrated by the rejection of European migrants from the southern and eastern countries: their admission was most keenly resisted by Americans whose own ancestors had journeyed from northern and western European countries. Illiteracy was one common deficiency imputed to the new arrivals. Thus, Archdeacon reports that "among immigrants who were at least fourteen years of age and who arrived between 1899 and 1909, the Germans, the Scandinavians, the English, and the Irish had illiteracy rates of 5.1 percent, .4 percent, 1.1 percent, and 2.7 percent, respectively. By contrast, the Italians, the Jews, the Poles, and the Slovaks had rates of 46.9 percent, 25.7 percent, 35.4 percent, and 24.3 percent, respectively."[4] Racist and prejudiced stereotypes of the new immigrants increasingly defined the post-1900 discourse employed by restrictionist organizations. In his *A History of the American People*, Woodrow Wilson, then a political scientist at Princeton University, alerted readers to the new source of immigrants manifest in the 1890 census, an alteration which "students of affairs marked with uneasiness." Overtaking the "sturdy stocks of the north of Europe" were "multitudes of men of the lowest class from the south of Italy and men of the meaner sort out of Hungary and Poland, men out of the ranks where there was neither skill nor energy nor any initiative of quick intelligence."

To Wilson's watchful eye, it was as if "the countries of the south of Europe were disburdening themselves of the more sordid and hapless elements of their population."[5] The Massachusetts Senator, Henry Cabot Lodge, characterized this wave of immigration as one bringing the "greatest relative increase from races most alien to the body of the American people." He added, "the shifting of the sources of the immigration is unfavorable, and is bringing to the country people whom it is very difficult to assimilate and who do not promise well for the standard of civilization in the United States—a matter as serious as the effect on the labor market."[6]

Following a brief review of some of the arguments of restrictionists, the bulk of the chapter provides a detailed analysis of the findings of the Dillingham Commission. Particular attention is paid to the importance of eugenic and anthropological research in the commission's report. The report's recommendations and conceptual categories influenced the immigration debate for the two decades after its publication.

Restrictionist Advocates

The American Protection Association, which was founded in 1887 and boasted a membership of over two million by the mid-1890s, was an energetic exponent of the need to limit the number and type of immigrants to the United States. In May 1894, it was joined by the Immigration Restriction League. The league was founded by three Harvard graduates, Prescott Hall, Charles Warren, and Robert DeC. Ward. The group was led by Ward, who was a professor at his alma mater and was destined to play a central role in restrictionist circles until the 1930s.[7] The league's self-proclaimed aims were the "limitation of immigration and a more careful selection, to the end that we shall receive no more aliens than can be properly assimilated."[8] The league was active until the 1920s, and the historian Barbara Solomon characterizes its role as one of creating an "ideology of restriction."[9] Its national committee included the economist John Commons; the eugenist Madison Grant (author of the grandiloquently titled *The Passing of the Great Race*); Lawrence Lowell, president of Harvard; and Franklin MacVeagh, who served as secretary of the treasury under President Taft between 1909 and 1913. It was enthusiastically restrictionist, warning against the "dangerous flood of immigrants" and advocating legislation for the "selection of those only who will make the most valuable citizens."[10] The league's members defined their task as raising consciousness about the level of immigration and the problem it posed, as its constitution stated: public opinion "must be made to recognize 'the necessity of a further exclusion of elements undesirable for citizenship or injurious to our national character.'"[11] In contrast to other restrictionist groups, such as organized labor, from its beginning, the Immigration Restriction League laid particular stress on the "racial" dimension of immigration, over and above the economic arguments in which the issue of immigrants was commonly discussed. Rather, the league's publications and arguments advanced what was to become a celebrated distinction between the "old" immigrants, of which their members' forebears were exemplary instances, and "new" immigrants. League secretary Prescott Hall posed the question starkly: did Americans "'want this country to be peopled by British, German, and Scandinavian stock, historically free, energetic, progressive, or by Slav, Latin, and Asiatic races, historically downtrodden, atavistic, and stagnant?'"[12]

The league's early years were concentrated on the literacy test that was pursued, at first unsuccessfully, in Congress by Senator Henry Cabot Lodge, whose congressional speeches contained plenty of racial language echoing the developing views of the league's members.[13] The latter's continued commitment to restriction fostered an alliance with the Junior Order of Mechanics, a descendant of the Know-Nothing party and virulently anti-Catholic. This "quiet entente" was, in Barbara Solomon's estimation, kept extremely quiet: "[I]n its own publications the League never referred to this questionable consorting. Anti-Catholic sentiment was at low ebb at the time the League cultivated relations with ignorant anti-Romanist groups. At home, Brahmin restrictionists never stooped to religious discrimination, but to aid restriction they willingly co-operated with Know-Nothing nativists elsewhere."[14] Solomon also documents how the league's concerns about the undesirability of the new immigrants increasingly converged with opinions and arguments proffered by social scientists such as John Commons, William Zipley, or Edward Ross, all of whom concurred in these views. Despite advancing economic theses about immigration, for "all these social scientists," Solomon remarks, "whatever their rational emphasis, immigration became a matter of the survival of the Anglo-Saxon stock."[15] The relatively few members of the Brahmins, such as Charles Eliot, onetime president of Harvard, who disagreed with the restrictionist approach to immigration did not capture the public debate, and indeed their views appeared increasingly exotic in the anti-immigrant tide: "as New Englanders shrank from the presence of immigrants in each successive decade, the older symbolic view of immigration vanished, until the exponents of an open, diverse world seemed strange and almost incomprehensible."[16]

From the fin de siècle, rationalization of hostility to the new immigrants was integrated with the pseudoscience of eugenists. It proved a successful alliance, which restrictionists such as the Immigration Restriction League promoted: "from 1890 to 1914, the racial ideology of the restrictionists built upon the older stereotypes, which New Englanders had shared, and imparted new meaning to them."[17] The application of biological principles of evolution to social development, so-called Social Darwinism, was hugely popular.[18] It not only reified the assumptions of racial calibrations within American society (including in respect to the marginalized African American population) but also provided explanations for social differences and for the United States's relative economic success compared with other countries. These ideas, expounded, for instance, in Herbert Spencer's writings, were valuable sources of belief for the well-off. Social Darwinism "could be used to defend cutthroat competition as natural, to condemn governmental interference in the economy as contrary to the more efficient action of natural laws, and to dismiss radical efforts to ameliorate social conditions as inconsistent with the inevitably slow improvement inherent in an evolutionary scheme."[19]

The diffusion of a Social Darwinian sociological pecking order coalesced with the stress, advanced by eugenists, on inherited sources of intelligence and ability. The scientific aim of eugenists was the determination of genetic sources of "feeble-mindedness" (associated with "racial degeneracy"), principles for its eradication, and the bases of selective breeding. Such concerns were widespread amongst academics, reformers, and politicians in the two decades before the First World War.[20] These concerns were strengthened by perceptions of immigrants: "[B]y 1900, one out of every seven Americans was foreign born. In the great cities of the east, this ratio was even narrower."[21] That President William McKinley was assassinated in 1901 by a naturalized immigrant who had a foreign-sounding name seemed merely to confirm burgeoning alarm about the scale of the problem posed by the new settlers. Political radicalism was frequently imputed to the new immigrants. By the end of the nineteenth century, many Americans doubted the ease with which immigrants could be assimilated with the existing (white) population, a point that Pole notes, if somewhat elliptically: "the intuition that men were equal and interchangeable . . . ran counter to the accumulating body of ethnic and religious prejudice, not to mention a good deal of social observation,"[22] though quite how "prejudice" and "social observation" coincided is not explained. One measure of political radicalism commonly cited by critics of immigration was radical newspapers in foreign languages. The numbers of these publications increased throughout the 1900s and 1910s; a survey in 1922 found that the number doubled after 1918 (see Table 3.1).

Table 3.1 Number of Radical Publications in Foreign Languages, 1922

Language	Number
Armenian	1
Bohemian	9
Bulgarian	3
Croatian	4
Danish	4
Estonian	1
Finnish	11
French	1
German	21
Greek	2
Hungarian	23
Italian	27
Jewish	20
Lettish	11
Lithuanian	15
Polish	7
Portuguese	1
Romanian	16
Slovenian	8
Spanish	8
Swedish	6
Ukranian	8
Yiddish	15
Total	222
Papers published in foreign countries	144
English papers in the United States	105
Grand total	471

Source: Derived from R. E. Park, *Americanization Studies: The Immigrant Press and Its Control* (New York: Harper & Brothers Publishers, 1922), p. 436.

Of the radical press, the sociologist Robert Park observed, "its object is to make its readers class-conscious."[23] Generally hostile to the United States and to capitalism, radical immigrant newspapers indicted their readers' new country, an approach that reached its fullest version in the anarchist press.

Thinly controlled intellectual disdain for the new immigrants was obvious in many petitions favoring the legislation. Thus, the Washington-based Waugh Chautaugua Literary and Scientific Circle's lament that "one of the gravest menaces to our country's welfare is the free and unrestricted admission of illiterate, incapable, and pauper immigrants within our borders"[24] mirrored the American Purity Federation's objection to "thousands of undeniably undesirable persons" arriving as immigrants.[25] Ecclesiastical support for the proposed restrictions came from some Protestant churches: the Cumberland Presbyterian Church in St. Louis rounded on "illiterate immigrants."[26]

Opponents of Restriction

Political and social pressure to limit immigration was marked by the 1890s; it did not abate as a political issue until 1930. The issue was intensely disputed, with the congressional committees on immigration subject to immense lobbying by both restrictionists and opponents of limits. Thus, the proposal, for a literacy test which was advanced in the Lodge Bill in 1897, provoked petitions both of support and of opposition. Any systematic educational test was likely to affect potential European immigrants. The German-American Society protested that demarcations between immigrants would deter the "better" migrants: "as provided by the bill, the fact that an immigrant, male or female, is able to read and to transcribe a passage from the Federal Constitution is to determine whether said immigrant shall be permitted to land." This mechanism would produce false economies: "[P]erhaps the half-educated foreigner who has nothing to lose in his own land will readily submit to such humiliating conditions. The conservative farmer, the sturdy laborer, will shrink from the same, however, and thus the country will be deprived of the most desirable class of immigrants."[27] Immigrants were also necessary to the expansion of the consumer market and to the creation of a set of distinct American values.

Another organization opposing the educational test wondered how many of the "founders" of the United States, themselves immigrants, would have been able to satisfy the new "illiberal" criterion.[28] The German Roman Catholic Central Society organized to have hundreds of petitions, which resolved opposition to the Lodge Bill, sent to Congress (some even in German, hardly a persuasive medium with the restrictionists).[29] The League of German-American Societies lambasted the bill for depriving America of "brawny arms and willing hands so very necessary for the development of our boundless resources." It added that "nothing in our estimation will harm our political, social, business and religious standing more than further restrictive legislation in the spirit of the proposed Lodge Bill, which we regard as wholly unamerican and unpatriotic." Employing a rather strained medical analogy, the petition's signatories declared that "the Nation's pulsation will grow weaker and weaker, as long as we resist the infusion of new blood into the arteries of public life and refuse to free ourselves from the shackles of knownothingism, which are hindering the restitution of the former progressive economic conditions of this country."[30] The Union of Free Communities of North America argued that restrictions on immigration contradicted "our country's history which, from its beginning until a short time ago, proves on every page, that one of our nation's most laudable virtues has been the hospitality offered to all comers."[31] It was joined by the New York City–based Arion Society, whose members resolved that immigration restriction abridged the "spirit of toleration and love of liberty bequeathed to us by the founders of this Republic."[32] The Polish National Alliance emphatically opposed the Lodge literacy scheme, claiming, not unreasonably, that the bill was principally "directed against the Slavonic nations." It cited distinguished immigrants (such as the composer Antonín Dvořák) in support of its interests, as well as the averred antisocialism of the Slavonic people: "[A]narchy forms no part of their character. Ultra-socialistic doctrines are not countenanced by them. They will compare favorably with the emigrants from other nations in Europe. We insist that it is not fair to judge the whole race by the condition of a limited number of unfortunate recent arrivals, whom stern necessity forced to live in hovels and work at starvation wages in coal mines."[33]

These opposing claims about the immigrants convey some of the emotions prompted by their arrival at the end of the nineteenth century.

The debates of the 1890s set the terms for those of the twentieth century: immigration was a source of intense controversy and often of vituperative opinion in the new century's first three decades. The arguments that were marshaled during passage of the Lodge Act continued to be rehearsed but were increasingly expressed in terms of racist and "scientific" claims; and indeed, Senator Henry Cabot Lodge himself anticipated this propensity in his attempt statistically to determine the distribution of ability among the American population according to national origin (a study that singled out the English racial heritage).[34] The connection between scientific arguments about race and patrician alarm about the new "hordes" received its first explicit formulation in the 1911 Dillingham Commission, whose report set the terms for the restrictionist measures incorporated in the 1924 law and favored by eugenists such as Charles Davenport, who zealously propagated eugenic arguments in the United States.

The Dillingham Commission

Data about American immigrants was provided by the comprehensive Dillingham Commission, which issued its forty-two-volume report in 1911 after four years of endeavor. The nine-member commission[35] was headed by Senator William P. Dillingham (Vermont), chairman of the Senate Immigration Committee. The bulk of the report presented valuable statistical and demographic data about immigrants. The scale of its undertaking and documentation, funded with a $1,000,000 appropriation from the U. S. Senate, was formidable. The huge project was a response to the 1907 immigration law whose drafters complained about the paucity of available reliable data regarding immigrants. The commission's two secretaries—who coordinated and completed the bulk of this vast project—were W. W. Husband and C. S. Atkinson, clerks of the Senate and the House Committees on Immigration respectively. Husband became an influential figure in U. S. immigration policy, later joining the U. S. Department of Labor and rising to the position of Commissioner General of Immigration.[36]

The study was corpulent because the Commission resolved on undertaking "an original investigation which, it was perfectly apparent, would necessarily be made far reaching and involve more work than any inquiry of a similar nature, except the census alone, than had ever been undertaken by the Government."[37] This is a good description. The commissioners examined a myriad of phenomena including patterns of immigration from Europe; conditions in the European countries from which the immigrants were drawn; the position and economic status of recent immigrants in the United States, including their occupations, residential patterns, levels of assimilation, and incidences of incarceration for pauperism, insanity, or criminality; the fecundity of immigrant women; and conditions in cities. The commission obtained original data about 3,200,000 individuals.

Old versus New Immigration

The commission advanced a conceptual dichotomy that had a profound influence on ensuing debate. It characterized northern and western European immigrants as constitutive of "old immigration,"[38] reserving the appellation "new immigration" for migrants from southern and eastern Europe; these categories were grounded in the significant shift in the source of immigrants from the nineteenth century. The dichotomy rested on a set of differences identified by the commission. The former group "was largely a movement of settlers who came from the most progressive sections of Europe for the purpose of making themselves homes in the New World." They entered a range of occupations, settled throughout the United States, and integrated with the existing population: "[T]hey mingled freely with the native Americans and were quickly assimilated, although a large proportion of them, particularly in later years, belonged to non-English-speaking races. This natural bar to assimilation, however, was soon overcome by them, while the racial identity of their children was almost entirely lost and forgotten."[39] For these immigrants, about whom the commission confidently described their "racial identity," America was the promised beau monde.

The character and experience of the recent arrivals was contrasted unfavorably to this model: "the new immigration has been largely a movement of unskilled laboring men who have come, in large part temporarily, from the less progressive and advanced countries of Europe in response to the call for industrial workers in the eastern and middle western States." The implication of this temporary status was inferred to be a reduced political commitment to the United States. The new immigrants rarely worked in agriculture.[40] They lived in ethnically concentrated communities in large cities, thereby evading systematic assimilation, a judgment retained in a 1920 Americanization study by John Daniels: "the great mass of immigrants who come to America settle first in urban 'colonies' of their own race." Such colonies "are looked upon as 'foreign' quarters, which cut the immigrant off from American influences and thus constitute a serious menace to the community. There is slight acquaintance with their inner workings and little comprehension of their real significance."[41] From a meticulous study of seven cities (New York, Chicago, Philadelphia, Boston, Cleveland, Buffalo, and Milwaukee), in which the commission's investigators visited 10,206 households comprising 51,006 individuals, the report anticipated Daniels's finding that the new "immigrant races live largely in colonies, many of whose characteristics are determined by the predominance of a foreign population";[42] the ability to speak English was often confined to school-age immigrants (a characteristic subsequently addressed by many employers who established English classes for their workers).[43]

The critical judgment that immigrants confined themselves unduly to particular neighborhoods and occupations overlooked the bars that were enacted by state legislatures to exclude immigrants from certain activities and occupations in the United States. From his study of immigrants and industry for the Carnegie Corporation Americanization series, William Leiserson castigated the federal government for failing to overturn state restrictions on immigrants' choices. Leiserson outlined an inventory of such impediments:

In Michigan an alien cannot get a barber's license. The labor law of New York requires that stationary engineers, moving picture machine operators, master pilots, and marine engineers shall be licensed, and non-citizens are disqualified by the license laws. Florida, Oregon, Texas and Washington prohibit aliens from catching and selling fish and oysters, while in Arizona, California, and Idaho license fees for fishing and hunting are from two and a half to ten times as high for the alien as for the citizen. Virginia prohibits aliens from planting oysters in certain river beds; and game laws, either placing prohibitions entirely on aliens or charging them higher license fees than citizens, are common in many states. In Louisiana an alien printer may receive no public printing to do. Virginia requires licenses for junk dealing and no non-citizen may receive such a license. In Georgia a person must have declared his intention of becoming a citizen before he can secure a peddler's license; and in Delaware a discriminating fee of a hundred dollars is charged to aliens for traveling peddler's licenses in addition to the fee charged for citizens.

In pre-prohibition days liquor licenses were issued to citizens only in many states, such as Ohio, New Jersey, Pennsylvania, Vermont, Texas, Florida, and Washington.[44]

These barriers were preceded by measures precluding immigrants' taking up unskilled jobs. The restriction of aliens' rights was applied in particular to the Chinese and Japanese, with some states, such as California, limiting the economic opportunities of Chinese aliens.[45] California barred aliens ineligible to acquire citizenship from purchasing commercial agricultural land, which, as noted in Chapter 2, excluded all nonwhites. The common defense of these measures and of licensing restrictions—that they were intended to encourage rapid naturalization by immigrants—failed to prevent the development of discrimination toward immigrants and consequently the resentment of the immigrants. These policies had the obverse effect of their stated rationale. As Leiserson concluded, "not by exclusion from American industrial opportunities and privileges will the immigrant be adjusted to American economic life. Such a policy, whatever its purpose, can result only in making it more difficult for him to establish himself on a basis of self-support and well-being."[46]

The new arrivals had a further, plainly debilitating characteristic. According to the Dillingham Commission, they were intellectually inferior:

> [T]he new immigration as a class is far less intelligent than the old, approximately one-third of all those over 14 years of age when admitted being illiterate. Racially they are for the most part essentially unlike the British, German and other peoples who came during the period prior to 1880, and generally speaking they are actuated in coming for different ideals, for the old immigration came to be a part of the country, while the new, in a large measure, comes with the intention of profiting, in a pecuniary way, by the superior advantages of the new world and then returning to the old country.[47]

This characterization of the new immigrants' low intelligence was periodically marshaled in debates in the ensuing two decades. It was anticipated in the attitudes and arguments of restrictionist groups such as the elitist Immigration Restriction League, which was based in the Brahmin community in Boston. From the league's foundation in 1894, its leading lights, including Prescott Hall, criticized the inferiority and undesirability of the new immigrants. As New England elite opinion became more accommodating of Irish and German immigrants, who previously had been the subject of considerable bile and prejudice, so its worries were transferred to the new arrivals, as Barbara Solomon notes: "by 1900, Yankee stereotypes of the old immigrant groups had become more sympathetic; but those of new immigrant groups, whom restrictionists wished to exclude, steadily deteriorated."[48] It was particularly southern Italians who were characterized so adversely. Anti-Semitism also developed, toward Russian Jews in particular, a tendency that aligned all too easily with eugenic categorizations. Thus, the eugenist Charles Davenport wrote of Russian and southern European Jews that "with their intense individualism and ideals of gain at the cost of any interest," they stood at the "opposite extreme from the English and the Scandinavian immigration with their ideals of community life in the open country, advancement by the sweat of the brow, and the uprearing of families in the fear of God and the love of country."[49] This was hardly impartial or scientific language.

Aside from intellectual inferiority, the assimilability of the new immigrants was questionable, causing a grave concern. The commission discovered that as much as 40 percent of the new immigration movement consisted of migrants returned to Europe, of whom about two-thirds remained in Europe, and so the commission contrasted this pattern unfavorably to that of earlier migrants, who had settled permanently. The "old immigration" group was judged by the Dillingham Commission to be assimilated and merged with native American stock. Of the new immigrants, the vast majority, as a corollary of their concentration in large urban centers, were employed in manufacturing and mining. They predominated in unskilled jobs, attaining, in effect, a monopoly of "unskilled labor activities in many of the more important industries." The commission argued that such unskilled labor did not affect skilled positions but, by forming a regular supply of cheap unskilled labor, had "kept conditions in the semiskilled and unskilled occupations from advancing."[50] New immigrants avoided trade unions (a disposition fostered by the consistent unenthusiasm of unions to organize immigrants, as Leiserson reported: "more unions have failed or neglected to organize the recent immigrants than have succeeded, and with the exception of the recent efforts in the stock yards and in the steel industry, the national headquarters of the American Federation of Labor have not stepped in to do the work which the constituent unions have left undone").[51] Such workers concentrated on making wages to send to their native country, kept close links with their fellow nationals, and eschewed assimilation. This latter blemish became a rallying point for restrictionists, who doubted their suitability to naturalize anyway. Barbara Solomon correctly emphasizes the extent to which the Dillingham Commission's report advanced and legitimated the types of ethnic distinctions and racial hierarchies privileged by the anti-immigrant, prorestriction movement, and its intellectual accolades: "[S]eemingly restrained in its ethnic judgments, the Report really fulfilled the restrictionist tradition initiated by [Francis] Walker and extended by the Immigration Restriction League and sympathetic sociologists. As a result, intellectuals and reformers associated ethnic and economic liabilities of the latest immigrants so loosely that the one set of impressions inevitably suggested and complemented the other."[52] The commission strengthened the notion that a vast array of new "racial" groups had landed in the United States.

There were voices of skepticism about these alleged flaws of the new immigrants. The settlement movement (designed to help immigrants adjust to American life), of whom a leading light was Jane Addams, assumed that the newcomers' differences arose from culture, not from "race." Addams and others attempted benevolently to assist immigrants to learn English and to adjust to their new country, aims submerged in the wartime and post-1918 Americanization movement when instilling Americanism was primary. In congressional hearings held a year after the publication of the Dillingham Commission, Grace Abbott, director of the Immigrants' Protective League (Chicago) and a defender of immigrants' interests, told congressmen of her organization's efforts to aid the "Americanization" of immigrants. She threw cold water on the ahistorical notion that the older immigrants had been perceived at the time of their arrival as any less assimilable than the new immigrants were now judged in 1912. Abbott reported that "when you come in close daily contact with the newer arrivals, you find that they are men and women just like the rest of us, some good and some bad, and it is impossible to discriminate against them as a whole." But, she added, "I am sure in the background of the minds of many who have visited the immigrant quarters is that feeling that the immigration has changed and that the present races of immigrants can not be assimilated and should not be admitted."[53] Abbott was skeptical about assimilation, querying both the precise content of "fundamental American ideals" and the time it took to absorb them. It was the resilience and determination of the new immigrants, often living in penury, that impressed Abbott, and not their threat to the American family or way of life. She argued that most immigrants arriving in the United States had a clear notion of the nation's distinct values and ideals and had been motivated to migrate partly as a consequence of this knowledge; this view was not widely shared. Abbott's humane reflections did not become the mainstream view. Indeed, such sentiments were outrightly derided and disregarded.

To assess assimilation, three measures were employed by the Dillingham Commission:[54] learning English, acquiring U.S. citizenship, and more nebulously, the abandoning of native customs. On all three criteria, the new immigrants were found wanting. In addition, patterns of home ownership were contrasted between new and old immigrants, with the Commission concluding that "as a rule the races of older immigration from Great Britain and northern Europe are more extensive home owners as a whole than the members of races of recent immigration."[55] The failure of new immigrants to assimilate was explained by the absence of families and the predominance of single men: "it is common practice for men of this class in industrial communities to live in boarding or rooming groups, and as they are also usually associated with each other in their work they do not come in contact with Americans, and consequently have little or no incentive to learn the English language, become acquainted with American institutions or adopt American standards." Immigrants with families, however, achieved a much fuller participation in American life, principally by their children attending school; children acted as "unconscious agents in the uplift of their parents."[56] Those immigrants who did assimilate were still looked on askance by the commission and other critics of immigration because of the allegedly harmful biological effects of intermarriage and interbreeding on the native American "stock."

The commission undertook meticulous research into the so-called racial composition of the new immigration. It devoted one of its forty-two volumes to the production of a "dictionary of races or peoples," which was prepared by Dr. Daniel Folkmar[57] (a volume that the eugenist Dr. Harry Laughlin praised for laying "the foundation for future biological work")[58]—and a precursor to U.S. Education Commissioner Philander Claxton's "calendar of racial incidents." In Robert Carlson's view, the dictionary "translated Anglo-Saxonism into a scientific classification system";[59] its political character was implied by the classification of the Irish as Anglo-Saxon rather than as Celt ("the race which originally spoke Irish, one of the Celtic group of Aryan tongues"),[60] a move reflecting this group's pivotal role in the restrictionist alliance opposing eastern and southern European immigration. This strategic importance was apparent in the dictionary's description of Irish attitudes to American democracy: "like the English, the Irish come to the United States speaking our own language and imbued with sympathy for our ideals and our democratic institutions."[61] This democratic commitment would have surprised many nineteenth-century critics of Irish immigrants who rejected them precisely for their lack of fitness to govern.[62] The commission mostly utilized the racial categories already employed by the Bureau of Immigration:[63] "the Commission uses the term 'race' in a broad sense, the distinction being largely a matter of language and geography, rather than one of color or physical characteristics such as determines the various more restricted racial classifications in use, the most common of which divides mankind into only five races."[64] These were Caucasian, Mongolian, Malay, Ethiopian, and American Indian. Despite commissioning this scholarly dictionary, the Dillingham commission focused principally on the traits of immigrants from southeastern Europe. These traits were addressed explicitly by the commission's anthropological study.

The Anthropological Research

Professor Franz Boas, an eminent anthropologist at Columbia University,[65] produced a study for the Dillingham Commission on "Changes in Bodily Form of Descendants of Immigrants."[66] This undertaking reflected in large part the prevailing ideas in biology, eugenics, and anthropology about the plausibility of specifying races and the belief in the ability to measure physical changes over time.[67] The focus here was the obverse of assimilation: rather than concentrating on how immigrants were assimilated into or affected by the new culture, the question posed was how immigrants and their descendants shaped the dominant population. Boas was a keen advocate of the effect of culture as a determinant of different societies, according it greater significance than race.[68] Applying anthropometric studies to subjects in New York City, Boas's findings were "much more far-reaching than was anticipated" and in the commission's judgment indicated "a discovery in anthropological science that is fundamental in importance." The findings had "awakened the liveliest interest in scientific circles here and abroad," and the commission urged continued investigation. The result exciting this scientific awakening was summarized thus:

> [T]he report indicates that the descendant of the European immigrant changes his type even in the first generation almost entirely, children born not more than a few years after the arrival of the immigrant parents in America developing in such a way that they differ in type essentially from their foreign-born parents. These differences seem to develop during the earliest childhood and persist throughout life. It seems that every part of the body is influenced in this way, and that even the form of the head, which has always been considered one of the most permanent hereditary features, undergoes considerable change.[69]

Boas's study is a vivid document. It is generously illustrated with cephalic indexes of head sizes and other measurements of different nationalities (a plan to assess the condition of subjects' teeth as the main indicator of changes in bodily form had to be abandoned because of a shortage of trained researchers). Boas's key premise was that the "form of the body seems to be the most suitable characteristic of any given race"[70] and hence is ripe for measurement. Boas cited evidence that "under a more favorable environment the physical development of a race may improve," and he wanted to determine whether the United States provided such a propitious context.[71]

Boas's investigations, in fact, did apparently unearth significant changes to immigrants' descendants. The head proved to be the crucial indicator of change:

> [I]n most of the European types that have been investigated the head form, which has always been considered one of the most stable and permanent characteristics of human races, undergoes far-reaching changes due to the transfer of people from European to American soil. For instance, the east European Hebrew, who has a very round head, becomes more long-headed; the south Italian, who in Italy has an exceedingly long head, becomes more short-headed; so that in this country both approach a uniform type, as far as the roundness of the head is concerned.[72]

The longer that immigrants lived in the United States before having children, the "better" the results for their offspring, a conclusion reached by comparing measurable features of individuals of a similar "race" who were either born abroad or born in the United States within ten years of the mother's arrival, or who were born ten years after the mother had migrated to the United States. A comparison of Hebrew and Sicilian cases seemed to provide overwhelming evidence.

Boas emphasized the cultural rather than the biological determinants of these results, though his analysis provided a framework for others to stress racial dissimilarities and to use this language of race. In this sense, the framework contributed to the legitimacy of eugenic-type research in debates about immigration.[73]

The study was carried further with a detailed examination of selected Bohemians, Slovaks and Hungarians, Poles, Hebrews, Sicilians, Neapolitans, and Scots, selected "because they represent a number of the most distinct European types"[74] and because they predominated among the new immigrants. All these groups evinced significant changes with both the stature increasing and the length and width of the head decreasing (Table 3.2). Boas observed that the data "show that the changes in the dimensions of the head do not depend by any means upon the absolute or relative measurements which are found among the foreign-born, but that heads which are nearly of the same length, like those of the Bohemians and of the Hebrews, behave quite differently in this country, the length of the one increasing, while the length of the other decreases."[75] Such conclusions naturally appear dubious to the modern reader.

These differences between the American-born descendants of immigrants and the European-born immigrants were traced by Boas and his colleagues to early childhood (the features of which continued throughout adult life). Weighing up the evidence regarding facial measurements, Boas leaned heavily toward environmental influences:

the development of the width of the face seems to my mind to show most clearly that it is not the mechanical treatment of the infant that brings about the changes in question. The cephalic index suffers a very slight decrease from the fourth year to adult life. It is therefore evident that children who arrive in America very young can not be much affected by the American environment in regard to their cephalic index. On the other hand, if we consider a measurement that increases appreciably during the period of growth, we may expect that in children born

Table 3.2 Measurements of American-Born minus Measurements of Foreign-born, Weighted according to Number of Cases

Race and Sex	Length of Head (in mm)	Width of Head (in mm)	Cephalic Index	Width of Face (in mm)	Stature (in cm)	Weight (in lb)
Bohemian						
Males	−0.7	−2.3	−1.0	−2.1	+2.9	170
Females	−.6	−1.5	−.6	−1.7	+2.2	180
Hungarians and Slovaks						
Males	−.5	−1.1	−.7	−1.0	+5.9	54
Females	−.3	−.9	−1.0	−2.2	+1.0	38
Poles						
Males	−.3	+.2	+.2	+.7	+4.2	22
Females	+.9	−1.6	−1.4	−1.3	+1.7	27
Hebrews						
Males	+2.2	−1.8	−2.0	−1.1	+1.7	654
Females	+1.9	−2.0	−2.0	−1.3	+1.5	259
Sicilians						
Males	−2.4	+.7	+1.3	−1.2	−0.1	188
Females	−3.0	+.8	+1.8	−2.0	−0.5	144
Neapolitans						
Males	−.9	+.9	+.9	−1.2	+0.6	248
Females	−1.7	+1.0	+1.4	−6	−1.8	126
Scottish						
Males	+1.4	−0.5	−0.8	−1.5	+1.8	39
Females	−0.3	+0.3	+0.2	+1.9	+3.9	33

Source: Derived from U.S. Immigration Commission, *Abstract of the Report on Changes in Bodily Form of Descendants of Immigrants* (Washington, D.C.: GPO, 1911), p. 28.

abroad but removed to America when young, the total growth may be modified by American environment. The best material for this study is presented by the Bohemians, among whom there are relatively many full-grown American-born individuals. The width of face of Bohemians, when arranged according to their age at the time of immigration, shows that there is a loss among those who came here as young children—the greater the younger they were. Continuing this comparison with the American-born, born one, two, etc years after the arrival of their mothers, the width of face is seen to decrease still further. It appears therefore that the American environment causes a retardation of the growth of the width of face at a period when mechanical influences are no longer possible.[76]

Boas concluded that settlement in large American cities and intermarriage patterns probably accounted for these trends.

Politically, Boas's findings, although hailed as startling and of scientific importance by the Dillingham Commission, in fact contradicted the burgeoning focus on hereditary factors in determining national characteristics.[77] Such factors were certainly given greater prominence by eugenists; indeed, skeptics of eugenics cited Boas's research.[78] If the U. S. environment had a positive effect on its residents, including recent immigrants, then agitation about the baneful consequences of the new immigration appeared misplaced and even pernicious. Indeed, Boas's own scholarly work was highly critical of race as a category for comparative analysis. His cultural anthropological framework eschewed the common assumption of the researcher's superiority over the investigated culture, an approach methodologically attained by acquiring the language of the studied group. This approach permitted an appreciation of culture—rather than simply of mental aptitudes and abilities—as a contributor to behavior and skills, a point that Thomas Gossett stresses: "when Boas speaks of race theories it is generally with the reluctance of a man who feels torn away from his essential task of examining the effects of a given culture upon a given people."[79]

Consequently, eugenists and others interested in such questions made little effort to build on or to incorporate Boas's results, though as Pole pertinently remarks, Boas's "methods did not contribute much toward liberating the popular mind from the notion that head forms and physical structure had something to do with what was inside the head."[80] The claims of Madison Grant in his book *The Passing of the Great Race*—forewarning of the end of the "great white race" because of interracial mixing—had greater influence than did the research of Boas in reinforcing the latent racial concerns of restrictionists. Such grand claims were comfortably wedded with the Mendelian laws of inheritance studied by eugenists. Boas's research contributed indirectly to eugenic debates because, by employing measurements of cephalic indexes, it could be engaged with in those terms. In Pole's phrase, it was "susceptible to attack by arguments based on his own continued respect for measurements of the cephalic index."[81] This judgment is in danger, however, of belittling the importance of Boas's research in the 1920s in laying to rest assumptions of scientific racism (even if advocates of restriction choose to ignore this implication).

Politically and intellectually, Boas fought racism both in politics and in scholarship, early championing the cause of African Americans' rights and subverting racist arguments: "it is very improbable that the majority of individuals composing the white race should possess greater ability than the Negro race." He recognized the dangers posed by pseudoscientific arguments for African Americans, warning that "the strong development of racial consciousness, which has been increasing during the last century . . . is the gravest obstacle to the progress of the Negro race, as it is an obstacle to the progress of all strongly individualized social groups."[82] As Thomas Gossett comments: "Boas was no cloistered expert. He spoke out again and again in the 1920's against racists like Madison Grant, Henry Fairfield Osborn, and Lothrop Stoddard."[83] He was an early and vigorous opponent of Nazi racism. In the public debate about immigration, however, Boas's work was less significant than other parts of the Dillingham Commission. Nonetheless, eugenists were highly suspicious of his work for the commission. When his name was proposed to the Immigration Restriction League as a potential member of a eugenics study committee, it was quickly rejected by Prescott Hall in a letter to the eugenist Charles Davenport. Hall, secretary of the league, wrote: "I must confess to . . . not very much confidence in Dr Boas. Of course, he has certain technical training for such work but I believe he is a relative of Emil Boas who was agent of the Hamburg-American line and was employed by the Immigration Commission as expert at the suggestion of Congressman Bennett to please the steamship companies and give him a fat job." He added, "while I am not of course competent to pass on the results of his work, and while his results are interesting, they seem to me far less important than investigation as to the mental traits—at least, if Dr Wood's theory is correct that the higher cellular lines modify last, and the lower ones, like the bones and muscular, modify first."[84]

Crime, Poverty, Mental Health, and the New Immigrants

The Dillingham Commission gave close attention to the immigration of criminals and the "mentally defective," as well as to the incidence of immigrants in receipt of charity or engaged in crime. These concerns resonated through immigration debates. In fact, it was the stories and claims about these features of southern and eastern European immigrants that had fueled the debate in the 1880s and 1890s, and indeed contributed to the founding of the commission. Exhaustive studies were undertaken by the commission's staff.

Few immigrants became charity seekers, despite commonplace assumptions to the contrary, a reflection, in the commission's view, of stringent immigration tests.[85] Of those with mental illnesses, the commission accepted that medical examinations already in force played a significant role in identifying sufferers but were less good at anticipating the development of such debilities. Legislation in 1882 and 1891, respectively, excluded the immigration of lunatics and of insane persons. A law passed in 1907 excluded "idiots, imbeciles, feeble-minded persons, persons insane within five years of the date of application of admission, persons having had two or more previous attacks of insanity, and persons suffering from mental defects, not otherwise specified, sufficiently serious to affect ability to earn a living."[86] These laws did not result, however, in increased number of exclusions, especially in the new century (Table 3.3). In a key section of its report, the commission claimed that immigrants were disproportionately represented in the asylum population: "[O]f the 150,151 insane persons enumerated in hospitals on December 31, 1903, 47,078 or 31.4 per cent, were foreign-born whites. The proportion of native-born whites of native parentage was 33.6 per cent and the proportion of native-born whites of foreign parentage was 10 per cent. Only 6.6 per cent of all the insane persons enumerated were colored."[87] Combining the numbers for the insane with the "feeble minded" gave a total of 47,934 "mentally unsound persons of foreign birth" in U. S. hospitals and institutions. These data permitted the commission to conclude that although significant numbers of hopeful immigrants were excluded on mental health grounds, nonetheless, "there are in the United States many thousands of insane or feeble-minded persons of foreign birth." From the commission's calculations, "it appears that insanity is relatively more prevalent among the foreign-born than among the native-born, and relatively more prevalent among certain immigrant races or nationalities than among others."[88] Of foreign nationalities' relative contribution to the insane population in hospitals in the United States, the descending rank ordering was Irish, Scandinavians, Germans, French, Scottish, Hungarians, English and Welsh, Italians, Russians and Poles, and Canadians. These sorts of conclu-

Table 3.3 Exclusion of Immigrants and Insanity, 1890–1909

Year	Lunacy	Insanity	Idiocy	Idiocy and Insanity	Imbecility	Feeble-mindedness	Total
1890	26		3				29
1891		36	2				38
1892		17	4				21
1893		8	3				11
1894		5	4				9
1895				6			6
1896		10	1				11
1897		6	1				7
1898		12	1				13
1899		19	1				20
1900		32	1				33
1901		16	6				22
1902		27	7				34
1903		23	1				24
1904		33	16				49
1905		92	38				130
1906		139	92				231
1907		189	29				218
1908		159	20		45	121	345
1909		141	18		42	121	322
Total							1,573

Source: Derived from U.S. Immigration Commission, *Immigration and Insanity* (Washington, D.C.: GPO, 1911), p. 7.

sions were clearly likely to be taken as further grounds for restriction by proponents of this position, though the first three groups were not part of the so-called new immigration. In the 1920s, the allegedly disproportionate number of immigrants in insane institutions triggered part of the restrictionist movement.

The data on immigrants in charity hospitals suggested contrary inferences: "the proportion of patients of races of recent immigration from southern and eastern Europe was much smaller than is popularly believed to be the case."[89] Alcoholism was the commonest cause of hospitalization. In respect to immigrants and crime, the populist linkage was again less manifest in the data compiled. Although statistics did demonstrate that convictions for crimes were higher among foreign-born than native-born Americans, they did not imply a greater criminal tendency among the former. The commission added, judiciously, that "it must be remembered that the proportion of persons of what may be termed the criminal age is greater among the foreign-born than among natives, and when due allowance is made for this fact it appears that criminality, judged by convictions, is about equally prevalent in each class."[90]

Such generosity was absent in its detailed discussion of Italian immigrants. The commission unequivocally argued—partly on the basis of results of a field trip to the country—that Italian criminals were gaining admittance to the United States. This assessment was interweaved with startling generalities about Italians: "an alarming feature of the Italian immigration movement to the U. S. is the fact that it admittedly includes many individuals belonging to the criminal classes, particularly of southern Italy and Sicily." Hence, the "prevailing alarm in this respect" did not rest simply on "the fact that a good many actual criminals come to the U. S. from Italy, but also by the not unfounded belief that certain kinds of criminality are inherent in the Italian race." Stereotyping of Italians was harsh: "in the popular mind, crimes of personal violence, robbery, blackmail, and extortion are peculiar to the people of Italy, and it can not be denied that the number of such offenses committed among Italians in this country warrants the prevalence of such a belief."[91] Such negative portraits of Italians were common, as the historian Humbert Nelli summarizes: "to Americans the Italian immigrants who poured into the country in the late nineteenth and early twentieth centuries . . . appeared to be the dregs of a broken and defeated race,"[92] a view also informing Woodrow Wilson's *History of the American People.*

A related study comes four years after the Dillingham Commission, in an address to the NAACP's annual conference. An analysis of the women's penal institution in Bedford, New York, found no particular association between nationality and crime: "each race contributed in proportion to its numerical strength . . . no one race can boast over another as to its moral character." However, the children of foreign-born parents did significantly outnumber native-born women confined at Bedford.[93]

Dillingham's Conclusions

The commission's copious data provided, in due course, grist to the eugenists' mill and others interested in differentiating between types of immigrants. Its analysis plainly distinguished new immigrants from old and appeared unequivocally to demonstrate the unsuitability, as potential citizens, of the new arrivals. Politically, these conclusions set the stage for legislation.

Archdeacon argues that the commission's analysis was biased: not only did the commission romanticize the "old immigrants," but also "its main failing came in the heavy-handed use of current racial theories in the analysis of data."[94] Although this sort of interpretation is too crude a summary of the massive research and data compilation undertaken by the Dillingham Commission (and in employing "racial theory," the commission was in step with most of the intellectual establishment), nonetheless, the commission's report played an important role in reifying stereotypes about immigrants, notably sentimentalizing the distinction between "old" immigrants from northern and western Europe and "new" immigrants from eastern and southern Europe, the latter portrayed as undesirable and unassimilable migrants.[95] Congressman Albert Johnson, cosponsor of the 1924 legislation on immigration, remarked that the Dillingham Commission's study constituted the "great impetus" that culminated in the 1924 law.[96] However, the eugenist Harry Laughlin, adviser to the House Committee on Immigration in the 1920s, criticized the Dillingham Commission for framing its researches, despite their thoroughness, "exclusively as an economic problem"; consequently, he maintained, the "biology of the task received relatively little attention."[97] Laughlin's assessment contradicts the scholar Keith Fitzgerald's claim that "the intellectual influence running throughout the commission's policy recommendations is clearly that of eugenics."[98] In Laughlin's favor, it is notable that the dictionary of race, which he praised, was not systematically integrated into the commission's lengthy analyses, and the commission's case for restriction was advanced principally on economic grounds. Boas's findings were also incongruous with the commission's general approach and out of step with populist demands for restriction, though the commission's remarks about the "criminality" inherent to Italians were a measure in this direction. Furthermore, the historian Ian Dowbiggin judges that "the fact that the report paid scant attention to the biologic nature of immigrants greatly disappointed nativists, who considered race and eugenics to be the heart of the matter."[99] Such a view understates the presence of eugenic assumptions in the report. Indeed, in the year that Dillingham's report appeared, the eugenist Charles Davenport wrote

Prescott Hall at the Immigration Restriction League proposing the "formation of a committee of the Eugenics Section on family traits of recent immigrants" on the grounds that the "time is ripe."[100] Hall responded enthusiastically. By publishing Boas's study, a legitimacy was imparted to analysis in terms of racial types and categories, even if such use commonly distorted the anthropologist's careful research and disregarded his caveats.

The commission reprinted the prolix submissions of restrictionist groups. In fact, it was a significant outlet for their views, almost all of which celebrated an Anglo-American conception of U. S. nationality often combined with an unequivocal nativism. The staunchly restrictionist and traditionally anti-Catholic Junior Order of American Mechanics (JOAM), whose membership was expanding dramatically during these years, told the Dillingham Commission that the "baleful influence of such a low type of immigration on our civilization, labor, morals, and citizenship is patent to every observer." The migrants were unassimilable: "[T]his country has wonderful assimilating powers and can assimilate and distribute through its body politic a great army of worthy and industrious people and those of the high moral type. But it can not assimilate the mass of lower Europe and protect its high standard of morality and good order."[101] It favored Celtic and Teutonic blood, representative of "that independent race of men of the Aryan blood."[102]

These sentiments were echoed by the Immigration Restriction League. Its secretary, Prescott Hall (a keen eugenist),[103] informed the Dillingham Commission that a literacy test was required urgently and that eugenic principles dictated the enactment of significant controls on immigrants. Hall advanced a crude eugenic framework, vitiated with the dangers of racial mixing:

> [R]ecent investigations in biology show that heredity is a far more important factor in the progress of any species than environment . . . Assuming what is by no means proved, that a mixed race is a better race, we should do as we do in breeding any other species than the human, viz, secure the best specimens to breed from . . . We should exercise at least as much care in admitting human beings as we exercise in relation to animals or insect pests or disease germs . . . [T]here are certain parts of Europe from which all medical men and all biologists would agree that it would be better for the American race if no aliens at all were admitted.[104]

Hall unproblematically explained a country's "backwardness" as arising from inherent racial failings, which the United States could not be expected to absorb: "[I]f these immigrants 'have not had opportunities' it is because their races have not made the opportunities. There is no reason to suppose that a change of location will result in a change of inborn tendencies."[105] These caricatures, soon complemented by eugenist arguments about racial delineations, bolstered critics of immigration during the ensuing two decades.

Dillingham's Recommendations

The Dillingham Commission recommended that Congress enact restrictions on immigration, principally because of what it claimed to be the unassimilable character of recent migrants. This unassimilability differentiated them from the older type of immigrants. It wanted tougher assessment of potential immigrants in their country of origin, to find out about criminal records and mental aptitude. Immigrants who became public charges within three years of arriving in the United States were to be deported. It wanted reform of so-called "immigrant banks" and of employment agencies, both of which tended to exploit and encourage immigrants. The continued exclusion of Chinese laborers was endorsed. Its major recommendations addressed the position of single, unskilled males migrating from southern and eastern Europe, whom the Dillingham Commission judged both uninterested in assimilation and mostly unsuitable for naturalization. To effect this reduction, it proposed several measures: a literacy test, a measure already enjoying considerable support in Congress (though not in the White House);[106] a fixed quota by race "arriving each year to a certain percentage of the average of that race arriving during a given period of years";[107] the exclusion of unskilled workers unaccompanied by dependents; annual limits on the number of immigrants admitted at each port; the specification of a fixed amount of money to be possessed by each immigrant on arrival; and an increase in the head tax, applied more leniently to men with families. Broadly, these recommendations both structured discussion and informed the detail of the immigration debate by 1929. They were a triumph for the arguments of restrictionists, salient in U.S. politics from the 1890s; indeed, Barbara Solomon suggests that these recommendations decisively "marked the advance of the [Immigration Restriction] League's cause."[108] Both the literacy test and the system of admission based on nationality quotas were adopted, the latter a mechanism that effected selection by assessment of individual suitability. Later reforms favored skilled over unskilled immigrants.

There was a lone voice of dissent on the Dillingham Commission, that of Congressman William Bennet. From New York, Bennet argued strongly against a literacy test and maintained that the commission's own research revealed that the problems of criminality, insanity, and pauperism among the new immigrants had been exaggerated. (This view seems well-founded in the commission's data, and I would concur with Keith Fitzgerald's assessment that "what little interpretation of this data the reports offered tended to undercut racial distinctions among immigrants on the grounds that their economic circumstances explained their living conditions and economic pursuits more than any other characteristic").[109] One probusiness lobby, the National Liberal Immigration League, was quick to stress the mixed picture painted in the Dillingham Commission (it had, in fact, strongly supported the commission's establishment[110]). It vigorously lobbied the executive to resist from enacting further restrictionist laws. Its president, Charles Eliot, gave several reasons for permitting generous immigration, including the abundance of land in the U. S. waiting to be settled and the need for labor to develop and expand industry, a process to which even unskilled workers contributed. The league opposed a literacy test "because ability to read is no proof of either health or character" and, in a telling phrase, observed that "in all races the most dangerous criminals come from classes that can read and write, and not from the illiterate."[111] The league argued that assimilation was a lengthy process that ought not to be judged or assessed prematurely: "experience during the nineteenth century shows that real assimilation will take centuries; and that amalgamation, or blending of races through intermarriage, is not only extraordinarily slow, but of doubtful issue as to the strength and viability of offspring." Eliot added that "the different races already in this country live beside each other, and all produce in time good citizens of the Republic; but they do not blend."[112] Behind such rhetoric, the league's principal motive was a liberal economic one. It opposed a literacy test because of the probable reduction of a regular labor supply.[113] The league proposed transporting unemployed workers from the large Eastern cities to points of employment throughout the country, particularly mill towns. Consequently, it found itself in conflict with organized labor, criticizing the efforts of the American Federation of Labor (AFL) president, Samuel Gompers, to secure immigration restriction through a literacy test.[114] Organized labor's converse interests made it a strong supporter of restriction.[115]

The Dillingham Commission's support for a literacy test, together with the pressures from restrictionist interest groups and activists, bore fruit in 1917—aided by American entry to the Great War—when such a test was legislated. This criterion required prospective immigrants aged over sixteen to read a passage in a language of their choice at the point of entry to the United States. The test was supported by both organized labor[116] (fearful of cheap workers) and pressure groups such as the Immigration Restriction League.[117] The latter maintained that the "reading test calls for only the most rudimentary education. Italy has started to improve its school system every time this bill has been pending. The Russian Jews can certainly learn Yiddish if they are willing to take the trouble, even if not always able to learn Russian."[118] The Immigration Restriction League had favored the literacy test from the end of the nineteenth century, energetically lobbying the federal executive to enact it. The league received support from the Bureau of Immigration at the Commerce Department, whose Commissioner-General had endorsed a literacy test since 1900.[119]

The literacy test had been vetoed once by President Taft[120] and twice by President Wilson, the latter having wooed immigrant voters in the 1912 presidential election. As Higham astutely notes, this action had placed Wilson in an invidious position: "Woodrow Wilson labored throughout the campaign under the embarrassing handicap of having to repudiate over and over again the contemptuous phrases he had written about southern and eastern European immigrants in his *History of the American People* a decade before."[121] These vetoes prompted copious correspondence from both proliteracy- and antiliteracy-tests groups.[122] The International Association of Machinists complained bitterly about the presidential veto in February 1915, as did a host of other labor organizations, including the Wood, Wire and Metal Lathers' Union; International Typographical Union; Brotherhood of Carpenters and Joiners; Tobacco Workers' Union; Pattern Makers' League; Paper Makers; Boot and Shoe Workers' Union; and Switchmen's Union.[123] Economic liberals supported the vetoes.

The political and electoral pressure for limits was too intense by

1917, and so Woodrow Wilson's veto of that year was overturned by Congress. For the scholar Robert Divine, the 1917 law marks a fundamental modification of the immigration law. It replaced the tenet of individual selection and suitability with one of group selection: "a new principle, group selection, was evident in such discrimination directed against the new immigration, and this concept of judging men by their national and racial affiliations rather than by their individual qualifications was to become the basic principle in the immigration legislation of the postwar period."[124] The literacy test exempted those who could demonstrate that they were escaping from religious persecution (designed principally for Russian Jews), and an immigrant's dependents were to be admitted regardless of their literacy. The 1917 Immigration Act formalized the Asia-Pacific Triangle, an Asiatic barred zone, which building on the previous restrictions in respect to Chinese and Japanese immigrants was intended completely to exclude Asian immigration to the United States.

The law's passage halted but did not end agitation for restriction. It is notable that the pressure for restriction by set nationality quotas, another recommendation of the Dillingham Commission, intensified. The clerk of the House Committee on Immigration speculated that "enactment of the first quota law was delayed because of the hectic and inflated prosperity which did not go to smash until the late summer of 1920. Immediately the lists of unemployed began to grow it was easy for restrictionists to have their way."[125] When the situation did "go to smash," the restrictionist pressure, reinforced by eugenic critiques, was unstoppable.

Conclusion

Three major conclusions arise from this consideration of the Dillingham Commission. First, the commission's report formalized and generalized the dichotomy between new and old immigrants, inflating the dangers of the former group and flattering Americans' depictions of the latter. Historically, such a dichotomy would have been observable in the mid-nineteenth-century with Irish and German immigrants constituting the dangerous category of new immigrant. This historical perspective was mostly lost in the political purpose of the Dillingham report, however, and it was the distinction proposed between northwestern and southeastern European immigrants that it promoted. The dichotomy proved to be a pertinacious one. Three years after its publication, the magazine *Outlook*'s editorial entitled "The Old Stock and the New" reproduced many of the assumptions of the Dillingham distinction and drew the inevitable conclusions: "with this widening of ideas and interests there has come another group of men and women from the Old World who are rapidly creating a 'new stock,' and many thoughtful Americans are asking whether in making the house so free to all who want to share its protection we are not endangering the ideas of the family and jeopardizing the spirit and faith which are the most precious possessions bequeathed by the men and women of the 'old stock.'"[126] Such distinctions and assumptions might also distort perceptions of the number of old and new groups, worried the sociologist Robert Park. Reflecting on efforts in the 1910s to make English the dominant language, Park observed that "possibly native-born Americans . . . think that the bulk of our population is made up of descendants of the Colonial settlers. In so far as this illusion holds, native Americans are likely to think there is a much greater demand than actually exists in the United States for uniformity of language and ideas."[127] Park recognized the determination of the Americanizers to impose a standard identity and single language. Park's additional concerns proved both sensible and prescient:

> [T]he fact that human nature is subject to illusions of this sort may have practical consequences. It is conceivable, for example, that if it should come to be generally regarded as a mark of disloyalty or inferiority to speak a foreign language, we should reproduce in a mild form the racial animosities and conflicts which are resulting in the breaking up of the continental imperiums, Austria-Hungary, Russia, and Germany. In all these countries the animosities appear to have been created very largely by efforts to suppress the mother tongues as literary languages.[128]

The distinction between old and new immigrants as a description of the trends between the 1890s and 1921 has proved durable, and one that scholars have had to employ. This initially political, and now academic, distinction influenced the Americanization process.

Second, the Dillingham Commission's exclusive concern with new immigrants from southern and eastern Europe by implication reinforced the political marginality of African Americans: conducting the debate in terms exclusively of white immigrants emphasized a vision of the United States's identity as a white one. This emphasis was ironic, since, as Mary White Ovington pointed out in her study of African Americans in New York, they were more fully assimilated than most new immigrants. Ovington concluded that "few of New York's citizens are so American as the colored, few show so little that is unusual or picturesque. The educated Italian might have in his home some relic of his former country, the Jew might show some symbol of his religion; but the Negro, to the seeker of the unusual, would seem commonplace." This acculturation arose from the length of time African Americans had been present in the U.S.: "[T]he colored man in New York has no associations with his ancient African home, no African traditions, no folk lore . . . He is ambitious to be conventional in his manners, his customs, striving as far as possible to be like his neighbor—a distinctly American ambition."[129] Yet the criteria of assimilability promoted by restrictionists seemed blind to these attributes because of the emphasis on an Anglo-Saxon Americanism, which was white. Here can be identified the origins of Toni Morrison's observation that "America means white."

Finally, and related to the second point, the Dillingham Commission's anxieties about the assimilability of the new immigrants rested on a model of the United States's dominant ethnic identity as an Anglo-Saxon one, traceable to the English settlers and subsequent northern European immigrants. It was not a melting-pot assimilationist model—despite rhetoric to the contrary—since there were clear views about who should be assimilated and who not. Although the melting-pot rhetoric served obvious populist interests, in practice, the key policy-makers had a clear idea of how the pot should be constructed and what its outcome should approximate.

Published in 1911, the Dillingham Commission's report illustrates how the issues of whiteness, assimilation, and Americanization were central to the formulation of immigration policy in American political development. The next two chapters examine how these efforts determined the definition of "American" in the crucial decade of the 1920s.

PART TWO

Defining Americans

CHAPTER FOUR

"The Fire of Patriotism":

Americanization and U.S. Identity

In this and the ensuing chapter, I examine the question of American identity as articulated in two policies toward immigrants. In Chapter 5, I concentrate on the notion of U.S. identity implied by eugenic arguments; in this chapter, the focus is on the Americanization movement, mobilized during the First World War and throughout the 1920s.

The sociologist Milton Gordon distinguishes three forms of assimilation in the context of American political development. The first is what he calls the Anglo-Conformity model, under which assimilation is biased toward instilling members of the polity with Anglo-Saxon values and interests. Second is the melting-pot model in which that group longest present or most dominant in the United States does not determine the overall character of national identity. And third is assimilation as a form of cultural pluralism, under which scheme a multiplicity of ethnic groups and identities coexist.[1] Gordon argues that the assimilation process that best describes historically the experience of the United States is the first type, Anglo-Conformity, an assessment with which I agree, particularly for the years under consideration in this study. It is a type convergent with the Anglo-Saxon group: based in the first English settlers and later northwestern European immigrants, and rooted in Protestantism. By the mid-nineteenth-century, a dominant group in the United States, who were derived from this heritage and who thought of themselves as "Americans," was identifiable. It was a white group. The political scientist Eric Kaufmann infers several characteristics of this group, including their commitment to Protestantism and liberalism, their sense of self-worth and prosperity making them a chosen people, and their cultural separateness from nonwhites and non-English.[2] These characteristics structured both the Know-Nothing movement in the nineteenth century and the Americanization drive.[3]

Between 1900 and 1929, a self-conscious effort was made to define this Anglo-American or American identity and to defend it as the product of a melting-pot assimilationism, and not simply as the maintenance of one group's dominance, while deliberately controlling who was to be eligible to assimilate. This identity was used politically in the Americanization movement.

One group who had already experienced assimilation for Americanization were Native Americans.[4] At the end of the nineteenth century, humanitarian and Christian "friends of the Indian" undertook Native Americans' "complete assimilation; the Indians were to be individualized and absolutely Americanized."[5] The Bureau of Indian Affairs provided education to induce a sense of "patriotic American citizenship" among Native Americans, which, combined with land reform, was designed to result in the "total Americanization of the Indians [and] at destroying Indianness."[6] A comparable commitment to "patriotic American citizenship" inspired Americanizers in the 1920s. Of the reformers of Native Americans, Prucha observes that "failing to perceive a single element of good in the Indian way of life as it existed, they insisted on a thorough transformation. The civilization which they represented must be forced upon the Indians if they were unwilling to accept it voluntarily."[7] In Abraham Polonsky's cinematic exploration of anti-Indian attitudes, *Tell Them Willie Boy Is Here,* Willie Boy's assimilated status is given as an example of democracy by a white man, George Hacker: "'I'll tell you what democracy is. You take that Indian over here. We let him go just as he pleases, just as if he still owned this country, just as if he was white and a man. That's what I call democracy, real democracy.'"[8] Judged a failure by the mid-twentieth-century when Native Americans returned to a collective lifestyle (reversing the Dawes Act of 1887), this Americanization of Indians was a powerful movement coincident with that addressed, through the public school system, for European immigrant children. In respect to Native Americans, this educational component reached its fullest form in the Carlisle Indian School in Philadelphia (opened in 1879), which Americanized Indian children both through the curriculum and by placing them with farmer families in Pennsylvania.[9] It is in respect to European immigrants, however, that Americanization was most intense.

This chapter is structured as follows. It begins with an examination of the origins of the Americanization movement during the First World War, together with consideration of the economic motives informing Americanism. The chapter then explains how what I term "educational" Americanization was transformed, after 1918, into a more intense form of "political" Americanization. The concluding section reports the varieties of Americanization, especially its partiality in respect to African Americans, and the recurrence of this approach in U.S. politics.

The Origins of Americanization

Organized Americanization arose for political reasons as the First World War and post-1918 years prompted an intensification in anti-immigrant feelings and in anxiety about the absence of "Americanism" among aliens who had made no declaration to naturalize as U.S. citizens.[10] Legislation that was operative from 1918 permitted the federal Bureau of Naturalization actively to propagate citizenship classes and to provide educational materials (in 1906 Congress had made competence in English a condition for naturalization), as Congressman Albert Johnson explained to a correspondent: "[F]ederal assistance began in the small paragraph carried in the Burnett Immigration Act passed in 1917. [It authorized] Federal aid toward promotion of citizenship."[11] The commissioner of the Bureau of Naturalization, Raymond Crist, explained in detail what measures for promoting citizenship were permissible under this legislation: "[T]he Act specifically provides for its [the Federal Citizenship Textbook] distribution only to applicants for naturalization who are in attendance upon the public schools. Quite a number of organizations of a public-spirited nature have been able to secure the book by bringing their English and Citizenship classes under the supervision of the public schools. It is true, also, that many of the foreign born who had not previously taken steps to become citizens, acquired a sincere desire to do so and made their applications because of the helpful influences of the classroom."[12] In 1920 alone, the Bureau of Naturalization distributed 98,958 textbooks on citizenship to public schools that administered classes for candidates for naturalization.[13] These textbooks were used throughout the country by instructors preparing aliens to petition to naturalize as Americans. The requirements for success were rigorous, demanding a detailed knowledge of federal, state, and local governments, as well as of the courts.[14]

To ensure that new immigrants had the opportunity to Americanize and to naturalize, some intellectuals, social workers, and politicians formed organizations dedicated to promoting their Americanization.[15] They received direct support from the Office of Education at the Department of the Interior. Americanization was undertaken in several ways: providing classes in English language where appropriate, ensuring that state and federal agencies addressed the specific needs of new immigrants unfamiliar with practices in the United States, and promoting literacy and knowledge of civic affairs. Schools and local governments, together with multiple voluntary organizations, took a lead role. This work at the Department of the Interior's Education Bureau was complemented by the citizenship education initiatives from the Bureau of Naturalization in the Department of Labor.

Public Schools

From the middle of the nineteenth century, the American public school system provided a powerful source of assimilation for immigrants and especially for immigrants' children. One Americanization director proselytized that "the public schools are the biggest Americanizing agency in the United States—they have been ever since we have had public schools; they are doing a marvelous work."[16] The Secretary of Labor described the role of the schools to one correspondent thus: "Americanization objects are substantially being accomplished by the work which the public schools and various organizations in different parts of the country are accomplishing, in conjunction with the Bureau of Naturalization of this Department." He elaborated that "the public schools are receiving monthly the names of the candidates for citizenship from the Bureau of Naturalization, and these candidates are at the same time being notified by the Bureau to avail themselves of the advantages which the public schools are increasingly offering for them. Through these agencies opportunities are being afforded for the spirit of America to be learned and absorbed by those who are coming into citizenship through the process of naturalization."[17] Public schools had also a symbolic content, according to Michael Olneck, who notes their role enunciating "the values, beliefs, cultural practices, and identities" of an American.[18]

Providing a common language and narrative of the history of the United States, school curricula and instruction initiated the foreign-born into being American. A visitor to New York in 1911 observed how public schools socialized immigrant children. Alfred Zimmern wrote his mother first about learning English: "one class consisted of boys and girls of all ages who had just landed in America and it was pathetic to see them learning English, not caring a bit in their eagerness how ridiculous they made themselves." Loyalty to the United States was rapidly instilled: "[B]ut the really impressive sight was the presentation and oath of allegiance to the American flag which takes place at 9 o'clock every morning. First they sang a number of American songs and some of the children recited and then came this ceremony at the end, every child stretching out its hand towards the flag. It really made one feel that America was a land of freedom."[19] Not surprisingly, the Americanization movement identified the flag as one of its most potent symbols.[20] Zimmern's observations come several years before the intense Americanization and the American First English language campaign unfolded. Furthermore, not all immigrants shared his high regard for intensive Americanism. Jennifer Hochschild notes that some immigrants resisted this educational inculcation: such immigrants "recognized that public schools often sought to beat foreigners' children into Protestant docility rather than to liberate their imagination through education. And they resisted, demanding schools in their own languages that would teach their own religions and values."[21] The success of public schools in assimilating immigrants was queried by some in the opening decades of the twentieth century (who cited, for instance, the continued use of German in some schools), and a more explicit form of Americanization was advocated.[22] Thus, in 1916, President Woodrow Wilson celebrated Americanization as a process of "self-examination, a process of purification, a process of rededication to the things which America represents and is proud to represent."[23]

The same public schools employed to socialize and Americanize new immigrants failed African American children, a discrepancy one member of the National Association for the Advancement of Colored People underlined in 1929: "[O]ur country boasts of her great free school system. There is no free school system in this country. Millions of American citizens are walking in dense mental darkness because our country denies anything like equal educational facilities to all of her citizens. In a state of the union where the black man constitutes thirty-nine per cent of the population he is given only one per cent of the appropriation for education and in a number of other states four times as much is spent for the education of a white child as is spent for a black child."[24]

World War I and Americanization

The First World War exacerbated hostility toward immigrants and boosted Americanization.[25] As one correspondent wrote the Secretary of the Interior, "if Americanization is to prevail not only must Germanization propaganda in this country be successfully combatted, but there must be established a positive and effective Americanization campaign that will bring home to the American people a positive, definite conception of the principles upon which a democratic civilization and representative government is based."[26] This intense Americanism approximated a crusade.

Prior to 1916, the work of the federal Office of Education impinged little on a public largely uninterested in the plight of immigrants. Interest was sharply aroused, however, by the advent of the First World War, when immigrants' sympathies and loyalties were often suspected by Americans.[27] The suspicion that immigrants—"with the detested foreign accent"[28]—frequently held anarchist or communist politics was commonplace. The Department of Justice fanned this suspicion of immigrants' behavior.[29] Deportations increased, and foreign-language newspapers were closely scrutinized.

The latent conflict among different immigrants, released by the First World War, was manifest in the exchanges about "hyphenated" Americans, that is, Americans who attached an ethnic identity prefix to their nationality were attacked by, for instance, the "one hundred percent" Americanizers, for which a national committee was formed. German-Americans and other groups promoted their mixed loyalties in this way. Presidential candidates Theodore Roosevelt and Woodrow Wilson became famous, at the time of the First World War, for their attacks on "hyphenated Americans." Such citizens were accused of lacking a complete commitment to the United States and of being insufficiently Americanized, charges laid principally on Irish-Americans and German-Americans, both of whom were considered weak supporters—if not outright opponents—of the British nation. July 4, 1918, became an occasion throughout the country for a celebration of intense patriotism.

In New York, a National Americanization Committee, under Frances Kellor, was established; and a director of Americanization was appointed in the Bureau of Education,[30] at the Department of the Interior in Washington;[31] the terms of cooperation between the Interior Department and the National Americanization Committee were formalized.[32] The states were divided into eleven districts, each of which had a regional director responsible for Americanization. In each state, a board was established that was made up of representatives from the various departments and organizations in that state who were engaged in Americanization work. The Bureau of Education began its involvement in education for immigrants in April 1914, providing English language classes.[33] In the autumn of 1915, the America First program was initiated, under which the U.S. Commissioner of Education appointed a National Committee of One Hundred. America First concentrated on getting non–English speakers to learn the language, but was always implicitly associated with the inculcation of Americanism.[34] The campaign identified five tenets necessary for national unity in a democracy. These were

> (1) a common use of the language of the United States; (2) a common understanding and appreciation of American standards, ideals, and responsibilities of citizenship; (3) a genuine allegiance to the United States, whether the land of the citizen's birth or of adoption; (4) active cooperation with fellow citizens in furthering the common welfare through government; (5) a universal consciousness of our national and social organization and the impelling forcefulness of its evolution.[35]

The bureau's work was coordinated by H. H. Wheaton, its specialist in Immigrant Education.[36] The Americanization division appointed racial advisers "to bring about better relationship among the races and to carry on the educational work." It submitted American copy to foreign newspapers, and the division issued a monthly *Americanization* bulletin, with 15,000 circulation, for "the workers of the country."[37] The bulletin's content illustrates just how extraordinarily extensive and energetic the Americanization campaign was across the United States. As the war ended, its intensity reached fever pitch, with states, cities, and a myriad of local voluntary organizations participating. This network offered a fertile base for the more overt political ambitions that became associated with the Americanization drive after the end of the First World War in response to communist and anarchist threats.

In a memorandum entitled "What Is Americanization?" the commissioner for Education in 1917, Philander P. Claxton, described official policy. The emphasis was on the U.S.'s immigrant composition: "except for a quarter million North American Indians, descendants of the natives whom the white settlers found here the people of the United States are all foreign born or the descendants of foreign born ancestors. All are immigrant or the offspring of immigrants."[38] The failure to distinguish between voluntary and involuntary immigrants is notable: "here, free from the domination of autocratic government and from the poisoning influence of decadent aristocracies, forgetting our fears and servile habits, we have elevated the best from all countries into a common possession, transfused and transformed it by our highest and best ideals and called it Americanism."[39] Claxton emphasized education in fostering Americanism: "Americanization is a process of education, of winning the mind and heart through instruction and enlightenment. From the very nature of the thing it can make little or no use of force. It must depend rather on the attractive power and the sweet reasonableness of the thing itself. Were it to resort to force by that very act it would destroy its spirit and cease to be American. It would also cease to be American if it should become narrow and fixed and exclusive, losing its faith in humanity and rejecting vital and enriching elements from any source whatever." Consequently, Americanization was a process which the foreign born "do for themselves when the opportunity is offered."[40]

The role of the National Americanization Committee, financed by private donations,[41] was central to this campaign,[42] as the Committee's chairman outlined in late 1918:

> [T]he Americanization work now being done by the Bureau of Education has been made possible by the National Americanization Committee. It is furnishing to the Department of the Interior a New York headquarters with full equipment for the racial and publicity work. It is furnishing a staff of 36 headquarters' workers in Washington and New York City, including field officers, translators, writers, speakers, and es-

pecially workers among the races. In addition to this, it is making it possible for a conference of twelve men of each of the races in America to advise and assist the government. These now number over 100 men who are helping to work out a sound policy and program of racial relations in America and carrying the message to their own people. It is supplying the funds to direct the work now being put into industries by the 1000 or more plant Americanization Committees appointed at the request of the Department of the Interior.[43]

"Races" in this account refer to the European immigrant nationalities. The same committee funded the Immigration Committee of the U.S. Chamber of Commerce, which encouraged Americanization by employers. This use of private funds[44] demonstrates a significant infiltration of a government agency by the private sector or, less dramatically, a marked degree of collaboration between public and private bodies. Commissioner for Education Claxton warmly praised Kellor's application: "[T]he National Americanization Committee is doing a very important work. It is a pity it could not have been begun many years ago. Had it been, conditions would be much better in the United States than they now are."[45] Claxton explained to the Interior Secretary that over three million of the thirteen million foreign-born men, women, and citizens in the United States spoke no English: "for their own good and our own we may not let these people remain among us either as citizens or aliens without giving them adequate opportunity and every proper inducement to learn the language of the country and whatever else may be necessary to enable them to understand the best in American social, industrial and civic life."[46] The bureau published detailed documents about how to teach English; later Americanization material included instructions in naturalization. By 1917 this work had become "a nation wide Americanization campaign,"[47] led by the Education Bureau.[48] It issued detailed proposals to teachers in public schools, made proposals to universities and colleges about their potential role in promoting Americanization,[49] supplied reading lists, and published a regular Immigrant Education Letter series. It certainly constituted a "nation wide" campaign.

The Bureau of Education's work was distinct from that of the Bureau of Naturalization (located in the Department of Labor), which, from 1916, began a program of providing education for foreigners wishing to naturalize.[50] In February 1918 the secretary of the interior agreed to the proposal that Americanization should be his department's "War Measure" and sought federal legislation and funding in support of this commitment,[51] an aim that failed.[52] The same interior secretary, Franklin Lane, was keen to retain Americanization work in his department's Bureau of Education (and not to lose it to the Bureau of Naturalization), informing one congressman,

[N]o doubt the Bureau of Naturalization can do much in the way of giving definite instruction in matters of citizenship to those who have applied for citizenship papers. I believe, however, that the larger task of educating all aliens in the use of the English language, in the history and resources of the country, in our industrial requirements, in our manners and customs and in our civic, social and political ideals, belongs rather to the Bureau of Education in the Department of the Interior, which was created for the purpose of promoting education in all its phases and which has through its half century of existence established intimate relations with State, county and city systems of education which incline school officers to look to this Bureau for advice in regard to all matters of this kind.[53]

Frances Kellor,[54] of the National Americanization Committee, encouraged these priorities, warning the commissioner of education that although teaching English and providing classes in citizenship were "basic and essential" activities, they were insufficient response to "the active anti-American influences at work" in the United States.[55] Kellor recommended an ambitious expansion of the Bureau of Education's work to counter anti-Americanism:

[A] thorough-going governmental Americanization policy and program is an immediate war necessity. I am deeply concerned by the realization that no existing Government agency is effectively reaching the non-English-speaking groups and that the most insidious forms of propaganda are making headway unchecked among them. There are literally thousands of foreign-language organizations in the United States fighting among themselves for independent and united native countries or to preserve their racial solidarity here. On the other hand, there are but few such organizations whose first interest is Americanization or to help America win the war.[56]

It was Kellor who proposed that the interior secretary give a public lecture on Americanization.[57] The wartime federal Council of National Defense prepared a memorandum in January 1918 that identified, in addition to more general issues about war mobilization, two problems with immigrants: a positive danger of sedition among the foreign-born and the lack of English among immigrant workers.[58]

where any considerable number of immigrants reside. These local committees should have charge of all local Americanization work, and should bring together in harmonious action the various agencies in the community already among the immigrant residents."[76] Local Selective Service boards were urged to ensure that new recruits sent to military camps should have demonstrated sufficient knowledge of English to follow basic orders.[77] The Council of National Defense repeated the need for foreign-born residents to learn English.[78] The council's Committee on Public Information published pamphlets explaining American ideals and urging aliens to naturalize.[79]

In the years 1917 to 1921, one strong emphasis of the Americanization effort was on "racial" groups, that is, immigrants distinguished by nationality. For instance, the November 1919 issue of *Americanization* included a bibliography entitled "for the study of races," which concerned exclusively immigrants of European extraction;[80] and in the second half of 1918, much effort was devoted to building up relations with nationalities' organizations, though Commissioner Claxton cautioned that "the difficulties are greater with the races that have come from countries with which we are now at war."[81]

Throughout 1917 and 1918, state and city governments were persuaded, in a wartime measure, to inaugurate hundreds of events to facilitate the Americanization of immigrants. Literacy and acquisition of the English language were consistently promoted, the second ambition aided by early data about draftees that found that of 10 million registrants, 700,000 could not sign their names or write English; these were overwhelmingly immigrants. These deficiencies were quickly identified as threats to American productivity and military preparedness.[82]

Indeed, it is difficult to underestimate the impact of the war on the Americanization drive, in two ways. First, the need of national policy leaders to galvanize support for the war permitted American populism work such as the "one hundred percent American" campaign. The aspersion "un-American" developed from the war's end, a criterion (combined, in 1919, with race riots, the Palmer raids, and intense anti-immigrant sentiments) that collectively weakened the aspiration of cultural pluralists.[83] Writing in 1919, Aronovici notes that the war made the issue of "national unity" a problem for the first time in the United States: "whether national unity means unanimity of opinion, whether it means unreserved recognition of a loyalty to all aspects of the present form and practice of government, or whether it means merely the breaking away from all foreign allegiance and the participation in the affairs of the government of the United State, is not always clear."[84] This ambiguity produced several responses, but the dominant official one, unsurprisingly, was an unequivocal Americanism. Second, in the postwar years, in frustration at the relative weakness of the Americanization movement, some Progressive reformers were increasingly drawn to stronger versions of this doctrine. The historian Gary Gerstle makes this latter point forcefully: rightward-leaning Progressives "lost their enthusiasm for reform altogether and reemerged, in the 1920s, as reactionaries—obsessed with restoring America to some imagined state of cultural homogeneity and moral purity."[85] The American Legion, founded in 1919, was an instance of these political and cultural developments. Americanizers had a clear view about the content of national identity. One publisher produced a regular "Americanism Poster-Folder" containing prayers and panegyrics to outstanding Americans. It was dedicated to the "100% Americanism" cause.[86]

The Economics of Americanization

For employers and industrialists, Americanization meant the acquisition of English, as a survey found: "among managers and employers we found a general feeling that industry must assume some responsibility for Americanization; but practically all of them identified this with the teaching of English and the naturalization of aliens."[87] Many employers ran Americanization classes in large plants, principally motivated by the need for their employees to speak English. Economic Americanizers combined an idealism about the virtues of the American way of life with fiscal hardheadedness, principally the belief that immigrants should be admitted in order for the economy to thrive. This belief may explain why the Carnegie Corporation sponsored a series of Americanization studies in the early 1920s.[88] The foundation allocated a sizable grant for the systematic study of immigrant experience in nine areas: schooling of the immigrant; adjustment of homes and family life; legal protection and correction; health standards and care; naturalization and political life; industrial and economic amalgamation; treatment of immigrant heritages; neighborhood agencies and organizations; and rural communities.

Writing in 1924, Leiserson infers a larger purpose to industrial Americanization: "[O]ne of the first needs that every intelligent manager notes, of course, is instruction in English for those employees who do not understand the language. This has led to quite a widespread organization of classes in industrial plants either directly by the management or in cooperation with public authorities or civic organizations." He continued, "but teaching English has not been the only work of these classes. Instruction in civics and American history has usually gone with the language lessons, and preparatory work for naturalization examinations has also been quite common."[89] Such exercises were most successful when undertaken in cooperation with local educational agencies. By 1919 over eight hundred industrial plants had some sort of Americanization program—either their own classes or ones held in conjunction with local public or voluntary organizations—for their employees.[90]

James Barrett has recently stressed the role of workplaces in stimulating a bottom-up process of Americanization, and he is certainly correct to focus on the role of employment. The organizers of the National Americanization Committee, for instance, speedily homed in on the necessity of Americanizing workers, as its chairman explained: "the real melting pot for the adult foreign-born is the industrial plants of America." The committee persuaded the U.S. Chamber of Commerce to appoint an Immigration Committee in December 1918.[91] The National Americanization Committee financed this Immigration Committee, which "carried on the industrial Americanization work among employers, including surveys of 244 industrial towns, appointment of Americanization Committees by 150 local Chambers of Commerce, preparation and distribution of 150,000 sets of leaflets in seven languages for enclosure in pay envelopes, the issuance of a semi-monthly Bulletin telling what industries are doing for Americanization and distributing information to many business organizations and industrial plants."[92] The Commonwealth Steel Company at Granite City, Illinois, for example, reported in its magazine *The Commonwealther* that it had classes for its non-American employees, among whom "a large proportion of accidents were happening"; consequently, "safety reasons necessitate their learning English . . . It is expected to bring this condition to the point that the learning of English will be eventually required of all foreign employees." Instruction in Americanism was also planned: "Americanization classes are being arranged for, and the foreigners are being led to know and love America."[93]

At a national level, the National Association of Manufacturers and the National Industrial Council both ardently supported the Americanization drive,[94] as did labor representatives such as the United Mine Workers[95] and the Labor Secretary James Davis's own union, the Iron, Steel, and Tin Workers.[96] The general superintendent of the Campbells Soup Company, whose produce was later made famous by Andy Warhol, told the Secretary of Labor that "I agree absolutely with your views on both registration and education, both of which should be compulsory."[97] Welcoming proposals for compulsory registration and Americanization of aliens, the manager of the Pittsburgh Provision & Packing Co. warned that "this country is full of aliens—people who have no desire or thought of becoming citizens of this country and who have no respect for our Constitution and Flag. Such people are a menace."[98] The monthly *Americanization* bulletin included a regular section on "Industrial Americanization," which dealt with developments in plants to Americanize foreign-born employees. There was thus a felicitous suturation of motives between political Americanizers and industrialists worried about the competence of their non-English-speaking workers.[99]

From Educational to Political Americanization

After 1918, Americanization was increasingly the preserve of those alarmed about the political threat posed by unassimilated foreigners. Thus, for Secretary Davis, Americanization was fundamentally linked to the political threat posed by aliens hostile to American values and government:

> I listened at Detroit to an argument presented for a Russian who was being held for deportation. He had been found guilty of distributing Communistic literature, etc., and they pleaded for him that he might remain in America. He had been here for eleven years and couldn't speak or understand the English language. He had not applied for citizenship and knew nothing whatever about our country, its institutions, or method of government. He had been brought up in Russia and taught to overthrow the Czar, and coming here he had that only in his mind—the overthrow of government. If he had been educated so that he could have known of

his rights, privileges and duties under our form of government no doubt he would have become a good citizen.[100]

Secretary Davis received many letters advocating the mandatory registration and education of aliens, which he copied to the chairmen of the House and the Senate Immigration Committees.[101] Davis (a foreign-born but naturalized American[102]—thereby an illustration of how quickly some naturalized citizens learned to distance themselves from succeeding immigrants) himself advocated such legislation, and in November 1921, his letter on this theme to Congressman Albert Johnson, chair of the House Immigration Committee, was widely circulated and commented on in newspapers. As Davis explained, "I am a foreign born citizen myself and have studied the problem of Americanization and proper education of these people. In my estimation the thing to do with all aliens is to register them and to see that they get the proper training under governmental supervision, which will fit them for the kind of citizens necessary to the welfare of the country."[103] To the Patriotic Sons of America, Davis remarked that "it makes me boil at times to hear of so many men who have been in this country from sixteen to twenty years and who have not even asked for their declaration papers and have no intention of becoming American citizens and have no desire to learn anything of American history and do not care anything about America at all. They have no American education or American ideals"[104] (and see table 4.1). Thus, after the First World War, as Barrett notes, the "Americanization campaign took on a distinctly nativist cast and a patriotic frenzy."[105]

Davis wanted registration of aliens, an expansion of Americanization education, and a fee levied on registered aliens: "[T]here is need for the proper education for citizenship of the millions of aliens now with us and the hundreds of thousands being yearly admitted to this country. To accomplish this the scope of the work of the present Bureau of Naturalization should be enlarged by providing a uniform registration of all aliens and a complete system of directing their education along lines which will make for Americanization."[106] Again Davis stressed the connection between the acquisition of language and political beliefs: "[T]he majority of our troubles from Red and anarchist activities are caused by lack of knowledge. Every citizen should know the language of the nation to which he owes allegiance. To speak our language, to know our institutions, and the principles

Table 4.1 Percentage of Naturalized and Unnaturalized Immigrants, 1920

Country of Origin	Naturalized (%)	Unnaturalized (%)
Luxembourg	75.4	26.6
Wales	74.4	25.6
Germany	73.6	26.4
Denmark	70.5	29.5
Sweden	70.0	29.5
Norway	68.2	31.8
Ireland	66.1	33.9
England	65.4	34.6
Scotland	62.9	37.1
Canada	61.7	38.8
Greece	17.4	82.6
Bulgaria	11.7	88.3
Spain	10.7	89.3
Albania	7.3	92.7
Mexico	5.5	94.5

Source: Derived from letter from Secretary of Labor James Davis to Senator Samuel Shortridge, May 4, 1922, pp. 11–12, in NA RG 174 Records of the Department of Labor, General Records, 1907–1942, Chief Clerk's Files, 163/127A-163/127D, Box 165, Folder: 163/127A Americanization, Sundry Files, 1922.

and ideals for which they stand, and to learn to love them—these alone constitute Americanization." He added that "little attention is paid to the education of aliens for citizenship—the greatest vocation and duty of every man!"[107] Of his aims, only the Americanization measure was acted on. Anticipating future arrangements, Davis urged the federal government to lead the Americanization drive, directing, instead of merely cooperating with, local patriotic and civic organizations. He argued that mandatory registration and Americanization would give the melting pot a new lease on life: such measures were "specifically designed," Davis maintained, "to encourage the alien, increase his respect of American institutions, uphold American ideals of tolerance, equality, human kindness and the spirit of cooperation, thus making more efficient our famous 'melting pot.'"[108] Many immigrant groups took the contrary view, however, seeing compulsion and Americanization as fetters on the melting pot.

Davis was keen on using singing as a medium to build patriotism. The labor secretary's expectations were nothing but high:

I can picture to myself the great army of foreign born banded together through the enrollment system as one great fraternal organization working toward the commendable end of fostering better citizenship and greater respect for American institutions, and in this work of Americanization there is a part for every American citizen individually and through the organizations of the church, fraternal, civic and patriotic societies . . . All have a duty and a privilege in spreading the gospel of truth about America and its institutions to counteract the radical propaganda of the few who dispense seeds of anarchism and of hate for selfish purpose of their own.[109]

This vision is not without modern imitators.

Davis did not take kindly to critics of his Americanization enthusiasms, dismissing a correspondent from the Americanization department in Connecticut: "[W]e are all agreed that citizenship is a matter of the growth of a desire to be created in the breast of the foreigners and that it cannot be forced. It must come from the heart. But why object to the enrollment for training to help create that desire? You register to vote, and I have to go to Pittsburgh from Washington and pay to register for the privilege of exercising the franchise. What more harm would it do for the good alien to have to register?"[110] And of the Union of American Hebrew Congregations, the labor secretary plainly despaired: "it is hard for me to comprehend that any one of the racial groups in the United States should so vehemently oppose a program of assimilation, least of all a race which has received so much at the hands of this nation which has become great through the strength of united peoples."[111] In his prolix reply, Davis challenged the union about its attitudes to Asian immigrants, in a passage that illustrates pellucidly how Anglo-Saxon and white this leading Americanization advocate's conception of Americanism was:

[A]re the American people to understand that the Union of American Hebrew Congregations does not believe in the exclusion of Orientals? Your Resolution clearly indicates that you would throw down the bars and admit the Chinese and other Eastern races indiscriminately, for you condemn its operation. It is not only evident to truly American peoples but even to these Orientals themselves that they will never become assimilated into a united American Republic. They are not of us. Their economic and moral standards are those of a thousand years ago. They live to themselves today where permitted to do so, as a nation within a nation. And now the Union of American Hebrew Congregations comes out openly against those who advocate the compulsory education of alien people in America in the English language, the traditions of our country, and the ideals for which we stand.[112]

Davis's aims were effected through the Naturalization Bureau. Its commissioner, Raymond Crist, explained his bureau's work: "this Bureau has, for about four years, carried on an increasingly wider-extending work with the public schools throughout the United States, to the end that the foreign population may be assimilated and ideals and loyalty to this Government developed within them." This work was undertaken in cooperation with public schools in 2,000 communities whose instructors the bureau had prepared: "the Bureau has published an outline course in citizenship instruction, which is being used extensively by the public school teachers in the citizenship classes which have been organized at the instance of the Bureau of Naturalization in these communities."[113] Congress had authorized the bureau to give textbooks to every foreigner aged over eighteen who was attending citizenship classes. It was an opportunity that the Bureau of Naturalization was ready to seize:

> [T]he Bureau has consistently held to the thought that it should not undertake a proselytizing campaign for the purpose of inducing aliens to take the step towards citizenship. While holding to the ideal, it is always confronted with the stern reality of the necessity for lending its support and stimulating to the highest activities those State organizations whose natural responsibility it is to see to it that the loyalty of the community is raised to the highest. In this work it believes it to be the essential and prime duty of such State organizations that they set into motion influences which will arouse and stimulate, if not kindle, the fire of patriotism in the minds of the aliens who are ready to devote themselves and dedicate themselves to this Nation and in particular during this trying period of its existence.

Crist continued with a dramatic statement about the problems facing the United States:

> [A]ll of our fundamental principles of Government are at stake. We cannot hazard them by being bound by too fine-spun ideals. This is a practical question that is before the entire Nation, and the Bureau of Naturalization appeals to your organization . . . to address yourselves to this burning question: Shall the aliens in your community remain in ignorance of American ideals? Shall they remain without the ability to speak our common tongue? Shall they continue to be estranged, or shall they

be won over and led to the final goal which is theirs individually as well as collectively, the goal of American citizenship? To this there is but one answer.[114]

This answer was presumably in the affirmative.

A conference on Americanization was convened in Washington by Secretary of the Interior Franklin Lane in conjunction with the Department of Labor[115] and the Council of National Defense in April 1918. Attended by representatives of every state, its sessions were dominated by denunciations of the foreign language press for "disloyalty" and the use of "enemy tongues" in schools.[116] Secretary Lane defined the conference's purpose as one of devising "ways and means by which the nation, states and local committees may co-operate to win the unqualified allegiance and full and effective support of persons of foreign birth residing in the United States, in our efforts in behalf of democracy, freedom, and a higher civilization."[117] A further conference on methods of Americanization dealt with such subjects as the best methods of teaching English, training teachers for Americanization, securing cooperation with "national and local racial organizations," influencing the foreign language press, and naturalization of aliens.[118] Similar events were held in the states.[119] In 1920 an "Americanization Exposition" was held in New York City by a coalition of Americanization committees and organizations. Its chairman wrote that "thoughtful Americans have come to realize that something constructive should be done to arouse the people to the consciousness of their Americanism and their responsibilities."[120] At the suggestion of the Massachusetts-based American School Citizenship League, the Bureau of Education organized a conference on citizenship and Americanization, with sessions arranged into topics such as "the teaching of history as a factor in Americanization" and "Americanizing Americans."[121] Its principal focus was on the teaching of history "in this critical period in our nation."[122] The American School Citizenship League created a History Committee to examine how history should be taught in schools so as better to enhance citizenship; the committee issued a report[123] and a set of books. A sixteen-day "All-American Exposition" was held in September 1919, with plenty of input from citizens of foreign birth or parentage.[124]

By the 1920s, failure to naturalize or to seek naturalization status was often taken as evidence of an unwillingness to fit into American

society or to accept its values.[125] By this decade, the humanitarian
efforts of early Americanizers associated with settlement movement
leaders such as Jane Addams, in cities like Chicago, Philadelphia, and
New York, were judged wanting by the proselytizers who considered
most of the new immigrants unassimilable except through a process
of explicit and highly directive Americanization. Whereas settlement Americanizers "attributed the alleged inferiority of Eastern and
Southern Europeans, not to inherent racial differences, but to cultural
background,"[126] their post-1918 successors, leaning on pseudoscientific arguments, harbored few doubts about the newcomers' "racial" inferiority. The new generation of Americanizers was also
mostly uninterested in how the new immigrants' values and cultures
could enrich or reshape U.S. identity, instead wanting to mold the new
arrivals into a preexisting Americanism. In modern parlance, it was a
"one-way," not a "two-way," street. This view is conveyed by Fred
Butler, director of the Americanization Division at the Bureau of Education: "[A]s I conceive the subject of Americanization, it is a problem
essentially of fitting every person within the boundaries of America,
men and women, to fulfill their duties as American citizens. It is essentially a process of citizenship training rather than a process of getting
hold of a certain group of foreign born people and making them
sufficiently American so that they will not be a danger to it. We are
not inspired by a danger of a menace against which we must guard
ourselves, but we are inspired by the vision of that America which will
come when every American citizen is as competent as a considerable
percentage of our citizens now are."[127] Somewhat contradictorily,
Butler worried about Americanization's becoming a limiting process
by pressing too uniform or too conformist a conception of Americanism, a fairly obvious danger of his division's work: "one of the things
that is most essential in this Americanization movement is so to control and direct it that instead of *setting* the minds of the people, it will
make the people intelligent on what the ideas of American people are
now and what the ideas have been, and will fit the people to go on
growing into a nobler and finer type of democracy . . . if Americanization is sanely conceived and intelligently directed, it should promote
rather than retard the development of the genius of America."[128] In
terms of achieving this aim, Butler declared that "there is only one
way to Americanize," which was to be done "through surrounding
our people with an environment in which any one of them and every

one of them will by their contact with American life learn, imbibe and assimilate the essential principles of Americanism."[129]

These Americanization steps were integrated increasingly with "citizenship training."[130] In 1923, President Warren Harding established the Federal Council on Citizenship Training, which was charged with designing ways in which federal government departments and agencies could foster and direct more effective citizenship training. The council formulated a community score card, with which local communities were urged to grade themselves on five criteria (mental development, health, vocational development, patriotism, and moral development) to measure relatively their success in making good American citizens.[131] Dimension four—patriotic development— concerned levels of Americanism among immigrants: "[P]atriotic attitude applies to both the foreign born and the natural born citizen, and is comprehended generally in the term 'Americanization.' It includes the imparting of an understanding of the Constitution of the United States, civics in its general sense, the English language, American history, American ideals and customs."[132] The focus of this drive was again, in part, immigrants whose commitment to the United States was considered wanting: that is, "all of those unassimilated elements in the empire of heterogeneous citizenship who adhere to customs and traditions which are not in conformity with American standards. These include the little Italys, Russias, Polands, Chinas, and other nationalities existing particularly in our large industrial centers, and other isolated classes."[133]

Americanization beyond Washington, D.C.

Americanization was promoted by organizations such as the Young Men's Christian Association (YMCA), whose local branches had designated Americanization secretaries,[134] the League of Women Voters' local organizations, the Kiwanis Clubs, and Chambers of Commerce. "Americanism" was one of the American Legion's principal activities, undertaken by its National Americanism Commission. Its exhaustive work consisted in "endeavoring to make America a better America." This task was defined as attempting

> to educate the alien for citizenship, and the citizen for better citizenship; to require the English language as the only medium of instruction in elementary and high schools, both public and private; to require the teach-

ing of American history and civil government in these schools; to devote a certain period of time each day to patriotic exercises; to fly the American flag over all schools; to cooperate with educators and raise the standard of education; to combat anti-American activities; to create better legislation for immigration; to add solemnity to naturalization; to cooperate with patriotic organizations; to restrict voting to citizens only.[135]

The commission recorded successes in getting state governments to pass laws implementing these aims. For instance, in respect to English as the required medium of instruction in schools, the legion's "Americanism Commission" claimed successes in twenty-five states.[136] The opposition expressed by the commission contributed to the defeat of a bill in Indiana that would have permitted the German language to be taught in private or parochial elementary schools.[137] The National Americanism Commission's specially prepared "charts of Americanism" were placed in 120,000 schools with the aim that this charter would "eventually be a medium of instruction" about the "underlying principles" of American values.[138] The commission lobbied Congress for immigration restriction, illustrating how restrictive legislation and Americanization converged.[139] The legion was joined by many other voluntary and government organizations in the Americanization drive. For instance, the Oregon State Federation of Women's Clubs, whose chairwoman was a member of the State Americanization Committee, set up classes in English and in citizenship in two counties in Oregon. The commissioner of naturalization, Raymond Crist, readily acceded to a request for textbooks and enthusiastically supported the initiative: "I wish to congratulate you upon the fine spirit which is evidenced by this action toward providing facilities for the education of applicants for naturalization and other foreign speaking persons who wish to learn to read and write English."[140]

In August 1921 the Governor of Oregon established a voluntary committee "for the purpose of developing a state wide plan of Americanization." Governor Olcott explained the purpose of the committee: "'it is important that every illiterate in America who has the privilege of voting be taught to read and write. Further, it is important that he know the underlying principles of our government and to come into full comprehension of our national ideals.'"[141] In March 1919 the State Federation of Pennsylvania Women devoted an issue of its monthly journal *The Messenger,* to Americanization. The federation advocated a more sophisticated understanding of Americanization than that implied by a melting pot: "substitute for the figure of the Melting Pot, which implies a fusion and blending by fire whereby elements change and lose their identity, a figure which will suggest the assembling or building into one harmonious structure many parts which have not entirely changed their characteristics, but which are distinguished by a native florescence here, an austerity there, laid upon the broad, deep foundation of real democracy and true freedom, and you express more nearly the ideal of Americanization."[142] The federation identified the twenty-two ways in which the federation believed that Americanizers should proceed. Like the federation, the National War Work Council of the American YMCA offered its services in the Americanization drive.[143]

The American Legion concentrated its efforts on education, the "keynote of Americanism," and for which knowledge of the English language was "essential."[144] Like comparable nativist organizations, it was alarmed that 25 percent of recruits in the U.S. Armed Forces could not read English, judging that inability to be a "dangerous menace to the nation's welfare."[145] Hence, the legion's Americanism Commission became determined to make English an obligatory language in state schools and expressed anxiety about those states lacking such a requirement. It also wanted to strengthen the English competence precondition for naturalization (a demand that would also weaken the multiethnic bases of labor organization).[146] "Patriotic education" necessitated general use of English. The commission wanted to catch Americans early and to inculcate national values: "[I]n education for citizenship, thorough training in the fundamentals should be emphasized. Ideals of service and cooperation for the common good should be developed particularly in the children . . . Civic playgrounds under proper directors are an exceedingly effective means of developing these ideals and educating children for citizenship."[147] Americanism was intimately linked to excising its opposite, radical, or un-American activities: in respect to schools, the commission recommended that the teaching of "disloyalty in any schoolroom" be made an offense. The commission deployed a range of media to endorse the Americanism message, including newspaper advertisements, billboards, movies, and specially prepared textbooks. Another organization in the Americanization movement was the North American Civic League for Immigrants (in which the ubiquitous reformer Frances Kellor was active[148]). The league was a voluntary body, supporting "the promotion of helpful legislation, the positive works required to protect the immigrant, and the teaching of the English language."[149] Its New York–New Jersey Committee was especially active, seeking "to whip up and sustain an interest in the immigrant and the need for his rapid assimilation."[150]

For the most ardent activists, Americanization was fundamentally about defining membership of the United States and of American life. It implied transcending immigrant diversity through assimilation into a uniform conception of national identity. Thus, the *Americanization Bulletin* spoke of measures to "'bring all races together.'"[151] This intermixing meant breaking up the ethnic communities into which many immigrants settled, a point made by the magazine *Outlook:* "the absence of intelligent methods of distribution has led to the practical segregation of great numbers of new comers into localities which are almost as definite in boundary as the old pales in medieval cities." The consequences of such poor planning were catastrophic: "[W]ith a lack of foresight which has been criminal in its stupidity we have brought in small armies of men and women ignorant of our language, laws, and habits, planted them in isolated colonies, done little or nothing to show them how to be Americans, left them to the leadership of agitators, and then, when they have become turbulent and lawless, have accused them of violating the hospitality of the Nation . . . They have been worked; *they have not been Americanized.*"[152] A study of immigrant neighborhoods, which was funded by the Carnegie Corporation in 1920, referred to them as "urban colonies,"[153] a common description echoing that of the Dillingham Commission.[154]

Occasionally voices were raised about the dangers of too heavy-handed an approach to foreign-born residents. For instance, one Americanizer in New Haven warned from his "work" with immigrants that "the contact the alien has with officialism as represented by government agencies often chills him and gives him a distinct dislike and suspicion of such agencies";[155] he was also skeptical about charging fees for instruction.

Un-American Language and Newspapers

Language was a central concern for Americanizers, the more intense of whom were deeply suspicious of non-English-speakers and publications. Secretary of Labor James Davis accused the foreign papers of "misinformation," saying that "one foreign language paper recently carried an editorial criticizing the contemplated [immigration] legislation which we are discussing as tending to make the alien discouraged, disgruntled and inimical to America and its institutions."[156] The Hundred Percent American committee declared the foreign language press to be "America's Greatest Menace" and urged Congress to enact "without delay a law prohibiting the publication of any newspaper within the United States *which is not printed in English.*"[157] Newspapers in non-English languages still enjoyed wide circulation after the First World War, as Table 4.2 shows. The table gives a broad overview of the circulation of foreign language papers. In terms of aggregate numbers of such papers, however, the figures in Table 4.3 are remarkable. Americanizers were not averse to using foreign newspapers to

Table 4.2 Circulation of Largest Foreign-Language Newspapers, 1920

Language		Circulation
	Dailies	
Italian	*Progresso Italo-Americano*	108,137
	Bollettino della Sera	60,000
	Weeklies and Monthlies	
German	*Frei Press*	121,749
	Deutsch-Amerikanischer Farmer	121,712
	Westlicher Herold	58,000
	Deutsche Hausfrau	50,000
Swedish	*Svenska Americanaren*	62,282
Norwegian-Danish	*Kvinden og Hjemmet*	52,083
Polish	*Zgoda*	125,000
	Ameryka-Echo	100,000
	Guiazda Polarna	89,785
	Narod Polski	80,000
Spanish	*Pictorial Review (Spanish ed.)*	125,000
	Dailies in New York only	
Yiddish	*Forward*	143,716
	Day-Warheit	78,901
	Morning Journal	75,861
	Daily News	57,784

Source: Derived from R. E. Park, *Americanization Studies: The Immigrant Press and Its Control* (New York: Harper & Brothers Publishers, 1922), pp. 91–92.

Table 4.3 Number of Papers in Foreign Languages in the United States, 1884–1920

	1884	1890	1895	1900	1905	1910	1915	1920
Albanian								4
Arabic			1	2	2	3	11	8
Armenian		1	1	2	5	6	9	
Belgian-Flemish								3
Bohemian	12	23	32	44	43	51	55	51
Bulgarian						1	1	1
Chinese		2	2	3	5	6	7	7
Croatian				3	2	8	16	9
Finnish		5	4	8	11	15	18	22
French	46	44	49	49	41	34	45	46
German	621	735	789	750	702	634	533	276
Greek			1	1	1	8	10	15
Hebrew/Yiddish		7	16	16	18	21	38	39
Hollandish	11	14	19	18	17	21	19	13
Hungarian	1	4	3	5	7	12	21	27
Italian	7	11	17	35	57	73	96	98
Japanese				1	5	9	16	15
Lettish							4	2
Lithuanian		1	4	6	8	11	18	16
Persian								1
Polish	3	15	24	39	44	51	68	76
Portuguese			3	4	6	8	12	18
Romanian						2	2	4
Russian		1	3	2	3	4	8	11
Scandinavian	53	96	137	127	134	139	134	111
Serbian				1	1	1	9	7
Slovak					9	16	19	28
Slovenian			6	7	4	7	10	14
Spanish	35	49	60	39	52	55	73	100
Ukranian						1	7	10
Welsh	5	5	5	3	2	2	2	2
Total	794	1,028	1,176	1,163	1,176	1,198	1,264	1,052
Total less German	173	278	387	413	474	564	731	776

Source: Derived from R. E. Park, *Americanization Studies: The Immigrant Press and Its Control* (New York: Harper & Brothers Publishers, 1922), p. 318.

place pro-American stories. Thus, James Davis proposed exploiting foreign newspapers to foster an interest in Americanization: "my idea is that we should run Americanization articles in the foreign language press and, along side of them, the English translation."[158] Similar initiatives were undertaken by the National Americanization Committee and Bureau of Education, whose "racial advisers" established extensive contacts with representatives of nationality organizations, holding conferences with them in Washington, D.C., or New York City and lobbying editors of foreign newspapers to take articles for their papers.[159]

Among local education agencies, evening classes flourished. Such initiatives were not simply benign. Many were prompted by hostility toward non-English-speaking immigrants, a pressure recognized by Edward Hartmann (and summarized in Table 4.4): "the years 1919–20 witnessed the passage of a good deal of state legislation in support of Americanization," often at the urging of the U.S. Bureau of Education's Americanization Division. He concludes that "there can be no doubt, however, that many states passed such legislation as a consequence of the wave of hysteria that swept the nation during this period resulting from the actions of the Department of Justice in conducting its crusade against the alien radical."[160] This intensified hostility to, and suspicion of, the immigrant, which was manifest in post-1918 American politics, fed directly into the Johnson-Reed Act of 1924 and into the national origins framework established in 1929.

In the early 1920s, a host of states—including Connecticut, Delaware, Illinois, Maine, Massachusetts, New Jersey, New Hampshire, Rhode Island, Arizona, Utah, Oregon, and California—passed legislation creating either special divisions of Americanization or Americanization programs, administered by local education departments. The American Legion played a significant role in lobbying for state laws requiring the teaching of American history and civil government.[161] Other groups set up public programs in citizenship education. Such measures contributed to the atmosphere in which the 1921 immigration restrictions were passed, an initiative that naturally weakened the case for ardent and regulated Americanization, since fewer immigrants were admitted and those arriving, by satisfying national quotas, were supposed to be more carefully selected. These measures also fostered the nastier sides of American "nativism" and hostility toward immigrants, epitomized, for instance, in the revival of the Ku Klux Klan during the 1920s.[162]

In general, the postwar years were distinguished by a fulsome commitment to the systematic Americanization of old and new immigrants alike, principally through the public school system. By 1922 one scholar could write that "there is not the shadow of a doubt but

Table 4.4 State-Level Americanization Laws, 1921

States That Had Implemented Laws Requiring:			
English as a Medium of Instruction in All Schools	Instruction in American History and Civil Government	American Flag on Schoolhouses	Patriotic Exercises in Schools
Alabama	Alabama	Arizona	Connecticut
California	California	California	Florida
Connecticut	Connecticut	Connecticut	Kansas
Delaware	Delaware	Delaware	Maine
Idaho	Florida	Florida	Maryland
Illinois	Georgia	Illinois	Minnesota
Indiana	Idaho	Indiana	New Jersey
Iowa	Illinois	Iowa	New York
Kansas	Indiana	Kansas	South Dakota
Kentucky	Kansas	Maine	Texas
Maine	Kentucky	Maryland	Washington
Massachusetts	Maine	Massachusetts	
Michigan	Maryland	Michigan	
Minnesota	Massachusetts	Minnesota	
Missouri	Michigan	Mississippi	
Nebraska	Minnesota	Montana	
Nevada	Missouri	Nebraska	
New Hampshire	Montana	Nevada	
New Mexico	Nebraska	New Hampshire	
Ohio	Nevada	New Jersey	
Oklahoma	New Hampshire	New Mexico	
Oregon	New Jersey	New York	
Rhode Island	New Mexico	Ohio	
South Dakota	New York	Oklahoma	
Virginia	North Carolina	Oregon	
	North Dakota	Pennsylvania	
	Ohio	Rhode Island	
	Oklahoma	South Dakota	
	Oregon	Tennessee	
	Pennsylvania	Texas	
	Vermont	Vermont	
	Wyoming	Virginia	
		Washington	
		West Virginia	
		Wyoming	

Source: Derived from Report of National Americanism Commission—1920–1921, pp. 24–25. In NA RG 233 Records of the US House of Representatives, Committee Papers, Committee on the Judiciary, HR67A-F24.1, Box 404.

that Americanization is the favorite pastime of America to-day. From every section of the country, from great cities, and from towns so small that their alien population is limited to one family, come reports of Americanization activities."[163] Fears of political extremists reinforced this development. In this context, Americanization was a narrowing activity. It was not until the 1960s that Kallen's sort of "cultural pluralism" found a responsive audience, by which time even he had dropped it.

Varieties of Americanization

Unquestionably the principal thrust of Americanization during the war and post-1918 years was a national campaign to Americanize non-English-speaking immigrants from eastern and southern Europe. Inevitably such an initiative had unanticipated effects, both directly for those affected and indirectly for those considered to lie beyond the assimilability implied in the Americanization program. Three such forms are examined in this section.

Cultural Pluralism

There were other voices in the public debates of the 1920s, which were less dismissive of the diversity bequeathed by the United States's immigrants and skeptical about the long-term benefits of Americanizing new arrivals. These voices included the arguments of John Dewey and Horace Kallen, advocates of the need to recognize the multiple cultures in the United States, and respectful of their intrinsic value. Such writers argued that if there was a "genuine" or "typical" American, he or she was a composite of different traditions, and that few Americans could not claim to be of the "hyphenated" type. Unlike contemporary multiculturalist debates, African Americans were not included by such cultural pluralists.

Some writers at the time expressed qualms about the degree of intervention implied by Americanization. Reflecting on the wartime Americanization propaganda, a community leader in Pittsburgh, Charles Cooper, advocated dropping the term itself: "Americanization savors too much of denationalization. Many races have resisted for centuries, and resisted successfully, every effort at denationalization." Consequently, "the term, Americanization, seems to me to be freighted down with the mistakes of the old world. Its elimination is a matter of wisdom."[164] Cooper proposed substituting it with the word "adoption" (notably a term employed by the 1997 Commission on Immigration Reform). This was a minority view. This attention to the individual was combined with a somewhat contradictory emphasis on community values and voluntary associational life.

An organization such as the United Neighborhood Houses of New York saw in Americanization an opportunity to instill defined values among immigrants, advocating that a "special system of instruction should be devised by which American ideals and customs should be taught in connection with classes in English."[165] Other studies were more sympathetic to values institutionalized in immigrant communities. One study of immigrant neighborhoods stressed the importance of locally based activities and organizations (such as benefit societies) that acted as media of Americanization: "the colony is thus a neighborhood in the truest and most human sense of the term, whose function is to serve as the normal medium for the immigrant's induction into the life of America." Aside from informal activities, immigrant organizations such as benefit societies or mutual insurance cooperatives had an Americanizing effect, according to John Daniels, who studied them: "these mutual insurance societies, though patterned after European models, represent co-operative initiative on the part of immigrants in meeting a serious problem which confronts them as soon as they reach America—namely, the possibility of calamity through the sickness or death of the wage earner." A case study of Lithuanians in the United States confirmed some of these patterns.[166] Voluntary institutions were established because immigrant Lithuanians "were oppressed by the exploitation of private stores;"[167] over time these came to be means of setting up economic organizations that helped Americanize these immigrants. Similar themes were emphasized by Allen Burns, director of the Carnegie Corporation study of methods of Americanization. Burns argued that spontaneous cooperative and voluntary arrangements characterized many immigrant communities and constituted a medium of socialization into American ideals: "the fundamental principles of Americanization are partnership and co-operation, and the immigrant is so thoroughly American that unless these principles of Americanism are observed, he will have nothing to do with the finest and most modern plans for his welfare." Burns cited athletic organization as presenting the "most complete Americanization," because the Amateur Athletic Union brought together immigrant athletic associations with existing American ones: "the result has been that all these immigrant athletic associations have become Americanized not because they had something handed out to them, but because they were asked to become partners with Americans in determining what the American standard of athletics should be."[168] This acknowledgment of community and local diversity was uncommon, however.

The National Americanization Committee also focused on the neighborhood, with Americanizing activities designed "to deal with homes and individuals, their conveniences and necessities, and related to living conditions, housing, protection, personal service by friendly visiting and breaking down the barriers between classes and races."[169] Frances Kellor produced a pamphlet about "neighborhood Americanization," the emphasis of which was on inculcation of Americanism among immigrants, with particular concern about the presence of "alien enemy activity" in immigrant communities. This latter concern defined the task: "Americanization is two-fold and is interwoven, and inseparable. It is the Americanization of the alien in a new country and the Americanization of Americans in their own country. This has pitilessly revealed the fact that we need both."[170] This pluralist approach was rarely reflected in national efforts.

Organic Americanization

John Daniels, in his 1920 volume for the Carnegie Corporation *Americanization Studies* series, characterized local cooperative arrangements as aspects of Americanization (mostly unacknowledged) because of the values they embodied: "[S]uch societies constitute the immigrant's first organized constructive contribution to America. Through them he relieves America of such public or private outlay on his account as would otherwise ensue, and at the same time expresses and further develops a quality which is regarded as fundamental in Americanism—the quality of thriftiness and self-help."[171] Most urban colonies had numerous such societies, with an average membership of 125, though some were much smaller. These organizations would later be thought of as sources of social capital, of the sort that the political scientist Robert Putnam has celebrated.[172]

Daniels stressed the importance of such community-based and ethnic-based organizations—which ranged from benefit societies to the church; foreign-language schools; libraries; and athletic, gymnastic, singing, and dramatic societies—as expressions of a "distinctly cultural character" of immigrant groups that, paradoxically, fostered Americanization: "the popular notion of 'Americanization,' when it recognizes at all the self-Americanizing activities of the immigrants, sees little value in their cultural societies, regarding them as obstacles in the way of assimilation."[173] However, Daniels rejected this latter characterization, instead maintaining that these locally based "nationalistic associations" constituted a form of "organic self-Americanization on the part of the immigrant himself."[174] Daniels summarized this important and overlooked process:

> [T]he natural inclination of the immigrant is to relate himself to American life, . . . this natural process of Americanization affects the individual immigrant largely through his colony group. Instead of breaking away from racial heritages and lines of association, attempting to don immediately a complete new outfit of things "made in America," and live among and associate with native Americans, immigrants of each race generally settle in compact colony neighborhoods, cohere closely among themselves, and form their own associations and organizations. Thus they get their bearings, build up collective morale and resources, and eventually identify themselves with the surrounding American community.[175]

Daniels concluded his detailed study by stressing how immigrants' activities directly contributed to Americanization, and he recommended that government Americanizing measures complement these community initiatives.

His approach is one that both views Americanization as an important process for social integration and promotes the commonly neglected contribution of immigrants' own organizations and social events to this achievement. This is certainly a different view from that of the commissioner of education who employed a "racial adviser" to navigate his way through the numerous European immigrant goups.[176]

Given the bile to which immigrants were subject by the most ardent Americanizers, especially those motivated by political or ideological aims, Daniels's study may well have appeared as one in which the author "had gone native." What is apparent is that his detailed investigation of ethnic neighborhoods impressed on Daniels the variety, richness, and innovativeness of existing organizational efforts among immigrants and the way that these activities themselves constituted a step toward Americanization, but one overlooked in national drives: "Americanization . . . is a process which begins as soon as participation in American life begins, which cannot be taught out of books or otherwise injected or bestowed, and which takes place only through and in pace with actual participation in community affairs."[177] These compelling conclusions were not generally shared, with many nineteenth-century writers condemning "race colonies."[178] Ironically, as Daniels notes, such immigrant activities simply repeated a historical process of Americanization: "the immigrant colonists of to-day organize to meet the problems which confront them in their new world in virtually the same way that the New England Colonists organized to meet the New World problems of their day."[179] The tenacity of ethnic or group loyalties in the US—manifest from the 1960s—supports the importance of Daniel's findings.

Complementing this analysis is the important research undertaken by James Barrett about the grassroots or "bottom up" sources of Americanization coincident with federal and voluntary drives. Barrett places a particular emphasis on working-class labor dynamics, whose organizers had to integrate different ethnic groups, normally speaking their own language. He argues that immigrants in the 1910s and 1920s Americanized selectively through labor and community organizations: unions, shop-floors, and parties "provided immigrants with alternatives to the world view and the values advocated in programs sponsored by employers and the government." Consequently, the immigrants "absorbed alternative views from their own ethnic communities, from cosmopolitans of various sorts, and from an earlier generation of older immigrants and native-born workers." These processes empowered immigrants, Barrett argues, to construct "their own identities, embracing those perspectives and ideas that made sense to them, rejecting those that seemed to be at odds with what they recognized as reality."[180] Although a partial process, it applied to many white European immigrants.

Part of the Americanization movement consisted of a generous attitude toward immigrants. One Bureau of Education memorandum, directed at women Americanizers, warned against helpers who were "merely seeking an outlet for your energies," since the "foreign-born are quick to sense and resent superciliousness and condescension." The memorandum suggested a more egalitarian approach: "[N]othing will Americanize so quickly as neighborliness, the friendly

visit of one woman to another. Treat the foreign-born woman exactly as though she were a native born newly moved into your neighborhood and a splendid work can be done."[181] Such subtleties, however, were lost in the 1920s, and the advice appears to have a rather
middle-class view of neighborhoods, out of place in the ethnic communities into which immigrants entered in American cities. Furthermore, Americanization, as defined and practiced by government departments, was premised exclusively on the principle of assimilation,
an absorption that identified lingering attachment to existing ethnic
values and communities as a tether on newcomers. Thus, a memorandum prepared by the Americanization Division at the Bureau of Education on "Making America" declared "that the process of assimilation can be hurried, that these people can more quickly be given the
vision of the real America and find their place in it, is easily possible if
the community will intelligently plan to that end." The same pamphlet objected to immigrants associating only with their own nationality: "[T]he great body of the new people are not taken into the life of
their community. Too often they have settled in groups containing
only their own race. These groups have grown by the addition of others of that race. The customs, the language, the dress of the old country have been retained. The isolation grows into solidarity. There the
new citizens live as foreign to the real America around them as they
were in their native land."[182] This memorandum urged tolerance toward immigrants and cultivated the ambition of bringing immigrants'
standard of living to an American one.

African-Americans outside Americanization

For the most part, Americanizers turned a blind eye to the position of
African Americans in the United States and expressed no concern
about their education or denial of full citizenship. This incongruity
struck the first president of the NAACP, Moorfield Storey. Addressing
the association's annual conference in 1921 in Detroit, Storey observed that "the poorest and more ignorant foreigner, just naturalized, has the right to fill any office in the country save that of President, but the most highly educated native citizen in whose veins runs a
little colored blood cannot even vote. Ignorance and worthlessness do
not unfit a man for suffrage, but the slightest shade of color will." He
added that "such a position cannot be defended."[183] Storey expatiated

on the ambitions of the Ku Klux Klan to render the United States "'a white man's country'":

> [W]hat a preposterous claim. Every country is a country of the people who are born in it and who make it their home. It may become also the country of foreign born persons who are allowed to become citizens, but no portion of its people can claim that it belongs to them alone. Christians cannot say "This is our country and no Jews shall have rights here." Catholic cannot say "This must be a Catholic country." Republicans cannot say "This is a Republican country." The Labor Unions cannot say "This is Labor's country and Capital shall have no vote." No body of white men can set at defiance our constitution and our laws and say that only white men shall have the right to vote, shall have justice in our courts, shall be protected by law in the U.S.[184]

Speaking in Congress to oppose a scheme to exclude all "members of the African or black race" as eligible for immigration, an Illinois Congressman railed against the injustices facing African Americans in the United States:

> [N]o other race numbering 10,000,000 of the Nation's population would submit to the indignities that have been imposed upon these people. Under this amendment citizens of America of African blood would be excluded from the right to return to America's shores. They have lived here for 250 years. They did not come here of their own accord. They have fought in every battle in which the Nation has been engaged. They have given their life blood for the preservation of the Union; they fought at New Orleans with General Jackson and in the Civil War 350,000 of these men volunteered that the Nation might be saved.[185]

The ironic divergence between the intense Americanization of foreign-born aliens and the disregard of the native-born population on occasions burst through to the surface in the post-1918 years. Wheaton's successor as Director of Americanization in the Bureau of Education, Fred Butler, reflected directly on this discrepancy, concluding that "it becomes clear to me that there are some American born who are not so clear upon the subject of citizenship as others; some of our citizens are not so intelligent as the rest on their duties to the republic."[186] He singled out African Americans as an instance of these deficiencies, marshaling commonplace prejudices in his analysis: "[W]e have millions of negroes who have practically no education and who have not had an opportunity to participate in our political life. They lack schooling and they lack experience. They are children in their mental and social development."[187] Butler also pointed to examples of intense poverty among rural whites, though he did not denigrate their mental capacities: "we have all through the Appalachian mountains many mountaineers of old English, Scotch or Irish descent, the descendants of old pioneers, continuing there among the mountains; people essentially sound in their religious and mental life, with great native capacity but who need training and education to enable them to fulfill their possibilities." Overall, for Butler, the gap between foreign-born aliens' lack of Americanism and the inherent limits of some native-born Americans was a cause for alarm: "[S]o we have many people in America who are born on American soil who are not able to perform their duties as citizens. These create as great a problem as the foreign-born—a problem in Americanization that we cannot afford to overlook."[188]

Butler's analysis is revealing in two ways. First, it shows how the Americanization process was principally focused on immigrants, since his remarks are a rare instance of an Americanizer considering other parts of the U.S. population. Second, his analysis illustrates the exclusivity of assimilationist Americanization (what he calls the "assimilation of the foreign-born and making Americans of them.")[189] It is not surprising that Butler's attention to the attribute "mental capacity" echoes the eugenic arguments being aired before congressional immigration committees. Yet Butler's definition of Americanism as "a very definite social philosophy" composed of core ideas—"such as freedom of speech, of religion, and of the press, the right of the majority to rule, full participation of the individual in government, and personal freedom"[190]—were palpably partially enjoyed in the United States at the time he was writing. These ruminations implied an agenda for Americanizers: "your task and mine is the improvement of the defective education, industrial, and social environment in which the negroes of the south and in some parts of the north, some of our mountaineers and backwoodsmen, and a multitude of foreign-born are living in America, that they may learn from a truly American environment true Americanism."[191] This is a pointedly top-down approach, in which Americanization is defined by a particular conception of those in need of it. Indeed, simply contrast part of a speech to the NAACP's annual conference in 1914, in which the speaker described African Americans' perception of their Americanism: "[N]o people in America have shown less prejudice and hatred against other people because of their race than have the colored people. And, yet, of all our mixed population, they have suffered keener anguish, have had to face greater difficulties and are to-day of all others more cruelly treated by our fellow countrymen because of this sinister and hateful thing which is over us when we sleep, which walks with us in our walking hours and so saddens the lives of all of us that our little children prattle at their toys with a sigh in the heart . . . We are constantly reminded by experience that race prejudice leaves secure no right."[192]

Butler was striving to avoid too crude a version of Americanization (even objecting to the word "Americanize" on the grounds that "it involved an imputation that is often objectionable. It has been used so often by those who assume a superiority in loyalty to America").[193] In fact, the needs of the categories of citizens that Butler identified were fairly basic and included particularly a proper education, or what he defined as "training for the fulfillment of American citizenship."[194] But this is also a curiously innocent claim, which disregards the legal and informal barriers to citizenship placed, for example, in the path of African Americans. Such views come perilously close to blaming Americans such as African Americans for lacking the "training" to be citizens. For instance, at the time Butler was writing, many black Southerners fell victim to lynchers every year.

Conclusion: The Ambivalent Triumph of Americanization

In the long run, Americanization was successful on its own terms, in part because the number of new immigrants was severely curtailed after 1929. By the end of the Second World War, naturalization was the normal choice of immigrants in the United States (and, by that date, most of the barriers to naturalization that faced some groups had been removed). In 1920, 47 percent of foreign-born persons were naturalized, compared with 63 percent in 1940 and 74 percent in 1950. In the twenty years before 1965, "over 2.15 million persons acquired American citizenship."[195]

Assisted incalculably by the First World War and the group animosities that it fostered, the Americanization movement has unavoidably been seen, in retrospect, as promoting a particular version of American identity and not as one open to national or ethnic diversity. In particular, the movement is charged with promoting an Anglocentric conception of the United States, a predictable strategy in the war-time atmosphere, though consistent with the motives of Anglo-Saxon Americanizers. Such a conception was, by definition, not inclusive of all members of the polity, for instance, excluding African Americans, Chinese- and Japanese-Americans, and some poor whites. The movement also required new Americans to detach themselves from ethnic groups, to sacrifice multiple allegiances in favor of a uniform national identity.

The impact of Americanization was a downgrading of group loyalties. Americanization was defined, at least implicitly, as the opposite of ethnic loyalties: it placed individual commitment to the United States above collective ethnic identities. Thus, the concern expressed in the Dillingham Commission report about the tendency of new immigrants to live in ethnic ghettos or foreign colonies leads directly into Americanization, as does the alleged "ignorance" and backwardness of immigrants who had therefore to be inculcated in American practices and culture. Such a message was conveyed, in unabashed terms, by Woodrow Wilson in speaking to new citizens: "[Y]ou can not dedicate yourself to America unless you become in every respect and with every purpose of your will thorough Americans. You can not become thorough Americans if you think of yourselves in groups. America does not consist of groups. A man who thinks of himself as belonging to a particular national group in America has not yet become an American, and the man who goes among you to trade upon your nationality is no worthy son to live under the Stars and Stripes."[196] Wilson's passage and its sentiments were widely cited in official texts about Americanization.[197] It was the "abstract, autonomous individual" whom Americanizers both praised and presented as the ideal citizen.[198] A judge told newly naturalized citizens in 1922 that in taking the oath of allegiance, the petitioners were assumed to "want to become a part and parcel of this great family of the nation; [and] that in seeking the privileges incident to American citizenship you expect to assume and respond to the burden."[199] The cumulative effect of this message in civics education, Americanization programs, and official ceremonies was to delegitimate ethnic or group values.[200]

These effects were part of a broader process, whereby Americanization retained the distinction (also popularized by the Dillingham Commission) between Americans descended from the original settlers (expanded to include nineteenth-century immigrants)—whose values were privileged in American national identity—and new immigrants—whose foreign customs and values rendered the Americanization process one of assimilation and acculturation with the dominant identity. Americanization functioned, as Olneck notes, to confer "prestige and authority on, and [to recognize] the authenticity of those who were or who emulated, the native-born."[201] Conformity with these latter was expected of immigrants. This expectation was stated explicitly by a political scientist, writing in 1906: "'Americanization' is assimilation in the United States. It is the process by which immigrants are transformed into Americans. It is not the mere adoption of American citizenship, but the actual raising of the immigrant to the American economic, social and moral standard of life." The writer, Grover Huebner, explained further: "[T]he American of today is, therefore, not the American of yesterday. He is the result of the assimilation of all the different nationalities of the United States which have been united so as to think and act together."[202]

Although its proponents considered Americanization equivalent to assimilation, in the sense of the melting-pot model, this identity was often less clear-cut in practice.[203] Ethnic traditions were not abandoned.[204] Their retention conflicted with de Crèvecoeurian expectations of extensive ethnic mixing and diverse identity formation. The melting pot myth's persistence arises in part from the "organic" Americanization process observable within such communities. But again it is important to appreciate the omission of African Americans from this Americanization debate. The post-1918 discussion of assimilation elided and ignored the position of African Americans. It was the assimilation of eastern and southern Europeans that exercised the assimilationists in the 1910s and 1920s; African Americans, if thought of at all, were considered unassimilable, despite their deep ties to the United States. Not only did Americanization prove a mixed process for those in targeted groups, but it heightened other inequalities. Both features derive from the narrow conception of U.S. identity on which Americanization was premised.

Fully to grasp both the impact of the Americanization movement and its historical resonance in the recent debates about immigration in the U.S. requires thinking about the position of immigrants and the way they experienced Americanizing measures in the 1920s. Most migrants arrive in their new country with a fundamental ambivalence: that is, there are regretful emotions about leaving a homeland mixed with apprehension and interest in the new country. These attitudes make it unsurprising either that immigrants from similar nationalities comingle in the same neighborhoods or that these centers become attractive points of destiny for new arrivals. Immigrants in the earlier part of the twentieth century were neither engaged on an American version of the classic European "grand tour" nor entering highly paid professional positions with associated prestige, but in most cases, they disembarked in a state of relative penury, often unfamiliar with the language of the new country, and had as immediate priorities locating accommodation and work. The experience of existing immigrants was invaluable in meeting these priorities, and such integration into a nationality-based neighborhood provided the basis—through self-confidence, acquisition of English, and assistance with work—from which a process of "organic Americanization" could occur, as it did overwhelmingly; in this context, James Barrett's identification of an Americanization process occurring from the "bottom up" is valuable, by which he means "the gradual acculturation of immigrants and their socialization in working-class environments and contexts—the shop floor, the union, the radical political party."[205] The urgency of Americanizers and their assumption of the immigrant's inferiority gave the Americanization a harshness and political aim that probably harmed assimilation, though the movement unquestionably hastened the formal integration of many immigrants who might otherwise have remained disengaged from U.S. life. This sharp edge of Americanization should not be overlooked. For example, a keen Pennsylvanian Americanizer described Americanization in brutal terms in 1921: "it is proposed to knock 1,000,000 hyphens out of Pennsylvania." This statement left no room for a Kallenian cultural pluralist vision of U.S. identity. The writer Herman Collins, director of publicity and education in Pennsylvania's Americanization program, continued: "[T]here is a new crusade to save in this State . . . One language and one country—the English language and the American flag for all native-born or foreign-born who dwell within our borders!"[206] This description of Americanization conveys its general characteristics: an exclusive process whose proponents wanted immigrants unequivocally to embrace Americanism and American values. African Americans were largely defined out of the dominant conception of Americanism in the 1910s and 1920s: Americanizers held Americanization to be about assimilating new arrivals into a white Anglo-American conception of U.S. identity. They were complemented by eugenists' definition of apposite immigrants and the "American race," to which the next chapter turns.

CHAPTER FIVE

"Frequent Skimmings of the Dross":

Building an American Race?

Is there a distinct American "race" or people? Despite Horace Kallen's unequivocal warning in 1915 that "the 'American race' is a totally unknown thing,"[1] this question nonetheless taxed policy-makers and intellectuals from the turn of the century as immigration achieved its greatest political salience. The question of identity was of profound importance, since restrictionists increasingly presented their arguments in terms of the incompatibility or unassimilability of certain groups of immigrants with existing Americans. The ardent restrictionist Senator Henry Cabot Lodge warned against the new immigrants who were, he argued, "from races most alien to the body of the American people and from the lowest and most illiterate classes among those races."[2] Throughout this discussion, the place of African Americans was ignored, and since almost all the key policy-makers presumed a "whites only" immigration policy, African Americans were assumed to be unassimilable with the U. S. "people." Retrospectively, "white" is a problematic concept: plainly, Africans were not welcome as immigrants, but neither were certain eastern and southern Europeans, who, despite nominal whiteness, were considered unassimilable. This intellectual climate was manifest at the time of the Dillingham Commission, a point made in Rogers Smith's characterization of the period: "overall, the design visible in education for citizenship during the Progressive Era etched in miniature the broader patterns of U. S. citizenship laws for these years". In these decades "most policymakers believed that, in order for American civilization to be preserved and advanced, the highest stations of U. S. intellectual, economic, social and political life must, for the forseeable future, be largely occupied by middle- and upper-class men of northern European descent. Most blacks, Native Americans, Latinos, Asian-Americans, immigrant working-class whites, and women were expected to be unfit for full and equal citizenship for generations to come, at best."[3] Throughout the Dillingham Commission's report, its authors give attention to the position of African Americans in the United States, with data about them included in several of its tables. However, since the immigration debate was confined to a discussion of migrants from European countries, discussion of African Americans assumes a secondary interest to the commission's authors. The discussion is insufficiently detailed to give a complete picture of African Americans in the United States.[4]

What the debates of the 1920s permitted was a sharpening of the dominance of the Anglo-Saxon group, presented in terms of a melting-pot assimilationist model. The ideology of assimilation was one that anticipated individuals coming to the United States and shedding their ethnic loyalties in favor of a general U. S. identity (a process reinforced by the campaign speeches and writings of Woodrow Wilson and Theodore Roosevelt against "hyphenated" Americans). In practice, the *product* of this melting pot conformed to a version of American identity consistent with the Anglo-American conception, one that belittled the ethnic or group values of those outside the northwestern European tradition. Thus I concur with Matthew Jacobson's conclusion that "race is not tangential to the history of European immigration to the United States but absolutely central." Shifting perceptions about white immigrants defined the debate about immigration in Jacobson's view: "the political history of whiteness and its vicissitudes between the 1840s and 1920s represents a shift from one brand of bedrock racism to another—from the unquestioned hegemony of a unified race of 'white persons' to a contest over political 'fitness' among a new fragmented, hierarchically arranged series of distinct 'white races.'"[5] Although who constituted white was contested and constructed in these decades, notably in court decisions regarding naturalization,[6] nonetheless, that the principal policy-makers wished to formulate a program privileging whites is clear.

Building on the analysis of Americanization in Chapter 4, in this chapter I examine the question of American identity through two developments. First, the arguments advanced by eugenists about the nationalities collectively constitutive of the "American race" are scrutinized. Both the Americanization movement and the eugenic arguments excluded African Americans, whose experience of segregated race relations, a powerful manifestation of many Americans' conception of the United States's identity, forms the second section of the chapter. The chapter concludes with an analysis of how the immigration debates of the 1910s and 1920s impinged on African Americans and black immigrants.

Eugenics and the Idea of an American Race

Coined by Francis Galton in 1883, the term "eugenics" (from the Greek for "wellborn") received its first institutional recognition in 1904 when Galton endowed a Research Fellowship in National Eugenics at University College, London. Karl Pearson, whose innovations in statistics facilitated the quantitative development of eugenic studies, was already well established there. Galton's gift financed the Galton Laboratory for National Eugenics, with Pearson appointed as its director.[7] The department's research included eugenic studies of heredity and medical questions. Daniel Kevles, an eminent historian of the eugenics movement, describes the work supervised by Pearson: "studies emanating from the laboratories typically explored the relationship of physique to intelligence; the resemblance of first cousins; the effect of parental occupation upon children's welfare or the birthrate; and the role of heredity in alcoholism, tuberculosis, and defective sight."[8] Such work centered on the general question of how to ensure mental and physical strength and improvement in the national "stock." For this very reason, one scientist, a geneticist, writing in a eugenics journal, differentiated his research from that conducted by eugenists: "[T]he eugenist and the geneticist will, I am convinced, work most effectively without organic connexion, and though we have much in common we should not be brigaded together. Genetics are not primarily concerned with the betterment of the human race or other applications, but with a problem of pure physiology, and I am a little afraid that the distinctness of our aims may be obscured. Alliances between pure and applied science are as dangerous as those of spiders, in which the fertilizing partner is apt to be absorbed."[9]

These careful distinctions were lost in the politics of eugenic research, however.

Eugenic research in the United States was conducted at the Eugenics Record Office established at the Cold Spring Harbor Laboratory, funded by the Carnegie Institution in Washington, D.C., and directed by the biologist Charles Davenport. Davenport's interest in inheritance in humans encouraged data compilation of life histories. In 1911, Davenport published *Heredity in Relation to Eugenics*.[10] Trawling the hundreds of life histories he had acquired through questionnaires, Davenport went in search of inherited sources of "feeble-mindedness," pauperism, and other traits. He reproduced the prevailing views about racial differences—claims that contributed to U. S. immigration policy—and the need to engage in the building of a strong national stock. This "positive" form of eugenics—fostering good marital choices, for instance,—was combined with an equally strong "negative" eugenics, the need to control the reproduction of the least desirable members of society.[11] This view fed directly into a restrictionist immigration policy, with selection based on individuals and families—tested appropriately for eugenic worthiness—to supplement the identification of nationalities to be excluded. Negative eugenics implied, in Kevles's phrase, "preventing the reproduction of the genetically defective, possibly by state-enforced sterilization. If the state could take a person's life, Davenport judged, surely it could deny the lesser right of reproduction."[12] Although unions of so-called "defectives" and a "normal" person could result in "normal" offspring, the risk of the obverse outcome fueled advocacy of institutional segregation of the "feeble-minded" and, ultimately, of their sterilization.

The appeal of eugenics was widespread in industrial democracies among policy-makers and intellectuals in the half-century before the Second World War. Organizations formed to promote eugenic research and arguments were established in the United States, Britain, France, Germany, and Denmark, among others. In terms of specifying the eugenic base of an American race or nationality, eugenists underlined the legacy of the English settlers in making Anglo-American stock. The English settlers' influence was dominant because it was the strongest and most fit. It was a view coincident with that of racists, as James Weldon Johnson illustrates from a conversation in 1908 with a Texan about the position of African Americans: "'[I]f he's inferior and weaker and is shoved to the wall, that's his own look-out,' said the

Texan. 'That's the law of nature; and he's bound to go to the wall; for no race in the world has ever been able to stand competition with the Anglo-Saxon. The Anglo-Saxon race has always been and will always be the masters of the world, and the niggers in the South ain't going to change all the records of history.'"[13]

In this context, the speculative work of Dr. Harry Laughlin was important.[14] Laughlin, expert adviser to the House Committee on Immigration in Congress and whose influence is the subject of Chapter Six, specified desirable traits in potential immigrants, a framework that logically implied that a distinct "American race" was identifiable (an opinion he tirelessly aired). Indeed, it was one of Laughlin's intellectual and political ambitions persuasively to make such an identification: "if the American people had the habit of using the term 'the American race' . . . we would have a standard to go by, and we could recruit to this standard from different European nationals."[15] There were international dimensions to this project. C. M. Goethe, based in San Francisco and Sacramento (and president of the Immigration Study Commission) reported supplying data to Australia, New Zealand, and Canada, and urging them to restrict immigration to the Nordic race: "[W]ith the exception of Quebec, these countries are overwhelmingly Nordic. They have great areas of unfilled land. We are trying to awaken public opinion therein. We are attempting to convince them that the problem of the Pacific, at least evolves [sic] holding these great unfilled areas for the natural increase of the Nordics—that herein lies perhaps our greatest responsibility to posterity."[16]

Harry Laughlin maintained that a race was biologically distinguishable. It was constituted through the ubiquitous melting-pot process: "the melting pot, with frequent skimmings of the dross, is a better metaphor than assimilation for a description of the actual results when races and family stocks come into contact."[17] Consequently, the "American nation" was "still in flux" because of immigration: "while the American white stock seemed fairly well fixed at the end of a generation after the Civil War, still, beginning with the early 1890's and continuing to the present, different races of immigrants have entered the country in great numbers."[18] This view of a new race resulting from the melting pot is a partial one, however, since not all groups were welcomed as potential constituent parts. The omission of African Americans that is evident in Laughlin's typology was reproduced in government policy. The Commissioner of Education's 1917 memorandum on "Racial Groups," for instance, dealt exclusively with European immigrants.[19]

It also sits askance with what Gunnar Myrdal would later term the "American creed," a morality rooted in equality, freedom, and opportunity allegedly available to all Americans.[20] Laughlin set out the constitutive elements of this American melting pot: "[T]he American race, then (omitting for the time being the descendants of persons who came to the United States involuntarily), is a race of white people who have fused into a national mosaic composed originally of European stocks (themselves mosaics), in rapidly descending proportion, as follows: Primarily, British, Irish, German, Scandinavian, French, and Dutch; secondarily, American Indian, Jewish, Spanish, Swiss, Italian, Austro-Hungarian, and Russian."[21] One predictable omission is African Americans, alluded to in Laughlin's first parenthetical phrase but clearly inconceivable for him as formative elements in or members of the "American race."

In other testimony, Laughlin's exclusion of African Americans from the "American race" is blunt:

> [H]owever unassimilable the negro is in race, he has, so far as he was able, adopted our institutions, our language, our religions, and essential law and customs, but the contrast in blood between the northwestern European settlers and the African negroes is so great that racial assimilation is impossible. If the European colonists in the New World wanted a European civilization, they should not have imported African slaves. But the negro is here. He paid the price of admission with two and one-half centuries of slavery. Negro slavery in America is another of the many cases in history in which a country, in trying to solve an economic problem, introduced a racial problem of gigantic proportions.[22]

Quite what form this "gigantic" racial problem assumed is left unstated in Laughlin's remarks, but he did observe, rather unoriginally, that "we abolished slavery, but we can not be said to have solved its consequent racial problem very satisfactorily, even up to the present time."[23] One senator was less reticent, telling his colleagues in 1914 that "we already have negroes enough in the South. We do not want any more," and supported any scheme whereby "they could go somewhere else, of their own free accord, and to that extent solve this great problem."[24]

Despite the apparent breadth of nationalities embraced within his formulation of the origins of the American race, Laughlin, in common with most eugenists and restrictionists, harped back to a conception of the "American" as constituted overwhelmingly by the English settlers and their descendants; and through the national origins scheme, he wanted policy to be premised on this primary conception. Thus, Laughlin declared that "there was an American race and an American culture of 1860, and this race and culture is being modified to some degree by the changed racial character of the immigration of the last two generations." The mid-nineteenth century was the peak of the Know-Nothing political movement, dedicated to retaining a dominant Anglo-American conception of the United States. But this new immigration had to be rendered compatible with the true race:

> [W]e can always use immigrants in limited numbers, provided their individual races to which they belong are compatible with our prevailing races for mate selection and that their family stocks are superior to our existing families. But unlimited immigration of races and types which have contributed very small percentages to the making of the original American people would supplant our fundamental race complex, and with the new race would come other cultures, languages, and traditions for the country.[25]

Such views were reflected in American society. For instance, the president of the Master Builders' Association of Boston reported his members' view that "there is danger, decided danger, of too far diluting our native (or should we say typically American) stocks by the introduction of other racial strains. It seems to be very definitely established, scientifically, that those races having Nordic blood are the ones which have forged to the front (among white races at least) in the development of modern civilization. Many of the races admitted freely to our country have had none of this valuable racial strain." In addition, "one of the greatest difficulties with many of the races admitted to our country is an absolutely lower moral standard."[26]

One example of Laughlin's aims was his comparison of the racial composition of the delegates to the Constitutional Convention of 1787 with those of the members of the U.S. Senate in the 69th Congress (1926–27). Finding that both were dominated by descendants of English immigrants—"as far as the political leadership of the nation is concerned, approximately the same racial blood is operating now as in the Convention"—Laughlin drew some robust conclusions: "[T]he lesson is that it behooves the American people to encourage the immigration and development of high political genius in our population. America must look forward toward raising the average intelligence of the whole people."[27]

Eugenists always insisted, regarding U. S. immigration policy, that their intention was to distinguish between individuals and not races;[28] such distinctions often got lost, however, in political debate. Thus, the warning issued by Carol Aronovici (chairperson of the Minnesota State Committee on Americanization) in 1919 about the danger of Americanization privileging one group over others was lost:

> [W]ithin recent years there has been much concern shown by anti-immigrationists regarding the dangers of mongrelizing the American people. The cry has usually come from Anglo-Saxons, who by pseudo-scientific discussion and by an appeal to the lower emotion of race superiority and the race struggle have advocated the exclusion of the so-called lower races, with the implication that only the Anglo-Saxon and Teutonic races are superior and, therefore, desirable. The present war with the discredit heaped upon the civilization and *kultur* of the Teuton leaves the Pan-Anglo-Saxon leaders with a clear conscience in claiming this country for the descendants of the original settlers from the British Isles, and with a large undigested mass of races to be either so absorbed and assimilated as to leave no trace of their original identity or to be kept on a low social level as a much needed industrial group which should have and keep its place.[29]

Laughlin argued that "racially, the American people, if we are to remain American, and to purge our people of degeneracy, and to encourage a high rate of reproduction by the best endowed portions of our population, can assimilate in the future many hundreds of thousands of northwestern Europeans, but even these only if carefully selected as to inborn family qualities superior to the average of our own people."[30] Laughlin not only wanted immigrants largely confined to persons from northwestern Europe who would be compatible with the American race but also advocated eugenic selection among prospective immigrants in these countries to ensure that only the eugenically superior were admitted. He feared racial degeneracy, particularly because of what Laughlin called "race mixtures," and warned against them: "radical crosses, whether in plants, animals or man, are useful in experiments to make new races, but it is an exceedingly extravagant and expensive process in which to indulge with the higher animals and man; the dross outmeasures many times the resulting material or value." For the United States, this analysis implied a program of positive eugenics, a prospect Laughlin embraced even in the late 1930s: "racially the American people, if they are to remain American . . . can successfully assimilate in the future many thousands of northwestern European immigrants, but only such of these as are carefully inspected and selected." Of course nonwhites were unsuitable: "but we can assimilate only a small fraction of this number of other white races; and of the colored races practically none."[31]

Speaking to a conference on immigration in New York in 1924, Laughlin lamented the problem of defining the "American race," a necessary concept for identifying suitable immigrants: "it is time to use the term 'American race,' and if we had the definition of American race . . . I think we would have a standard that would serve us well for the future progress." He outlined his order of nationalities constitutive of this "race": "If the American race is composed, first, of descendants of immigrants of the British Isles; then immigrants coming from Germany, Scandinavia, from the Netherlands, from France, then the Jewish group, then from Spain, then, possibly, Hungary, Russia, and the group from other countries, if that is the stuff out of which the American race is made, and if we maintain those proportions, I think we would make a great step in advance."[32] This formulation rehearsed the framework about to be enacted in the Johnson-Reed law. Laughlin's statement describes the logic from which the nationality quota provision was derived. He continued to explain this premise:

> [T]he quota law is trying to include the proportion, not connected with any one race, that has an integral part here. They [its drafters] have attempted to exclude races that are not subject to naturalization, because they are not integrals in the American race. I feel, after we determine what the American race is, and the biological components of it in the proper proportion, then our immigration policy should be to recruit each element of these races, and only to bring in such individuals of personal qualities and good family stock qualities whose progeny will improve the natural talents, the emotions, instinct, intellect, quality of the American people. We ought to breed up the American people by immigration.[33]

The nationalities deemed to be "not integrals in the American race" presumably alluded not only to southeastern Europeans but also to African Americans and Asians. The chairman of proceedings heaped praise on Laughlin's views as representing the "heart and essence of the whole movement in Washington," adding that the 1924 law was designed to "produce in America in one hundred years from now the America of today as determined by a study of the Census of 1920, and an admixture, by immigration only of such elements as will preserve those proportions, as far as it can be done."[34] This was a bald summary of the logic of 1924.

More discursively, Laughlin stated that "the criteria for permission for an immigrant to land in America, should be whether he is of an assimilable race, and whether he brings with him some hereditary quality which in his children, would constitute a decided asset to the American people. This asset must be in the nature of superior hereditary physical soundness, of special hereditary intellectual ability, or of hereditary temperamental qualities of a high order."[35] For Laughlin the national origins scheme was a mechanism to make immigration consistent with the "racial makeup of the entire people," which would, in a phrase echoing Americanizers, "keep America American."[36] It was an agenda readily embraced by Congressman Albert Johnson, chairman of the House Committee on Immigration, who concluded that "the task of our committee is to prepare proposed duties which will develop the American people along the racial and institutional lines laid down by the founders of the country, so far as the control of immigration can do it."[37] For Laughlin, determining "the future American race" required three measures: first, immigration control; second, mate selection that could be "controlled or directed to a small degree by the several individual states in their marriage laws, but mainly it is a matter of national ideals and custom and social value as to 'whom marries whom'"; and third, controlling reproduction of "the degenerate section of the population."[38]

Laughlin endeavored to oppose any objective notion of racial superiority or inferiority. He simply believed in keeping "races" distinct, though the calibrations he drew were extremely fine: "[I]t is, then, this matter of degree of racial difference that governs the degree of racial assimilation of the immigrant to the receiving races. In selecting immigrants, racial similarity and the possession of hereditary ability to perform the work of the receiving country are necessary primary considerations." He added, in a clause that tied these views into the science of IQ measurement, that "hereditary ability is equally as important as similarity of races."[39] Eugenically, racial mixing outside broad groups meant emasculation: "[R]adical crosses are useful in experimenting to make new races, but it is an exceedingly extravagant and expensive process. The dross outmeasures many times the resulting material of value."[40]

In his own account of "the major racial problems in the development of the American people," Laughlin provides a narrative purely from the point of view of white immigrants of British origin. His seven instances in which immigration by individuals or groups who disrupted this narrative of a developing white American nationality were as follows:

> 1. The effort of the white pioneer-colonists along the Atlantic seaboard to prevent destruction by racial mixture with the American Indian; 2. The conflict for racial and institutional supremacy between the British colonists on the one hand and the French, Dutch and Spanish on the other; 3. The importation of Negro slaves; 4. Oriental immigration; 5. Radical change in racial and individual character of immigrants beginning with the great rise of American industry following the Civil War; 6. Mexican immigration into the southwest; and 7. The substitution of the biological for the asylum and economic bases of the nation's immigration-control policy.[41]

Stage 7 was the one achieved by the Johnson-Reed Act of 1924. Laughlin conceded that the arrival of African Americans was an instance of "involuntary immigration" but discounted this factor in assessing the effects: "but in the long run the racial consequences were the same, whether the immigrants come as free colonists or as slaves." The eugenist plainly considered African Americans not to be full Americans: "[N]ow there are 11,891,143 colored persons in the United States (1930 Census). That makes a racial problem of the first order, and one extremely difficult to solve." He expatiated on this last point: "however unassimilable the negro is in race, he has, so far as he has been able, adopted American institutions, language, religions and essential laws and customs, but the contrast in blood between the European settler and the African negro is so great that racial assimilation is unacceptable to the European."[42] It would be difficult to locate a more precise statement of the perceived relationship between immigration and American identity, among those defending an Anglo-Saxon conception, than this one proffered by Laughlin. Employing a now curiously dated conception of "blood" and limited biological premises, Laughlin made his racial classifications central to immigration policy: "America can furnish the environment and the opportunity, but the immigrant must furnish the blood—that is, the inherent qualities and capacities that will respond favorably to our environment. Such response must show in sounder bodies, in better trained minds and in nearer approach to American ideals of conduct." Consequently, "a successful policy of immigration-control would sort out and admit only such would-be immigrants who are definitely capable of making such constructive response personally, and whose children would be Americans beyond question."[43]

In sum, Dr. Harry Laughlin developed two sorts of arguments derived from his eugenic research. First, he advanced a claim about what national groups formed the principal part of American national identity, beginning with the English settlers. Second, eugenic considerations encouraged him to prioritize certain groups as apposite for inclusion in the national "race" and others for exclusion. I turn now to the consequences of this narrow conception for African Americans, both immigrants and natives.

African Americans and Anglo-Saxon Americanism

Both the conception of American identity promoted in the Americanization movement and the immigration restrictions enacted in the 1920s rested on a view of U.S. society as white and homogenous. In this section I consider the way that this presumption affected African Americans and their responses to the legislation, through a discussion of segregation, black immigration, and national origins. Preliminarily, Du Bois's seminal description in *The Souls of Black Folk* of African Americans' dual identity applies fully to this era:

> One ever feels his two-ness—an American, a Negro; two souls, two thoughts, two unreconciled strivings; two warring ideals in one dark body, whose dogged strength alone keeps it from being torn asunder. The history of the American Negro is the history of this strife. . . In this merging he wishes neither of the older selves to be lost. He would not bleach his Negro soul in a flood of white Americanism. . . He simply wishes to make it possible for a man to be both a Negro and an American, without being cursed and spit upon by his fellows, without having the doors of Opportunity closed roughly in his face.[44]

The anxieties and concerns raised in Du Bois's analysis can but be strengthened by the way in which American identity was discussed by Americanizers and proponents of immigration restriction in the 1920s. It is here that we see the effects in domestic politics of a "whites only" immigration policy.

Despite the legal and informal restrictions imposed on African Americans in this jim crow era, there were numerous autonomous African American communities in the U.S. constructed from individual actions and choices in these decades. Many African Americans achieved prominence in American life and not just within the demarcated spheres of segregated life. And they organized politically. Aside from the work of the NAACP, in the 1930s the National Negro Congress attempted to organize African American workers in order to seek political rights and full participation in the New Deal program and to fight against segregation and discrimination.[45] Its president was A. Philip Randolph. The congress was repeatedly accused of being communist, a claim that was rejected by its leaders but that tarnished the congress.[46] It contributed decisively to the antilynching campaign.

African Americans organized in industrial work. Although oppressed by segregated work practices and by usually racist trade unions, this treatment did not mean that no African Americans organized during the interwar decades. In fact, there were instances of interracial worker alliances, as documented in Robin Kelley's study of Alabama.[47] Kelley observes of the International Labor Defense's work in Alabama, the dominant black organization in Birmingham in the mid-1930s, that whereas most whites dismissed it as a form of outside agitation, "many black working people saw the organization as a sort of public defender for the 'race.'" Its popularity exposed divisions within the African American community: "the ILD was not just one additional voice speaking out on behalf of poor blacks; it was a movement composed of poor blacks."[48] What is important in Kelley's analysis for my study is the exposure of class and other divisions within the African American community, cleavages that became the basis of political movements and organization. Such activities and organizations were often unrecognized but nonetheless crucial precursors to the civil rights movement of the 1950s and 1960s.

Many scholars and writers have stressed the extent to which apparent acquiescence in segregation camouflaged bitter African American opposition to its institutional manifestations. Commenting on the "tremendous struggle which is going on between the races," James Johnson declared that "it is a struggle; for though the black man fights passively, he nevertheless fights; and his passive resistance is more effective at present than active resistance could possibly be. He bears the fury of the storm as does the willow-tree."[49] Robin Kelley has taken the implication of such observations further empirically by examining what he terms "the hidden social and cultural world of black working people"[50] and by assessing the political importance of such activities and communities that were created within a generally hostile and indeed oppressive milieu. The crucial point is that the existence of autonomous worlds in African American communities, whose members actively created their own interests, cultural resources, and styles of political engagement is apparent. That the NAACP and other groups or individuals working for civil rights for African Americans assumed a distinct and identifiable part of the population should not, however, lead to exaggerated understandings of African Americans' racial essentialism. This point has been well made by Anthony Appiah and Robin Kelley among others.[51] Furthermore, despite the gross inequalities of segregation, African American communities, such as that in Harlem, had no difficulty in the 1920s in demonstrating creative and autonomous values.[52]

For some African Americans, cultural and political autonomy implied separatism, and here the Caribbean influence was important.[53] In the 1920s, Marcus Garvey's separatist movement, the United Negro Improvement Association (UNIA), celebrated the distinct position, inheritance, and identity of blacks in the United States political system, and also eschewed assimilation with white America.[54] David Cronon underscores Garvey's opposition to black leaders committed to integration: "Garvey denounced other Negro leaders as being bent on cultural assimilation, cravenly seeking white support." The NAACP was his favorite target: the association "was the worst offender in Garvey's mind because, he said, it 'wants us all to become white by amalgamation, but they are not honest enough to come out with the truth . . . To be a Negro is no disgrace, but an honor.'"[55] This radical separatism—intended to culminate in a dedicated state in Africa,[56] which was gently mocked in Chester Himes's novel *Cotton Comes to Harlem*—was plainly at odds with the integrationist and civil rights oriented NAACP movement (a tension depicted in the Denzel Washington film *Hoodlums*). Focusing on urban working-class and poor African Americans, Garvey's political stance was militant and confrontational, and it sits with a tradition of what Komozi

Woodard terms the "historical process of black nationality formation in the United States."[57] Garvey focused on industrial issues, including discrimination by white employers against blacks in the labor market, their exclusion from unions, unequal wages compared with whites, discrimination in the military, and the constraints facing black businesses. Garvey's UNIA emphasized racial pride, reclaiming ghettos for African Americans and generally building a sense of autonomy and self-control in black communities.

African Americans and the Federal Government

During the 1920s, while eugenists such as Harry Laughlin and their congressional allies were promoting arguments about how to restrict immigration and to build an American race, the position of most African Americans was dictated by the system of segregated race relations, which was permitted in the 1896 Supreme Court judgment *Plessy v. Ferguson.* This ruling enabled the federal government (and state and local governments) systematically to discriminate against African Americans under the pretext of the spurious "separate but equal" doctrine that *Plessy* had pronounced. In one of the many poignant scenes in Spike Lee's film *4 Little Girls,* Chris McNair recounts having to explain to his six-year-old daughter, Denise, later one of the victims of the 16th St. Baptist Church murders in Birmingham, Alabama, that because of their color, black people could not use certain facilities. This scene conveys powerfully the injustice and inequality of segregation. *Plessy v. Ferguson* legitimatized racial segregation in American society.[58] The court's decision echoed the discussion of the Founding Fathers in respect to slavery and confirmed that African Americans' place in the U.S. polity was one resting on inferior citizenship.[59]

This inequality was introduced into the civil service in 1913, overturning meritocratic criteria of admissions.[60] Senior appointees of the new Woodrow Wilson administration permitted (and in many cases colluded in) segregated race relations in their departments.[61] President Wilson justified the practice as a mechanism both to relieve tension in the bureaucracy and, since the promotion of African Americans over whites was unthinkable, to provide limited opportunity for the advancement of some African Americans. Wilson wrote to one African American activist, in July 1913, that "it is true that the segregation of the colored employees in the several departments has begun upon the initiative and the suggestion of several of the heads of departments, but as much in the interest of the negroes as for any other reason."[62]

These two developments—Supreme Court endorsement of "separate but equal" arrangements and a segregationist administration—together had an immense effect on the federal government's treatment of African American citizens, as the ensuing cases illustrate. The following examples demonstrate the mechanisms with which federal government officials implemented segregation under the *Plessy* doctrine. They also reveal these practices in several contexts: first, in federal government departments where the electoral success of the Democrats in 1912 quickly translated into segregation; and second, in restaurants operated in government departments, which publicly demonstrated African Americans' differentiated, second-class citizenship. These are not exhaustive examples but are representative of practices common in other parts of the federal government, such as prisons, the Armed Services, or National Parks. These examples are followed by that of the failed antilynching legislation to illuminate congressional intransigence. The consistent theme of opponents of segregation was that it both violated the constitutional right to equality enjoyed by citizens of the U. S. and implicitly created discrimination. And as Thurgood Marshall later wrote, efforts to "draw a line between a policy of 'discrimination' and a policy of 'segregation'" were inherently problematic since "segregation is in itself discrimination. The moment you tell one citizen that he cannot do what another citizen can do, simply because of his race, you are maintaining a policy of discrimination."[63] Even where critics sought equality within the segregationist framework, the fact of its fundamental injustice remained.

The Civil Service. In August 1913 the NAACP sent to President Wilson a formal letter entitled "On Federal Race Discrimination" to protest his administration's support "in segregating the colored employees in the Departments at Washington." Wilson's acceptance reflected "a failure to appreciate the deeper significance of the new policy; to understand how far reaching the effects of such a drawing of caste lines by the Federal Government may be, and how humiliating it is to the men thus stigmatized."[64] One NAACP member described changes in 1919 at the Library of Congress: "the new superintendent of buildings and grounds at the Library of Congress has segregated the colored employees in the employees' lunch room, and excluded the colored public from the public restaurant altogether."[65] A protest was lodged with the House and Senate library committees responsible for the library's operation.[66]

Employees of the federal government found themselves divided into two classes, according to race, and one of the classes was dominant over the other: "it has set the colored apart as if mere contact with them were contamination." To African Americans "is held out only the prospect of mere subordinate routine service without the stimulus of advancement to high office by merit."[67] Such practices by the federal government provided an all too obvious pretext for racist behavior in society.

Although NAACP protests received substantial press reportage and editorial comment, they failed to stem the segregationist tide unleashed in the federal government by Wilson appointees.[68] By January 1919, the District of Columbia (DC) Branch of the NAACP observed in its annual report that "few days pass without an appeal of someone to the branch for assistance" regarding segregation and discrimination in the federal government.[69] One description of conditions in the Register section of the U.S. Treasury is representative: "[T]he floor is used by all classes of clerks, but on one side, partitioned off and closed from the outer room by a door is the colored section comprising about sixty-six women and men. There are, however, ten more colored men on another floor used by white clerks. These are caged in on coupon work with a white clerk over them."[70] By 1922, a year after the immigration restrictions of 1921, the NAACP observed that "segregation is more prevalent in the Departments at Washington today than ever before."[71]

The results of segregation in government departments were apparent throughout the 1920s, with Republican presidents and congresses showing no inclination to halt segregation.[72] A letter to Warren Harding in August 1920, when he was the Republican presidential nominee, sought his support in opposing the "humiliating policy of segregation in the civil service of the government,"[73] but to no avail. This inaction caused great bitterness, as Richard Sherman notes: "nothing had engendered as much bitterness against Wilson in American Negroes as did the segregationist policies introduced during his administration." Consequently, African Americans hoped for reform: "[M]uch could be corrected by executive order, and much was hoped for when the Republicans returned to power. But to the chagrin of the colored population in the two and a half years of Harding's presidency little seems to have been accomplished."[74] There was no improvement a year later, as James Johnson informed President Calvin Coolidge: "[T]he situation in some of the government departments at Washington has for a number of years been a smirch on the very name of democracy. Colored Civil Service employees, regardless of their classification, rank, service or efficiency, have purely on account of race been herded, segregated and Jim-crowed under the very nose of the government." He added that with segregated employment, "the government itself is made a party to such rank discrimination."[75] In 1927 a new wave of segregation was unleashed in federal departments in Washington,[76] and as the NAACP concluded in 1928, "rather than abolishing segregation the Republicans had maintained it or actually increased it."[77] A member of the DC Branch of the NAACP, Neval Thomas, described the new practice in a letter to President Calvin Coolidge: "the colored clerks in the Pension Office have been taken from their desks . . . and congregated in a Negro division called the File Room, where some of them are doing laboring work, and all of them in danger of remaining in the lower salary grades by reason of such placement." He concluded that "it is the overshadowing issue of government that is involved, for any group stigmatized by the nation as inferiors and pariahs is subject to further inroads upon its liberties."[78] Among the political elite, African Americans were viewed as "inferiors and pariahs." Fear of reprisals prevented many African Americans from complaining about segregation.[79]

A modest reversal of the changes at the U.S. Department of the Interior[80] did not excise segregated race relations elsewhere in the federal government, as a dispiriting description several months after Secretary Work's decision demonstrates: "to date you will find Segregation in every department where there are enough Negroes to fill a room, or other segregated area."[81] Segregated race relations remained at the post office, treasury, interior, and war departments, among others.[82] Support for segregation among white employees was high. Since segregation was condoned in official policy, this reaction was hardly surprising. Tentative steps to desegregate the cafeteria at the Treasury's Bureau of Engraving and Printing provoked a boycott by whites: "white employees of the bureau have instituted a boycott because Negroes are not rigidly segregated in the diningroom."[83]

In sum, from 1913 (until the 1940s and in some cases the 1950s) many federal departments operated segregated race relations—jim crow departments—among their employees. That a world of greater equality was displaced during this period is suggested from James Weldon Johnson's memories of the pre–Woodrow Wilson Washington: "[T]he social phase of life among colored people is more developed in Washington than in any other city in the country. This is on account of the large number of individuals earning good salaries and having a reasonable amount of leisure time to draw from. There are dozens of physicians and lawyers, scores of school-teachers, and hundreds of clerks in the departments."[84] This world of modest employment and social creativity was eroded from the mid-1910s and did not recover until the 1960s.

Restaurants in Public Buildings. If African Americans were admitted to restaurants in the federal government, it was to segregated seating. When the new Supreme Court of the District of Columbia building opened in 1919, its status as a source of justice and redress proved vacuous for African Americans. An NAACP member, Neval Thomas, discovered this inequity directly: "today . . . I was plainly told that it was the order of the Court that no colored were to be served" in its public restaurant.[85] In response to a protest from the NAACP, the Chief Justice of the Court wrote that "the person who runs the restaurant in the Court House of the District of Columbia has been notified by the Court that all persons have the right to equal service therein."[86] Enforcement of this dictum was precarious, however, and a further letter produced no response. African American lawyers were informed that the restaurant, although located in a public building, was a "private" one and therefore immune from federal law (this judicial argument was invoked frequently legally to justify the exclusion of African Americans from facilities).[87] Within a month of the NAACP's complaint, a separate restaurant was created for blacks. This new facility was placed behind a screen in order that, as Neval Thomas surmised, "no white person would be hurt by the unsightly sight of a Negro eating in his own building."[88]

The African American member of Congress, Oscar De Priest, was active in combatting discrimination in federal policy. The matter of restaurants came to De Priest's attention when his secretary, Morris Lewis, who was accompanied by his son, was expelled from the restaurant:[89] "my son and I were seated in the coffee shop when the cashier came over and tapped me on the shoulder, announcing that the restaurant was exclusively for white people and that colored people would not be served."[90] Such exclusion from a public cafeteria illustrates how segregation operated on racial lines independently of class. The NAACP's secretary, Walter White, rejected proposed arrangements based on segregation since "the setting aside of a jim-crow table for Negroes . . . is as discriminatory as barring altogether of Negro patrons. Such action is a difference in degree and not in kind of segregation."[91] This arrangement was the solution proposed by Senator Royal Copeland. Protest letters from the NAACP to all senators and congressmen about the restaurant ban prompted some bizarre responses. The Texan representative, Sterling P. Strong, managed to invert the inequities of segregation to present it as a model of benevolent treatment toward African Americans in the South:

> [T]he railroads have been compelled to carry separate coaches for colored people and white people are not allowed in these coaches to consume room or in any way cause discomfort to the colored people. The colored people are also provided with a separate waiting room at all railroad stations where the same rules apply as to the separate coaches on the trains. They are also provided with separate apartments on street cars and no white person is allowed to encroach upon this space set aside for colored people.[92]

This was a cruel and cynical description of segregation. Citizenship for many African Americans meant second-class status: they were excluded from certain areas of public institutions and educationally relegated to separate (and as it later transpired, inferior) treatment. Strong also pointed out that a separate table had been offered to Congressman De Priest in the House restaurant, an offer understandably rejected by the congressman. Roy Wilkins speedily replied to the senator's letter, noting that whites avoided carriages reserved for blacks because "nine times out of ten [they are] inferior to those sections reserved for white people." Such segregation rarely resulted in equality of facilities: "in fact, the only excuse for separation is the enforcement of inequality." He added that "it is no wonder that the white people do not wish to 'intrude' upon this type of accommodation."[93]

In January 1934, Congressman Oscar De Priest introduced a resolution in the House of Representatives to end discrimination in the House restaurant.[94] The resolution was referred to the Committee on Rules.[95] The committee was slow to consider it; consequently, in mid-February, De Priest orchestrated a petition in the House, seeking the discharge of the committee on this resolution.[96] One hundred and forty-seven congressmen signed this motion, two above the necessary number to get the matter discussed on the House floor, where the resolution[97] was passed, though it proceeded no further. Cafeterias that were operating in federal departments thus reproduced segregation.

Antilynching Measures. The U.S. Congress and Executive failed to enact antilynching legislation until after World War II. Attempts to end lynching dominated the work of the NAACP from its foundation in 1909, as the association resolved at its 1922 conference: "[T]he first and great question before American Negroes is lynching. We are still the one land in the world which shows itself powerless to prevent the burning of human beings."[98] Protests against lynching included the silent march in New York City on July 28, 1917, led by James Weldon Johnson (who also memorably described the brutality of a lynching that he witnessed).[99] Between 1869 and 1922, there were 3,436 lynchings committed in the United States with less than a dozen of the perpetrators ever punished.[100] In 1922 alone, there were 61 lynchings,[101] and 28 in 1923, a figure equaled ten years later in 1933.[102] Over several decades the NAACP led campaigns to enact federal legislation against lynching.[103] The NAACP convened a conference in May 1919 on antilynching legislation, published numerous pamphlets about this cause,[104] and organized writing campaigns when appropriate to members of Congress and to newspapers. Also, the NAACP lobbied for a congressional investigation of lynching,[105] though not at the expense of legislation. In the 1920s, African Americans had hoped for some support on antilynching from the Republican Party.[106] President Warren Harding's failure specifically to recommend passage of a bill was indicative of a general Republican malaise toward the circumstances of African Americans.

The first success of the NAACP's Anti-Lynching Committee[107] came with the 1923 Dyer Bill (named after Congressman Leonidas Dyer), which passed in the House and in the Senate Judiciary Committee, but the bill was never brought to the Senate floor despite much support.

Missourian Congressman Leonidas Dyer's commitment to antilynching legislation was tenacious. In May 1918 he delivered a powerful speech against the practice and called for federal action. He anticipated arguments employed by the civil rights movement in the next few decades, highlighting, for example, the discrepancy between the deployment of U.S. troops overseas "against tyranny and oppression" and the toleration of "lynching and attacks upon persons" at home: "this country alone stands in shame and disgrace before the civilized bar of public opinion in that it has for years tolerated lynchings."[108] Lynching was the "most damnable crime known to civilized man." He cited the Fourteenth Amendment to justify federal activism: "the principle is that persons so assailed are within the peace of the United States; that the United States owes them the duty of protection; and that the power of protection follows upon the duty."[109] He listed a string of judicial decisions in support of this interpretation of the Fourteenth Amendment. Dyer liaised with the NAACP. In April 1918, Dyer sent the association his draft bill and invited "any suggestions and comment" before he introduced it in the House.[110] Dyer wanted the NAACP to publicize his endeavor, "to counteract efforts that have and are being made to make the colored people believe that this is not a Bill designed for their protection."[111]

The NAACP's legal committee provided assistance. The association also assisted in identifying supporters to testify in support of the bill before the Judiciary Committee, since Dyer plainly intended to publicize lynchings and to educate the public through statements in the Congress.[112] The NAACP's secretary, John Shillady, promised a national campaign "to create a tremendous public sentiment in favor of the bill," coincident with Dyer's initiative.[113] In May 1919, Dyer introduced another bill, HR 259; and Senator Charles Curtis, also a stalwart against lynching, introduced a resolution in the Senate (S. Res. 189) in September. Thus, by the time of his 1923 bill, Congressman Dyer had devoted several years and considerable energy to antilynching legislation.

Politically, the NAACP concentrated on Senator Warren Harding, Republican presidential candidate in 1920. James Weldon Johnson, together with Harry Davis, a Cleveland member of the NAACP Board of Directors, visited Harding at Marion, Ohio, in August 1920, and highlighted the racial issues that they wanted the Republican platform to include. The NAACP identified, in Moorfield Storey's words, "seven points relative to the Negro on which it was desired that he make specific statements before a delegation of colored citizens."[114] These points included extracting a commitment to federal antilynching legislation, an issue that Harding had previously supported. This effort was unsuccessful. Further visits with Harding, now elected president, by Johnson and Storey resulted in a small dividend:[115] Harding's message to Congress included a reference to "wipe out the stain of barbaric lynching from the banners of this democracy." This statement transpired to be the only substantial support provided by the White House for antilynching legislation until the 1940s.[116] In July 1921, however, with little progress in Congress (despite a Republican majority),[117] James Weldon Johnson wrote to Harding again, reminding him of the importance of a federal initiative on lynching, especially in the light of Harding's earlier statements: "[T]he colored people are looking to the Administration for some remedy. . . If Congress should simply plead that it has no power to act, the colored people would not only be disappointed but disheartened."[118] As Congressman Dyer told the NAACP's annual conference in 1922, "it is recognized everywhere that this crime of lynching is principally against the colored people."[119]

From the beginning of his antilynching campaign, Dyer aimed to shore up the constitutional argument, emphasizing it over the horrific data on lynchings, as James Johnson noted: "Mr. Dyer is more interested in having arguments to support the constitutionality of these measures than in having the presentation of data regarding lynchings and race riots."[120] In the Senate, Senator Curtis paralleled Dyer's efforts, holding hearings on antilynching legislation and introducing draft bills. Opponents of the Dyer Bill, led by Southern Democrats such as Hatton Sumners (a Democrat from Texas), argued that the new measure would unreasonably weaken local law enforcement responsibility.

A new Dyer Bill was favorably reported by the House Committee on the Judiciary on October 20, 1921, though no further progress was made during that session despite efforts to bring the bill to vote. Opponents of the legislation concentrated on the old chestnut of the constitutionality of a federal role in antilynching. This issue dogged all the proposals to use federal power against lynching.[121] The issue was discussed at the House Judiciary Committee in July 1921, when the Assistant Attorney General, Guy Goff, told committee members that the bill was constitutional. Dyer's Bill H. R. 13 proposed "to assure to persons within the jurisdiction of every State the equal protection of the laws and to punish the crime of lynching." Goff stated that "states could by neglect or omission 'deny the equal protection of the laws' to its citizens, as guaranteed by the 14th Amendment. He also stated that Congress had the right, under the police power which it has in connection with any expressed power granted to Congress, to enact this sort of legislation."[122] This view was supported by the Attorney General.[123] The Committee reported H. R. 13 on October 27, 1921 (despite prevarication at various stages by the committee[124]).

President Harding's support was withheld. James Johnson stressed the gravity of lynching to the president: "I need not tell you of the political disappointment and dissatisfaction which the masses of colored people, especially in the voting states of the North, have been feeling." He added that "it would be an act that would affect not only the thinking colored man and the colored man on the street, but would reach even the Negro on the plantation."[125] Johnson urged Harding to make passage of the Dyer Bill a keynote in his message to Congress in December 1921.[126] In the new year (1922), the NAACP tackled the constitutional concerns head-on, particularly the claim that if federal authorities could deal with lynching, they would also have the power to legislate in respect to murder:

> [T]he analogy is not a true one. Lynching *is* murder, but it is also *more* than murder. In murder, one or more individuals take life, generally, for some personal reason. In lynching, a mob sets itself up in place of the State and its actions in place of due process of law to mete out death as punishment to person accused of crime. It is not only against the act of killing that the Federal Government seeks to exercise its power through the proposed law, but against the act of the mob in arrogating to itself the functions of the State and substituting its actions for the due processes of law guaranteed by the Constitution to every person accused of crime. In murder, the murderer merely violates the law of the State. In lynching, the mob arrogates to itself the powers of the State and the functions of government. It apprehends, accuses, tries, condemns and executes by meting out death as the punishment—a very different thing from murder.[127]

On January 25, 1922, the Dyer Bill was passed in the House of Representatives by a vote of 230 to 119, following adoption of a special rule on the bill and fourteen hours of debate. Hearings were held before a subcommittee of the Senate Judiciary Committee in March 1922 about the constitutionality of antilynching legislation. Its chairman, William Borah (R-Idaho), disputed the constitutionality of a federal antilynching role, and prodigious NAACP efforts to dissuade him of this view were uneffective. Borah was motivated in part by personal animosity toward the Majority Leader, Henry Cabot Lodge,[128] a long-standing opponent of immigrants who subscribed to an Anglo-Saxon conception of U.S. nationality but who was now compelled to support the NAACP cause.[129] Lodge's precarious electoral position in the 1922 elections enabled the NAACP to target his constituents if he failed to support the Dyer Bill, and Dyer himself "spoke under NAACP auspices to a Boston audience in May and urged that his listeners work for Lodge's defeat that autumn unless he got the antilynching bill through."[130] Lodge responded by putting pressure on Borah and his subcommittee to report, and the full Judiciary Committee accepted the bill by 8 to 6 on June 30 (with Senator Borah as the sole Republican to join the 5 opposing Democrats). The Dyer Bill was favorably reported by the Senate Judiciary Committee. All now depended on a floor vote. The NAACP continued to lobby the president, urging him to use the opportunity of a meeting with leaders of the Senate in August about the legislative program to make antilynching a priority.[131] At the end of August, the Senate Steering Committee decided to place the bill on the legislative program to be taken up before the close of the session.

Opponents of antilynching legislation continued to cite its potential unconstitutionality as grounds for rejection. In September 1922, James Johnson found himself having to explain, yet again, to Harding's secretary the implausibility of this defense. Johnson wrote that "the Anti-Lynching Bill now before the Senate has been favorably passed upon by the Judiciary Committees of both Houses of Congress; it has been endorsed by the Attorney General of the United States, who is the legal advisor of Congress. A recent petition presented to the Senate was signed by two former attorneys general of the United States, 19 justices of Supreme and Superior courts in the various states and a number of eminent lawyers."[132] Despite these efforts, on December 2 the Republican senators' caucus decided permanently to withdraw the Antilynching Bill until March 1923.

Although bitterly disappointed, James Johnson privately took a philosophical view of this decision: "[T]he fight has been a magnificent one. We have succeeded in making lynching a political issue and a national and international issue as well, and we have also placed the plain facts about lynching before the American people."[133] A few years later at the NAACP's 1929 annual convention, Johnson described the Dyer Bill, part of a continuing campaign, as "its most spectacular height"; furthermore, the vote rendered Congress "a forum on the subject of lynching . . . and what was said on that floor was heard through the nation and around the world. We thereby had a chance to put the facts, the vital facts, the underlying facts, about lynching for the first time before the whole American people and before the civilized peoples of the world."[134] Writing to Harding's secretary, Johnson adopted a confrontational tone: African Americans felt not merely disappointment but also "chagrin and resentment" about the bill's failure. Johnson rounded on the inadequacy of Republican support: "if the Republicans had been in actual collusion with the Democrats to have the latter pull their chestnuts out of the fire, the appearances could not have been worse."[135] Thus, the federal government—whether controlled by Democrats or Republicans—failed to act to address inequality of treatment toward African Americans. The tactics used to abort the 1923 Dyer Bill illustrate the problems confronting proponents of equality for African Americans at that time and the inferior status accorded African Americans' interests in federal policy.

After the failure of the Dyer Bill, the NAACP maintained its campaign to address lynching by lobbying successive presidents[136] and congresses. It assiduously documented lynchings and burnings of African Americans, publicizing these incidents. The NAACP came close to success in the 1930s with the Costigan-Wagner Bill, but it was not until the 1940s that federal legislation was finally enacted. As Zangrando correctly notes, African American interests were always a lower priority for congressmen than other interests: "as the NAACP would discover year after year, many congressmen treated antilynching as an expendable issue."[137]

Immigration Policy, Black Immigrants, and African Americans

That immigration policy between the 1880s and the 1920s focused on southern and eastern Europeans meant that African Americans were seen by policy-makers as irrelevant to their decisions. In fact, both the focus on the United States's white ancestry and the categories with which immigration policy was discussed had important consequences for African Americans. In addition, despite restrictionists' and eugenists' ambitions to build a whites-only immigration policy, black immigrants arrived in the United States throughout this period.

Excluding Black Immigrants

A systematic attempt to proscribe black immigration came as an amendment to the immigration bill considered in Congress in December 1914; it was Southern-inspired and was designed to exclude people from the Caribbean who had been working on the Panama Canal and had settled in the United States. Senator Reed proposed to add the phrase that "all members of the African or black race" be excluded.[138] In support, Senator John Sharp Williams made clear that this proposal was aimed at West Indian immigrants:

> [W]e are beginning to receive now some very undesirable immigration of the African race from the West Indies. A great many Jamaican negroes have been employed upon the Panama Canal; and after the termination of that work, having become accustomed to American wages, which they received down at Panama, a great many more of them began to come to the Gulf ports. Florida and Louisiana have already received a considerable proportion of African immigration from the French and English West Indies; that is to say, immigration of West Indians who are wholly or partly Africans in race.[139]

Williams compared the West Indians unfavorably with Asians, articulating a common racial triangulation, whereby Asian immigrants, while defined as unassimilable, were characterized further to oppress African Americans:[140] "[Y]ou have already a law whereby you exclude Chinese. Chinese are as much superior to negroes as can be, almost. You have a gentlemen's agreement with Japan by means of which you excluded Japanese." His argument rehearsed commonplace claims about the bases of assimilation in a homogeneous society:

> [Y]ou can not have free institutions grounded upon anything in the world except a homogeneous race. You can try it all you please, but you simply can not have it. You have got to have a population which is at least potentially assimilable in lawful wedlock. If you do not have a population all elements of which are potentially assimilable in lawful wedlock, then you have in the very midst of the Republic a disintegrating force, undemocratic, unrepublican.[141]

Williams, who was from Mississippi, also feared West Indian immigrants because they might not respect the strict segregationist and marriage codes within which white Americans defined the circumstances of African American communities and lives. He warned that the "West Indian negro, as a rule, is a man who is accustomed to political and social equality, because the races intermarry in the West Indian Islands; and every West Indian negro who comes to the South comes with that idea in his mind and becomes a source of race conflict and a source of race oppression upon the white man's part, or an invitation and temptation to it, which is as bad for the white man as it is for the negro."[142] The amendment, proposed by Senator James Reed of Missouri, was carried by 29 to 25 votes, with 42 senators not voting.[143]

The House rejected the amendment, however, with 74 congressmen supporting, 253 opposing, and 99 not voting.[144] The vote was preceded by a lengthy discussion. Martin Madden, representing a constituency in Chicago with numerous African American voters,[145] noted that if accepted, the measure "would seem to make it impossible for a negro, a citizen of the United States, to reenter this country if he happened to be abroad for any reason." This proposed version of ethnic cleansing was not incompatible with the amendment's proponents' motives. Madden dismissed the legislation as "the most drastic I have ever seen proposed. It is discrimination of a kind that can not be justified."[146] To a round of applause, Madden declared that "it would be unjust beyond measure to adopt this amendment to the immigration law. One-tenth of the American people are of the black race, and no people in all the world's history has ever been more loyal to a Government than have these people to this."[147] A congressman from Pennsylvania remarked that the proposed "strange" amendment removed "the black man out of the 'alien' class," an "extraordinary proposition."[148] Another congressman described the amendment as "having been designed for the specific purpose of singling out one particular race from among all the people of the earth, and then to heap upon this designated race and each member thereof the odium of complete exclusion under all and every condition, and this, too, without any direct benefit to our own people."[149] Congressman William Calder of New York maintained that the amendment's supporters would "class the negro with the criminal and undesirable," and since "very few of the Negro race come here from foreign lands" anyway, he opposed it.[150] Like others, he commented on the high education standards of most West Indians coming to the United States and worried about how such a measure would damage American missionary efforts in Africa.

There were willing supporters of the amendment in the House, one congressman informing his colleagues that "of all the barnacles that the civilization of the United States has fastened to it, of all the leper sports, of all the sores, of all the misfortunes that the civilization of this Republic has fastened to the body politic it is the African race, which stands as the worst." Black Americans threatened Anglo-Saxonism: "[I]t is this black race, this black death, this parasite of race destruction that is fastened upon the Anglo-Saxon people and upon the civilization of the United States. You had just as well to begin to understand that the white people are going to rule this country."[151] These racist comments, elaborated in hideous detail, also provoked applause. Echoing the same conception of American nationality, a Louisianian congressman argued that the amendment was "in the interest of the American people, in the interest of her own people first, and then justly excluding those whom you and I could not invite to our shores."[152] Intense NAACP lobbying played a role in killing the amendment,[153] but that it received such serious consideration is noteworthy.

Black Immigrants

Despite the injustices of segregation heaped on African Americans—operative throughout the United States—and the attempts by Congress in 1915 to exclude "all members of the African or black race," blacks did immigrate in the first decades of the twentieth century, overwhelmingly from Caribbean countries ruled by British or French colonists (and therefore eligible under those country's quotas).[154] Caribbean immigrants were part of the nonquota countries unrestricted by the legislation of the 1920s (when policy-makers resolved against restrictions of either Canadians or South Americans).

Between 1900 and the mid-1930s, close to 150,000 such immigrants were admitted, though considerable numbers departed,[155] and there were periodic efforts to halt the migration to the United States (such as the restriction placed on Jamaicans in July 1924).[156] The story of these Caribbean immigrants—politically and culturally enormously consequential as their numbers included such figures as the political leader Marcus Garvey, the writer Hubert Harrison, and the poet Claude McKay—has been recounted by Winston James,[157] building on Ira Reid's 1939 study.[158]

Winston James demonstrates the influence of Caribbean immigrants on radical African American politics in the first three decades of this century. Despite colonialism, many Caribbeans were highly educated, and even the Mississippian senator, John Sharp Williams, had to record his surprise when he was informed in the Senate that only 23 percent of West Indian immigrants were illiterate: "[H]aving heard those figures, I confess myself somewhat surprised. My own impression was that a majority of the West Indian negroes could not read. It seems from this that only 23 per cent of those of them who came into the United States could not read. That is perhaps owing to the fact that the very best element—I mean by that the intellectually highest element—of the West Indian negroes comes to the United States, rather than the most inferior of them."[159] James correctly underlines the severe racism encountered by blacks in the United States. The poet Claude McKay reflected in 1918 that "'I had heard of prejudice in America but never dreamed of it being so intensely bitter.'"[160] A similar point was made by Ira Reid, who observed that "probably the most striking experiences upon arrival is the awareness of race that is soon discovered;"[161] he added that "the Negro immigrant is at a disadvantage after a brief experience on the American racial front. He becomes sensitive to criticism, self-conscious and uncertain of himself and his values. He is conscious of opposition and of the persistent attempts to belittle his presence here. Yet, being ambitious and possessed of a desire to succeed, he tackles the problem and leaves as mute evidence a transfer of culture values that has made the Negro immigrant less foreign, and the American Negro less provincial in his approach to racial and economic problems."[162] James's more recent study illustrates that the influence of Caribbeans in black politics far outweighed their actual numbers. As Howard University's Kelly Miller remarked in 1927, "'[A] Negro radical is an *over*-educated West Indian without a job.'"[163] Caribbean immigrants carried a sense of majority consciousness, that is, "they were accustomed to negotiating a world in which they constituted the overwhelming majority of the population,"[164] and this consciousness served as an effective instrument with which to respond to racist discrimination in the United States in a way often unimaginable to African Americans. Ira Reid concluded in his 1939 study that black immigrants confronted severe racism and were spared the worst excesses of such prejudice by their relatively low profile. They endured their own form of Du Boisian duality:

[T]he Negro immigrant enters the United States in the dual role of Negro and immigrant. Moving into a few centers of Negro population in large numbers, threatening the existing order of Negro adjustments he brings the bases for intra-racial conflict. One factor only prevents the conflict from becoming intense, the visibility of the Negro immigrant is low. Except for those who are Spanish and Portuguese-speaking, and who usually move into their own language groups, the external characteristics of Negroes, native and foreign, are the same. Looking alike, they are not inherently estranged; differing in mores they are isolated.[165]

There were comparable strains within the Black American community,[166] as the NAACP's Walter White pointed out in 1923, when he complained about the way in which Northern blacks resented "the influx of their southern brothers." As he pointedly observed, such divisions were foolish in a society riven with hostility toward African Americans: "when mobs start forth, as they did in Washington, Chicago and Omaha, they attack every person who is dark and do not take the time to enquire whether or not the Negro they have caught is a southern or northern one." Consequently, the "race problem is one which affects every man who is colored and we are going to rise or fall together."[167]

Gaining assimilation with African Americans, though often a complicated process marred by tensions, gave some respite to black immigrants in their adjustment to the United States but (as the previous section explains) also confirmed them in a second-class position in American society, since, as Reid concluded, "neither the immigrant nor the native is accepted as part of the dominant white society."[168] The fate of black immigrants illustrates further the exclusionary terms in which the U.S. immigration debates of the 1910s and 1920s were conducted. Because black immigrants were instantly equated by white Americans with the native African American population—despite the significant differences of traditions between Caribbeans and African Americans—Caribbean immigrants were alarmed about how this perception defined their status in the U.S. political order. The reluctance of Caribbeans to be so equated explains both the tensions often observable between the two groups and the more politically militant initiatives of Caribbean immigrants. Caribbean political radicals had rich educational and political experience on which to draw, and their unwillingness to be assigned to an inferior status of citizenship must have contributed to the significant separatist movements orchestrated by immigrants from the Caribbean countries.[169] Caribbean immigrants not only were active politically but "also provided some of the most distinguished radical black intellectuals at the time."[170] Such activities were conducted within the social and political limits to which all blacks in the United States were subject: jim crow segregationist discrimination.

Black immigrants, especially in New York, were often keen to naturalize as U.S. citizens. The secretary of the Negro Foreign Born Citizens Alliance wrote to a congressman in August 1921, reporting that his organization "has been engaged for the past two years in preaching Americanization to the vast number of alien negroes of Harlem and elsewhere in Greater New York, estimated from twenty to thirty thousand." The alliance had succeeded, "after considerable outlay of time, energy and money . . . in preparing successfully just a little over two hundred who have obtained citizenship."[171] The director of citizenship at the Naturalization Bureau welcomed this initiative, telling the secretary that "I am much interested in the efforts of your organization to bring a comprehension of American institutions and ideals to the members of your race group."[172] He urged the alliance to contact the chief naturalization examiner in New York to coordinate its Americanization classes.

The 1924 immigration act, the subject of Chapter 6, explicitly excluded the "descendants of slave immigrants" from entitlement to immigration and excised them from the population of the United States on which quotas were to be based. This discrimination was proposed in 1952 directly in respect to Caribbean immigrants. The 1952 McCarran-Walter Bill proposed restrictions on certain Caribbean countries, as an analysis of the legislation explained:

> [T]o ensure that only a token number of colored persons may enter the United States, the proposed legislation further strikes directly at the major modern source of this population flow. Most Negro immigration to our country today comes from Jamaica, Trinidad and other colonies of the British West Indies; on the whole, this immigration has contributed thousands of good workers and loyal citizens who now fill important positions in the national economy. The McCarran-Walter Bills, by dissociating colonial immigration from the quota of the mother country, would cut down Jamaican immigration from about 1,000 to 100 immigrants annually, and would fix 100 as an iron-clad maximum limit upon every other colony. When it is recognized that the inhabitants of Can-

ada, Mexico or any other independent country in the Western Hemisphere may enter freely as non-quota immigrants, the racially discriminatory aspects of this provision are placed in proper perspective.[173]

The ambition that was displayed by certain policy-makers to establish a whites-only immigration policy was entrenched.

Immigration and Migration

Within the United States, for many African Americans, the major migratory experience was that of moving from the Southern to the Northern states. Walter White explained in 1923 the major push and pull causes of this great population movement: "[T]here are at least two reasons for this movement. First, the opening up of industrial opportunities in the North incident upon the increased industrial activity and the working of immigration restrictions; and second, the growing intolerance in certain Southern states resultant upon the activities of the Ku Klux Klan and other lawless organizations."[174] The experience of crude "work or fight" policies, introduced by some Southern states and municipalities in 1918, added to the incentive to leave. This rule formally required able-bodied adults between sixteen and forty-five, both men and women, to be in some occupation for fifty hours a week. It was applied partially. Walter White reported that "in Wetumpka, Ala. a small town fourteen miles from Montgomery, the mayor had a colored cook. She quit one Saturday night, because she could get better wages elsewhere. On Sunday morning the mayor had her arrested. On Monday morning she came up for trial in the *mayor's* court before the mayor, who fined her $14.00, paid the fine himself, and then told the woman to go on out to the house and go to work and quit her foolishness." White added that "a disgusting feature of these officials is that they are being successful in keeping the Negroes quiet by masking their dastardly efforts under the guise of patriotism."[175]

Thus, for African Americans, immigration restrictions both coincided with and helped foster the migration of hundreds of thousands to the North. The 1921 restrictions opened up employment prospects in the North. However, residence in the North did not obviate discrimination or prejudice,[176] a point Walter White underlined in a press statement in July 1923, commenting on the Northern migration of African Americans:

[T]here is one other thing that the Migration is proving and that is the fallacy of the argument that if the Negro solves his economic problem all other phases of his difficulties will be eliminated. Thirty, even ten years ago, practically all white people and most colored people believed such a doctrine. We are seeing today, however, that the object of the mob's and the Ku Klux Klan's wrath is not the Negro who by his thrift and industry has achieved economic independence. Poor whites resent seeing greater prosperity on the part of this member of a supposedly inferior race; other whites in the South feel that such a Negro is too dangerous an example for other Negroes; and third, they drive Negroes of property away and take their possessions for themselves.[177]

The African American migration was at times linked to the immigration debate. For instance, in 1918 the commissioner of immigration, Frederic Howe, speculated that the 15 million aliens present in the United States were likely to return to Europe after the conflicts subsided. Howe warned that "there are 15,000,000 aliens here who have not seen their relatives and friends in Europe for four years and are anxious to return to them"; furthermore, European aliens could anticipate improved conditions in their home countries: "[M]any of them came here because of the oppressive property laws of their native lands. Now, with a more equitable distribution of land assured, they are eager to hasten back."[178] Howe drew a parallel with the mistreatment of African Americans in the Southern states: "[A]s an instance of conditions in the United States, take the migration in the last few years of hundreds of thousands of negro workers from the South to the North. Had the South maintained as good working opportunities as the North this exodus would not have occurred."[179] Howe envisaged not only an exodus of aliens but also restrictions in their home countries on emigration, resulting, in combination with the internal migration, in a labor crisis. Immigration was curtailed by the war period, and it is this falloff in the annual inflow of new European laborers—replaced by Southerners—that seemed to alarm Howe and others. It was a development picked up on by African Americans. Eugene Kinckle Jones told the NAACP in 1919 that "we have in this country an immigration situation directly opposite to that which existed a few years ago; instead of a large immigration coming into the country we have three hundred thousand more departures of persons from our shores than arrival." He anticipated "another strong call for Negro labor by the North" and counteractivity "on the part of the South trying to retain Negro working men and women for work."[180]

Both this disruption to Northern industry and the shortage of labor in the South prompted a disingenuous campaign by Southern white employers to attract African Americans to return, a strategy exploited after the postwar riots in 1919 in Chicago. One newspaper story captures the dual pressures: "such men as Senator Pat Harrison of Mississippi and Congressman John McDuffle of Mobile, Ala, who grew up surrounded by negroes, who were cared for by the old negro 'mammies' and whose parents owned negroes in the days of slavery and who have employed large numbers of them since reaching manhood, heartily indorse [sic] the movement set on foot in Chicago by Harry D. Wilson, commissioner of agriculture of Louisiana, for the return of the negroes to the south." The contrary view was expressed by a congressman in Chicago "where the most serious race riots recently occurred resulting in the migration of a large number of negroes back to their southern homes, declared that negro laborers are wanted in Chicago and will be protected from white men."[181]

The connection between immigration reform and African Americans' labor market participation was made the centerpiece of a talk by the commissioner of conciliation at the U.S. Department of Labor in 1923. Adopting "a colored view of every situation," Phil Brown addressed the subject of "The Negro Migrant." Brown, an African American, emphasized both the pressure of postwar industrial reconstruction combined with immigration reform and the persistence of discrimination.[182] The close to 610,000 African Americans migrating to the North between 1917 and 1922 were "classified as emergency labor, rather than preferred." The connection with the reduced number of immigrants was direct: "[T]he Negro is sought to fill the unskilled functions of alien labor. To the industries the inclusion of his labor is an experiment; to him it is the realization of a century of dreams."[183]

In common with other observers, Brown stressed the deep assimilation or Americanization observable among African Americans: "[A]s an American, conceived in the continental processes of soul and soil, the Negro is unsurpassed by the proudest products of our best American antecedents. In all our wars he has borne arms for, but never against his country."[184] In terms of socializing new workers, Brown noted that employers and industrialists were principally experienced in respect to non-Americans organized in "groups controlled by nativity and language and living in ghettos entirely from preference." The new Southerners presented a contrast. They posed an equal challenge to exclusionary trade unions, since, in Brown's words, "there is no organic reason for the exclusion of Negroes from labor unions."[185] Eugene Kinckle Jones rather hopefully cited Samuel Gompers's establishment of an AFL committee in 1918 to meet with "a like committee representing the colored workers to consider and prepare a plan of organization."[186] It would take more than a committee, however, effectively and willingly to encourage local unions to organize black workers; indeed, most adopted exactly the reverse approach.

African Americans and National Origins

Throughout the 1920s, most African Americans engaged politically with the problem of segregation and the discrimination and racism it induced or sustained. But this concentration does not mean that the major immigration debates and legislation of this decade were unconsidered by African American activists or organizations such as the NAACP. Indeed, at the NAACP's 1929 annual conference—one of especial significance, since it celebrated the association's twentieth year—reflections on the previous decade's immigration decisions were apparent. One author used the national origins legislation enacted in the Johnson-Reed Act and by the Quota Commission to illustrate the fallacy on which attempts at racial distinction and classification rested, a prescient voice in this pre-Nazi era: "[I]t is to be remembered that race classification in itself is still naive and untechnical. This is the rock upon which the national origins legislation to control immigration has foundered." Anticipating other critics of racial categories, he noted that "the learned ethnologists do not know how to divide the races and the layman who acts upon the assumption that race differences can be instinctively sensed follows merely his uncritical sights, and some fantastic convenient groupings as 'African race,' 'Bohemian,' Irish, Canadian race etc."[187] The same author characterized the metamorphosis of identities and the use of racial categories that were evident in the immigration debate:

> [O]nce we heard much of the virtues of the melting pot and the rich heritage which immigrants brought to America. They were needed for our rapidly expanding industries. The employing whites welcomed them freely. The middle classes were completely tolerant. It was only in the lower levels where their labor constituted a competitive factor that the South Europeans met difficulty. They succeeded the Irish in inheriting opprobrium. They were the 'wops,' 'dagos,' 'guineas,' to be properly

shunned. With the war came a new theory of race and as suddenly as they were taken in they were thrown out of the family of the chosen races. The intelligence tests proved that they ought to be not only thrown out but kept out. The new residential sites now excluded not merely Negroes but members of the Baltic and Mediterranian races.[188]

Another NAACP member, Nannie Burroughs of Washington D.C., complemented these points with her excoriation of the prejudice mobilized against both African Americans and immigrants. Burroughs told the conference that "our country has fought harder to keep men in physical and moral slavery than any of the so called Christian nations of modern times. America has several millions of Jews, whom she shuns and scorns; over five million Poles and Czechs whom she fears and confines to ghettos; great tribes of Indians whom she backs into the western wilds; Mexicans who are next door neighbors, whom she chases across the border; Chinese and Japanese to whom she refuses to sell a foot of ground in the land of the free; European emigrants whom she lets in to work; and twelve million Negro citizens from among whose number she has snatched over four thousand to tar, feather, and burn alive at the stake."[189] Because "these millions" were viewed as "problems" rather than "fellow-countrymen to be cultivated," for these citizens constitutional rights were irrelevant.[190]

Conclusion

In sum, the immigration legislation enacted in Congress in the 1920s was far from insignificant to African Americans, as many at the time recognized: the efforts to exclude certain "undesirable" or "inferior" European immigrants had direct implications for the position of non-whites in the United States. Although the treatment of African Americans and immigrants was often not commonly associated by policy-makers in the 1920s, policy toward each expresses two manifestations of a discriminatory regime—domestically and externally—that underpinned the assumptions of elite decision-makers in this crucial decade. In terms of creating inequities with which future policy-makers would have to grapple, both types of discriminatory policy were significant. African Americans and American Indians were the two invisible communities whose political position was affected detrimentally by the immigration legislation of the 1920s. The former group had their second-class citizenship reinforced; and the political mobilization of African Americans in the 1960s confirmed the significance of the U. S. government's immigration policy that was enacted in the 1920s in contributing to their unequal citizenship. In dramatically limiting the number of nonnorthwestern Europeans eligible for immigration, the 1924 law and the 1929 national origins quotas reinforced the second-class position of African Americans in the U. S. polity. From 1896 when the Supreme Court legitimated the "separate but equal" doctrine, segregated race relations had become the norm in the United States. This doctrine established the marginality of African Americans; the national origins system of immigration strengthened it. U.S. immigration policy attempted to end black immigration but in fact did not do so, as a steady stream of West Indians arrived between 1900 and 1930.[191]

Building on the previous chapter's analysis of Americanization, the present chapter has illustrated how the discussion of immigration policy was premised on a conception of American identity with two key characteristics: first, the dominance of an Anglo-American, or English settlers' descendants, component; and second, the exclusion of African Americans from the ingredients of the assimilationist melting pot process. This was the political and sociological context of the immigration law enacted in the 1920s. The Americanization drive of the 1920s epitomized these pressures, since its activists had a narrow and an exclusionary conception of American identity. They sought to "Americanize" those foreigners already present and carefully to limit the arrival new immigrants. Milton Gordon's Anglo-Conformity model of assimilation captures this dynamic, though the reality of this process was more exclusionary than this theoretical framework recognizes.

The political success of this dominant group model should not be underestimated. It is widely entrenched institutionally and culturally, certainly manifest fifty years later. Thus, Michael Cimino's accomplished post-Vietnam film *The Deer Hunter* ends memorably with a forlorn group of characters singing "God bless America" after the burial of their friend Nick (Christopher Walken). It is a striking conclusion to an affecting movie about American identity. The film's protagonists live in a Ukranian-American community in steel-producing Pennsylvania, respecting codes and norms from this white, working-class ethnic background (recorded in the wedding scene and Orthodox Church services), yet they powerfully convey attachment and loyalty to the United States. This version of U. S. identity—a combination of nationalism and ethnic rootedness—is not the melting-pot assimilationist dream of the Americanization movement or the purism pursued by eugenists, but may nonetheless rather more accurately equate with American reality. It is presumably the ability, or willingness, to believe in a distinct "Americanness" that enables the characters in *The Deer Hunter* to retain their patriotism (and that can be contrasted to the chaos and uncertainties of Terrence Malick's *The Thin Red Line*). In this latter quality, Cimino's film echoes the often simple patriotism captured in John Ford's Westerns (such as *My Darling Clementine* or *Liberty Valance*), though both versions veer dangerously close to sentimentality (a quality that does not necessarily invalidate either their poignancy or their popularity), a tendency not absent from dramatizations of African Americans' wartime participation (such as that on the Tuskegee airmen). Nonetheless, these works are engaging with a white, European conception of American history and identity, neglecting the United States's multiple cultures and diverse traditions. It is this lacunae that has been addressed in recent decades, since the failure to acknowledge a richer version of U.S. ethnic and group composition proves increasingly unsatisfactory as either political analysis or historical record.

CHAPTER SIX

"A Very Serious National Menace":

Eugenics and Immigration

Racial categories and eugenic arguments were commonplace among intellectual and political elites in the late nineteenth and early twentieth centuries. Writing in 1912, Leonard Darwin, an activist in British eugenics circles, described the eugenics project as one that displaced the "slow and cruel methods of nature" with "some more rational, humane and rapid system of selection by which to ensure the continued progress of the race." He anticipated an "all-wise government" identifying whom to "prohibit from figuring amongst the parents of the rising generations" and whom "to encourage to marry."[1] In the United States, this eugenic agenda was closely associated with the formulation of immigration policy in the 1910s and 1920s.

The alleged threat of racial degeneracy stimulated much eugenic research. In the United States, eugenic research was conducted at the Eugenics Record Office established at the Cold Spring Harbor Laboratory on Long Island, New York, directed by the biologist Charles Davenport. In 1910, Davenport secured funding from a philanthropist for a dedicated eugenics office at this laboratory.[2] The office was well endowed from several sources. Davenport awarded scholarships to an army of research students and ran summer schools imparting skills in human heredity and statistical techniques of field research. Trained researchers collected a copious supply of records on the life histories and inherited traits of diverse groups and families throughout the United States.

Eugenics provided the justification for advocates of sterilization policy. Sterilization was a mechanism to address inherited "feeble-mindedness." Writing the majority decision in the 1927 *Buck v. Bell* case, which upheld a Virginia state law permitting sterilization of Carrie Buck, a "feebleminded" and "moral delinquent," the U. S. jurist Oliver Wendell Holmes declared that "three generations of imbeciles are enough" and that it was legitimate for the state to prevent the reproduction of so-called "degenerates."[3] Buck was duly sterilized, as were many citizens in other American states that enacted comparable laws.[4] Long-term reduction in the number of such citizens would have fiscal dividends for society, it was claimed, and would result in a more robust population.

This eugenic approach is now widely criticized. The limits of its scientific base and the implications it had for drawing inferences were insufficiently attended to by Davenport and his colleagues. Although Davenport was a scientist, his approach suffered from "shallow carelessness."[5] Davenport's "negative eugenics" simply encapsulated, in Kevles's view, "in biological language the native white Protestant's hostility to immigrants and the conservative's bile over taxes and welfare."[6] Nonetheless, the influence of eugenics in U.S. society and of American eugenists internationally was considerable. For instance, American eugenists significantly influenced German policy and practice in the interwar years, as Stefan Kuhl has persuasively documented. Dr. Harry Laughlin, whose role is discussed later, received, along with other American scientists, an honorary degree from the University of Heidelberg in 1936, at a time when the policies of both Germany and German universities were increasingly criticized in the United States (by Franz Boas, for instance). Kuhl reports that "despite his wariness of being regarded publicly as allied with the Nazi government, Laughlin was proud of the honorary degree. He received congratulations from several colleagues in the eugenics movement and was acknowledged in both the German and the American press."[7] Kuhl documents how American eugenic laws (such as those for sterilization and aspects of its immigration policy) were cited approvingly by German eugenists—"the Nazi administration referred to the 'model U. S.' as playing an important role in shaping its own race policy"[8]—and emulated in German legislation. Kevles observes that Californian sterilization laws "helped inspire the Nazi measure, which was passed in 1933."[9]

Eugenic organizations were formed to promote the new science and its policy proposals.[10] It had a broad political appeal, as Frank Dikotter underlines: "far from being a politically conservative and scientifically spurious set of beliefs that remained confined to the Nazi era, eugenics belonged to the political vocabulary of virtually every significant modernizing force between the two world wars."[11] Eugenists provided advice that was eagerly sought in newly urbanized and industrialized societies, many of whose members were skeptical of religious principles and enamored of experts. Exploiting the "prestige of science,"[12] political elites cited eugenic research in support of policies to sterilize selected patients and—as this study illustrates—of restrictionist immigration based on a purportedly scientific hierarchy of "races." Such motives are evident among the eugenists advising on U. S. immigration policy. This role interacted favorably with the claim that not just physical traits were reproduced generationally but that behavior had biological sources. Social Darwinism pandered to this tenet, with claims about the extent to which the offspring of the poor or the criminal or the feeble-minded were themselves likely to reproduce these parental defects. This approach leads directly into the family histories undertaken and popularized in the United States from the 1890s. It resonated among progressive reformers in that country. But eugenic arguments had pernicious racial implications. Thomas Gossett rightly observes that "racism thrived as the ideas of biological evolution began to make themselves felt" in the United States. Natural selection was viewed as a healthy struggle between nations, individuals, and races: "this conflict, far from being an evil thing, was nature's indispensable method for producing superior men, superior nations, and superior races."[13] The eugenists' alarm about racial degeneration consolidated, in the United States and other countries, around the popular term "the menace of the feebleminded." This priority led to promotion of arguments about sexually segregating, sterilizing or excluding (in the case of immigrants) the "feebleminded."

Eugenists displayed an illiberal propensity to judge some members of the community as less worthy of equality of treatment than others. Such views were arguably logical consequences of the eugenics framework, since eugenists, in Gossett's words, "did not believe in laissez faire . . . It was around this program of increasing the 'fit' elements of the population and decreasing the 'unfit' elements that the eugenics movement developed."[14] Kevles puts the same point more harshly:

"an unabashed distrust, even contempt, for democracy characterized a part of eugenic thinking in both Britain and America." He adds that "socialist, progressive, liberal, and conservative eugenicists may have disagreed about the kind of society they wished to achieve, but they were united in a belief that the biological expertise they commanded should determine the essential human issues of the new urban, industrial order."[15] The ahistoricism of such characterizations is criticized by Ian Dowbiggin, who, from his study of psychiatry and eugenics, argues that psychiatrists were attracted to eugenic research for "professional reasons" and that it was the progressive potential that appealed to them: "they were psychiatrists who found themselves living in an age of rapid and unnerving change, a time filled with both promise and acute uncertainty." Consequently, "eugenics emerged during this period as a quintessentially progressive reform."[16] This defense may hold for populists but is much less valid in respect to eugenists such as Laughlin and Davenport, at least as revealed in their ardent advocacy of selective immigration.

In 1920s America, this "biological expertise" achieved a striking ascendancy in the making of immigration policy with, for instance, presidential candidate Calvin Coolidge asserting that "biological laws tell us that certain divergent people will not mix or blend."[17] Prescott Hall of the Immigration Restriction League corresponded regularly with Charles Davenport,[18] and Barbara Solomon observes that "the activities of the eugenicists converged with those of the restrictionists and, in the end, left a permanent effect on the anti-immigration movement."[19] For both Social Darwinians and eugenists, the racial imperative found a focal point in immigration trends of the sort documented in the Dillingham Commission. It was racism that became the dominant element in post-1918 anti-immigration rhetoric and campaigns, with racial objections becoming, in Gossett's judgment, "by far the most powerful source of objection" to immigrants.[20] Eugenics was a powerful arsenal in this campaign.

The First World War increased racial animosity in the United States and stimulated the Americanization movement. The years after 1918 were fertile ones for eugenic arguments about inferior and superior racial stocks, and how the former could be eliminated or controlled. The wartime period also bequeathed an intelligence test (the I.Q., intelligence quotient measure, which was developed in 1912 by William Stern to compare a person's mental age with his or her chronological age) that was employed by the armed forces to test its recruits. This test was initially termed the Stanford-Binet measure of intelligence, as formulated by Lewis Terman. The influence of these techniques in fomenting racist views is superbly analyzed by Thomas Gossett, who concludes that "intelligence testing was to give racist theorizing a new lease of life—in fact, in the minds of many to make race the crucial determinant of human progress or retrogression."[21] Over 1.7 million male recruits to the armed forces were tested by a team of psychologists. Much misrepresentation and inaccurate interpretation followed the publication of the results of these studies; unquestionably, they excited alarm about the mental ability of aliens and Americans of foreign birth. Since much was made of the impartiality of the tests and their concentration on innate ability irrespective of background, Gossett concludes that the U.S. Army studies constituted a "powerful tool" that "was placed in the hands of the racists." He emphasizes further that

> the great lesson which many of the psychologists drew from the army tests was that intelligence is influenced relatively little by environment. The conclusion readily reached was that great numbers of people—in fact, the majority—were not capable of benefiting from improved education. The Negroes were the farthest removed from any possible hope. The tests, said Dr Yerkes, "brought into clear relief . . . the intellectual inferiority of the negro. Quite apart from educational status, which is utterly unsatisfactory, the negro soldier is of relatively low grade intelligence." This discovery was "in the nature of a lesson, for it suggests that education alone will not place the negro race on a par with its Caucasian competitors."[22]

This rejection, or downplaying, of environmental factors was at odds with the findings of Franz Boas's research commissioned by the Dillingham Commission.

Such harsh assessments fed into a political environment increasingly hostile toward foreigners, particularly those whom eugenists were able to characterize as of "inferior" stock. Nonwhites, such as Asians, were already effectively barred from immigration; the debate now turned to placing controls on those allegedly less desirable European sources of immigrants. Wartime experience gave racial and hereditary theories a new legitimacy in the United States, and consequently, as Gossett remarks, the 1920s "became the time when racist theories achieved an importance and respectability which they had not had in this country since before the Civil War."[23] Eugenics provided a direct link between racists' opposition to interracial mixing and scientific arguments for such beliefs. Thus, Charles Davenport, director of the Eugenics Record Office, was "probably the most positive advocate of the theory that race intermixture led to biological abnormalities."[24] But it was his energetic assistant, Harry Laughlin, who spread this message to immigration policy-makers.

The Eugenic Bases of Exclusion

The national origins scheme, adopted in 1929, represented the convergence of quotidian stereotypes about immigrants and the pseudo-science propagated by eugenists. Attitudes and prejudices hithertofore directed toward African Americans were now aligned with the new immigrants. Patrician and "old stock" American descendants feared the "racial imbroglio" posed by the new immigrants. Eugenists favored severe restrictions on immigration as part of a general program to prevent dilution of the American "race" or "stock." This issue was widely aired. In 1914 both the Medical Society of New York State and the Massachusetts Medical Society complained to the U.S. House of Representatives Immigration Committee about the failure adequately to screen immigrants to exclude what each termed the "mentally defective." The latter body warned of the "direful consequences of their being allowed to marry and to propagate and so deteriorate the mental health of the Nation."[25] Over a decade later, the president of the Eugenics Research Association warned Congressman Albert Johnson of the high fecundity of women immigrants, which affected the "character of our people." He added that "it is necessary to protect—as far as possible—our best stock" from the fecundity of the lower classes and probable undesirable farrago of races;[26] the Dillingham Commission had examined this alleged fecundity of the new immigrants, finding higher average numbers of children borne to women of foreign parentage than of those borne to white American women.[27]

Eugenic arguments played a decisive role in transforming the immigration policy from a concern with absolute numbers to one about the suitability and assimilability of immigrants whether considered individually or as families.[28] As Garland Allen observes, employing subjective criteria, American eugenists "classed as superior those people descended from Nordic or Aryan stock or those from wealthy classes.

Conversely, inferior people were those from eastern European, Mediterranean, Asian, African, native American, or Jewish stock, along with the chronically poor . . ." The implication was plain: "to American eugenicists, the old Anglo-Saxon, Nordic stock was in danger of being swamped by a massive increase in the number of hereditary degenerates."[29] The legislation implemented from the 1880s already provided opportunity to restrict the entry of sufferers of mental illness, and these restrictions were applied by admitting officers. Thus, between July and December 1922, aside from 3,811 aliens refused admission because they were likely to become a public charge, 39 were debarred as "idiots, imbeciles and feeble-minded," 38 as suffering from "insanity or epilepsy," and 18 because they suffered from the vaguely defined condition known as "constitutional psychopathic inferiority." Two were debarred on grounds of alcoholism.[30] However, in terms of eugenists' priorities, these categories of ineligibles were too limited and the numbers excluded risibly small (and as Table 6.1

Table 6.1 Causes of Rejection by U.S. Immigrants, 1907–1917

Cause of Rejection	1909	1912	1914	1917
Idiocy	18	10	14	9
Imbecility	42	44	68	19
Feeblemindedness	121	110	995	224
Insanity (including epilepsy)	167	133	197	146
Constitutional psychopathic inferiority				3
Likelihood of becoming a public charge	4,458	8,182	15,784	7,893
Affliction with contagious diseases	2,308	1,674	3,143	1,383
Affliction with tuberculosis	82	74	114	119
Physical or mental defectiveness	370	2,288	6,537	1,734
Chronic alcholism				10
Criminality	273	592	755	257
Prostitution and other immorality	323	263	380	510
Procurement of prostitutes	181	192	254	371
Contract laboring	1,172	1,332	2,793	1,116
Inability to read (over age 16)				391

Source: Derived from *Reports of the Department of Labor, 1917,* Report of the Secretary of Labor, and Reports of Bureaus (Washington, D.C.: GPO, 1918), p. 126.

shows, had not grown significantly). And the climate of racist beliefs fostered in the 1920s implied greater restrictive legislation. This climate was shared and engineered by, as Gossett writes, both "emotional bigots" such as the Ku Klux Klan and "academic writers on racial differences," the latter chiefly responsible for making "racism respectable."[31]

Eugenic Research and Immigration Policy

The eugenist[32] with the greatest influence on immigration policy during the 1920s was Dr. Harry H. Laughlin, who worked at the Eugenics Record Office at Cold Harbor Laboratory. The office was funded by the Carnegie Institution of Washington, whose administrators took a positive and financially supportive interest in this eugenics research, including that on immigration,[33] though Laughlin's eagerness to establish formal arrangements to collaborate with the State Department, on occasion, exercised the Carnegie Institution.[34] The Eugenics Record Office had been founded in 1910 to establish a database of the American population for eugenic research. Laughlin was hired by its director, Charles Davenport. Laughlin's expertise was subsequently solicited by Congressman Albert Johnson, chairman of the House of Representatives Committee on Immigration and the key congressional policy-maker.[35] Immensely hardworking, Laughlin made numerous influential presentations to the House Immigration Committee about the "social inadequacy of aliens" and the formulation of policy to prevent their immigration.[36] Laughlin was employed, as expert eugenics agent, by the House Committee from April 1920 (until 1931) to research and prepare data about the eugenic characteristics of immigrants and potential immigrants to the United States,[37] studies that we will examine in detail. The questionnaires gathering data for his studies were circulated under the Committee on Immigration's "franking privileges," an entitlement of his expert position.[38] One of Laughlin's studies, claiming to find a disproportionate percentage of foreign-born people in prisons and asylums, was widely publicized in 1923.[39] Laughlin described his work to a colleague: "[W]e are studying, from first-hand sources, immigrant stocks by nationality and specific type of defect—the feebleminded, the insane, the criminalistic and the like. We are also comparing immigrant nationalities with the older American stock and with other alien races."[40]

Dr. Laughlin's[41] first major contribution to specifying the appropriate eugenic bases for a national immigration policy was given to a hearing before the House Committee on Immigration, in 1920, on "Biological Aspects of Immigration." Laughlin, an adroit lobbyist of his preferred causes,[42] used the occasion to rehearse arguments that were familiar in eugenic circles but that were probably less well-known to policy-makers or the public. He also introduced the first of his several documentations about the high public cost of maintaining immigrants who needed professional care or were incarcerated. This fiscal calculation was a salient strand of eugenic thought in the 1920s.[43] Laughlin told the committee that "the character of a nation is determined primarily by its racial qualities: that is, by the hereditary physical, mental, and moral or temperamental traits of its people." This feature set the agenda for research at the Eugenics Record Office, which was to assess, by acquiring detailed records from insane hospitals and prisons, the relative importance of heredity and environment in forming "degenerate Americans."[44]

Congressman Albert Johnson, chairman of the House of Representatives's Committee on Immigration, commissioned Laughlin to undertake a series of reports for the committee, which he used as a basis for the formulation of U.S. immigration policy.[45] In 1922, Laughlin produced a 100-page analysis of America's melting pot; in 1924, he reported his extensive field research (120 pages) on the main emigrant-exporting countries in Europe; and in 1928, he discoursed (from an 80-page study) on the "eugenical aspects of deportation," building on his earlier work. Each of the studies was widely distributed and discussed. Many sold out several print runs. Laughlin continued to appear before the committee after the enactment of the 1924 law; he was summoned, for instance, in 1928 to give his biological views on Mexican immigration;[46] he also journeyed to Europe on several occasions, sometimes as an accredited U. S. immigration agent, other times at personal expense, to examine the so-called "stock" of emigrants bound for the United States.[47] Laughlin favored pedigree studies on immigrants, as he explained to one colleague: "by doing pedigree work in the field abroad we can judge the family-stock of the immigrant but, if we let him come in without pedigree study we have to wait until his children and grandchildren come on before we can judge his worth."[48] In 1930 he told the U. S. secretary of labor that the aim of his trip was "to throw some light upon the biological nature of the emigrants as breeding stock for future American citizens."[49] Madison Grant and Albert Johnson interceded with the labor secretary to secure this appointment.

Harry Laughlin's eugenic research promoted two claims about the danger of unregulated immigration: first, it posed a fiscal burden because immigrants were more likely to be "degenerate" than were native-born Americans and thus to require institutional care; and second, were likely to be a racial cost, by diluting the quality of the national stock. Dilution, in this context, alluded both to degeneracy resulting from intermarriage and to cultural contamination, dangers often considered associated.

The Financial Burden of Immigration

A major eugenic theme about immigration throughout the decades after 1900 was the fiscal burden posed by the disproportionately high percentage of immigrants in asylums, prisons, and poorhouses. Such views were regularly aired before congressional committees. The director of the New York State Hospital System complained in 1924 that of its "41,000 patients, 25 per cent, or over 10,000, are aliens with no legal claim upon the bounty of the State."[50] Dr. George Kline, commissioner of the department of mental diseases in Massachusetts, told Congress in March 1926 that out of 22,000 "defectives" and epileptics in state institutions, "approximately 40 per cent will be found to be foreign born, and perhaps 55 to 60 per cent will be found to be of foreign-born parentage." At any given time, the state had about 130 such immigrants awaiting deportation.[51] Kline emphasized the public cost of maintaining these inmates: "[T]he cost of maintenance of the insane, both alien and otherwise, is borne almost wholly by the State. Of course, an attempt is made to collect from the estate or whatever source we can, but the amount collected by the State institutions for the support of mental cases is relatively small. It is less than 11 per cent, and practically nothing from alien insane."[52] Similar evidence was reported about the financial burden of the insane in New York and other states. From his study of psychiatrists, Ian Dowbiggin concludes that "the psychiatric consensus was that the laws governing medical inspection and deportation of immigrants had to be reformed and vigorously enforced if the country was to avert a crisis in state charity."[53] The House Committee on Immigration heard about the cases of individual children classified as "mental defectives" at another hearing and the burden they imposed.[54] In response to these concerns, the 1924 Johnson-Reed Act had imposed a deportation constraint on immigrants admitted to such publicly funded institution within five years of settling in the United States (a restriction that aliens often proved able to sidestep). Eugenists took solace from the national origins plan, believing it would result in immigrants of a quality and nationality apposite to the improvement of the "American race."[55]

Harry Laughlin presented estimates to the House Immigration Committee in 1920, about the cost of the maintenance of what were termed "social inadequate" aliens, composed of ten groups: (1) feeble-minded; (2) insane (including the nervous and psychopathic); (3) criminalistic (including the delinquent and wayward); (4) epileptic; (5) inebriate (including drug habitués); (6) diseased (including those with tuberculosis, the syphilitic, the leprous, and others with chronic infectious segregated diseases); (7) blind (including those with greatly impaired vision); (8) deaf (including those with greatly impaired hearing); (9) deformed (including the crippled); and (10) dependent (including children and folks in homes, ne'er-do-wells, tramps, and paupers).[56] In case these data were not in themselves sufficient evidence, Laughlin added an example to support his contention: "[I]n the census of 1900, the foreign-born [over ten in age] population of the country was 19.5 per cent; and they contributed 34.3 per cent of the total insane population. Now, if that foreign stock was just as good as the stock already here, it ought to have contributed only 19.5 per cent."[57] The decision to add "constitutional psychopathic inferiority" as grounds for nonadmission to the United States won Laughlin's endorsement since, in his view, the category is a "scrap-basket term . . . it implies poor stock in the family; and in the particular individual, it implies degeneracy." The historian Ian Dowbiggin notes the support of many psychiatrists for the inclusion of this term, a professional endorsement that had failed to convince congressmen in 1914: "some senators were suspicious of assurances that psychiatrists using the term truly knew what they were talking about." The psychiatrist Thomas Salmon's definition of the term did not entirely allay congressional concerns: "'a congenital defect in the emotional or volitional fields of mental activity which results in inability to make proper adjustments to the environment'";[58] the term was included in the 1917 immigration act, which also established a literacy test.

Laughlin wanted the vague description "general shiftlessness" incorporated legally; his definition rivaled the concept's generality: "[I]n every little Italian, or Scandinavian, or English, or Scotch town, there are village ne'er-do-wells who have not made good among their fellows. That is the type of immigrant which we want to exclude, even if he can stand up and get by the immigration officials and is able to pass the reading test, and can pay the head tax and may legally come into this country; we do not want him anyway. He is poor immigrant stock."[59] The imprecision of this description and hence the potential for its uneven application are striking. All such decisions about exclusion and suitability were, in the eugenic scheme, to rest on examination of family histories by trained experts, of the sort popularized by Goddard and Dugdale.[60]

The *Saturday Evening Post* published one of its restrictionist articles, by Kenneth Roberts, about Laughlin's report. It stirred up public alarm. Complaining that permanent legislation had been unduly delayed, the journalist reported from Laughlin's study that "the cost of supporting these socially inadequate people of alien stock is so great that nearly 8 per cent of the total expenditures of all the states must be devoted to their upkeep in state custodial institutions."[61] The U. S. Department of Labor made Laughlin's research the centerpiece of a memorandum about the enforcement of immigration laws. Advertising Laughlin as "one of the world's best known scientists," the department reported the results of his survey of "state institutions housing the feeble-minded, the insane, the criminals, the epileptics, the inebriates, the chronically diseased, the blind, the deaf, the deformed, the crippled and the dependent." Laughlin's results were disturbing: "this expert finds that while the foreign born constitute 14.70 per cent of the nation's population, they furnish 20.63 per cent of the population of these institutions, and that 44.09 per cent of the inmates of these institutions are either of foreign birth or born of parents of foreign birth." In one large state, "47 per cent of the inmates in that state of institutions for the care of public dependents are foreign born, and that 27 per cent of them are still alien."[62] The maintenance of public dependents consumed 30 percent of that state's taxes. This theme of the excessive cost of the "pauper insane and criminal classes" was hammered home by the eugenic-inspired Immigration Protection League, which, in February 1928, proclaimed that the United States had been "expending approximately 27,000,000 dollars" on such inmates' maintenance.[63]

Laughlin continued to undertake such studies[64] and was convinced that they influenced policy. He modestly observed that "I believe that these reports to the House Committee have done a great deal toward molding legislation and governmental policy in the direction of the eugenical basis for immigration control."[65]

Immigrants and Degeneracy

Eugenists, including Laughlin, worried that the immigration of "inferior" stock would, through interbreeding, erode the quality of the American people: in a word, it would induce degeneracy. Eugenic investigators worried about "racial degeneracy" (one conceived of in terms of "the relative soundness of recent and older immigrant stocks,"[66] the dichotomy formalized by the Dillingham Commission). Identifying and expunging its sources were defined as a basic aim of immigration policy.

To explain the principle of degeneracy, Laughlin introduced a three-fold categorization of the mentally ill. The "feeble-minded" consisted of three classes:

> [T]he lowest are the idiots—the men can not attend to their own wants; they have to be clothed in dresses, and wear diapers. Then, above the idiots, there are the imbeciles, who can not be trained to do ordinary work; they, too, have to be placed in institutions. Then, above the imbeciles, come the morons. They are the border-line cases; they have the bodies of adults but the minds of 9 and 10 year old children; they can be trained to do useful pick and shovel work of a certain type, but they can not get along in school, no matter how long they attend. Nor do they acquire social responsibility.[67]

The appellation "moron" (replaced later by that of "mental defective") was new to several of the congressmen, and Laughlin warned them that "the moron is really a greater menace to our civilization than the idiot" since the deviousness of the morons enabled them to evade immigration inspectors; furthermore, the combination of fecundity and few inhibitions made moronic women "highly fertile sexually."[68] Questioned by one congressman as to whether it had been "scientifically demonstrated" that morons were intrinsically "incapable of much advancement" even when provided with appropriate care and opportunity, Laughlin replied in the affirmative, citing Goddard's research at Vineland, New Jersey.[69]

In respect to U. S. immigration policy, Laughlin asserted that "it is now high time that the eugenical element, that is, the factor of natural hereditary qualities which will determine our future characteristics and safety, receive due consideration."[70] He wanted eugenic tests on immigrants in their home cities to identify and weed out degenerates. Furthermore, immigrants had larger families than nonimmigrants: "the importance of this condition of admission is driven home when we recall that immigrants are going to add to the breeding stock of the American people in greater proportion than their immigrant numbers bear to the total population, because statistics have shown that immigrant women are more prolific than our American women."[71] Later in his testimony, Laughlin returned to these themes, adding a note of urgency: "[B]y setting up eugenical standards for admission demanding a high natural excellence of all immigrants regardless of nationality and past opportunities, we can enhance and improve the national stamina and ability of future Americans. At present, not inferior nationalities but inferior individual family stocks are tending to deteriorate our national characteristics. Our failure to sort immigrants on the basis of natural worth is a very serious national menace."[72]

In defense of the eugenic approach to family records and the search for "degenerate" forebears, Laughlin cited the cases of the Jukes, Ishmaels, and Kallikaks families, all of whose dismal life narratives were aired widely by eugenists in the 1910s and 1920s (though the study of the Jukes by Richard Dugdale dated from 1877). Among eugenists, these studies were accepted as demonstrations of how "degeneracy" was passed from one generation to the next. Laughlin claimed that similar studies of immigrants would permit the prevention of "any deterioration of the American people due to the immigration of inferior human stock."[73] He explained the importance of the findings of the family histories: "[Y]ou have to recognize the fact that although we give opportunities in this country, everybody is not educable. This backwardness is not all due to environment, because our field studies show that there is such a thing as bad stock . . . while these three families [Jukes, Ishmaels, Kallikaks] have been famous in magazines and newspapers, our field workers every month send in case histories that deal with the same human types and conditions. The lesson is that immigrants should be examined, and the family stock should be investigated, lest we admit more degenerate 'blood'".[74] The casual use of terms such as "stock" and "blood" is common in this period and among elite policy-makers. Laughlin reported that the Jukes and Ishmaels were simply the tip of what might be termed the "family degeneracy iceberg," since field workers usually encountered "a great network of degenerate families. The Jukes and the Ishmaels and others are noted simply because they have been studied. They are members of degenerate classes, but they are not novel. There are hundreds of such families. The task is to trace such families to their origin. The present-day lesson for the Nation and for each State, community and family is to prevent the entrance of members of such families as human seed stock."[75] Unlike other students of immigration, eugenists were interested in the consequences for the American "stock" of immigrants, not their economic effects. Laughlin recommended that "highly specialized and skilled" eugenists be employed as American consulates to examine immigrants and declare them mentally and physically fit for a visa. This proposal was rehearsed throughout the decade and, in part, implemented.

Elsewhere Laughlin criticized the effects of modern institutional care. Institutionalization prolonged lives of the "weaker" members of the "stock": "I think the tenderness with which modern civilization and charity care for many of its so-called defective classes has been biologically unfortunate in that it has bolstered up individuals who under a lower civilization would have perished."[76] Laughlin ruminated worriedly about reproduction in poorhouses where the terminologically imprecise "almshouse type" was found: "the moron girl that goes to the almshouse generally gets there because she is pregnant or has a baby, and as soon as she is able to work again she goes out into the community, and the next year she comes back and has another baby."[77]

A class distinction was also imputed to the distribution of mental deficiencies:

Chairman (Congressman Johnson): are there not some cases where the moron has not come from a low family but has been checked though disease? Laughlin: Yes. That does not show degeneracy of stock, however. . . It is simply an unfortunate happening or accident to the individual. Scarlet fever may stop the mental development; but that does not show that the individual comes from bad stock. But the average moron that you find in the institutions has had fair opportunities and has not been marked with extraordinary diseases, but has brothers and sisters and cousins and uncles of the same type; *it is the stock.*[78]

Laughlin informed the committee that there was, furthermore, an ethnic disparity in the distribution of morons: "in reference to foreigners, one notices, by the names of individuals who are found in institutions, that the lower or less progressive races furnish more than their quota."[79] The consequences of this pattern for the American race were serious, as interracial mixing seemed unavoidable to Laughlin.

Laughlin's analysis of the melting-pot U. S. population looked in detail at nine categories of "socially inadequate" (that is, feeblemindedness, insanity, crime and delinquency, epilepsy, tuberculosis and leprosy, blindness, deafness, deformity, and dependency), across a range of nationalities, or what he termed "races." A more general definition of the socially inadequate was formulated: "a socially inadequate person is one who by his or her own effort, chronically, and regardless of etiology or prognosis, fails in comparison with normal persons to maintain himself or herself as a useful member of the organized social life of the State."[80] The "social inadequate," a "liability of the State," attained that condition for a range of reasons: "a socially inadequate person is one who can not adjust himself as an asset to the social organization; consequently he has to be taken care of by society, either by commitment, voluntarily or involuntarily in an institution, or by outside charity, or at home as a burden, by his own family." Laughlin was entranced with the cost-benefit analogy: "social inadequacy is a double debit: not only do the inadequates not pull their own weight in the boat, but they require, for their care, the services of normal and socially valuable persons who could well be employed in more constructive work."[81] Pecuniary calculation was indeed a guiding principle of eugenics.

For the melting-pot study, Laughlin derived a set of predictions (termed quotas) from the 1910 census about what number of each nationality should—on a normal distribution—be found in state institutions (about each of which data were collected for January 1, 1921).[82] Analyzing a huge database, Laughlin suggested that the "outstanding conclusion" of his analysis was that "making all logical allowances for environmental conditions, which may be unfavorable to the immigrant, the recent immigrants, as a whole, present a higher percentage of inborn socially inadequate qualities than do the older stocks."[83] From the data he singled out a number of European countries that vastly exceeded their predicted quotas and were guilty of "dumping" their socially inadequate on the United States. In respect to insanity, these included Russia, Finland, Poland, Ireland, Bulgaria, and Turkey (findings consistent with the Dillingham Commission's researches). Some results surprised the committee but were glibly explained by the eugenist. For instance, on the measure of dependency, African Americans were the lowest, a finding counterintuitive to perceptions of this group's social inadequacy. Chairman Albert Johnson's formulation—that "in other words, their conditions of living are so low that dependence does not show itself"—was endorsed by Laughlin, who appended his own gloss: "in the United States, represented principally by the South, the American negro fulfills his quota in dependency in institutions by only 25.27 per cent but here, as in other types of social inadequacy other than crime, the dependent or inadequate negro is taken care of by the plantation." Such ad hoc explanation does not inspire confidence in this scientific framework. At the other extreme, the Irish in America were found to have a high dependency ratio, again best accounted for by stereotypes rather than evidence: "[T]he Irish have shown a quota fulfillment astoundingly high, 633.53 per cent. They are not thrifty, as a racial group in the United States; drink and dissipation were common, so that in many cases, especially in old age, their economic status was so low that many of them were thrown on the resources of the State."[84] That the data might have been flawed was not considered by Laughlin.

Laughlin's calculations were criticized (mostly by supporters of a more open immigration policy); in particular, his early estimates of aliens in state and federal prisons and asylums were challenged. Laughlin's researchers surveyed 445 of the total 657 such institutions. Congressman Johnson was fiercely defensive of the value of Laughlin's study and of the accuracy of its content: "[W]e were able, as Dr. Laughlin states, to secure returns from 445 out of 657, and every return, it should be borne in mind, required a great deal of voluntary research on the part of the institutional authorities. It was a first-hand survey in nature and extent never before undertaken among the eleemosynary institutions of the country."[85] Laughlin subsequently presented to the committee new data from public institutions, which he argued confirmed his earlier analysis. In general, Laughlin's researches were subject to little scrutiny, though there were criticisms voiced about the purposes to which these eugenic findings were put. As Matthew Jacobson points out, several critics in Congress in the

1920s questioned why such efforts were expended to demonstrate the inferiority of certain immigrants.[86] Such anxieties did not deflect the eugenic thrust in restrictionist legislation, however, or interrupt the stream of research reports from Laughlin and his colleagues.

One critic, H. S. Jennings, who was a professor at Johns Hopkins University, was sympathetic to eugenic research but alarmed by the political use made of Laughlin's analyses. Although the argument in favor of the 1890 census over the 1910 census (as the basis for national origins calculations) seemed valid to Jennings, the case for it "drawn from Laughlin's studies seems to me clearly illegitimate."[87] Jennings tendered his resignation from the Eugenics Society, believing that "this was not a good connection for me, as a worker in pure science." Professor Irving Fisher, chairman of the Eugenics Society's committee on immigration, in responding to Jennings, conceded the inaccuracy of Laughlin's statistical analysis[88]—excusing its employment by the Eugenics Society as a result of a deadline pressure—but justified by the organization's influence on immigration policy: "[O]ur committee [of the Eugenics Society] did succeed in getting into the public consciousness the important principle of sifting immigrants about eugenics. In the end, that idea however much it failed, in first trial, is more likely to win now that the thought is being held by millions of people who never thought of it before."[89] Other criticisms were usually cavalierly dismissed.[90] As Elliott Barkan observes, in general Laughlin's researches and arguments received remarkably little scrutiny: despite Laughlin's periodic testimonies before Congress, "almost no one challenged him."[91] And Thomas Gossett, acknowledging that scientific racism had begun to dissipate fundamentally by the end of the 1920s, remarks "one can hardly help wondering—now that the claims of the racists are widely recognized as having little or no scientific backing—why the opposition to racism was so long in developing. Were not the effusions of nineteenth-century racists, for example, extreme enough to call for a more sober scrutiny among serious thinkers?"[92] It is a pertinent question. But acceptance of eugenic-type arguments was not unique to the United States, and it took the horror of Nazism finally to implode this pseudoscientific doctrine. The eugenists' very use of scientific language and claim to expertise insulated them against potential critics, as Frank Dikotter notes: "defenders of eugenic reforms rested their case on scientific arguments, which few opponents had the intellectual means to combat."[93] And considering recent scholarship on eugenics, Robert Nye notes that such research illuminates the "sheer complexity of the scientific and political issues at the heart of the eugenic movement"; he adds that "in view of these contradictions, many of which deepened in the 20s and 30s, the one thing on which all eugenicists of good will could agree was that 'like produces like.'"[94] And indeed, rejection of eugenics by scientists in the 1930s did not occur simply for scientific reasons but reflected also political anxiety about its implications.[95]

Eugenics and the Selection of Immigrants

The upshot of Laughlin's researches, together with that of other eugenists, was a blueprint for U. S. immigration policy that was influential with policy-makers in the 1920s. Eugenists wanted much tougher selection procedures for the admission of immigrants, procedures that would utilize eugenic "family history" studies to identify signs of explicit or latent "degeneracy" in migrants and to exclude weaker "members of the stock." As Laughlin explained, "in our future immigration legislation it will be necessary to include the element of family history or biological pedigree, if we are to improve the American human stock by immigration." The federal government had a pivotal role in such selective breeding: "the surest biological power, which the Federal Government now possesses to direct the future of America along safe and sound racial channels is to control the hereditary quality of the immigration stream."[96]

Laughlin argued that the instrument of national origins quotas for admitting immigrants had to be combined with "selection based on family stock quality."[97] This biological principle was much more important, he asserted, than either the United States's economic needs or its place as an asylum for the persecuted: "the economic and asylum factors have not disappeared but are relatively unimportant compared with the dominating biological principle."[98] Laughlin urged an extension of the eugenic principles first included in immigration policy in 1917: "[I]f 'America is to remain American' we shall have to perfect the principle of selective immigration based upon high family stock standards. By national eugenics we shall have to correct the errors of past national policies of immigrants, but by new statutes which are sound biologically we can cause future immigration to improve our native family stocks."[99] In 1924, Laughlin urged the House Immigration Committee urgently to establish a new commission to undertake fresh biological studies of immigrants: "the principal instruction to the commission should be to keep constantly in mind the future benefit to the American people, as a unit, based upon the improvement of the hereditary qualities of family stocks in accordance with American ideals."[100] Laughlin contended that only a proper eugenic policy could forestall degeneracy of a race: "institutionalization is the immediate palliative, but national eugenics is the long-term cure for human degeneracy."[101]

From 1924, U. S. inspectors had a significant role in vetting potential immigrants in their home country, a procedure Laughlin wanted strengthened (though it is unlikely that questionnaire results could predict accurately which individuals would become public charges). Laughlin and the House Committee linked the improvement of these mechanisms directly with the need to reinforce eugenic principles in immigration policy:

Laughlin: The time will come when this country will have to face, more courageously than it has at the present time, the matter not only of race and of individual quality, but also of pedigree or family stock, and we will have to face boldly and courageously the matter of race. It is a matter of conservation of nationality. After the Chinese exclusion act, the greatest step that the American people took in relation to the nationality of race was, of course, the quota laws of 1921 and 1924. It is now clear that the country has in its recent legislation entered definitely upon the biological basis, a farsighted policy, of immigration control.

Chairman Johnson: The mere fact that we have a 2 per cent quota law is a long step in the right direction.

Laughlin: Yes, sir.

Johnson: And you think it led us to the conclusion that we ought to weed out within the 2 per cent, or any other per cent we have?

Laughlin: Yes, sir.

Congressman John Box (TX-D): In your opinion, what would be the ultimate result upon the people of America and upon the country if we should continue indefinitely the policy that had controlled us prior to the enactment of the 2 per cent law?

Laughlin: The racial constitution of the ultimate American would, before many generations, be very different from the American of to-day. It would be certain in time to upset our ideals of law and government, and it would cause also a severe social upset. Out social ideals would be changed because the fundamental instincts of the people would be different. They might be better, but they would be different, most probably inferior.

Box: I want to have the opinion stay in the record.

Laughlin: I will be very glad to have it stay.[102]

Without having strict controls on immigrants, monitoring their mental health from the time of their arrival, and deporting those who fell victim to some of the "socially inadequate" flaws, Laughlin asserted that "immigration will tend to work not toward the improvement but toward the degeneration of the American people."[103] He told the American Eugenics Society that "eugenical principles alone should constitute the basis for our future immigration laws and rules."[104] Laughlin was exercised by the alleged racial degeneration of the "American stock" as a consequence of inappropriate immigration. Referring to the increasing proportion of so-called "new" compared with "old" immigrants, he reflected that "unless the source of its immigrants be of a constant race and quality, no nation can suffer many such turnovers in population origin and retain its essential character."[105]

On the basis of a six-month field research to eleven European countries,[106] Laughlin devised ambitious plans for a selection policy. This proactive strategy was designed not only to preclude admission of the "undesirable" immigrant but also to establish a basis for selecting immigrants who would be "a valuable addition to our national family stocks."[107] He combined this advocacy with characterizations of the apolitical work of a scientist such as himself: "a scientific study which has a bearing upon current political issues is always conducted under the greatest difficulty; but the scientist must, nevertheless, confine himself to facts and their analysis and must take into consideration only criticisms of scientific work."[108] This was a somewhat unconvincing juxtaposition of advocacy and impartiality. Asked explicitly in Congress whether the immigrant from northern Europe was more attractive than the immigrants from southern and eastern Europe, Laughlin declined to give an unequivocal response. However, it was difficult, as Laughlin's questioner Congressman Dickstein implied, not to draw this conclusion from both the data presented and the premises explicated in Laughlin's scientific research.

Laughlin identified some of the traits that these preadmission questionnaires and tests would be designed to elicit, qualities of a "biological order," about which it was "possible to make biological studies . . . and to make our sifting of the immigrant stream more effective by eliminating those applicants in whom the undesirable traits are disclosed."[109] The qualities were "truth-loving"; inventiveness and initiative; industry and common sense; the "quality of responsibility"; and social instinct, the "natural sense of a square deal." Mirroring eugenists in other countries, Laughlin wanted to move from a negative eugenic base in immigration policy—that is, one designed merely to "eliminate the defectives"—to a positive and proactive one that selected desirable immigrants according to agreed-on eugenic criteria: "in brief, besides the quota limitation of the law of 1921 and the causes for rejection enumerated in the law of 1917, our future laws, if the country is to be protected against inferior immigrants and is to select and welcome superior strains, should provide by statute for the determination of individual and hereditary qualities by requiring modern pedigree examination in the home territories of the would-be immigrant."[110]

In 1928, Laughlin reported on eugenics and deportation, using a recent survey of the "socially inadequate" located in 684 state and federal prisons and asylums (of a total of 688 such institutions). He aimed to compare the relative proportions of deportable and nondeportable foreign-born inmates. Deportation was the "last line of defense against contamination of American family stocks by alien hereditary degeneracy."[111] The 684 institutions disaggregated into 53 for the "feeble-minded"; 173 for the insane; 203 for criminals and delinquents; 12 for epileptics; 82 for tuberculosis sufferers; 1 for the leprous; 42 for the blind; 30 for the deaf; 5 for the deformed or crippled; and 87 for dependents. Collectively they held 74,184 foreign-born inmates in 1925 and 1926, a testimony to the failure of immigration policy, in Laughlin's view: "[I]f our immigration laws had worked as was intended, none of the present 74,184 inmates would have been admitted. But our first lines of defense were so broken by the alien attack that over 70,000 inadequates were found."[112] Table 6.2 summarizes the findings. The range of "problems" included is notable. For Laughlin the figures signaled an unacceptable failure of immigration policy, for which "the principal remedy would seem to provide for more thorough examination into the individual and family histories of the would-be immigrant."[113]

Table 6.2 Institutional Inmates, 1925–26

Type	Number of Institutions	Native-Born		Foreign-Born		Total*
		Number	Percentage	Number	Percentage	
Feeble-minded	53	36,347	84.2	1,602	3.71	43,167
Insane	173	148,484	60.43	53,986	21.97	245,724
Criminalistic	200	85,057	78.76	11,224	10.39	107,996
Epileptic	12	7,391	72.52	749	7.39	10,192
Tubercular	82	13,478	74.85	2,608	14.48	18,006
Leprous	1	143	73.33	52	26.67	195
Blind	42	5,684	93.06	130	2.13	6,108
Deaf	29	6,382	91.84	57	1.82	6,949
Deformed and crippled	5	662	75.48	16	1.82	877
Dependent	87	21,254	54.28	3,746	9.57	39,155
Total	684	324,882	67.91	74,170	15.50	478,369

* Includes 79,317 (16.58%) for whom nativity was unknown.

Source: Derived from "The Eugenical Aspects of Deportation," hearings before the Committee on Immigration and Naturalization, HR, 70th Congress, 1st Session, February 21, 1928, p. 6.

In practice, few foreign-born inmates in these institutions were deported, although many were eligible for expulsion. In 1925, 4 persons were deported for "feeble-mindedness" out of 1,612 eligible for expulsion. Therefore, the United States needed to "deport defective aliens in greatly increased numbers,"[114] in Laughlin's view; the United States's "liberal" deportation laws were "administered with great charity and considerable laxity."[115]

Laughlin wanted three criteria, which would reflect these eugenic imperatives, to be added to the immigration policy: first, a higher intelligence level standard for immigrants; second, a rigorous family stock test; and third, a restriction to white races only (something already in the law).[116] He envisaged a questionnaire requirement for potential immigrants to the United States, on which they would supply information about their individual history, physical examination, mental and educational examinations, and "family stock" values (secured by a "eugenic study of 15 or 20 of the near kin"). Laughlin had high expectations about the value of this investigation into potential immigrants' family lineage:

[B]y means of these short pedigree studies, it is possible to throw some light upon the character of the individual, or enough to determine, much more surely than is done by personal examination alone, whether the individual is sound, whether he is likely to become a "waster," whether he is of good stock, and from the soundness, initiative, natural intelligence, respect for law and order, industry, and the like, of his near kin, whether he would probably make a desirable addition to the population of the United States.[117]

Laughlin proposed a national registry of aliens, to "follow up the immigrant's process of naturalization and Americanization,"[118] a proposal dovetailing eugenics with the Americanization movement. Espousal of the need for such a national registry illustrates how the purported scientific interests of eugenists converged with more political or nationalist ends: "a national registry of aliens would not only protect the Nation against anti-social conduct on the part of aliens whose interest in becoming Americans proves to be lacking but this service would make also the deportation of aliens who show certain anti-social qualities a feasible administrative possibility." In addition, aliens falling victim to mental illness could be targeted, thereby ensuring that "the country would be protected against reproduction by these racially defective aliens."[119] The mobilization of science for political judgments and ends is plain here. Since the "descendants of immigrants" would form the United States's "future citizenry," Laughlin intimated that "we should therefore make the possession of desirable natural qualities one of the conditions for the admission of sexually fertile individuals."[120] Such leitmotivs dominated the discussion of immigration policy throughout this decade. Sufferers of mental illness (and other illnesses) were not treated as equal citizens. Eugenists believed that, in respect to race-mixing, certain groups were immiscible.

The National Eugenics Society's subcommittee on selective immigration issued a report about screening prospective immigrants in their country of departure. It was an arrangement supported by Secretary of Labor James J. Davis (one of the three commissioners charged with determining quotas after the 1924 law and a keen Americanizer). "From the point of view of national eugenics," the report's authors advanced the argument for inspection of immigrants.[121] Much of the report's content was confined to addressing arcane aspects of international law in order to establish a right to inspect immigrants in the departing country. Nonetheless, eugenists wanted the powers of examination of potential immigrants greatly expanded: "we believe that it would be entirely proper to demand that he [the immigrant] produce reliable witnesses to support his own statements, even to the extent of demanding medical and other expert testimony to the effect that he is mentally and physically up to the standard required by our laws and that he belongs to sound family stock."[122] They wanted to exclude immigrants who failed to equate with American physical, mental, and moral attributes, an aim that necessitated a "knowledge of his family as well we as his individual history."[123] These proposals were consistent with those of Laughlin.

The Eugenics Committee maintained that established inspection procedures were inadequate as demonstrated by the prevalence of immigrants in prisons and poorhouses: "[T]here is an altogether undue proportion of aliens and of persons of foreign birth in our penal and eleemosynary institutions. Particularly is this true with regard to the criminal and the insane who, theoretically, are barred by our laws from entry into the United States if the defect exists at the time of their arrival."[124] Inspection officers needed more information about the mental condition of immigrants in order to exclude these undesirable aliens. The research of Harry Laughlin was cited in support of these assessments, notably his claim that incidences of "latent insanity" among immigrants were unacceptably high, justifying additional background research: "without the personal history of the immigrant and of his near kin there can be no certainty of discovering latent physical and mental defects." Laughlin recommended acquiring additional information about immigrants in four categories: "(1) concerning the immigrant's individual history. (2) Physical qualifications. (3) Mental and educational qualifications. (4) The pedigree of the near kin of the immigrant."[125] There was preference for such examinations to be conducted in the United States, however, rather than overseas, because of the belief that U.S. inspection facilities were superior, particularly for detecting latent diseases.

Laughlin pursued eugenic research until his death in 1943. He prepared a report in 1939 on "biological aspects of immigration," for the New York City Chamber of Commerce's immigration committee. The report echoed his earlier themes about racial qualities and marriage.[126] From the late 1920s, he devoted increasing attention to the registration of aliens, often being supported by the Immigration Service at the U. S. Department of Labor,[127] and to Mexican immigration. In the 1930s, the role of immigration as a contributor to unemployment was examined, though many of the so-called "unemployables" were not immigrants[128] and the restrictive legislation excluded most immigrants.

Other Eugenists and Immigration Policy

Laughlin was the most energetic and influential, but not the only, eugenist advising the House Committee on Immigration. Congressman Albert Johnson solicited views from eugenists.[129] He was elected president of the Eugenics Research Association in 1923.[130] Because Johnson was an ardent supporter of the national origins plan, eugenists saw in him a well-placed and dependable ally. The American Eugenics Society established a Committee on Selective Immigration in the mid-1920s, a proposal for which Charles Davenport had aired ten years earlier.[131] Leading committee members included Harry Laughlin and Francis Kinnicutt. The committee praised the national origins policy as the "most scientific, soundest in principle and fairest to all elements in the population of any method of quota limitation which yet has been proposed." It ensured that immigrants who were descended from colonists and early settlers would be treated preferentially. The committee sought greater selectivity in the assessment of potential immigrants to ensure admission of "only those who are superior to the median American in mental endowment as far as this is shown by approved psychological tests." Immigrants were to be examined medically in their countries of origin before departing and should ideally be subjected to "consideration of the hereditary history of all aliens proposing to emigrate to this country."[132]

In 1924, Robert DeC. Ward, a Harvard professor and member of the Immigration Restriction League, wrote President Calvin Coolidge to declare that "in signing the immigration bill you have approved one of the most important measures which has ever been put upon our statute books. You have done a very great service to the country. You have lived up to the words of your Message of last December, that America must be kept American."[133] The Immigration Restriction Association assiduously maintained pressure not to abandon the national origins scheme enacted in 1924, circulating a thirty-page pamphlet entitled "National Origins and American Immigration," to all members of Congress in late 1928. It was written by Edward R. Lewis, a member of the league's executive committee.[134]

An important influence on Johnson and his committee was Captain John B. Trevor, whose views overlapped with those of eugenists. Johnson and Trevor worked closely in the period before and after the enactment of the 1924 legislation, consulting on the drafting of bills and responding to amendments. Enclosing a plan for the "ultimate elimination of immigration," Johnson told Trevor in 1927 that the National Origins proposition "has been a thorn in the flesh of this Committee." Johnson added that the "discussion over National Origins has given final proof of the futility of attempting to maintain national unity or to develop as a Nation in the face of Nationalistic groups."[135] Lothrop Stoddard, eugenist and author of *The Rising Tide of Color against White Supremacy,* wrote Johnson that the "Immigration Act of 1924 is the second great turning point in America's national and racial destiny."[136] Stoddard, a Harvard law graduate who took a Ph.D. there in 1914, argued that the white races, especially the Nordics, were being weakened by interracial mixing. Thomas Gossett judges Stoddard as "one of the most active propagandists for racism" ever active in the United States.[137] Another eugenist, Norman B. Livermore, encouraged Johnson to remain steadfast on national origins: "I am satisfied from my own studies of racial problems and eugenics that such a move [rescinding national origins] would be a very great backward step and open the flood gates again to an enormous lot of subnormal people, who are in the long run but a great liability to this country."[138]

Henry Fairchild, a sociologist and the author of *The Melting-Pot Mistake,*[139] was another intellectual concerned with the racial degeneration posed by immigrants. He praised the system of national origins admission because of its rejection of the melting-pot approach.[140] Gossett observes that "one detects in him a dislike for certain ethnic groups, particularly for the immigrants from southern and southeastern Europe,"[141] a disposition he must have shared with other restrictionists. Of unregulated immigration, with no attention to the characteristics of the new migrants, Fairchild was scathing: "[I]t took fifty years of vigorous teachings to produce the first federal action in the exclusion of the undesirable classes . . . We today are reaping the benefits of the failure of what was called the 'liberal spirit' two generations ago; and can you imagine what the situation would be in the United States today if that so-called liberal side had won out."[142] Despite eschewing calculations of racial superiority and inferiority, Fairchild opposed mixing of the races: "[W]e have nearly sixteen million both of whose parents are foreign born, and we have another seven or eight million, one of whose parents is foreign born. I wonder if that is not as much foreign mixture as we need to lend to this alleged variety and richness to our population for a given time to come."[143] In addition to his worries about racial mixing, Fairchild argued that immigration had detrimental consequences for the United States's "national unity," threatening the country's "distinct national existence." He elaborated, saying that "nationalities, you know, is a very different thing from race, although they are very frequently misused. Race is a biologic fact. Nationality is a social or spiritual class, and the menace of the immigrant, in my opinion, is fully as much a menace to our national unity as it is to our racial purity or the hope of its being."[144] These remarks illustrate how much the debates of the 1920s were about the distinctions that eugenists drew among the white nationalities. Fairchild keenly endorsed the national origins framework.

Despite the immense difficulties in statistically determining the accurate quotas, Fairchild concluded that "the national origins principle is the only basis for the restriction of immigration yet proposed that is entirely sound in theory, invariably fair to all groups concerned, and defensible by obvious logic as a feature of a permanent immigration law."[145] Fairchild maintained that assimilation was harder because the most recent immigrants were not descendants of those he called native Americans. The change was a dramatic one: "[T]he American nationality was in all essential respects closely akin to the English nationality, and not far remote from the nationalities of the countries of northwestern Europe. To-day, the immigrants represent as diverse and inharmonious nationalities as are to be found among all the branches of the white race." These latter groups "find assimilation hardly even a remote possibility."[146] Such views echoed the conclusions of the Dillingham Commission. Even after the Second World War, Fairchild harbored doubts about the suitability of some peoples to imbibe democratic values and institutions.[147]

Conclusion

The making of American immigration policy in the 1920s arose from a multiplicity of pressures, including economic interests, racism, ethnic cleavages, and eugenic propositions.[148] The close relationship established between the eugenic proselytiser Dr. Harry Laughlin and the chairman of the House Committee on Immigration, Congressman Albert Johnson, demonstrates the direct representation that eugenic research and arguments established in Congress. As the next chapter shows, the national origins plan, together with the preceding quota scheme and literacy tests, incorporated a eugenic influence by differentiating between prospective immigrants. Although the quota scheme established in 1921 can perhaps be interpreted as a reasonable policy response to a difficult question (and the resolution of which would inevitably upset some citizens), even though eugenic support for it was considerable, the shift to national origins appears in a different light, since its premises were rooted unequivocally in issues of race and difference. As Fitzgerald argues, this shift introduced a new language into immigration policy reflecting the influence of racial and eugenic ideas. Restrictionists in the decades culminating in 1929 shared a consensus about the evils of immigration: "[P]opular opinion held that people born in America, especially those of Anglo-Saxon or Nordic stock, were the nation's unique source of strength. Immigration was diluting that strength. As these foreigners became less similar to previous immigrants, however, the terms of these objections shifted from a concern over religion and morality to one of scientifically justified assertions about genetic inferiority. . . Genetic rationalization became an administrative goal."[149] It was this last claim that dominated the debate over immigration in the 1920s, a remarkable achievement for scientists and their expertise. Ian Dowbiggin also pinpoints eugenic pressure in the consolidation of the 1921 quotas three years later: "[B]ecause of pronounced opposition from the transportation companies and industry, the 1921 act proved to be only a temporary measure. The eugenicists, fearing that this national origins test might not last long, mobilized quickly to introduce new legislation. Their efforts were rewarded by the 1924 Immigration Act,"[150] which as the next chapter reports, both reduced the number of immigrant places and tied them to the 1920 census.

For eugenists the legislation of the 1920s was a triumph. Writing at the passage of the 1924 law, the committee's Eugenics Expert, Harry Laughlin, declared that, as a consequence, the American nation "unless it takes a very great backward step, is now committed to the biological or eugenical basis for its immigration policy." He explained the eugenic significance of the policy:

[W]ithin this policy there are three factors in selection: first, the total number to be admitted in any year; second, the distribution of this number among foreign nations, in accordance with an American formula; and third, the sifting out of would-be immigrants within the quotas in accordance with two standards—first, high individual mental, physical and moral worth, including the possession of American ideals of the American race, and second, adding to this individual standard the requirement which calls for sound pedigree or family-stock values. These are, of course, only the boldest outlines.[151]

These "boldest outlines" made an indelible impact on the United States's immigration policy and on its politics. For the scholar Matthew Jacobson, the eugenic presence in the 1920s legislation is both a historical manifestation of racial categorization and the construction of such categories, observable in different guises in earlier periods. Jacobson writes that "the exclusionary logic of the 1924 legislation represented not a new deployment of race in American political culture, but merely a new refinement of how the races were to be defined for the purposes of discussing good citizenship."[152]

This conclusion, although a useful corrective to the danger of ahistorical consideration of the 1920s, underestimates the peculiar legitimacy achieved by scientific racist theories, including eugenic ones, that occurred in this decade and that was manifest in the powerful international eugenic community. That such arguments fitted so comfortably into the United States's political circumstances (and its Anglo-Saxon-biased melting-pot ideology) and were exploited to construct legislation appeasing identifiable constituencies, certainly exposes the historical openness of the United States to such racialist frameworks. But eugenics had a distinctive appeal that was based in the convergence of its alleged scientific authenticity with populist racist stereotypes, which, in the hands of unreflecting promoters such as Laughlin, enabled it to influence legislation. The assumptions about types of immigrants and racial calibrations, embodied in the Johnson-Reed Act, formalized the views that had dominated political rhetoric and debate since the late nineteenth century.

PART THREE

Legislating Americans

CHAPTER SEVEN

Enacting National Origins
The Johnson-Reed Immigration Act (1924)

Despite the enactment of a literacy test in 1918, the pressures to limit the number of immigrants arriving in the United States did not cease, and the publication of the 1920 census demonstrated continued population growth from immigration.[1] Proponents of restriction returned to the battle with renewed vigor after the First World War and succeeded in getting Congress to enact quota-based limits on immigration in 1921. This achievement set the stage for the struggles over immigration that characterized the 1920s, manifest in both the 1924 Johnson-Reed law and in the adoption in 1929 of a national-origins-based quota system.

President Calvin Coolidge gave a restrictionist message—broadly endorsing an "America is for Americans" rhetoric—to the Congress in December 1923. It was a prelude to the 1924 law. The Immigration Restriction League urged him to remain steadfast.[2] Congressman John Cable congratulated President Coolidge on his efforts "to stop the seepage of aliens" entering the U. S. and recommended a larger appropriation for the immigration office.[3] The U. S. Department of Labor maintained that there were "millions of unnaturalized [immigrants], outside of the unnaturalizable races," who were living undetected.[4] It wanted tougher enforcement laws and increased funding for inspectors. Both the association of some immigrants with anarchism (manifest in the discovery of bombs in May 1919, including one outside the Attorney General's house) and labor conflict galvanized anti-immigrant sentiments. Alleged communists were arrested and deported. In 1921, Congress, overturning a presidential veto, imposed a temporary limitation on new immigrants from Europe that was organized in terms of nationality quotas. Immigrants could constitute only 3 percent of their country's extant population in the United States as counted in the census of 1910; total immigration was restricted to 357,000 per annum. The prospect of tens of thousands of poor Europeans, victims of the postwar economic crisis, arriving in the United States unleashed anti-immigrant sentiment. The congressional debate about the potential immigrants was heated, providing ample ballast for the prejudiced and stigmatizing characterization of the "new" type of immigrant, castigated by the Dillingham Commission. Terms such as "barbarian hordes" or "alien flood" found generous use in Congress. Commissioner General of Immigration W. W. Husband found himself in Congress, defending modifications to the national quotas.[5]

Two preliminary points about the decisions made in the 1920s require specification. First, the debate was concerned exclusively with Europeans and with divisions among Europeans. The demarcations drawn between northwestern European immigrants (deemed desirable) and southeastern European immigrants (largely unwelcome) were set in this period. The eugenic arguments focused principally on Europe, since a whites-only policy was assumed. Indirectly this focus contributed to the marginalization of nonwhites in U.S. politics.

Second, the National Origins formula enacted at the end of the 1920s had as a model the exclusionary measures previously adopted toward Chinese and Japanese immigrants, particularly the former group.[6] The sociologist Peter Rose remarks fairly that "no people who came to these shores of their own volition ever suffered as much discrimination or ostracism as did those from China and Japan. None were [sic] made to feel less welcome."[7] From the mid-nineteenth century, the Chinese who settled in California faced increasing hostility, barred, for instance, after 1854 "from testimony in the courts in cases involving whites."[8] Hostility toward Japanese immigrants was also strong.[9] One correspondent of Congressman Albert Johnson, self-described as a "pronounced friend of the Chinese and Japanese," told Johnson that "I am sure we agree that the immigration of Chinese and Japanese to Hawaii or the mainland of the United States should be closely restricted," a view that seemed accurately to catch Johnson's disposition.[10] In the case of both of these Asian communities the restrictions upon immigration, while gradually eased after 1945,[11] were such that the number of Asian American immigrants did not grow significantly until the 1970s.

Albert Johnson and the House Immigration Committee

From May 1919 the chairman of the House of Representatives Committee on Immigration and Naturalization was Albert Johnson. He mobilized the restrictionist lobby decisively for the passage and enactment of the 1921 law, introducing nationality quotas and absolute limits for immigrants. Johnson, who was from Washington state, was the key congressional actor in both the passage of the law and in shaping the final form of the national quotas arrangement established in 1929. Before entering Congress, he made his reputation as a small-town newspaper editor, implacably opposed to organized labor, particularly the Industrial Workers of the World (IWW, the Wobblies). As historian John Higham records, in responding to an IWW-led strike in 1912, "Johnson made a state-wide reputation by leading an armed citizens' movement which broke the strike, ran the leaders out of town, secured the recall of the mayor, and tried to punish the foreign laborers who obeyed the strike call by announcing that preference in re-employment would be given to native Americans."[12] On this basis, Johnson was elected to Congress as a staunch restrictionist. By 1924 he had become the éminence grise of American immigration policy, dominating the seventeen-member House committee (of whose members only two, Congressmen Samuel Dickstein of New York and Adolf Sabath of Chicago, ever opposed restriction). Johnson served in the Congress from March 1913 until March 1933, acting as chairman of this committee from the 66th to the 71st Congress.

Albert Johnson orchestrated passage of the 1924 law. He harbored few doubts about restriction, as he made clear to his committee: "I have come to the conclusion through readings and studies of the situation in the larger cities that no matter who the members of this committee may be in the next few Congresses, or who will be the chairman, the movement will keep on until there is just as complete a suspension of immigration to the United States as is possible to be had." Echoing popular themes (and the report of the Dillingham

Commission), he contrasted the new wave of immigrants to the United States's original settlers:

> I believe that all the people that came [initially], with comparatively few exceptions, felt that they were Americans the day they put foot on this soil. They felt that they were the people, part and parcel of the new government of the new country—United States of America. But the traditions that they brought were theirs; they were not the traditions of the country that had come up from the Colonies, so that as they came on in ever-increasing numbers the conditions in the United States changed, traditions changed, customs changed—at first hardly noticeable—until suddenly we find that everything is changed, literature is changed, language is changed, methods in the schools have changed, the stage has changed, relations of parent and child has changed.

It is doubtful that "all the people who came" shared in this general warm sense of belonging. The concurrent Americanization movement was in fact premised on varying degrees of assimilation. Johnson's characterization was racially bounded.

The tensions fomented by the new immigrants alarmed Johnson: "I know that the feeling of the House of Representatives to-day is for more restrictions. I do not believe it is possible to stop the movement for more restriction." He implied dangers arising from a multicultural medley: "it is not only in addition to the desire to maintain this country and build it as a nation with the traditions that go with the nation, but it is also the desire on the part of those only one generation away, to not have this country in the way Europe went, break up into conglomerations of people speaking various languages and hating each other."[13] This concern about internal conflicts and cleavages within the United States excluded from consideration relations between African Americans and white Americans of whatever ethnic background. It was conflicts arising solely within European immigrants that concerned Johnson.

Congressman Johnson was the link between eugenists' research and immigration policy-making. His contacts with Prescott Hall of the Immigration Restriction League predated 1914,[14] and the league regularly provided information to the House Immigration Committee. Johnson corresponded with Madison Grant, after the latter published his 1916 book on race decline, as well as with other eugenists. He was active in the American Eugenics Society.

Johnson spent a great deal of energy defending the legislative success in 1921, when restrictions were established temporarily. He had no doubts about the pressures to which that legislation was subjected, particularly in respect to the nationality clause. He told the president of the National Society of the Sons of the American Revolution (SAR) that "pressure upon us to modify the law to enlarge the non-quota exemption and to alter the preference provision has been tremendous." Close to a hundred bills were received by the committee to enlarge the nonquota exemptions or to revise the preference provision. Aside from such lobbying, Johnson believed that there were at least 200,000 aliens illegally in the United States who should have been deported. He thanked the society for its consistent and welcome support: "I am grateful to the organization for its numerous resolutions and endorsements; and to all officers and members who have expressed their views in support of the enactment of adequate laws on immigration, deportation, and naturalization for the protection of the people of the United States."[15]

To constrict further the numbers of southern and eastern Europeans, activists lobbied Congress to make the percentage of resident nationality groups 2 percent and to use the 1890 census for which enumeration these groups made up a much smaller proportion of the U. S. population.[16] This combination, originally proposed by a Vanderbilt University political scientist, Roy Garis, in 1922,[17] was enacted in the Johnson-Reed Immigration Act of 1924.[18] The 1924 legislation reduced the annual total number of immigrants to 150,000. Opponents of restriction recognized that quotas were unavoidable but resisted shifting to the 1890 census as a benchmark (which would have given two-thirds of the places to immigrants from northwestern Europe), aiming to retain the 1910 census. In an attempt to preclude the claim that the 1890 census discriminated against certain immigrant groups, the "national origins" plan (itself a reflection of racial ideas) was formulated in the 1924 law, since it was supposed to produce an immigration policy consistent with the "true" ethnic elements of the U. S. population. The national origins plan designated quotas according to a calculation of group size at the Republic's foundation, excluding the "descendants of slave immigrants." The implementation of the new arrangement was delayed until 1927 (and then again until 1929).

Writing to a eugenist in 1927, Congressman Johnson described the gestation of the quota principle as follows:

In 1912, Senator Dillingham introduced a percentage restriction bill, proposing that 10% based on the number of aliens in the United States on the 1910 census be admitted. I became interested in that idea and campaigned for Congress in 1912 on the percentage restriction plan. [In 1919] Senator Dillingham, aided by the present Assistant Secretary of Labor, W. W. Husband, who had been Secretary of the Commission in 1909 and later Secretary to Senator Dillingham, produced the temporary 3% quota act.

The House Committee then began an intense study of the quota plan of restriction and evolved the 2% of 1890 idea. The 2% of 1890 almost exactly divides the population as between the two great groups in accordance with the origins of the people of the United States, but does not make quite true divisions as between peoples of the various nations of the two grand divisions.[19]

This account underplays why the 1890 base appeared to be such a "desirable year" for calculating the immigration quotas.

From Nationality Quotas to National Origins

By accepting (in clause (b) of Section 11) that immigration should be regulated in terms of nationality quotas, derived from the 1920 and not the 1890 census, the 1924 Act not only unleashed intense lobbying by various ethnic groups to enlarge or defend their probable quota but also opened up quarrelsome debate about the suitability of different nationalities for residence in the United States. The 1924 Act raised the issue of desirable and undesirable immigrants. Thus, in April 1924, President Coolidge was urged to enact the law (and at all costs not to veto it) by the Immigration Restriction League, who warned that failure to do so "would be playing into the Democratic Candidate."[20] The president received a plaintive letter from Congressman Johnson warning him against vetoing the bill: "[I]n my opinion, the House is likely to pass that bill over executive disapproval by a vote of at least 3 to 1. I think the Senate would show a similar proportion of votes to pass over a veto. I have examined the matter carefully and am in close touch with the great bulk of those favoring restriction."[21] In 1927 the quota system established in the 1924 Johnson-Reed Act was substituted with a national origins plan (implemented in 1929), which was calculated by a special executive board on the basis of the 1920 census. (American consuls in European countries were to make the decision about visas.) Both the temporary quota system and the national origins plan shared an important characteristic, as Divine observes: they replaced the principle of individualism as the basis of admittance to the United States with one of group selection, a modification whose authors "failed to realize the violence this form of nationalism did to a concept of a democratic society in which men were free to assert their own individuality."[22] The substitution of group principle over individual selection rested on contentious eugenic hierarchies of race.

President Coolidge was unsuccessfully lobbied by congressional opponents of the restrictionist legislation. Congressman Samuel Dickstein (D, N.Y.), a staunch opponent of restriction, objected fundamentally to the quota scheme, articulating a view shared by other opponents: "[T]he preference provided for in the bill is a camouflage and is discriminatory. It may work well insofar as England and Germany are concerned because of the greater number allotted them for their quota, but it practically bars the rest of the world; particularly so under the National Origin scheme. . . This is another section that is wholly discriminatory."[23] In another letter the same congressman observed of the bill that "it involves the reputation of millions of our citizens as to whether or not a stamp of inferiority is to be placed upon them,"[24] a characterization accurately capturing the invidious implications of the 1924 Act and its racialist progenitor. The proposal to use the 1890 census, in place of the 1920 one, to calculate quotas, excited criticism. Congressman Sabath, another antirestrictionist, wrote immediately to President Coolidge, arguing that use of the 1890 benchmark would discriminate "against all the southern and southeastern European nations," as did the national origins scheme (to become operative from July 1, 1927), and he pleaded for the extension of the act "for two years" in order that "scientific study [could be] made before permanent legislation is enacted."[25] Congressman Sabath added that "we should restrict immigration along sane, humane and scientific lines, instead of branding millions of our citizens as inferior and deliberately hurting the pride of nearly all friendly nations."[26] Sabath's use of the term "inferior" regrettably captures exactly the aims of the restrictionists. Dickstein and Sabath were the leading congressional critics of the new law.

Within his own administration, Coolidge won fulsome praise for signing the law from his secretary of labor, James J. Davis. A naturalized American, Davis was an arch restrictionist, who became a mem-

ber of the commission, established by the 1924 legislation, to set national origins quotas. Davis declared, with studied obeisance, that
"history will record it as one of the greatest acts of your administration." Davis's hostility was pronounced toward Japanese immigrants,
whose "total exclusion" he supported, since "during my whole life I
have been opposed to the mixture of Orientals into our national life."
He argued that his position reflected not racism but the belief "that
the mixing of races, even though they might themselves be of high social, moral and intellectual standing, is not a good thing." He stated
nonchalantly that "we know that the Jap is unassimilable." Davis
believed that the U. S. already contained "a great racial problem,"
which arose from imported foreign labor: "the question of expedi-
ency or temporary advantage either to trade, industry or sentiment is
unimportant in comparison with the determination in favor of the building here of a homogeneous, easily assimilable, characteristic American race."[27] Davis thought there would be considerable disappointment about the timidity of the restrictions included in the 1924 law.
The secretary of labor remained implacably set against unrestricted
immigration, endorsing amendments after 1924 to toughen restriction and supporting the National Origins plan.[28] Davis's robust views
about the bases of the "American race" and the dangers of racial mixing were coincident with those of eugenists and must, of course, be
judged in the context of their time. That caution does not belittle their
invidious consequences or excise their unattractive premises.

The Immigration Restriction League also saluted the 1924 legislation and the president's role in its enactment. The league judged the
law a full realization of the historic ambition set out at the end of
the previous century by the league's members: "those still living of the
handful of men who, at the call of Mr. Robert DeC. Ward, first met
thirty years ago on May 31, 1894 to form the Immigration Restriction League . . . have thus at last seen their belief embodied in what
promises to be effective and permanent legislation."[29] The league
however, wanted further restriction, epitomized in the quota clause of
the 1924 law.

Specifying the National Origins Quotas

The 1924 Act postponed the implementation of the national origins
quota, based on the 1890 census, until 1927, when it was again temporarily delayed; the system finally began in 1929. In January 1927

the commission established by the 1924 act (known as the Quota Board, with seven members overseen by the Secretaries of Labor, James Davis, of Commerce, Herbert Hoover, and of State, Frank Kellogg[30]) to set nationality quotas reported.[31] The commission was charged with determining the national origins of the American population as a basis on which to make calculations about quotas. A table compared the quotas based on the 1890 census with the quotas derived from national origins (Table 7.1). The data were mostly derived from census sources, as the committee appointed by the three secretaries explained: aside from annual immigration data from 1820 to 1920 and the classification of the white population in the census of 1790, "the reports of the decennial censuses which have classified the foreign-born population by country of birth at each census from that of 1850 to that of 1920, inclusive; the native white population of foreign or mixed parentage by country of birth of parents at each census from that of 1890 to that of 1920, inclusive; and, both the foreign-born white population and the native white population of foreign or mixed parentage by mother tongue at the censuses of 1910 and 1920."[32] The analysis concentrated on white immigrants. The committee attempted to distinguish two groups. The first group was the "original native stock," for which the committee used records in the 1790 census, as documented in the government publication *A Century of Population Growth* (published in 1909); this had categorized the estimated population in 1790 into nationality groups and whose more prosperous patrician descendants inhabited the turn of the century world depicted in Edith Wharton and Henry James novels. And the second group was the "immigrant stock," who entered the country subsequently. From this dichotomy, "of the 94,820,915 white population of the United States as enumerated in 1920, approximately 53,500,000 were of immigrant stock and 41,000,000 of original native stock."[33] The smaller size of the later figure was bound to sound alarm bells among restrictionists: in 1890 the immigrant stock number was 24,668,792 compared with 30,432,466 original native stock (Table 7.2).

This calculation was arrived at through a "scientific plan," according to the statistician responsible, Dr. Joseph Hill.[34] Residents who were recorded in the 1790 census were considered native stock. The methodology of ascertaining descendants of white Americans from the 1790 census was not uncontroversial, as the following committee exchange illustrates:

Mr Dickstein (D, NY): In other words, this so-called particular national origins scheme . . . is more or less of a discrimination against certain classes of people in the United States, is it not?
Mr Hill (Bureau of the Census): No.
The Chairman (Johnson): Let us counter that question. How does it discriminate?

Table 7.1 Immigration Quotas, 1927

Country	Provisional Quotas from National Origin	Present Quotas from 1890 Census	Estimated Number in 1924
Afghanistan	100	100	
Albania	100	100	100
Andorra	100	100	100
Arabian penisula	100	100	
Armenia		124	100
Australia, etc.	100	121	100
Austria	1,486	785	2,171
Belgium	410	512	251
Bhutan	100	100	
Bulgaria	100	100	100
Cameroon (British)	100	100	
Cameroon (French)	100	100	
China	100	100	
Czechoslovakia	2,248	3,073	1,359
Danzig	122	228	100
Denmark	1,044	2,789	945
Egypt	100	100	100
Estonia	109	124	325
Ethiopia (Abyssinia)	100	100	100
Finland	559	471	517
France	3,837	3,954	1,772
Germany	23,428	61,227	20,028
Great Britain and Northern Ireland	73,039	34,007	85,135
Greece	367	100	384
Hungary	967	473	1,521
Iceland	100	100	100
India	100	100	
Iraq (Mesopotamia)	100	100	
Irish Free State	13,862	28,567	8,330
Italy, etc.	6,091	3,845	5,716
Japan	100	100	

Dickstein: It discriminates against Germany apparently, whose quota was 61,227 and cuts it down to 23,428.

Chairman: How is that a discrimination, if they have the blood stock here to warrant those figures?

Dickstein: That is what I am trying to find out from Mr Hill.[35]

Table 7.1 (continued)

Country	Provisional Quotas from National Origin	Present Quotas from 1890 Census	Estimated Number in 1924
Latvia	184	142	384
Liberia	100	100	100
Liechtenstein	100	100	100
Lithuania	494	344	458
Luxembourg	100	100	100
Monaco	100	100	100
Morocco	100	100	100
Muscat (Oman)	100	100	
Nauru	100	100	
Nepal	100	100	
Netherlands	2,421	1,648	2,762
New Guinea, etc.	100	100	
New Zealand, etc.	100	100	100
Norway	2,267	6,453	2,053
Palestine	100	100	100
Persia	100	100	100
Poland	4,978	5,982	4,535
Portugal	290	503	236
Romania	516	603	222
Ruanda and Urundi	100	100	
Russia	4,781	2,248	4,002
Samoa, western	100	100	
San Marino	100	100	100
Siam	100	100	
South Africa, Union of	100	100	100
South-West Africa	100	100	
Spain	674	131	148
Sweden	3,259	9,561	3,072
Switzerland	1,198	2,081	783
Total	153,541	164,667	150,000

Source: Derived from U. S. Senate, 69th Congress, 2d Session, Document No. 190, "National Origins Provision of the Immigration Act of 1924," message from the president of the United States, January 7, 1927.

Chairman Albert Johnson was unequivocal in supporting the statistician's methods, defending Hill against his colleagues' skepticism. (Hill made appearances before congressional committees until the legislation was settled in 1929.)[36] Questioned about ambiguities in the allocation of original native stock from the 1790 census, Johnson pronounced that "errors one way would be balanced by errors the other."[37] Queried about the probable accuracy of the 1790 census, Dr. Hill argued, improbably, that because the United States was a rural society at that time, records were more dependable. In response to critical questions about the calculations, he argued that the consequences of errors were marginal: "[I]t is only fair to say and you ought to know that 150,000 immigrants means one immigrant to 600 inhabitants. So an error of 600 would make a difference of only 1 immigrant, an error of 6,000 would mean 10 immigrants, and an error of 60,000 would mean 100 immigrants."[38] This calculation was cited frequently and vigorously by Johnson in defense of the national origins scheme, though Margo Anderson reports that privately, Hill had "serious reservations about whether reliable figures on national origins could be determined."[39] Robert Divine notes, correctly, that the sheer complexity of the Quota Board's calculations contributed to a perception of the national origins scheme's impracticality and strained the plausibility of its authors' assertions to scientific rigor.[40]

The shift to national origins was contested. Whereas the 1921 and 1924 laws discriminated—through the quota system—against southern and eastern European immigrants in favor of northwestern ones, the national origins scheme, within a similar aggregate number of immigrants, greatly increased the immigrants from Britain, while other northwestern countries (Ireland, Germany, Norway, Sweden,

Table 7.2 White Population

Census Year	Original Native Stock	Immigrant Stock	Total
1890	30,432,466	24,668,792	55,101,258
1900	34,272,951	32,536,245	66,809,196
1910	38,101,175	42,630,782	81,731,957
1920	41,288,570	53,532,345	94,820,915

Source: Derived from National Origins Provision Immigration Act of 1924, hearings before the Committee on Immigration and Naturalization, HR, 69th Congress, 2d Session, January 18, 1927, p. 12.

and Denmark) suffered reductions in quotas. Organizations representing the latter's interests consequently mobilized against national origins, whereas ardently nativist ones, emboldened with eugenic evidence, maintained the pressure to retain the plan. Thus, on top of the division between northwestern and southeastern Europeans (Dillingham's "old" versus "new" immigrants) was imposed a fresh cleavage within the first group between original settlers and nineteenth-century arrivals. That the latter were now equated with the former would have surprised most nineteenth-century Americans.

A key thinker behind the national origins plan was Captain John B. Trevor (who graduated from Harvard in 1902 and took a masters degree there in 1903), former head of the American Defense Committee. He calculated the "national origins" of the U. S. population concurrently with, but independently of, both Senator Reed and Congressman Johnson. He was active in eugenic circles. John Higham credits Trevor with the strategy of excavating national origins, a "brilliant solution."[41] Speaking to the House Committee hearings, Trevor declared, "I started in January, 1914, to see whether it was possible to make an analysis of the population of the United States on the basis of national origin. That was my own idea. It was not suggested to me by anybody. My purpose was to see if such a thing could be done, and to determine what proportion of immigration southern and eastern Europe was entitled to."[42]

Trevor, who had been an intelligence officer with the U.S. Army in New York City during the First World War, gave a lengthy disposition on the national origins plan to Johnson's congressional committee.[43] Trevor wanted an immigration law that would maintain the U. S. population's racial composition as close to the Anglo-Saxon model as possible. He was already admired by Congressman Johnson. As Margo Anderson discusses, Trevor devoted considerable effort to keeping the statistician Joseph Hill committed to national origins: "Trevor made it a point to keep in contact with Hill, to visit him in Washington, to entertain him in New York. He thus made sure that progress was being made in producing the appropriate numbers."[44] He had become a confidant of the House Immigration Committee, as John Higham records: having made a "strong impression on Johnson . . . before long Trevor was drawn into intimate association with the committee. He sat in on informal meetings of the restrictionist majority, fed ideas to it, and contributed to the drafting of reports, all on a voluntary, unpaid basis."[45] Not as intellectually significant as Harry

Laughlin, Trevor was nonetheless an important source of ideas for the House Immigration Committee, especially its chairman Albert Johnson. Trevor pursued a patriotic line: "[I]t is inevitable that any arbitrary census date is going to discriminate against somebody. It so happens, under the present law that the particular favorites are the Germans and the Irish, and they naturally do not want to have their privileges taken away from them." However, he argued, that "in none of the material I have seen . . . has the interest of the United States been taken into account. It is always the interest of somebody else outside the United States that is being considered."[46] This "interest of the United States" was not entirely neutral but happened to be coincident with that of the British descendants, as he later implied: "however classified, the evidence is incontestable that the British stock predominated to a huge extent, particularly prior to 1700."[47] By 1750 there were a million residents in the colonies, overwhelmingly, Trevor argued, of English, Welsh, and Scottish extraction. Hence the apportionment provided for in the recent quotas seemed fair. Ironically, Trevor dismissed the melting-pot model as "a myth."

The maintenance of American democracy—"our institutions are distinctly of an English character"—necessitated restriction:

> [W]hen the act of 1924 was passed, it was obviously felt by the committee that northwestern Europe should receive such a proportion of the quota as that area had contributed to our population as a whole. That proposition is not only just, but is essential for the maintenance of our form of government. As you know, dictatorships are in existence in practically every country which claimed it was being discriminated against by the 1890 census date. However, we do not want that sort of government in this country. Mussolini has done marvels for Italy, but nobody here would want a form of government of that kind which seems to work well with Italians, but not work well with Americans.[48]

Southern and eastern Europeans were apparently intrinsically incapable of democratic government or of functioning under one. Trevor's rejection of the melting-pot model underlines how contested a framework it has always been.

The Campaign for and against National Origins

The debates after 1924 were complex and rebarbative, culminating in a bitter few months before the national origins scheme was finally implemented in 1929. The recommendations of the Quota Board proved divisive. The proposed scheme upset the northwestern Europeans—other than the British who gained substantially—since their quota, made public when the Quota Board reported in January 1927, fell significantly. Furthermore, it was an argument based on a reading of the U. S. nation as composed of certain "stock." Prorestrictionists were eager to retain the 1890 census base, their opponents seeking to substitute it with the 1920 census. The thirty-year difference would have a considerable effect on the ethnic composition admitted after the quota regime commenced. Language was often emotive, the *Saturday Evening Post* declaring in an editorial entitled "Time to Put Up the Bars" that "hosts" of immigrants "swarmed" into the United States.[49] This publication gave ample room to the restrictionist cause, commissioning Kenneth L. Roberts to visit and write about potential European immigrants; his findings were not flattering, since he judged most of the hopeful migrants unsuitable for naturalization or citizenship.[50] Such views were supported in the petitions and resolutions sent to members of the congressional immigration committees.[51] However, on February 13, 1929, the Senate Committee on Immigration ended its hearings on the quota issue and voted against reporting a resolution that would further postpone the date at which the National Origins Clause became operational. President Hoover signed the law on March 22 and stipulated that the clause become law from July 1 1929.

Supporters of the 1890 Baseline

Submitting a memorial to the president and Congress, an eminent group of American scientists and eugenists urged rapid implementation of the nationality quota that was based on the 1890 census, since it was "sound in principle and fair to all elements in the population. Only by this method can that large proportion of our population which is descended from the colonists and other early settlers, as well as the members of the newer immigration, have their proper racial representation in the quotas." The scheme would promote racial harmony: "[W]e believe that Congress wisely concluded that only by such a system of proportional representation in our future immigration could the racial status quo of the country be maintained or a reasonable degree of homogeneity secured. Without such basic homogeneity, we firmly believe, no civilization can have its best development."[52] The signatories included six professors of biology at Princeton; five other Princeton professors; Harvard biologists; Robert DeC. Ward; Madison Grant; the economist John Commons (whose 1908 book *Race and Immigration* had extolled the virtues of Nordic Europeans compared with inferior southern Europeans); Harry Laughlin; Henry Fairchild, sociology professor at New York University; Leon Whitney and Roswell Johnson, field secretary and president of the American Eugenics Society respectively; and Charles Davenport, director of eugenic research, Carnegie Institution.

Johnson's House Immigration Committee certainly preferred the 1890 baseline.[53] Critics of the proposal made little headway. Joseph Carey, president of the American-Irish Republican League, attacked the national origins framework as "unfair": "[I]t allots virtually one-half of all the immigrants coming in to one country [that is, Britain]— all the immigrants coming from the countries governed by the quota. That in itself looks bad to us. It savors of unfairness . . . we believe that the national origins scheme can not be taken as a fair and scientific basis, because the statistics available are faulty and incomplete."[54] Carey wanted the 2 percent rule based on the 1890 census to be retained because "we want a country that will be purely American. . . I am an American citizen, and I believe we should do that which is best for the future of our country."[55] Carey's advocacy of the 2 percent rule was prompted by his desire to guarantee access to Irish immigrants, who he believed were sacrificed under the national origins scheme to the benefit of British immigrants.

The Act and Political Divisions in the US

Immigration policy rested on and exposed fault lines deeply entrenched in American society. Thus, Congressman John Box (D, Tex.), plainly frustrated with Carey, challenged him: "[G]overnments and civilization spring from impulses of the people. If our institutions have had their origin in, and thus far have had their lives shaped by, English impulses, then is it not a great risk if we allow, say, Russia to inject a big element into them?"[56] Carey's claim, that non-English-speaking immigrants should be as welcome as any other immigrant and that the second and third generations of such immigrants were assimilated, was rejected by Chairman Johnson. The chairman cited unassimilated communities in Pennsylvania: "I could take you to settlements in the United States that have existed for 150 years and where the predominating language is still Pennsylvania Dutch. That is all right. But those people have not made progress, and have not done what you say these other people have done. They are good citizens, but they continue to speak a broken Dutch language."[57] This was a new variant on the melting-pot philosophy of American citizenship: being a "good citizen" was not sufficient for assimilationists who had a clear image of the desired outcome of the melting pot, an assumption of the Americanization movement. Theoretically, this situation raises an important issue about whether a common language is necessary to the political culture of a democracy. The chairman's dismissal of the Pennsylvanian community as lacking progress is combined with both acceptance of their separate language and acknowledgment of them as "good citizens." Yet the immigration committee was working to exclude comparable persons.

Proponents of national origins liked to impute foreign interests to their opponents and judged this tendency itself to be a measure of their opponents' weaker attachment to the American "race." Thus, one academic observed to Johnson that "it is, perhaps, natural that those whose interests are more closely associated with some foreign country that would benefit by the change should be more vigorous as proponents of repeal than those whose interests in any foreign country are more remote should be as opponents. It is partly because I think it probably true that the 'established' native stock are less active that I am writing this letter."[58] The language deployed by this correspondent—"native stock"—is also instructive. Congressman Johnson was happy to reply in equally picayune terms: "[H]aving finally adopted the 2% of 1890, the proposal to change from that basis to the National Origins basis seems to create confusion and disturbance among all affected races and a similar disturbance in the United States from the fact that one-third of our people are either immigrants or the first children of immigrants. Nearly all of these have ties or alien associations sufficient to create a very considerable disturbance."[59] Advocates of the national origins scheme hoped to gain political support from opponents of the 1890 basis—principally southern and eastern Europeans—who lost out to the German, Scandinavian, and Irish Americans favored by the 2 percent quota scheme of 1890. One national origins supporter and eugenist, Edward Lewis, observed with convoluted logic to Johnson that "the origins basis does not favor the 1790 stock. It merely decides to count the native stock." However,

Lewis's own impeccable lineage rather qualified his views: "it happens that my father's people in a straight line go back to 1670, that my mother's people go back in a straight line beyond the Revolution, that my wife's mother's people go back to the Mayflower."[60]

Many groups, such as the American Legion and the Swedish Lutheran and Methodist Episcopal churches, sought a return to the 1890 criterion.[61] At its annual meeting in 1929, the American Legion resolved in favor of the "continuance of the method of restriction upon immigration in the 1924 Immigration law with its fundamental national origins provision,"[62] a restatement of its previous annual conference endorsements.[63] A massive campaign was organized to send petitions to members of Congress, calling for the full implementation of the 1924 law.[64]

Nativists for 1890

The Sons of the American Revolution lobbied energetically for restriction, vigilantly monitored federal policy, and vociferously articulated the restrictionist cause. The SAR hailed the 1924 law as America's "Second Declaration of Independence" (an appellation much favored by Congressman Johnson). In May 1926 the SAR complained about the "fight" between the House and the Senate to limit the restrictions enacted the previous year. Its language pulled no punches: "[T]he chief opposition is found in a certain racial group and the alien blocs, the purpose being to increase their numbers and their political strength by flooding the country with their own kind. From their point of view this can best be accomplished by destroying the present quota law."[65] Its lobbying efforts were well supported by Congressman Johnson, who on one occasion arranged for two-hundred copies of a two-hundred-page SAR pamphlet to be "distributed under his frank." The SAR was adamant that "the statute as it stands is sound and beneficial from an American viewpoint, and that the Congress would very justly be condemned should it weaken the restrictions by yielding to the various frontal and flank attacks made upon the law."[66] One of the secretary generals of the SAR, Howard Rowley, submitted to Johnson a long-winded letter supporting implementation of the national origins plan, since this would get a "fundamental principle established." Rowley marshaled eugenic arguments: "restrictive immigration must also be selective if we are concerned with the future stock of America and not some present economic concern."[67]

The nativist Order of United American Mechanics (OUAM), a remorseless proponent of limits whose views had been included in the Dillingham Commission, believed the 1924 regulations were "just and equitable" and appropriate to "govern the future immigration of those races naturally assimilable."[68] The order's local branches tirelessly petitioned the House and Senate Immigration Committees opposing any weakening in the 1924 regulations. Hundreds of such petitions were organized and sent to Congress.[69] The Patriotic Order of the Sons of America gave fulsome support to the 1924 law. One branch explained that "this country cannot assimilate the advanced hoards [sic] of immigrants who would come to the country if restrictions were not pressed on them . . . We believe that American institutions rest solely on good citizenship and good citizens are only made by the best of people and we realize that the best of people do not come from foreign shores." Expressing a common sentiment, it implored that "America must be kept American."[70] The order wanted legislation registering all aliens in the United States.[71] Business interests did not side with labor but instead advocated a broad immigration policy ensuring a consistent supply of new workers.[72] Theirs was a lonely and mostly isolated voice.

A consistent supporter of the national origins clause, and indeed an organization that lobbied for its adoption, was the blandly named Immigration Study Commission. It congratulated President Coolidge when he signed the 1924 act (ranking the date with Thanksgiving and Armistice Day), the commission's president speculating that "one wonders, however, if the final enactment of your measure into law does not mean perhaps even more to the American people of the tomorrows, because it fixes the type of the American Race."[73] The commission promised to maintain a stream of propaganda in support of the new law, resolving to "continue the fight by education of the American people."[74] Its aim[75] was to retain a "Nordic" dominance in the American population. The commission noted that both New Zealand and Australia were likely to replicate American legislation: "stimulated by what you have been doing in Washington there will probably come two great, almost purely Nordic, Australasian nations with a combined potential population eventually almost equal to that of the present United States."[76] It planned a similar campaign in Canada, invoking the writer Madison Grant's view that Canada and the United States constituted the "purest Nordic areas."

Grant's book *The Passing of the Great Race,* which was published in 1916, had been widely embraced by restrictionists. Erudite and highly educated, Grant was also an officer of the American Eugenics Society and vice president of the Immigration Restriction League. His book, much influenced by the writings of Arthur de Gobineau and Houston Stewart Chamberlain, was both a panegyric for the Nordic race and a warning about its corruption or dilution by uncontrolled interrace mixing. As Thomas Gossett remarks, Grant "believed that the superior races in the United States were in danger of being overwhelmed by inferior immigrants."[77] Grant distinguished three races in Europe, the Alpines, the Mediterraneans, and the Nordics, differentiating them in predictable ways and singing the praises of the last. The commission characterized the 1928 presidential election as "a combat between the old American stock and the hyphenates"; Hoover's victory implied the "political strength of the former." This outcome placed the 1924 law in context, giving it unequivocal strength: "[T]he National Origins Clause is merely justice to the old American colonial stock. Their ancestors gave us our institutions."[78] This argument converged with many of the eugenic claims about keeping the American stock pure.[79]

"New Immigrant" Opponents of the 1924 Act

Critics of the 1924 law were concentrated among groups representing Americans with links to southern and eastern Europe. They were politically weak. Thus, the Women's Zionist Organizations argued, reasonably, that the legislation "unfairly" discriminated against "nationalities from particular sections of Europe." Furthermore, the premises of such differentiation were bogus ones: "this discrimination implies an acceptance of a pseudo scientific theory of racial superiority and is moreover contrary to American ideals of equality and justice."[80] The Massachusetts Jewish Committee argued that the 1924 law was intended to "discriminate against the Jews, the Slavs, the Greeks, the Italians, and all the people of Eastern and Southern Europe, and that therefore it is alien to the principles of a free and liberal America."[81] The Polish-American-based Citizen's Club of New Britain, Connecticut, concurred that Albert Johnson's legislation "would prove to be a discriminating, rather than a limiting, law."[82] Americans of Italian birth and descent took a similar view of the law, organizing through the Italian Americanization Clubs. The Sons of Italy argued that the clause discriminated "entirely out of keeping with the tradition and practices of the United States." The groups wanted to use either the 1910 or the 1920 census instead of the 1890 for calculating the number of eligible immigrants, since the latter criterion depicted Italians as "undesirable" and endangered "Americanization."[83] The St. Calogero Society reiterated these concerns about Italian-Americans,[84] as did other groups.

Opposition to the Johnson bill was understandably intense among Italian-Americans because of the way in which the debate characterized southern European immigrants in general and because of the likely future restrictions that it implied. One group summarized these views to the Senate committee: the national origins provision "is the culmination of five years of intensive propaganda . . . seeking to establish the proposition that southern Europeans, Italians included, are an inferior product, mentally and otherwise, and incapable of being made into one-hundred per cent Americans while, the Nordic races are inherently superior and hence more desirable as immigrants."[85] This description was not without foundation.

"Old Immigrant" Opponents of the 1924 Act

Both Scandinavian and Irish-American groups lobbied against the national origins scheme because, although immigrants with these backgrounds would do better than those coming from southern and eastern Europe, they still did less well proportionately than under the 1921 regulations.[86] The American Irish Historical Society's chairman, John Murphy, argued somewhat disingenuously that the society did not seek more places for Irish immigrants but disapproved of the methodology of the new framework: "we oppose the entire 'National Origins' plan because of our conviction, founded upon substantial research, that no such determination of national origins can be based on other than a more or less unscientific hypothesis which is susceptible of distortion in prejudiced hands."[87] This opposition might have been weaker if 1890 instead of 1920 were the proposed census baseline. The society rejected the purported scientific methodology on which the calculations were based, objections already aired before the House Immigration Committee. The society distributed a pamphlet advocating the repeal of the national origins clause. The pamphlet opened with a telling quotation from the three Secretaries of State, Commerce, and Labor when they delivered their report to Congress in January 1927: "the statistical and historical information available raises grave doubts as to the whole value of these computations as a basis for the purposes intended."[88] This sentence was taken from a letter that itself is of interest. President Coolidge sent the report from the Quota Board, with the secretaries' accompanying letter, to Congress on January 7, but on January 10 he forwarded a new letter to Congress that was intended, the President reported, to "replace an inaccurate copy" inadvertently transmitted to the Senate; the secretaries, reflecting on these "grave doubts," added, "we therefore cannot assume responsibility for such conclusions under these circumstances."[89] Robert Divine infers that these modifications arose from political pressure placed on the president by Republican congressmen worried about the elections of 1924.[90] Coolidge was reported to be concerned about the effects of the national origins quotas on American voters descended from northwestern Europe.[91] Congress was thus offered grounds for repealing this clause of the 1924 law.

Congressman August Andresen (from Minnesota) introduced a bill to repeal the national origins system citing concerns that no good reasons were provided for depleting the number of Germans, Scandinavians, and Irish to be admitted ("I can therefore see no justice in the arbitrary method under the 'National Origins' provision to shut our doors to a class of immigrants, which experience and history plainly shows, now make up some of our best citizenship"); he also highlighted the three secretaries' reservations.[92] The Sons of Norway opposed the national origins provision;[93] the Swedish-based Vasa Orden af Amerika and the Danish Brotherhood of America campaigned against the clause.[94] The proudly named Grand Lodge of Independent Order of Vikings communicated its opposition to the national origins clause.[95] Opposition was also voiced by Americans of Scandinavian and German origin. The Swedish-American Republican Club objected to the 1890 quota and sought its repeal, praising Nordic values.[96] German Americans endorsed such views.[97] American Jewish organizations, such as the Council of Jewish Women and Assembly of Hebrew Orthodox Rabbis of America and Canada, were also hostile.[98]

The Anti-National Origins Clause League

The most systematic campaign against the 1924 quota rules, as measured by, for instance, the quantity of petitions forwarded to members of Congress, was launched by the Anti-National Origins Clause League, which was based in Detroit. Referring to the "obnoxious national origins scheme," its secretary described the League's campaign: "I have been in touch with over fifteen hundred organizations throughout the country by direct mail, and we now have a nucleus for a strong national body of societies to continue the work for the fall if this first session of the 71st Congress does not repeal the national origins scheme."[99] The league rejected the premises of the national origins clause established in the 1924 law, dismissing them as "unworkable" and unfair, and as methodologically "unscientific." The scheme's defects were numerous: "[T]here is not available sufficiently complete statistical and historical information to determine exactly the national origins of the peoples of the United States. Its provisions for numerical calculation of immigration quotas lead to assumptions, guesswork, deductions, conjecture, with arbitrary conclusions, with the result that any set of quotas by such attempted calculation will always be open to continual public criticism." The league introduced a devastating observation from Herbert Hoover uttered before he became president: "'As a member of the Commission whose duty it is to determine the quota basis under the National Origins Law, I have found it is impossible to do so accurately and without hardship. The basis now in effect carries out the essential principle of the law, and I have favored repeal of that part of the act calling for a new basis of quotas.'"[100] The league's campaign to rescind the national origins quota did not imply an opposition to immigration controls but an aversion specifically to their derivation. This was a self-serving argument, as the league secretary's letter to Senator Royal Copeland reveals: "[T]here is more opposition to the *method* of determining quotas as attempted by the national origins than is manifested by petition or letter, and the opposition is on the increase. Very few object to the idea of restrictive immigration and it is the method of calculating the quotas which is so objectionable."[101]

Business groups were wary of the national origins framework. They generally favored immigration. The U. S. Chamber of Commerce told Johnson that it recommended retaining the quota limit system but opposed national origins.[102] The chamber's immigration committee produced a fourteen-page report in support of repealing the national origins scheme. The report argued that the quota system enacted in 1924 worked effectively and that the national origins system—which by that date had twice been postponed by Congress—would be harmful: "[T]he putting into effect of any restrictive immigration policy is bound to stir up racial antagonisms and misunderstandings. There is plenty of evidence that changing over to the national origins plan would revivify these antagonisms without any large commensurate gain to our final purpose, which is the building of a homogeneous and united nation."[103] The report was surprisingly candid, if conceptually confused, about the machinations necessary to implement this scheme: "the difficulty is that the national origins plan requires apparently the use of a very fine tool to try to accomplish what can only at best be a very rough judgment of the relative importance of European seed stocks in our present white population."[104] Hundreds of petitions that opposed national origins were orchestrated by Irish-American groups and submitted to the Senate Immigration Committee.[105] Ultimately such protests failed, however.

The political divisions stirred up by immigration restriction in terms of nationality were thus deep ones. Congressman Johnson was not immune to these petitions and protests. As early as 1926, he cautioned President Coolidge about the electoral damage of the national origins provision among Republican voters: "my opinion is that a pronouncement by you in plenty of time before the general elections will save to our party not less than twenty districts in states where German, Irish, and Scandinavian people are disturbed over possible further restriction under National Origins section."[106] Johnson sponsored the bill, which passed by 234 to 111 votes in 1927, postponing implementation of the national origins scheme for two years.[107] In March 1928 Johnson was able to write one Scandinavian that the national origins scheme was again postponed by resolution until 1929.[108] In other correspondence with a supporter of immigration restriction but an opponent of national origins, Johnson gave an extended account of the policy's development. He stressed the Senate's role in promoting the new scheme: "in securing an agreement between House and Senate on the 1924 Immigration Act, the House conferees were obliged to accept the amendment of Senator Reed which provided for National Origins, although the House conferees endeavored to place in the amendment delaying and qualifying steps under which we thought the National Origins provision might never come into action." Johnson believed that the United States would gain "by the admission of some 73,000 immigrants from Great Britain (not counting the Irish Free State) out of a possible 150,000 to be admitted annually. On the other hand, the 2% of 1890 census quota system now in use gives about one-third of possible immigration from Europe to Germany, which has been the cause of some feeling." Evidence of Johnson's recognition of the complexities of the national origins scheme was apparent elsewhere in the letter: "I am of the opinion that if National Origins goes into effect, the pressure in the next Congress for a change will be so great that the restriction of immigration will be more likely to be weakened than if the 1890 [baseline] is continued."[109] Since Johnson backed national origins, these caveats were presumably politically motivated.

Johnson retained a resolute opposition to immigration, even considering an absolute ban to be preferable should the search for national origins categories abort: "the 'national origins' plan serves to divide the Nordics, practically all of whom should not be divided, for we need a solid front in order to combat the forces of restriction."[110] The national origins scheme had the potential to dissolve the robust restrictionist coalition, successfully mobilized for the passage of the 1921 and 1924 laws; Johnson saw this alliance disintegrating before his eyes under the new faultlines generated by national origins calculations. To one constituent, Johnson explained that the committee members "felt that the national blood stock feeling aroused by National origins would be as a mere Puget Sound zephyr compared to a Kansas cyclone if we attempted to take away one-half of the British, Irish, German, and other northern quotas, for the benefit of relatives of those from the southeastern countries."[111] Johnson's political doubts about the national origins measure were picked up by Herbert Hoover, who criticized the measure when nominated by the Republicans as their presidential candidate in 1928. This opposition was insufficient, however, to prevent the scheme or to permit its repeal.

Conclusion

The arguments of opponents and proponents were rehearsed in the final congressional debates on the issue, held between February and June 1929.[112] The scheme was enacted by both chambers, after a House bill—narrowly passed—to postpone its implementation failed to garner support in the Senate. President Herbert Hoover, publicly an opponent of the clause, declared it would be in effect from July 1, 1929.

National origins was a significant triumph for a view of the American people as white and racially homogenous, whose integrity should not be compromised by inappropriate immigrants.[113] This success is reflected in both the debates about the new policy and its suitability, and in the thoughts of the leading congressional policy-maker, Albert Johnson. The new arrangement consolidated the United States's self-image as a white nation, unenthusiastic about nonwhite immigrants and with a particular conception of assimilation, derived from the Americanization idea of the Anglo-Saxon identity. Since the national origins regulations enacted in 1929 explicitly excluded "the descendants of slave immigrants" from any computation of the population of the United States in 1920 for the purpose of determining quotas and quota eligibility, an obscure but nonetheless discriminatory provision in respect to African Americans, it is difficult to dissent from the view that policy-makers wanted to make Americans in a white image.[114] Another commentator made this point, writing in 1952: "[I]n determination of the total population in the 1924 Immigration Act Negroes were coupled with Asiatics (who were barred from citizenship), and with American Indians (who could not be proved to be immigrants). Such an exclusion was not an innocent accident; the 1924 law early achieved notoriety for the racist sentiments which engendered it and the Ku Klux Klan support which ensured its passage." This deficiency was perpetuated in the McCarran-Walter bills of 1952, thereby reaffirming "a bias against Negro immigration which should have been repudiated long ago."[115]

Official accounts of the 1924 immigration law straightforwardly acknowledged its racial intentions and the conception of American identity that it promoted. Thus, the Immigration and Naturalization Service's monthly review explained in 1947 that "in its broader sense, the National Origins Plan was intended to preserve the racial composition of the United States through the selection of immigrants from those countries whose traditions, languages and political systems were akin to those in this country."[116] To some extent, a concern about alienating southern and central Americans exempted these countries from the 1924 legislation. Senator Reed, for instance, was a committed Pan-Americanist, and at the time of the legislation, immigration from south of the U.S. border was modest.[117] This commitment enabled South American countries and Canada to win exemption from the Western Hemisphere national quotas.

A White Nation

The discussion of immigration policy in the United States during the period 1900 to 1929 (manifest in the Dillingham Commission's work, congressional committee hearings, and the national origins plan) is vitiated with a fear of inferior "stock" or "races" or "nationalities" invading and comingling with the "real American stock," that is, white descendants of the northwestern Europeans, especially the English, who first settled the New World colonies. African American descendants are considered as involuntary members of the U. S. population and as basically unassimilable—hence the system of segregation. The arguments about the true or genuine "stock" making up Americans had malign implications for African Americans: the debates were about types of European immigrants. By defining these citizens, if only en passant, as in essence unassimilable, the debates and decisions about immigration policy contributed powerfully to the definition of the place of African Americans as lacking full rights of citizenship in the U. S. polity.[118] It exposed the enmity with which these citizens were viewed by the dominant white population, specifically those viewing themselves as eugenically superior to and direct descendants of the pure stock of colonial settlers. Individualism is now presented unproblematically as an American constitutional and ideological convention; yet its formulation in this period of eugenic-inspired debate about immigration was far from race-neutral.[119] This racial bias complemented the entrenched system of segregated race relations operative in the United States from the end of the nineteenth century and endorsed by the Supreme Court's 1896 decision in *Plessy v. Ferguson*.

The ethos that immigrants should be assimilable with the dominant "American race" underpinned the debates about immigration; assimilation occurred through de Crèvecoeur's melting pot, but the ingredients of this dish were to be predetermined, and blacks were not included. Thus, the national origins quota system purported to set immigration quotas on the basis of the national origins of the U.S. population. In fact, as a later presidential commission acknowledged, this was not the case: "[T]he act . . . uses the national origins of the population of 1920, not of 1950. It excludes from consideration Negroes, American Indians and other non-white people. Thus, it fails to take into account the national origins of the current population,"[120] and always presumed these biases. However, this very same 1953 report perpetuated the myth that between 1776 and 1921, immigration was "unrestricted,"[121] ignoring the exclusion of Chinese and Japanese migrants, and rather oddly asserted that "there is considerable mystery shrouding the development of the national origins plan."[122] As this chapter has demonstrated, there were entirely identifiable sources driving this legislation.

Immigration policy-makers were determining who would be entitled to become members of the polity and thereby be empowered to exercise the right to naturalize. The discussions ineluctably affected perceptions of and attitudes toward those already present in the community: new immigrants—Europeans from southern and eastern Europe—were treated as less than equal in the eyes of the preceding generations of immigrants, the "old immigrants." This fundamental division between two sorts of potential immigrants from Europe—those easily assimilable with extant Americans and those from a distinct background (allegedly burdened with an array of imperfections and flaws)—structured the formulation of the 1924 Johnson-Reed Act and the system of quota-based admission initiated in 1929. Consequently, immigration policy compromised the United States's doctrine of equality; as Congressman Adolph Sabath, a member of the House Immigration Committee, remarked, the 1924 law "would be the first instance in our modern legislation for writing into our laws the hateful doctrine of inequality between the various component parts of our population."[123] It was an illiberal decision based on notions of worth and desert incompatible with a political ideology constructed from classical liberal sources or with the principle that oppressed peoples could find refuge in the United States. With visas to be issued for European immigrants by U. S. consuls in the immigrants' home country, the "racial and ethnic composition of immigration was now legally regulated by the state."[124] In Ian Dowbiggin's judgment, the 1924 and 1929 measures exactly satisfied eugenists' aims: "Johnson, [Madison] Grant and their followers were jubilant because the new legislation penalized southern and eastern European immigrants most heavily. They considered the 1924 act their greatest victory."[125] Among psychiatrists, however, eugenic principles were already in significant decline, according to Dowbiggin.

The Danger of New Divisions

Fitzgerald points out that such a legislative success, in terms of racial and eugenic ambitions, obviated the need for the political coalition which had strived for such an immigration policy in the preceding four decades.[126] However, the political struggle over national origins gave such advocates a continuing role for the five years after the Johnson-Reed Act was enacted.

As chair of the House Committee on Immigration and Naturalization and as key architect of the 1924 law, Congressman Albert Johnson had to field the myriad of petitions, resolutions, letters, and lobbying conducted in the five years after the law's enactment, as the disputatious issue of quotas was publicly debated. His own correspondence over these years reveals a transformation from a firm commitment to the national origins clause to one of increasing anxiety about the potential political consequences of this measure, yet there persists a determination to effect the law. Initially, Johnson viewed the criticisms of the national origins clause as constituting a "grand assault";[127] to one correspondent, he wrote that "the effort to modify the Immigration Act of 1924 is perpetual. It takes form principally in proposals to widen the non-quota or exempt classification."[128] Nonetheless, Johnson's worries should not be exaggerated and, to restrictionists, he remained the firmest of their allies in Congress. In June 1924 the Immigration Restriction League told Johnson that "what you are doing is one hundred times more important than a lot of things that are making one hundred times as much noise."[129] The league viewed Johnson as an ardent restrictionist, which he certainly was in 1924. The Ku Klux Klan "congratulated" Johnson on his "effort to maintain strict immigration law in our glorious country."[130]

Over time, Congressman Johnson seemed more conscious of the conflicts and divisions ineluctably stirred by the national origins plan. Increasingly strained by the issues raised in enacting the national origins provision, Johnson informed Captain Trevor that "agents" of the

Catholic Church had been "probing this office for several months past, making inquiries about the National origins but not showing their hands."[131] In 1926 when the results of the committee of experts were still awaited, the committee's clerk informed one colleague that "Mr. Johnson is disposed to let the 1890 quota basis stand"[132] and not to shift to national origins. By February 1927, he concluded that were a proposal to abrogate the national origins scheme introduced to Congress, "I am of the opinion that two-thirds of the House would vote to repeal the Origins provision if given an opportunity."[133] Politically, Johnson also recognized the costs of the national origins scheme, recording that "the opinion prevails among many of the restrictionist members of the Committee that to carry National Origins into effect is to add the opposition of organizations representing Northwestern European immigration to the continued assaults to the Southeastern European people, thus increasing a force that will continue to hammer away and ultimately break down restriction."[134] Awaiting a report from the Learned Societies on the system, he wrote to one erstwhile supporter in Massachusetts that "personally, I am afraid that National Origins in effect will bring about greater racial antagonisms than any of us have anticipated." He also thought that the pro-1920 census advocates would be exploited "by the other and greatly enlarged groups for revising National Origins on a 1930 basis as soon as the next census figures are available."[135] To another voter, Johnson was surprisingly contrite, as the country awaited, in March 1929, President Hoover's resolution of a "most awkward situation": "I cannot rid my mind from the belief that National Origins in effect will create racial antagonisms among those of the second and third generations far beyond anything that has been anticipated."[136] Part of the reason, which was unacknowledged by Johnson, for such "racial antagonism" arose from the eugenic assumptions of "race" informing the new measure. The differentiation between members of the U. S. polity introduced by this framework could not but induce "racial antagonism." Of course, Johnson's concerns were simply in respect to tensions among different European nationalities and not to the mistreatment of nonwhites.

CHAPTER EIGHT

"A Slur on Our Citizenry":
Dismantling National Origins: The 1965 Act

The upshot of the divisive debates during the 1920s about immigration policy was the passage of legislation designed to structure the ethnic composition of immigrants to the United States. The number of immigrants was measured against a quota of national origins set for each country. This arrangement meant that immigrants were placed against a total of their country of ethnic origin, not necessarily of birth. Only ethnic groups whose forebears were deemed to have reached the United States voluntarily were permitted a quota under the national origins scheme, a device that automatically excluded Africans (whose enslaved forebears arrived involuntarily), Chinese, and Japanese. The national origins scheme was purposefully designed to build up a northwestern European vision of American identity and nationality, a vision whose architects wished to have no truck with other groups or races: segregated race relations complemented this external strategy.

In practice, the 1920s legislation worked in several ways. First, the number of immigrants entering the United States annually was reduced, a trend undoubtedly helped initially by the ravages of the Great Depression, which froze the American labor market's pulling powers. Second, the bias toward European immigrants succeeded, since few Asians or Hispanics entered the United States in these decades. By 1965, under the national origins allocations, three countries—the United Kingdom, Ireland, and Germany—were entitled to

Table 8.1 Immigration Levels, 1951–1960

Country	Present Quota	Average immigration, 1951–1960
Europe		
Austria	1,405	2,968
Belgium	1,297	1,292
Czechoslovakia	2,859	2,880
Denmark	1,175	1,370
Finland	566	668
France	3,069	3,802
Germany	25,814	34,545
Greece	308	4,844
Hungary	865	6,455
Ireland	17,756	6,455
Italy	5,666	18,700
Latvia	235	1,913
Lithuania	384	1,186
Netherlands	3,136	4,719
Norway	2,364	2,467
Poland	6,488	12,798
Portugal	438	2,043
Romania	289	1,743
Spain	250	1,072
Sweden	3,295	1,886
Switzerland	1,698	1,719
Turkey	225	684
United Kingdom	65,361	20,887
U. S. S. R.	2,697	4,650
Yugoslavia	942	5,866

70 percent (108,931) of the places (from a total of 158,503). The remainder of Europe was entitled to 40,483 quota places, and for all other countries, the total of quotas was 9,089 (Table 8.1). However, the bald effect of these allocations over time was mitigated. Within the national origins quota, there was much greater demand from the European nationalities that were awarded the smaller quotas (that is, central and southeastern countries) than from the privileged nationalities of northwestern Europe. Between 1932 and 1950, the former groups contributed twice as many immigrants as permitted by their quotas, whereas northwestern ones contributed less than half their entitlement. The tendency of immigrants from southeastern European

Table 8.1 (continued)

Country	Present Quota	Average immigration, 1951–1960
Asia		
China	205	3,274
India	100	314
Indonesia	100	1,012
Iran	100	291
Iraq	100	190
Israel	100	935
Japan	185	4,467
Jordan	100	511
Korea	100	702
Lebanon	100	337
Philippines	100	1,809
Africa		
Morocco	100	216
South Africa, Union of	100	232
Tunisia	100	137
United Arab Republic	100	618
Oceania		
Australia	100	500
New Zealand	100	189

Source: Derived from data presented in the *Congressional Record—Senate,* August 23, 1963 vol. 109, p. 15770.

countries to be single males, who later brought in their wives and families, underpinned these patterns. Nonetheless, as Reed Ueda notes, the Western Hemisphere overall remained the principal supplier of immigrants between 1929 and 1965: "[W]ith the exception of the Depression years the Western Hemisphere sent large waves of newcomers throughout the restrictionist era because it was exempted from quotas and ceilings. Responding to the labor needs of industry and agriculture, lawmakers had left a gateway open for labor migration from the Western Hemisphere. Canadian and Mexican immigration was especially high, supplying new reserves of labor to fill the shortages caused by restrictions on immigrants from Europe and Asia."[1] In addition, the pressures of the Cold War forced numerous administrative regulations to permit refugees from communist countries the right of entry (see Table 8.2).[2]

Table 8.2 Immigrants Admitted by Special Legislation, 1953–1964

Type and Legislation	Number
Refugees	
Displaced persons (Displaced Persons Act 1948, nonquota)	1,030
Refugees (Refugee Relief Act, 1953)	189,021
Hungarian parolees (act of July 25, 1958)	30,701
Azores and Netherlands refugees (act of September 2, 1958)	22,213
Refugees and escapees (act of July 14, 1960)	6,111
Special legislation nonquota immigrants	
Orphans (act of July 29, 1953)	466
Skilled sheepherders (act of September 3, 1954, nonquota)	385
Immigrants (act of September 11, 1957)	61,948
Immigrants (sections 2 and 3, act of September 22, 1959)	29,337
Immigrants (act of September 26, 1961)	15,525
Other nonquota legislation (special legislation)	412
Immigrants (act of October 24, 1962)	18,944

Source: Derived from "National Quotas for Immigration to End," *Congressional Quarterly Almanac,* 89th Congress, First Session (Washington, D.C.: CQ, 1965), p. 460.

These empirical trends did not eliminate support for the 1920s system of national origins quotas, however, which remained the operating framework until 1965. The erosion of discriminatory immigration laws occurred in a piecemeal fashion: a 1934 memorandum by the Commissioner of Immigration and Naturalization praised the laws of the 1920s as an embodiment of "the sentiment of the country, including that of the racial and alien groups, and have been effective in the execution of our policy of restrictive and selective immigration."[3] In 1943 the Chinese Exclusion Laws were repealed as a sop to wartime contingencies. The removal of Chinese restrictions was the first inroad into the racial immigration framework. Significantly, the decision reflected foreign policy calculations rather than concerns about domestic politics or the illiberality of immigration policy; it was orchestrated by the Citizens Committee to Repeal Chinese Exclusion.[4] Racial restrictions were excised in respect to India and the Philippines in 1946.

The chapter concentrates on the efforts to dismantle the national origins regime established in the 1920s. It begins with a discussion of the exemption of Mexico from this latter legislation and then examines the defense of national origins, concluding with the enactment of the 1965 law.

The Fluidity of Whiteness

The Johnson-Reed act of 1924, as effected in the 1929 regulations, made no specifications about immigrants from Mexico and Canada. Legislating for Mexicans, without enacting limits for the rest of South America and Canada, was politically unwise, as a member of Calvin Coolidge's administration recognized in 1927: he considered it "inconceivable" that "for the sake of preventing a relatively insignificant migration from Mexico, the undesirability of which is at least questionable, we should endanger our good relations with Canada and Latin America."[5] Those Mexicans who did migrate between the United States and their homes provided valuable cheap labor and were especially welcomed during the First World War, which was causing a labor shortage. Robert Divine calls attention to Senator Reed's commitment to Pan-Americanism as an important motive for these exemptions. Divine observes that the majority of senators "believed traditional American policy toward Latin America demanded favorable treatment of these countries in immigration policy. Senator Reed, the leading restrictionist in the Senate, appealed to the idea of Pan-Americanism as justification for exempting Canada and South America."[6] The extremely modest scale of immigration from Latin America, including Mexico, ensured that the sorts of concerns articulated in the 1980s and 1990s were remote from policy-makers' concerns. Mexicans, however, were rarely welcomed as permanent residents in the United States, and during the years of the Great Depression in the 1930s, hundreds of thousands of Mexicans were expelled by immigration officials. A similar pattern was repeated during the Second World War and its aftermath: welcomed during the period of wartime labor shortage, Mexicans in the 1950s were subject to Operation Wetback, a Justice Department initiative that was devised to repatriate them forcefully.[7]

Omitting Mexico and Canada, especially the former, alarmed eugenists (such as Harry Laughlin) and other policy-makers who feared that unregulated immigration from Mexico would damage the national origins principle successfully embodied in the new law.

Americanizers had also been exercised by the failure of Mexicans to learn English and to assimilate. In one study in 1920, Mexican immigrants were castigated as one of the "exceptions" by failing to join "the great melting pot of American Amalgamation." The same observer, Colonel Mans, noted that "this exception has not only been well marked among that large portion of the Mexican population absorbed with the territory acquired as a result of the Mexican War, but also holds true with the hundreds of thousands of Mexicans, who since 1848 have emigrated to the United States and become identified with America."[8] He described the attitudes and practices of Mexicans settled in Texas:

> [F]rom a careful study in Texas, where over 500,000 of the Spanish-American people live, I find but a small percent among the adults who speak English, although many of such families have lived in Texas for generations. Not only is this true but there are thousands of such native born Mexicans who are still celebrating the national holidays of Mexico and regarding the flag of that republic as theirs.

The report continued:

> There are hundreds of small towns scattered throughout Texas where the population is almost entirely Mexican, where English is rarely spoken. Indeed in some of the towns along the Rio Grande all of the County officials are Mexican, and Spanish is not only the official language in those towns, but juries are empanelled from men who do not understand a word of English. Necessarily the entire proceedings of such courts are transacted in the Spanish language.[9]

A report for the Chamber of Commerce in 1939 took a less benign view of Mexican immigrants, identifying "the failure to extend its provisions to countries of the Western Hemisphere" as "the outstanding defect" of the Immigration Act of 1924. It added that "the restrictions imposed upon entries from Europe stimulated an influx of a most undesirable class of aliens from Mexico, Central and South America and from our own possessions in the West Indies."[10]

Mexicans were not excluded from rights of citizenship: "[T]he Mexicans in the border states are classed with the white population and allowed by law the same privileges of voting, schooling, riding in the cars, entering hotels, theaters and public places. Generally speaking, Mexican children attend the public schools with American children without class discrimination."[11] This is a further illustration of the historical and sociological constructions of racial categories and distinctions. Mexican children failed to learn English mostly because they left school at a very early age (since "as a rule the Mexican child is bright, intelligent and measures up with the American child quite well").[12] Colonel Mans believed that the clash of cultures—"gentle, courteous and timid" Mexicans with the "brusque and hard driving Anglo-Saxon"—created barriers to Americanization, and he clearly envisaged this latter as a two-way street: "in order to Americanize the Mexican portion of our population we must humanize the Americans."[13]

Despite such periodic concerns about Mexican immigrants, in point of fact, until the 1950s, few Mexicans moved permanently to the United States. Many came as migrant workers but did not make the United States a permanent residence. Nonetheless, for the eugenist Harry Laughlin, exempting the potentially damaging Mexicans was an error. Those who were used to employing Mexican immigrant labor, principally farmers and other employers in the Southwest, proved sufficiently well organized to resist the demands of eugenists and others (including organized labor and the patriotic societies) to end Latin American immigration. Mexico and the other Latin American countries benefited from their membership in the Western Hemisphere, a sphere that many in Washington wished to safeguard. Divine points to the considerable difficulties facing advocates of Mexican restriction (Canadians were more or less welcomed): if restrictionists "advocated a quota for all Western Hemisphere countries, as they did at first, they were faced with opposition from northern border states which were sympathetic to Canada and from the many advocates of Pan-Americanism. On the other hand, if they supported a quota for Mexico alone, as they later did, they were open to the charge of flagrant discrimination against a neighboring country."[14] The charge of "flagrant discrimination" was probably not one of great concern to most restrictionists, but politically orchestrating a majority in favor of their proposal proved elusive.

More recently, political scientist Clare Sheridan argues that the debate about Mexican immigration in the 1920s was one that bore fundamentally on the "whiteness" of American identity and citizenship. Sheridan writes that "anti-immigration forces raised the specter of a permanent Mexican presence in the United States not as citizens, but as a peon class injurious to national character or 'Americanness.'"

The alarm about Mexicans was exploited to reinforce American identity as white: the restrictionist debates was "about American identity and citizenship—not the citizenship status of Mexicans, but about the meaning of citizenship for *whites*."[15] Such a view, well supported in Sheridan's analysis of racialist and eugenic arguments concerning Mexican immigrants in the 1920s, is further testimony to how the immigration debates in this decade contributed to American political development, in this instance to eligibility for full membership and the advantaging of whiteness. More generally, Table 8.3 illustrates just how successful U.S. restrictionist legislation was in respect to designated nationalities.

Defending National Origins

The national origins system was regularly defended and not infrequently praised by politicians in the 1940s and 1950s. A report of the Senate Judiciary Committee in 1950[16] concluded that despite the experiences of the Second World War, the system was the one most appropriate for U. S. immigration policy: "without giving credence to any theory of Nordic superiority, the subcommittee believes that the adoption of the national origins quota formula was a rational and logical method of numerically restricting immigration in such a manner as to best preserve the sociological and cultural balance of the

Table 8.3 Immigrant Aliens of Specified Races Admitted to the United States from June 30, 1899 to June 30, 1949

Years Included	Chinese	East Indian	Japanese	Korean	Pacific Islander	Filipino*
1900–1909	19,182	3,989	142,536	7,749	788	
1910–1919	18,885	3,184	77,257	996	132	
1920–1929	25,523	1,286	40,482	643	82	
1930–1939	2,687	179	2,367	85	6	247
1940–1949	7,764	153	904	86	18	3,039
Total, 1899–1949	75,679	8,806	266,941	9,581	1,198	3,286

* Filipinos were counted as aliens only from the enactment of the Philippine Independent Act of 1934.

Source: Derived from *Monthly Review*, Immigration and Naturalization Service, January 1950, and NAACP Washington Bureau, Part I, Box I-107, Folder: Immigration, 1952.

United States."[17] Keith Fitzgerald concurs with this interpretation, observing of this substantial Senate inquiry, based on extensive testimony and compilation of statistical evidence, that it "betrayed a sympathy with the goals of the National Origins Act: to preserve the numerical dominance of Northern and Western European ethnic groups within the population as a whole." Crucially, "the report criticized the failure of the law to achieve these ends rather than the ends themselves."[18] These assessments came two years before the passage of the Immigration and Nationality Act (1952), which also placed a ceiling of 2,000 on immigrants coming from the Asia-Pacific triangle.[19]

The 1952 Act gave little direct credence to the racial and eugenic arguments in support of the national origins system, as Vialet notes, simply allowing the system in place to continue and thereby permitting such assumptions to persist: "[I]n contrast to the 1920s, the case for the national origins system in the early 1950s was not generally argued on the grounds of racial superiority. Instead the argument was based partly on sociological theories of the time relating to cultural assimilation."[20] But this interpretation may be too kind. In its evaluation of the legislation, the NAACP was critical of its racialist premises: "McCarran says his Bill has eliminated racial restrictions. Don't Let Him Fool You. It Hasn't. In a very subtle way, this Bill draws the racial line even more tightly for people from the Asia-Pacific area and the West Indies."[21] The legislation erected "additional barriers to entry" in respect to applicants from the West Indies.[22] Discussions of assimilation assumed a melting-pot process, or as senators critical of the 1952 law concluded, "the McCarran Bill looks backward to 1920 and uses our population of thirty years ago as the basis for computing quotas today."[23] Thus, the 1952 law not only failed to abrogate the national origins system but also augmented it with additional racist measures, as President Truman's commission underscored: the 1952 Act adds

> some important racist provisions which, in fact, depart from the basic theory of the national origins system itself. The 1952 act requires the establishment of separate subquotas for colonial dependencies in the Western Hemisphere, a provision which has generally been regarded as discriminatory against the colored people of the Caribbean area. The 1952 act likewise defines a special geographic area known as the Asia-

Pacific Triangle. The people of that area are given a special limited racial or Oriental quota, regardless of the place of their birth—a departure from the origins principle.[24]

Defenders of national origins in Congress in the 1950s and 1960s rehearsed the earlier claims of their predecessors in the 1920s.

The 1952 Act also reflected the political pressures of the Cold War, these thwarting efforts by President Truman and congressional allies to liberalize the restrictions inherited from the 1920s. This fact is interesting since external pressure at the same period did contribute to the desegregationist movement.[25] Nonetheless, the national origins system garnered its critics. Vetoing the 1952 Bill (a veto overwhelmingly overturned by Congress), President Truman remarked that the "basis of this quota system was false and unworthy in 1924. It is even worse now. It is incredible to me that, in this year of 1952, we should again be enacting into law such a slur on the patriotism, the capacity, and the decency of a large part of our citizenry."[26] Emanating from the president, this is a strong statement, and it vindicates the critics of the 1924 law who maintained that its designers used spurious grounds to differentiate between desirable and undesirable immigrants. Truman's intervention implies a fundamental opposition to the immigration policy established in the 1920s: the 1952 act "embodied the political choice of limiting immigration by continuing the national origins quota system which had become an institution, albeit a controversial one, after 30 years of existence."[27] The 1952 act introduced a new emphasis on highly skilled immigrants, who were to receive 50 percent of the quota places. A second preference, for 30 percent of the immigrants, was created for parents of U. S. citizens over the age of twenty-one and unmarried adult children of U. S. citizens. Permanent resident aliens wishing to bring in spouses and unmarried children received 20 percent of places.[28]

The Walter-McCarran Act finally ended the bar on certain races' eligibility for naturalization. Naturalization was now made open to all. The act also formally removed race as a bar to immigration. Nonetheless, the 1952 legislation was itself subject to intense criticism in the report of a presidential commission established by President Truman after his veto (of what some critics daubed "this Bill of Abominations"[29]) was overturned; the report wanted the immigration law "reconsidered and revised from beginning to end." Its authors recommended abolishing the national origins system and replacing it with a "unified quota system, which would allocate visas without regard to national origin, race, creed or color."[30] The authors concluded that the existing immigration and nationality law "rests upon an attitude of hostility and distrust against all aliens" and "applies discriminations against human beings on account of national origin, race, creed and color."[31] They wanted greater openness in the numbers of immigrants admitted and elimination of restrictive categories. These laudable proposals had no immediate effect on policy, though. There were strident voices in the Congress who opposed the racism of the 1924 Act, however, and who urged radical reform in 1952. Notably, Adam Clayton Powell, commenting on the proposal in the 1952 legislation to set up quotas for Jamaica, Trinidad, and other colonies in the British West Indies, declared that "nothing could be more damaging to our world prestige than the alienation of the support of the one bill for the peoples of the colored race in this most critical period."[32] Powell was drawing attention to the postwar international context in which decolonization and antiracist movements had become significant voices.

Efforts by the Eisenhower administration, keenly supported by the president, to reform the regime that was consolidated in the 1952 legislation largely failed. Reforms creating a more generous policy toward political refugees, especially from communist regimes (including the Refugee Relief Act of 1953),[33] were enacted, but the basic elements of the immigration framework remained untouched. Substantial amendments were crushed by persistent congressional support for the system created in the 1920s. Supporting legislation in 1957[34] to extend the refugee system, Senator James O. Eastland, chairman of the Senate Judiciary Subcommittee on Immigration, assured his colleagues that "in making these adjustments the bill does not modify the national origins quota provisions which have been a part of our immigration and nationality system since 1924, and which were carried forward in the Immigration and Nationality Act [1952]."[35] Such temporary reforms were necessitated by the humanitarian casualties of political repression, particularly in communist countries.

The controversial nature of the national origins system was evident in congressional debates about immigration policy. Introducing a bill to reform it in 1963, Senator Philip Hart (D-Mich.) told his colleagues that the "essence of our democratic credo is the dignity of

man. Our constant effort to implement fully this credo, and our vigi-
lant protection of America's heritage, require that our immigration
policy be brought in line with the moral and ethical principles upon
which our democracy is based."[36] Hart argued that the policy inherited from the 1920s compromised American democratic institutions:
"[O]ur present quota system's discriminatory provisions continue to
generate skepticism relative to America's practice of democracy. In
these anxious times it is important that we bring our basic immigration law into line with our more tolerable practice, and with our traditions and ideals."[37] Hart was a consistent proponent of immigration
reform, seeking both the elimination of national origins quotas and a
rationalization of the myriad of amendments and laws passed, in the
1950s and early 1960s, to aid political refugees and asylum seekers.
He introduced letters and other documents of support into the *Congressional Record* throughout 1963 and 1964 as part of his campaign
for reform.

The chairman of the House Judiciary's Subcommittee on Immigration and Nationality until 1963, Congressman Francis E. Walter (D-
Penn.) was a staunch defender of national origins. He served in the
House between 1933 and 1963 and, by 1962, had "blocked all previous efforts at revision."[38] In 1962 he initiated hearings in Congress on
immigration to inform future policy, an exercise that resulted in eighteen volumes of reports but no legislation.

Minor revisions to the national origins quota were included in
the 1952 law, but the numbers allocated to Asian countries were remarkably small, precluding a significant growth in the number of
Asian immigrants eligible for naturalization as U. S. citizens. "Race"
was less obviously a barrier to naturalization, but the numbers entitled to exercise this option were small. Asians were allocated against
their country of origin rather than of birth, ensuring that the potential
number of immigrants was decisively limited. This measure also affected some Europeans. In his autobiography, the historian Peter Gay
records how his family's efforts to leave Nazi Berlin were trammelled
by his father's birth in the part of Silesia that was given to Poland in
1918: "he had been born in that narrow sliver of Silesian territory
turned over to Poland in the peace treaties following the First World
War." This place of birth affected his application to the United States,
since American law required a petitioner for admission to be classified
according to the status of his country of birth when the application

was made. The consequence was plain: "[A]ccording to American immigration authorities, then, my father was a Pole, making him one of fewer than six thousand to be eligible each year. That this provision of the law was sheer nonsense made no difference."[39] In his statement vetoing the 1952 bill (which was overriden by Congress), President Truman expressed appreciation of the dangerous convergence between the national origins system and the discredited racial doctrines underpinning German Nazism: "[T]he greatest vice of the present quota system is that it discriminates, deliberately and intentionally, against many of the peoples of the world. The purpose behind it was to cut down and virtually eliminate immigration to this country from Southern and Eastern Europe. A theory was invented to rationalize this objective. The theory was that in order to be readily assimilable, European immigrants should be admitted in proportion to the numbers of persons of their respective national stocks already here as shown by the census of 1920."[40] Not only was the system discriminatory, argued Truman, but it subverted U.S. foreign policy objectives in fighting communism: "Today, we have entered into an alliance, the North Atlantic Treaty, with Italy, Greece and Turkey, against one of the most terrible threats mankind has ever faced . . . But through this bill we say to their people: You are less worthy to come to this country than Englishmen or Irishmen."[41] An initiator of investigative committees on civil rights and racial inequality in the Armed Services,[42] President Truman was fully acquainted with the inequities of U. S. immigration policy. As Reed Ueda observes of the 1952 law, it "perpetuated the legacy of restriction out of fear that immigration would undermine national strength. The act expressed an isolationist nationalism."[43] Since Truman was no amateur in foreign affairs, his opposition to the legislation is all the more significant.

Ironically, despite the huge political effort expended on implementing the national origins system in the 1920s, its practical effectiveness had evaporated by the 1950s and 1960s. Most obviously, the preferential treatment provided for Western Hemisphere countries was not taken advantage of after World War Two. Only one of three immigrants came from the national origins system. A report in the House of Representatives on the 1965 legislation made this pattern clear: "[T]he national origins system has failed to maintain the ethnic balance of the American population as it was designed and intended since the nations favored with the high quotas have left their quotas largely unused. Immigration statistics establish that only one of every three immigrants, during the last two decades, actually was admitted to the United States as a quota immigrant under the national origins system."[44] After 1945, American immigration trends failed to realize the ambitions of either the 1929 national origins system or the 1952 McCarran-Walter Act: "[B]etween 1946 and 1965, only 57 percent of all immigrants admitted to the United States were from Europe; the percentage was well below that by the early 1960s. Due to the various refugee laws, more southern and eastern Europeans were admitted than was provided for under the quota system."[45] The Western Hemisphere did dominate immigrant numbers, however. Of the two-thirds total annual quota allotted to Great Britain, Ireland, and Germany, many places were unclaimed: in 1964, as one senator remarked, "more than one-half of Great Britain's quota of 65,361 was unused, and more than one-third of Ireland's quota of 17,756 was unused." In contrast, countries with small quotas, such as Greece or Italy, "have lengthy waiting lists of eligible people. The fact that such discrimination is written into the law, in a country which basically believes in equal justice under the law for all men, raises severe doubts about our sincerity."[46] Political refugees received an increasing number of places, and immigrants from Western Hemisphere countries were able to claim the places left under the national origins quotas. Despite this failure to realize the ethnic and racial aims of the 1920s system, its formal abolition was far less automatic.

Domestically, of much greater consequence was the internal migration of African Americans between the 1930s and 1950s from the South to the North. Combined with wartime pressures to desegregate[47] and the civil rights movement of the 1950s, these developments redefined the question of race in the United States as solely one of black-white relations and inequalities.[48] Although the racism of Nazi Germany and the values of victors of the Second World War all pointed to the spuriousness of differences based in unpersuasive biological essentialism—and the fundamentally sociological character of such distinctions—nonetheless, "race relations" after 1945 developed as an intellectual field and policy framework concerned with black-white issues.[49] That this simplistic binary was both consequential and of lasting significance is made plain by the renewed interest in "whiteness" examined in Chapter 2. As Matthew Jacobson points out, the issues that so alarmed Americanizers in the 1920s—about assimilability and the persistence of isolated communities based around ethnic loyalties—had evaporated. This transformation was itself a racialized one, however: "[A] complex system of races had given way to a strict scheme of black and white, which itself implied an absence of race on the white side and a presence of race on the black. The 'ethnic' experience of European immigrant assimilation and mobility, meanwhile, became the standard against which blacks were measured—and found wanting."[50] In this context the new restrictions of 1952 in respect to black immigrants were striking.

Abandoning National Origins: The 1965 Act

The 1965 law was several years in the making. President Eisenhower's initiatives proved abortive. In 1961, President John F. Kennedy, a critic of national origins when he was a senator in the 1950s, entered the White House with a commitment to end the system. He supported bills introduced in Congress in 1961 and 1962 to scrap the system. Before his assassination, Kennedy drafted legislation to phase out the national origins quotas at the rate of 20 percent a year. Echoing the very criticisms leveled at the system when it was established in the 1920s, Kennedy lambasted immigration policy, identifying it as his "most urgent and fundamental reform." He explained that "the use of a national origins system is without basis in either logic or reason."[51] These criticisms go to the heart of why the national origins system operated as a racial mechanism.

President Lyndon Johnson picked up the mantle—informing Congress in January 1965 that an immigration bill was planned—and pushed through the 1965 law (or technically amendments to the 1952 law). In his 1965 State of the Union address, President Johnson declared, "let a just nation throw open the city of promise to those in other lands seeking the promise of America, through an immigration law based on the work a man can do and not where he was born or how he spells his name." Submitting his bill on immigration, Johnson described the national origins framework as "incompatible with our basic American tradition."[52] The legislation nicely complemented his other two major democratic reforms, the Civil Rights Act of 1964 and the Voting Rights Act of 1965. Together, these three pieces of legislation consolidated democratic principles and institutions in the United States, as one observer correctly comments: "[P]ublic support for the repeal of the national origins quota system reflected genuine changes in public attitudes toward race and national origins. The 1965 immigration legislation was as much a product of the mid-sixties, and the predominantly Democratic 89th Congress which also produced major civil rights legislation, as the 1952 Act was a product of the Cold War period of the early 1950's."[53] This account rather neglects the sources of the scheme operative in the 1920s.

Speaking in the Senate in 1963, Senator Hiram Fong (from Hawaii) remarked that "America's agonizing reappraisal of her racial policies and practices is manifest in our Birminghams and Cambridges, our New Yorks and Chicagos, in the demonstrations and disturbances stirring many communities across the Nation." He counseled a reconstruction of immigration policy to complement the domestic attempts to establish equality, "because the racial restrictions inherent in our present immigration laws disparage our democratic heritage." These restrictions contradicted "the spirit and principles of the Declaration of Independence, the Constitution of the United States, and our traditional standards of fairness and justice."[54] Fong expatiated on the connection between domestic inequality and a discriminatory immigration policy:

> [A]t home, we have wiped out racial barriers. . . We are making significant progress in desegregating our public schools, housing, business, and public accommodations, and protecting the voting rights of all citizens. It is imperative that we, as a Nation, recognize this great upheaval in our Nation and throughout the world for equal status. . . We have erected racial barriers that deny equal dignity and respect to more than one-half of the world's population. These racial barriers are bad for America. They hurt America's image as the leader of the free world. For example, do Senators know that under present American immigration quotas for Asia and the Pacific areas more than 50 percent of the people who populate our newest State could be almost totally excluded from the United States? That Ireland, with a population of 2,815,000 has a larger quota than all Asia, with a population of nearly 1.5 billion?[55]

Fong itemized eight ways in which extant immigration policy discriminated between foreign groups (and see table 8.1). First, national origins quotas in 1965 were given only to white nations: "Polynesians, orientals, and Negroes were totally excluded."[56] The 1952 law modified this restriction modestly by giving 100 places each to oriental, Polynesian, and African countries. In the House of Representatives, Congressman Libonati (D-Ill.) made a similar point, complaining that the national origins system "excluded the descendants of slave immigrants from total population figures—a sad commentary upon honest thinking to disclassify in citizenship almost the entire Negro population."[57] Second, the 1952 Act gave only 1.53 percent of annual immigration quotas to countries in the Asia-Pacific triangle. Third, "while place of birth determines the quota under which a white person would fall, race, or ancestry is determinative for Polynesian and oriental persons."[58] Fourth, a special quota of 100 existed within the Asia-Pacific category for the thousands of oriental and Polynesian people living around the world. Not surprisingly, there was disagreement about who should be included in this small quota. Fifth, the law in respect to China was idiosyncratic. It had two quotas: one of 100 for the white persons born in China and one of 105 for Chinese people irrespective of where they were born. Sixth, orientals living in Eastern Hemisphere countries were charged to a general quota. Seventh, the law continued to penalize immigrants from central and southeastern Europe: "the combined quotas for Greece, Turkey, and Spain, for example, come to 783, which is roughly one-third of the quota we allot to Norway."[59] Eighth, the treatment of dependents differed by race: "under the 1952 act, an Asian family of mixed blood may be separated in migration if the wife is accountable to an oversubscribed quota, although her husband is chargeable to an open quota." This treatment contrasted with a non-Asian wife accountable to an oversubscribed quota, who could be given the quota of her immigrant husband, if he had access to an open quota.[60]

Michigan's senator, Philip Hart, praised Fong's inventory of the discriminatory clauses in U. S. immigration policy as "definitive," and he restated his conviction that "an immigration policy with different standards of admissibility for different racial and ethnic groups, a policy with unjust strictures against family unification, in short, a policy with built-in bias, should have no place on our statute books."[61] Senator Paul Douglas (D-Ill.), speaking in 1965, criticized American immigration law for discriminating "against Asians and southern Europeans who wish to come to the United States to live, by allotting to them unreasonably small portions of this quota."[62] He somewhat icily reminded the senators of the foreign-policy implications of the national origins system: "I hope the well-meaning people who support the present law as a guardian of the national character will take heed of the problem which it poses for our representatives abroad, who must reconcile the national origins system with our claims of equality for all."[63] Similar inconsistencies had faced U. S. diplomats in respect to the country's segregated race relations.

The ideological and political support that underpinned the enactment of the national origins system in the 1920s had dissipated by the mid-1960s. It is not coincidental that the 1965 Immigration Act was enacted in the wake of the country's civil rights movement: the incongruity between racial exclusion of designated immigrants and the inadequacy of domestic democratization measures was never more graphic. Massachusetts Senator Edward Kennedy told the Congress that the old patriotic societies no longer defended the system: "[A]ll recognized the unworkability of the national-origins quota system and at the close of the meetings agreed to cooperate in finding a new formula for the selection of immigrants. No significant opposition to eliminating the national-origins quota system was organized by any of their organizations."[64] In 1979, Senator Kennedy denounced the inheritance bequeathed by the 1952 law, declaring that "it was flawed from the beginning with discriminatory and anti-alien provisions. Some of the more blatantly racist and objectionable sections—such as the national origins quota system and the Asia-Pacific Triangle provisions—were repealed in 1965. But not much else was changed."[65]

President Johnson's bill[66] was introduced by Representative Emmanuel Celler (D-N.Y.) and Senator Hart. Both Francis Walter's replacement with Michael A. Feighan (D-Ohio) and the massive Democratic victory of 1964 (producing an almost 2 to 1 majority for the party) augured well for change (despite Feighan's long-standing feud with Judiciary chairman Celler). Feighan's support was important to the passage of the Act. He was committed to ending the national origins quota system, particularly in contrast to his predecessor, Representative Francis Walter, who had consistently deflected initiatives to reform it.[67] Feighan had previously introduced legislation to reallocate unused quota places on grounds other than race or nationality. His decision in 1964 to schedule hearings on the revision of the national origins system provided the opportunity for the first such hearings in twelve years. Tensions between Celler and Feighan marred but did not prevent the legislative process.[68]

The bill was signed into law by President Johnson on October 3,

1965, after a lengthy and frequently contentious legislative process. The 1965 act abolished national origins as the basis for quota allocation between immigrants. This fundamental change was not designed to open the United States to increased numbers of immigrants but simply to end inequities in the selection of immigrants. The new law stated that "no person shall receive any preference or priority or be discriminated against in the issuance of an immigrant visa because of his race, sex, nationality, place of birth, or place of residence," thereby ending national origins quotas and the Asia-Pacific triangle. The new arrangements regarding national origins became operative on July 1, 1968. The 1965 law set an annual aggregate of 170,000 immigrants from the Eastern Hemisphere (within a total of 270,000), though no single country could claim over 20,000 places, and introduced a new preference system under which immigrants could apply. (As with previous legislation, these numbers did not include spouses or children of immigrants.) The new preferences favored highly skilled immigrants, though efforts systematically to restrict Western immigration numbers failed.[69] Political refugees received formal status. The national origins arrangement was abrogated, though the new emphasis on kin-based immigration continued to favor groups already present in the United States, and the new system was criticized for this reason (see later). Restrictionists and nativists who had driven previous immigration decisions were mute,[70] except for organized labor, which was suspicious of the preference accorded to the highly skilled. The 1965 bill replaced the term "feebleminded" with "mentally retarded" to refer to those excluded on grounds of severe learning disability.

Ending the national origins system was opposed by Senators Everett Dirksen (Republican) of Illinois and Sam Ervin (Democrat and later chair of the Senate Watergate hearings) of North Carolina; however, after Johnson's landslide victory for the Democrats in Congress in 1964, the oppositional power of the Republicans was depleted. They wanted a ceiling set on Western Hemisphere immigration, claiming that existing trends implied a rapid escalation, especially from South American countries. President Johnson acceded to this demand, while also won over about the argument for family- or kin-based preferences. The ceiling was put at 120,000 for the Western Hemisphere, operative from 1968. Backlogs in this quota and undersubscription in the Eastern Hemisphere quotas forced changes in 1976 and 1978 that ended the distinction between the hemispheres and set a world ceiling of 290,000 immigrants per annum.

Dirksen's and Ervin's support for the family-based preference system was crucial: it permitted a modern version of the national origins system in that it naturally favored nationalities *already present* in the United States. In the Senate debate, however (between September 17 and 22, 1965), Senator Ervin expressed more annoyance with anti-national origin lobbying tactics than with the argument that it should be replaced. Ervin's reasoning was often tortuous (including the implausible claim that "one of the chief virtues of the national origins quota system . . is the fact it places the control of quota immigration in the hands of the mathematicians rather than in the hands of the politicians").[71] He favored "retaining our basic immigration law in substantially its present form."[72] Other southern senators (such as Thurmond, South Carolina; McClellan, Arkansas; Ellender, Louisiana; and Eastland, Mississippi) were much more critical of the new bill and robustly defended the national origins system.

Texan Congressman O. C. Fisher also defended national origins criteria, though the logic of his position was not compelling; it rivaled some of the more perverse defenses of segregation: "[T]he alleged discrimination is, of course, ridiculous. Since admissions from various European countries is now based upon the ratio of people from those nations who were here in 1920, it would be just as sensible to contend that the Italians, the Russians, the French, others discriminated against this country because more of them did not choose to emigrate here prior to 1920."[73] His congressional colleague Richard S. Schweiker (R-Penn.) took the obverse view and urged enactment of the new law in order that "all the discriminatory aspects of our immigration policy" would be eliminated: "let us fashion a new law which eliminates all discrimination on the basis of national origin and asks only of a man what he can contribute to the American civilization of 1965."[74] This view was shared by a New York congressman who complained that "for all too long America's immigration and naturalization laws have been in conflict with our national history and ideals . . . our present policy actually discriminates among applicants for admission into the United States on the basis of accident of birth. The national origins system thus implies that people from one country are more desirable than people from another."[75] In fact, the system did not "imply" this; it enshrined the principle in law. These were not isolated voices; such views garnered widespread support in the House of Representatives, from both Democrats and Republicans. The sorts of groups who had lobbied most intensely for the national origins system in the 1920s offered only mild opposition to the new law, apparently placated by the proposed numerical limit on the number of immigrants from either the Western or the Eastern Hemisphere. An impressive list of organizations—including the American Federation of Labor and Congress of Industrial Organizations (AFL-CIO), the National Committee for Immigration Reform (whose members included former Presidents Truman and Eisenhower), the American Immigration and Citizenship Conference, and various organizations representing ethnic groups (especially Italians, Greeks, and Japanese) in the United States—campaigned for the reform. An opinion poll conducted in the summer of 1965 found support for removing the national origins system, though not for a significant increase in the number of immigrants.[76] The chairman of the National Americanism Commission of the American Legion (an organization intimately involved in the Americanization of the 1920s), Daniel J. O'Connor, favored retaining McCarran-Walker but recognized the probability of reform; consequently, the organization wanted Congress to ensure that no one country had a disproportionate number of immigrants.

Opposition to abandoning the national origins system came from predictable sources, often aligned with the sorts of organizations that had driven the restrictionist reforms of the 1920s. Thus, the American Coalition of Patriotic Societies had an Immigration Committee, chaired by John B. Trevor, Jr., which strongly favored retention of the McCarran-Walter Act. Employing outdated language, Trevor told the House Immigration Committee that the national origins quota system was "based upon our own people" and that "national origins simply attempts to have immigration into the U. S. conform in composition to our own people," precisely the language and arguments of the 1920s. Such assertions received little overt support in 1965, however, and the phrase of "our own people" was quite at variance with the politics of the 1960s.

Overall, the dominant mood in Congress favored reform, with many congresspeople contrite about the discrimination permitted by the national origins system. This view defeated opponents of change. Despite the importance of ending national origins, its replacement with family-based criteria diluted the force of the 1965 reform. The new law "did not do away with selectivity in admission; it only substituted new and less invidious criteria for admission." These new criteria were, "first and principally, relationship to a citizen or lawfully resident alien; second and less heavily weighted, personal qualifications of ability and training; and finally, chronological order of application for admission."[77] This last factor influenced the distribution of admissions significantly in the years after 1965. Japanese Americans had little reason to celebrate the shift to kin-based immigration, for instance, their representatives telling Congress that "there are very few of Asian-Pacific origin in this country who are entitled to provide the specified preference priorities to family members and close relatives abroad." Consequently, "although the immigration bill eliminates race as a principle, in actual operation immigration will still be controlled by the now discredited national origins and the general patterns of immigration which exist today will continue for many years to come."[78] Some critics charged that the diversity lottery, included in the Immigration Act of 1990 (whereby nationals of identified countries could submit applications to the Department of State from which a random number would be awarded a limited number of visas independent of family ties) revived a modest form of national origins, given how it favored groups present in the United States. It was supported by white ethnic groups, notably Irish Americans, and opposed by organizations representing Asian and Hispanic Americans.

The new law provided for a three-year phasing out (from July 1, 1965, to June 30, 1968) of the national origins quota system. Each country outside the Western Hemisphere was limited to an annual total of 20,000 immigrants. In spite of the caveats attached to the law, the legislation constituted a significant change in immigration policy, at least in respect to criteria of race or ancestry: these factors were excluded as grounds for the selection of immigrants.[79] The 1965 act was certainly denounced in later decades by restrictionists,[80] who complained about its effects in opening U.S. immigration to those previously excluded.[81] The 1965 Act (formally an amendment to the 1952 law) was intended by the Johnson administration to abrogate the national origins criterion and the Asia-Pacific limits. These aims were accomplished, but Congress coupled their erosion with new restrictive measures, a ceiling on Western Hemisphere immigration and a labor certification requirement. Such restrictions were not part of the bill's drafters' intent and were in fact opposed by the White House. Congress was able to wield sufficient political pressure to require the inclusion of such restrictions as conditions necessary for the bill's enactment. Furthermore, as one scholar notes, "[A]lthough the administration had overwhelming majorities in both houses of Congress, immigration bills notoriously raise divisive issues that do not follow party lines. So there may well have been reluctance to put party loyalty to the test, a reluctance underlined by the conspicuous defection of conservative Democrats in the Senate."[82] President Johnson's renowned legislative skills[83] undoubtedly facilitated lawmaking in an area that had notoriously become a quagmire for other policymakers.

Conclusion

Among European immigrants, central and southeastern Europeans gained from the 1965 reform, building on their successes in getting immigrants into the United States by exploiting the undersubscription for places under the national origin quotas. The other major trend after 1965 was a veritable explosion in the number of immigrants from the Eastern Hemisphere. Between 1970 and 1990, the Asian-American population grew from 1.5 to 7.3 million, whose members were mainly immigrants and whose country of origin was diverse. Politically, Asian Americans have become a significant force since the early 1980s, in a way largely independent of the past discriminatory experience of Chinese and Japanese Americans. This result was unanticipated. Simultaneously, immigration from Mexico and Central America rose, as did the numbers coming from South America. Once in the country, these groups immediately affected the backlog system (until 1963, Asian immigrants labored under an absolute limit of 2,000 per year). Mexicans had unlimited access until 1976.

The changes to Western Hemisphere immigration enacted in the 1965 legislation permitted an increase in the numbers from the countries in that hemisphere. A ceiling of 120,000 was set in the law, operative from July 1, 1968, and these places were rapidly taken up. In fact, a backlog of applicants for permission to enter as immigrants quickly formed: by 1976, the backlog meant that there was a waiting period of two-and-a-half years for a visa for applicants from this hemisphere.[84] In 1978, ceilings by hemisphere were abolished, and a worldwide ceiling was instituted.

Between 1966 and 1991, 15.53 million immigrants were admitted to the United States, mostly regulated by the 1965 law. In the thirty-six years predating 1965, the national origins system admitted a total of 5.8 million immigrants.[85] Exempted from both the 1924 and the 1952 laws, Mexicans migrating to the United States faced relatively easy entry. Thus, although tens of thousands of illegal immigrants or aliens were deported by the U. S. Immigration and Naturalization Service (INS) in the 1950s, the numbers of Mexican migrants steadily grew: in 1952, 200,000 temporary Mexican bracero workers[86] and over 300,000 in 1954 were admitted;[87] there was also substantial illegal immigration from Mexico and elsewhere (Table 8.4). The migration of temporary Mexican workers from the mid-1940s did not interest the principal restrictionists in Congress, such as Senator Pat McCarran, the cosponsor of the 1952 legislation. Later trends are considered in the next chapter.

Two concluding points bear underlining. First, the national origins system failed in practice to structure immigration patterns to the degree hoped for by its architects. This failure arose from unanticipated circumstances rather than from opposition to its discriminatory principles or from inadequate implementation. Furthermore, the contradiction between its discriminatory framework, supplemented in 1952, and U. S. democratic principles was clear. Second, the urge to distin-

Table 8.4 Aliens Apprehended, Deported, and Required to Depart, 1941–1976

Years Included	Number of Aliens Apprehended	Total Number of Aliens Expelled	Number of Aliens Deported	Number of Aliens Required to Depart
1941–50	1,377,210	1,581,774	110,849	1,470,925
1951–60	3,584,229	4,013,547	129,887	3,883,660
1961–70	1,608,336	1,430,902	96,374	1,334,528
1976	875,915	793,092	27,998	765,094

Source: Derived from U. S. Department of Justice, *Annual Report of the Immigration and Naturalization Service*, 1976, p. 126.

guish between types of immigrants has been a persistent one in U. S. immigration policy since the 1880s, most powerfully manifest in the legislation enacted in the 1920s but restated in 1952 and, initially, retained in the family-based system established in 1965. Such a propensity sits uncomfortably with the claim that the United States is a society reluctant to differentiate between its members.

PART FOUR

Legacies

CHAPTER NINE

After Americanization:

Ethnic Politics and Multiculturalism

The earnest Americanizers of the interwar years now appear dated. Not only would the idea of systematically instilling a rigorous form of Americanism constitute an improbable political agenda, but also the political developments since the 1960s effectively preclude such an approach. The vast array of individualist and group politics, which are organized across an extraordinary range of causes, renders remote the notion of a mono-Americanization. In part, it was the ascriptive restrictions coincident with this movement that accounts for its datedness. Responses and reactions to the narrowness of traditional Americanism are the subject of this chapter.

Prior to the 1920s, the United States had already undertaken important decisions affecting who were acceptable as members of the polity. Both the Chinese Exclusion Law of 1882 and limits on other Asian immigrants underlined a hostility to non-European immigrants that enjoyed some legislative expression until the middle of the twentieth century. The debate in the 1920s was principally about distinctions between European immigrants. This concentration had obvious implications for the place of both non-European immigrants and African Americans in the United States. By the 1960s and 1970s, the legacies of these biases fed into the group consciousness that fueled the civil rights movement and so-called revived ethnic group politics.[1] That new group consciousness set the context for what Joseph Rhea terms the "Race Pride Movement," which he finds manifest among

Asian Americans, Indian Americans, Latinos, and African Americans[2] and which fueled multiculturalism. The discourse or language of the immigration debate created categories of "desirable" and "undesirable" immigrants, the rejection of which has featured in post-1960s political debate. As the previous chapter reported, the 1920s regulations remained in place, despite their discriminatory character, until the mid-1960s, at which point their abandonment coincided with a more general and national concern with civil rights. These factors interacted: for instance, stressing the attractiveness of old immigrants compared with that of new ones indirectly supported the second-class position of nonwhite Americans, especially African American victims of discriminatory segregation.

For some commentators, these political movements do not dent the achievement of immigration in the United States, in two senses: immigration has improved the lot of vast numbers of people who migrated to that nation; and second, a genuine melting pot has developed, not simply a reflection of Anglo-Saxon values. The historian Reed Ueda takes this latter position: by the 1960s, he argues, "[A] real historical melting pot that was neither Anglo conformist nor homogeneous had formed . . . It produced a shared national culture and a heterogeneous and constantly changing set of ethnic cultures." He adds that "even Anglo-Saxons were in the mix, and they were blending with others too. The changes in the melting pot occurred in a cumulative way, but not with linear simplicity, over a succession of generations. New cultural elements, once recognizably foreign, over time became quintessentially American. Thus the melting pot itself changed irresistibly and unpredictably."[3] This view runs the danger of reifying the "melting-pot" concept itself, since Ueda appears implicitly to acknowledge that the concept of a melting pot promoted in the 1920s was spurious because of its Anglo-Saxon bias. Whether this earlier melting pot can subsequently be transformed is far from self-evident.

This chapter considers two of the consequences arising from the Americanization movement and from the restrictive immigration policy of the interwar period. The first consequence is the revival of ethnic politics since the 1960s, mainly among Americans whose immigrant forebears came from European countries and whose identity was undervalued in the surge to Americanize. The second is the development of multiculturalism, a programmatic ambition of those groups in the United States who conclude that their historical experiences have been belittled or ignored in conventional narratives of U.S. history and who were largely written out of the Americanization process. To return to the issues introduced at the beginning of the book, the proposition advanced in this chapter is that both trends arise, in part, from the way in which immigration policy in the 1920s defined membership of the U.S. polity. In particular, the relatively narrow model of assimilation promoted in that decade's Americanization movement could not but be tested in later years as those Americans who felt unduly marginalized by its assumptions struggled to be recognized politically: the regime underpinning this discriminatory immigration policy was roundly imploded in the 1960s.

A New Ethnic Politics

The reform of immigration in the 1960s and the enactment of the Civil Rights Act of 1964 and of the Voting Rights Act of 1965 proved collectively to be a backdrop to a new politics.[4] Some citizens, defining themselves in terms of groups based often on ethnicity, began to demand a fuller political role. These included both so-called minority groups, such as Native Americans or Latinos or Asian Americans, who were sometimes eligible for special treatment, and older ethnic groups (earlier targets of the antihyphenated American campaign, for instance). For these latter groups, the articulation of a pronounced ethnic identity was both a celebration of their tradition and later a response to affirmative action.

The Resilience of Ethnic Loyalties

Some observers have identified a "white ethnic revival" in the United States since the 1970s. Part of an articulation of a backlash against affirmative action programs, such ethnic soul-searching was also, in Elliott Barkan's view, the "culmination of a cultural searching by second-and-third generation European Americans that coincided with their efforts to secure at last their material gains in contemporary America."[5] Since this alleged "revival" occurred before conflict over affirmative action intensified, Barkan's interpretation is persuasive. Indeed, Oscar Handlin had observed in 1951 that American identity did not imply the "simple conformity to a previous pattern, but the adjustment to a new situation. In the process the immigrants became more rather than less conscious of their own peculiarities."[6] The historical evidence about degrees and types of assimilation is mixed,[7] and the extent of group identity should be not overdrawn. Indeed, Richard Alba warns from his study of ethnic identity that "the transformation of ethnicity has not run its full course among Americans of European ancestry."[8]

An influential interpretation of ethnic politics was developed in 1963 by Nathan Glazer and Daniel Patrick Moynihan, from their study of New York City.[9] They identified five ethnic groups in the city (African Americans, Puerto Ricans, Italians, Jews, and Irish), observing, however, in their revised edition that the inclusion of the first group made little "political" sense and that their prediction about African Americans were flawed: "where the book failed was in determining what **kind** of group Negroes would form. As an ethnic group, they would be one of many. As a *racial* group . . . they would form a unique group in American society." Glazer and Moynihan's reduction of African Americans to an ethnic group was false. Their ethnic group model overlooked the tradition of black nationality movements. They observed that "when we wrote *Beyond the Melting Pot* [in 1963], the alternatives seemed to lie between assimilation and ethnic group status: they now seem to lie somewhere between ethnic group status and separatism."[10] Informing this discussion is recognition of both the distinct position of African Americans in the United States and the unexpected tenacity of ethnic group loyalties and memberships; thus, the authors remark that "the long-expected and predicted decline of ethnicity, the fuller acculturation and the assimilation of the white ethnic groups, seems once again delayed—as it was by World War I, World War II, and the cold war."[11]

A politically influential statement of the white ethnic revival was provided by Michael Novak in his book *The Rise of Unmeltable Ethnics.*[12] This tendency, in Novak's version, can be seen as the return of the issues provoking the national origins framework in the 1920s: the devaluing of some nationalities or ethnic groups (principally southern and eastern Europeans) in comparison with others (northwestern Europeans) and a desire to stress national unity over ethnic traditions. Novak worried about the damage done to ethnic identities and traditions by the individualism conventionally heralded as the centerpiece of American political culture. In this view, the family, religious, and community sources of identity and loyalty were victims of the United States's proclaimed individualism: if individualism was central to identity and success in the United States, then combining it with group loyalties was immensely difficult. Such individualism was the especial providence of the dominant Anglo-Saxon group whose values were central to the Americanization movement and shaped the national origins immigration system. By implication, this deracination of ethnic group loyalty not only arose from "the prevailing American value system, with its dominant myth of self-help," but also had "divided America more deeply even than the issues of war and race."[13] This view of a narrow, European-based, and exclusionary conception of U.S. identity has its defenders still.[14]

Ironically, the renewed interest in their origins and ethnic traditions signified a challenge by these white ethnic groups to the melting-pot ethos, complementing the challenge that was mounted, partly through the civil rights movement, by African Americans. Thus, in his study of white ethnic groups in the United States, Richard Alba alights on a "paradoxical divergence" since the mid–twentieth century: he finds a divergence "between the long-run and seemingly irreversible decline of objective ethnic differences—in education and work, family and community—and the continuing subjective importance of ethnic origins to many white Americans."[15] Alba is drawing attention to the continued and strongly held commitment to an ethnic loyalty articulated by some white Americans. From this finding, Alba posits the emergence of an overarching category of "European Americans" that is in possession of "its own myths about its place in American history and the American identity." He argues that "the transformation of ethnicity among whites does not portend the elimination of ethnicity" but does portend a new one composed of Americans of European background: "the persistence of ethnic identities can thus be understood as an outcome of assimilation in a societal context that remains fundamentally multiethnic and multiracial, and where, therefore, competition between groups defined in ethnic terms remains a powerful force."[16] The renewed interest in ethnic traditions was part of a common interest in retaining a distinct identity and sense of self in an increasingly mass society.

For white Americans with European ancestry, the attachment to ethnic traditions is highly variable, important for some but less so for others. By the 1990s, one scholar, Mary Waters, could conclude that among such individuals, acknowledging an ethnic loyalty varied person by person: "ethnicity is increasingly a personal choice of whether to be ethnic at all, and, for an increasing majority of people, of which ethnicity to be."[17] For white Americans, ethnic background was utterly irrelevant to life chances. The benign effects of retaining ethnic values frequently does not hold for nonwhites, however. Furthermore, the ethnic loyalty that all of Waters's sample opted for constituted, if only indirectly, a further barrier to sharing a common Americanism, reinforcing group divisions. This effect was strengthened by the resurgence of white ethnic values and politics in the 1970s. Waters appreciates this point and writes that "a Polish-American who 'knows he is a Pole, who is proud to be a Pole, who knows the social costs and possibilities of being a Polish worker' is less able to understand the experience of being black in America precisely because of being 'in touch with his own ethnicity.'" She explained, "that is because the nature of being a Pole in America is [one] lacking in social costs, providing employment, and chosen voluntarily."[18]

There are thus two views about the ethnic groups' revival: for Novak and others, it is about defending a traditional European-based notion of Americanism; in contrast, for Waters and Alba, ethnicity is a voluntary identification. It is uncertain which interpretation most accurately characterizes the strong ethnic groups identifiable, if only crudely through housing patterns, in Northeast cities such as Boston and Providence, and middle Atlantic cities such as New York and Philadelphia, where many neighborhoods—self-consciously Irish-American, or Polish-American, for instance—are visible. The sociologist Stephen Steinberg, writing in 1981, opted for the second: "the ethnic revival was a 'dying gasp' [which] did not signify a genuine revitalization of ethnicity, but rather was symptomatic of the atrophy of ethnic cultures and the decline of ethnic communities."[19] Steinberg argues convincingly that the apparent ethnic revival reflected a deep-rooted loss of genuine ethnic values and loyalties, consequential on Americanization, and in order "to pursue the American Dream, to escape from grinding poverty, immigrants realized they would have to shed at least the more obvious marks of their immigrant background."[20] Richard Alba seems to share this view, concluding that "the popular notion of a third-generation return to ethnicity is incompatible with the progressive decline across the generations in the salience of ethnic identities"; consequently, claims about ethnic reinvigoration do "not square with the scanty attention most whites seem to give to ethnic political issues."[21] Yet the pertinacity of a fundamental ethnicity underpinning American identity, which is expressed, for instance, in residential neighborhoods, is striking. The indifferent film *Good Will Hunting* depicts a wholly white Boston, in which the central character's background in a South Boston working-class Irish-American community expresses nothing but confidence in this tradition. No indication of the demise of such ethnic loyalties is presented, though indirectly the narrative underlines the shared whiteness of the community. There may well be a class dimension to the relative significance or insignificance of ethnic loyalties that needs to be conjoined with assessments of ethnic group revival or demise. Labor historians have argued that Americanization occurred along class lines in the 1940s and 1950s,[22] a process that constituted the basis for subsequent community solidarity.[23]

Even if these revived ethnic loyalties are principally symbolic, this possibility does not necessarily render than politically trivial either for those holding them or for others in American society observing them from an excluded position. These ethnic loyalties are certainly part of the factors defining the relationship between whites and nonwhites in American political development, and the decisions of the 1920s acted over the long run to confirm the significance of ethnicity.

These tensions underline the limits of assimilation in the United States.[24] Two responses are possible. Barkan hopes for an "accommodative pluralism." However, such a scheme would be an anathema to a traditional assimilationist such as Arthur Schlesinger, Jr., who derides the idea of an ethnic revival, substituting the term "upsurge," and characterizes its origins as a "gesture of protest against the Anglocentric culture." Schlesinger despairs of the disintegrative effects of ethnicity: "it became a cult, and today it threatens to become a counter-revolution against the original theory of America as 'one people,' a common culture, a single nation."[25] For adherents to an individualist, liberal political tradition, a forceful and strident group-based politics is irreconcilable with the core values of the United States, which has maintained and reinforced itself by assimilating new arrivals into those core values. In respect to immigrants voluntarily migrating to the United States, this is a reasonable expectation, although a greater articulation of ethnic traditions and identities need not be as destructive of the central values as some critics anticipate.

Ethnic Revival and Affirmative Action

The assimilationist model implicit in American politics from the 1920s to the 1960s had worn thin in significant part because of the definitional choices taken in the 1920s about the suitability for membership of the polity and the persistence of discriminatory segregation of African Americans. In that decade, African Americans had to watch national policy-makers pursue a vigorous Americanization program and implement an immigration policy, both of which assumed that the U.S. was a white society.

The renewed interest in ethnicity among descendants of European immigrants posed a serious challenge to the core assumptions of the melting-pot assimilationist model as understood, for example, by Americanizers in the 1920s. Such groups were considered quintessential candidates for "melting," their differences eroded in the process of creating the distinct American identity. Yet it was these very groups who now attempted to emphasize or at least to specify the distinctive values, traditions, and customs that singled out their ethnic heritage, and whom Alba characterizes collectively as "European Americans." There was perhaps a richer tradition of diversity *within* the groups assumed to be most successfully assimilated in the United States polity than commonly appreciated. However, these intragroup divisions appear to collapse in the face of a challenge to the aggregate's whiteness, thereby suggesting that they are less deeply embedded than this latter factor. Ian Haney López, who argues that the rise of new white ethnic groups should be analyzed "as a means of opposing non-Whites," makes a similar point forcefully: although "most Whites entertain a subjective belief in their commonality based on descent from European immigrants," this common heritage assumes political significance "only insofar as it contrasts with that of non-Europeans, that is, non-whites."[26] The retention of a European-American ethnic loyalty, however diffuse its constituent elements or voluntary its adoption, assumes significance as a source of identity directly defined in opposition to nonwhites.

In the 1990s, grievances over affirmative action have accentuated the ethnic identity among some whites.[27] This points to the importance of the redefinition of race in black-white terms in the decades after 1930 when the immigration restrictions were in place. As the quotation from Toni Morrison in Chapter 2 noted, for some nonwhites "American means white," and the terms of this association were strengthened, not loosened, in the 1920s and in 1952. The revival of ethnic groups has to be placed in this context, a point Matthew Jacobson stresses: "the white ethnic revival of the 1960s and 1970s may have been a backlash-creation of the modern civil rights movement; but 'white ethnicity' itself, much earlier on, was in part the creation of a newly invigorated black-white social dichotomy."[28] Delgado and Stefancic argue, that despite the Supreme Court's reversal of "separate but equal" segregation, the language of judicial decisions has returned to that of the late nineteenth century. Comparing the 1896 *Plessy v. Ferguson* decision with the 1981 case *City of Memphis v. Greene* (permitting the construction of a wall separating a white neighborhood from a black one), they conclude that "in both cases, separated by nearly a century, during which much progress in race relations was said to have been made, blacks have been presented with a rhetorical legerdemain that tests both their ability to participate in societal self-deception and their inclination to prevail in the face of it."[29] Haney López also notes that the revival of ethnic traditions "coincided with and came in response to the civil rights movement."[30]

The electoral consequences of affirmative action for racial divisions are addressed by Gilens, Sniderman, and Kuklinski. They conclude that affirmative action—despite the heterogeneity of programs covered by this term—generates immense hostility among white Americans. They write that "even in its mildest form, affirmative action for African Americans generates opposition among a substantial number of whites: almost two out of five (37.4 per cent) oppose making an 'extra effort' to ensure that qualified blacks are considered for college admissions." White opposition increases with other forms of racial preference: "for example, three out of four whites oppose reserving a certain number of job openings for blacks," and the same number reject giving preferences to qualified blacks in decisions about college admissions. Affirmative action measures have an emotional effect, Gilens and his colleagues discover: "not only do most whites express opposition to most affirmative action policies, but many express anger over racial preferences as well." On a scale of 0 to 10 designed to measure anger at affirmative action in jobs and schools, whites have a mean response of 6.3, and 42 percent of Gilens et al.'s sample give responses in the "three most angry categories (i.e., 8–10)."[31] Employing a sophisticated unobtrusive methodology, these scholars find that the level of "anger" is higher than these initial data suggest, with an additional 20 to 30 percent of whites "angry" with such program revealing this hostility when responding to unobtrusive questions. Thus, the aggregate level of hostility is considerable and points to the importance of whiteness in the formation of some Americans' views. Some of the historical sources of this trajectory in American political development lie in the way in which policy-makers conceived of American identity and implemented it in immigration legislation between 1882 and 1965.

Multiculturalism

Multiculturalists advocate equal respect for all cultural and ethnic identities in a political system. Politically, these multiple identities have been integrated into public policy in a way purported to respect the inherent value of each tradition and not to privilege any one tradition over another. Multiculturalism also reflects historical demarcations between different peoples in the United States, as Linda Kerber remarks: "behind the emphasis on multiculturalism lurks the knowledge that not everything melted in the melting pot, that the experience of difference has been deeply embedded in the legal paths to citizenship."[32] Cultural pluralism was its precursor, and some of the anxieties that cultural pluralists expressed in the 1920s have resurfaced in multiculturalism.

The ethnic heritage studies program, authorized by Congress in 1972,[33] was a portent of the multiculturalist agenda. The proposal for such a program, first made in Congress in 1970, was the subject of hearings held by the House Education and Labor General Education Subcommittee. The hearings received testimony from academic historians and ethnic group activists, all of them supporting the proposed program, and citing the historic neglect of ethnic groups' traditions. For example, a sociologist from Notre Dame University told the committee that "most elementary and secondary education stresses the accomplishments of Americans of Anglo-Saxon origin and often ignores other groups. Although studies of ethnic groups have been made, continuing research of their histories and their present roles in society are needed."[34] The executive secretary of the National Council for the Social Studies complained that schools "generally have failed to encourage self-pride in minority students' ethnic groups," thereby understating the "nature of America's pluralistic society."[35] A history professor linked the proposal directly to the events of the 1960s: "[T]he conflict and violence of the 1960s shattered the illusions that America is a 'melting pot' of different ethnic groups. Study of history has equipped Americans badly to deal with present turmoil."[36] Speakers in behalf of African Americans and Mexican Americans concurred in these assessments.

Multiculturalism has been influential (and divisive) in education policy.[37] Nathan Glazer describes the rewriting of the history of the American West for the California school system. The new curriculum "puts everyone in the covered wagons," Asian Americans, Hispanics, and African Americans.[38] Stanford University's decision in 1989 to replace its "Western civilization" paper with a less Eurocentric foundation course attracted considerable publicity, adverse and complimentary. The motive for the reform seems to have been a desire to respond imaginatively and intelligently to the issues raised by multiculturalists. Individual high school teachers, caught up in stark classroom realities, take a low-key view of these revisions, as Glazer learned from one instructor: "he didn't care that much *what* his students read, as long as they could read and write."[39] For critics of multiculturalism, such initiatives, observable in many schools and universities, constitute a direct assault on American values.[40] These critics claim that such initiatives instill a misleading account of U. S. history, distorting the role of influential historical figures and the motives for their choices.

This pressure for multiculturalism has given the question of group rights an urgency in American politics. It complements a more general concern identified by several political theorists with "recognition," the principle whereby a group wants the rest of society to accept or "recognize" it publicly as part of a process of legitimating its place in the polity.[41] The late political theorist Judith Shklar argues, among others, that this ambition for "recognition" is a response to past misrecognitions.[42] Therefore, "recognition" consists principally of the extension of equal rights to those previously excluded and does not inherently require the establishment of special rights or status. For Shklar, it is the granting of equal civil and political rights that is important, not the use to which these rights are put.

This politics of recognition extends to a considerable number of cases in the United States,[43] spanning both ethnic and lifestyle groups, and as more groups are "recognized," so more are likely to be formulated. Historically and politically, the dominant Anglo-Saxon group, which was behind the Americanization movement, that was encountered earlier and whose conception of U. S. identity was a white one, did not require recognition, since their values were coincident with those most prominent in public discourse. This coincidence has been of profound significance for American political development.

Multiculturalism and African Americans

One powerful motive for multicultural curricula was the school desegregation decisions of the 1950s and the historical inequalities made salient by the civil rights movement.[44] These episodes exposed how little attention was given to African American history.[45] In *We Are All Multiculturalists Now,* Nathan Glazer interprets multiculturalism as a manifestation of the United States's failure toward its African American population. And whereas the aim of African Americans until the 1960s was to destroy segregated race relations and to achieve integration and assimilation, since the 1970s the inadequacies of this integrationist project[46] has spurted separatism among some and encouraged multiculturalism. Multiculturalism is a fundamental rejection of the melting-pot ethos. African Americans stand, in Glazer's words, as "the storm troops in the battles over multiculturalism."[47] Providing historical models and reference points in the new curricula is designed to address the neglect of African Americans' experience.

Historically, African Americans were excluded from conceptions of the assimilated American. Woodrow Wilson's and Theodore Roosevelt's attack on so-called "hyphenated Americans" entirely omitted blacks from the realm of American citizenship. These remarks succeeded in offending ethnic Americans *and* ignoring African Americans. It is the legacy of this oversight combined with that of segregated race relations that explains why African Americans are, in Glazer's words, the "storm troops" of multiculturalism, some of whom reject assimilation.[48] In Glazer's view, the explanation for this rejection of assimilation lies "in black experience in America, and in the fundamental refusal of other Americans to accept blacks, despite their eagerness, as suitable candidates for assimilation."[49] Consequently, the assimilationist model as a template for all Americans looks distinctly tarnished.

The historical mistreatment of African Americans until the 1960s undoubtedly gives them a key place in the multicultural debate, as does the way in which their history was included in national narratives. Thus, Leon Litwack correctly underlines how embedded a view of inferiority was among the generation of academic historians dominating education between 1900 and the end of the 1930s: "if mobs lynched blacks with calculated sadistic cruelty, the academic sciences were no less resourceful in providing the intellectual underpinnings of racist thought and behavior, footnoting the subhumanity of black people and helping to justify on 'scientific' grounds a complex of racial laws, practices and beliefs," views not incompatible with the eugenic arguments informing policy in Washington at this time. Litwack continues with particular attention to the academy, indicting historians: "the scholarly monographs and textbooks they authored perpetuated and reinforced an array of racial stereotypes and myths and easily justified the need to impress and quarantine black people."[50] This tendency culminated it the 1930 textbook *The Growth of the American Republic,* by Samuel Eliot Morison, which portrayed slavery as a happy idyll.

Greater attention to African American history should not result in a neglect of the way that other groups were defined out of the mainstream, or whose members suffered numerically under the national origins quotas put in place in the 1920s, and who also have an interest in a broadening of educational curricula. The immigration policy choices of this decade introduced distinctions into the U. S. polity that necessarily weakened the assimilationist ideal, devaluing southeastern European immigrants to the benefit of Europeans descended from northwestern countries. The modern upshot is an ambivalence (among groups outside the Anglo-American group) about both assimilation and Americanization, an ambivalence that has provided some of the political support for multiculturalism.

Responding to Diversity

Ethnic politics and multiculturalism both posit a greater diversity at the core of the U.S. polity than was commonly assumed prior to the 1960s. The civil rights movement of the post-1945 years, whose efforts culminated in the legislation of the mid-1960s, complemented the claims of multiculturalists about the partiality of aspects of U.S. politics as recounted in conventional histories. These developments have provoked responses from both detractors and supporters. Among those opposed to recognizing diversity and plurality as so pervasive in the United States as to prevent a single identity other than one imposed, critics of multiculturalism have been prominent. Supporters of a broader understanding of the U.S.'s political development have attempted to restructure arguments to absorb these recognitions by proposing ways of transcending group distinctions.

Opposing Multiculturalism

Arthur Schlesinger's trenchant critique of multiculturalism centers precisely on its devaluing of the integrative and assimilative elements coalescing the United States's diverse peoples together. In his view, the United States was a "brilliant solution" to the "inherent fragility of a multiethnic society": it created a "brand-new national identity, carried forward by individuals who, in forsaking old loyalties and joining to make new lives, melted away ethnic differences." This historical account is the stuff of conventional school textbooks. For the first immigrants or settlers to the United States, the aim was "not to preserve old cultures, but to forge a new *American* culture." This ambition resulted in a "vigorous sense of national identity."[51] But this view tells the story only from the point of view of voluntary settlers and ignores the plight of those landed involuntarily in the United States. Schlesinger, of course, recognizes this defect and unreservedly admonishes those unwilling to appreciate how deeply racism dented the American ideal and sense of national identity. The difficulty, however, is whether this latter sense of national identity can still be discussed independently of the groups its designers *purposefully* excluded: if it was so successful, then would multiculturalism, ethnic division, and racial hostilities have formed as intensely and deeply as they have? Schlesinger argues that America has seen itself as a "nation composed of individuals making their own unhampered choices," but this self-conception was a misnomer, given the ways in which the choices of immigrants and African Americans were consistently hampered, and the choices of white people promoted, on the basis of group membership. The individualist account presented by Schlesinger may be a good ideal, but to imagine that it dictated historical events or actions is delusionary.

Later in his book, Schlesinger provides an attractively simple defense of this approach: it rests on the "unassailable facts" that, "for better or worse, American history has been shaped more than anything else by British tradition and culture." Such an admission does not, as Schlesinger immediately points out, justify ignoring the malign aspects of this tradition—including "callous discrimination against later immigrants, brutal racism against nonwhite minorities"—but this admission does provide a rationale and explanation for the dominance of the Anglo-American tradition.[52] Criticizing new patterns of self-segregation among some African American students,[53] Schlesinger observes that "institutionalized separatism only crystallizes racial differences and magnifies racial tension,"[54] which is exactly the argument used by opponents of the "separate but equal" framework that operated between 1896 and 1954! The fact that these latter objections fell mostly on deaf ears should alert Schlesinger to the strength of feelings of modern multiculturalists. Indeed, Michael Rogin points out that Schlesinger's own use of blackface, in his history of Jacksonian democracy, is rather innocent, and he advises Schlesinger, the critic of multiculturalism, "to remind himself of what he once embraced as the fancy dress of nationalist popular revival."[55]

In his critique of multiculturalism, James Ceaser stresses the unintended ironic intolerance of its advocates: demanding a broadening of educational curricula and cultural values, such advocates commonly reject Enlightenment liberal principles as the ultimate source of oppression and distinctions of the sort associated with racialist frameworks.[56] This logic results in an absolutism seemingly inconsistent with the very broadening implied by the term "multiculturalism": "given the multiculturalists' rejection of reason and their emphasis on the experience of being Other, their standard presents itself more or less as a passionately held moral conviction." He adds that "victimization is the transfer point where theoretical relativism is laundered and turns into moral absolutism."[57]

Ceaser examines how multiculturalism conflates two terms—race and culture—that earlier generations of writers and academics, not least Franz Boas, strove to keep apart, precisely to avoid "racialism" in academic disciplines: "today multiculturalism has reconnected the concepts of culture and race, if not inside anthropology itself, then in such disciplines as history and literary criticism."[58] Ceaser maintains that this reuniting of the two terms produces a crude coagulation, such as the term Asian Americans, whose constituent members—including, for example, Japanese Americans, Chinese Americans, Korean Americans, and Vietnamese Americans—differ vastly in terms of language and national traditions, a comment applicable to the term "European American" too. Consequently, it is multiculturalists—not some dominant Americanist group—that create these generalizations: "what makes them all members of one culture in America today is the racialist preconception of multicultural theory; it is culture by intellectual ukase and bureaucratic decree."[59] Ceaser does, of course, recognize that any multiculturalist use of racial language is intended to be quite distinct from earlier generations of racialists, such as Madison Grant or Harry Laughlin, for whom biological hierarchies were fundamental and definitional. But Ceaser finds in multiculturalism a moral absolutism; a confusion about the nature of culture ("[C]ultures themselves are usually not multicultural. Cultures tend to be proud of their particularity, which they often regard as superiority");[60] and the absence of empirical knowledge in multiculturalist arguments, of the sort necessary for devising practical policies.

Bilingual education points to some of the difficulties posed by the multiculturalist agenda. On the one hand, many people will salute the principle of providing children with working knowledge of two languages from childhood; in this way, it should open up, rather than close, more doors, as opponents of multiculturalism tend to argue. On the other hand, as practiced, bilingual education has been the preserve of those immigrants' children lacking English as their first language; and rather than providing immersion in English to get them up to a comparable level of the native speakers, bilingualism has often seemed to limit the educational development of its participants. In June 1998, California voters supported the latter view, by a two to one majority, endorsing Proposition 227 to replace bilingual teaching with English immersion classes for immigrant children. The positive vote included a majority of Hispanic voters. Nationally and at the state level, lobbying for laws to make English an official language has garnered considerable support with either statutes or constitutional amendments enacted in over fifteen states.[61] The debate over bilingualism in schools has been divisive. Bilingualism, mostly in respect to Spanish, challenges the assimilationist model of Americanization—just as it was so charged before the First World War when the Americanization movement developed. Its critics claim that (despite the terms of the 1968 Bilingual Education Act and the Supreme Court's

1974 judgment in *Lau v. Nichols* regarding a Chinese-speaking pupil) it ill-prepares children for citizenship. Arthur Schlesinger is driven to apoplexy by this institution: "[B]ilingualism shuts doors. It nourishes self-ghettoization, and ghettoization nourishes racial antagonism";[62] he cites testimony from teachers and observers in support of this assessment.

The criticisms articulated by Schlesinger against multiculturalism find considerable resonance in Peter Salins's recent polemic in favor of traditional assimilation and criticism of multiculturalism. Salins argues that the three principal features of multiculturalism—bilingual education, multicultural curricula and the often explicit disparagement of American institutions and values—weaken the United States's unity and political stability. Because multiculturalism "promotes an agenda of ethnic grievances," and its proponents preclude a "balanced and complex presentation of American or world society and make it unthinkable ever to reverse the good guy, bad guy, it weakens the U.S. polity."[63] The damage is overwhelming in Salins's judgment: "the multiculturalist trashing of America should concern Americans . . . because it robs our children of their most precious birthright: a justifiable pride in the American Idea and the generally enlightened and idealistic trajectory of America's domestic and foreign policies."[64] Yet in common with many critics of multiculturalism, this view shows too little appreciation of how that very "American Idea" has been politically manipulated and just how exclusionary it has often been historically.

Culture and Race

A different sort of criticism has been marshaled by scholars alarmed by the simplicity of assumptions about "cultures" in the multiculturalist debate. The work of Anthony Appiah is especially important here. That the multicultural debate is in part a racial issue is underlined by Appiah. Rather than considering how immigrants became assimilated as Americans in the opening decades of this century, Appiah suggests, in common with other writers, that they became white, a process that did not occur for African Americans; this claim returns to one of the three ways in which immigration structures American political development introduced in Chapter 2, that is, through its promotion of whiteness. It is a point complemented by Justice Thurgood Marshall's dissent in the *Bakke* decision when he observes that "it is unnecessary in 20th-century America to have individual Negroes demonstrate that they have been victims of racial discrimination." This is the situation because "the racism of our society has been so pervasive that none, regardless of wealth or position, has managed to escape its impact." Consequently, "the experience of Negroes in America has been different in kind, not just in degree, from that of other ethnic groups . . . The dream of America as the great melting pot has not been realized for the Negro."[65] The melting-pot assimilationist model has been a racially partial one, premised on the whiteness of those assimilated. Appiah writes that on one reading, "the families that arrived during the turn-of-the-century wave of immigration have assimilated, become American." But there is another interpretation: "[W]e might say that they became white. When the Italians and the Jews of Eastern Europe arrived, they were thought of as racially different both from African-Americans and from the white Protestant majority. Now hardly anybody thinks of their descendants in this way. They are Americans: but unless their ancestors include people from Africa or Asia, they are also white."[66] Whiteness proved a source of commonality among European immigrants, an identity transcending ethnic groups but excluding nonwhites. Culture is itself a historically constituted process: consequently, African American culture is a process that includes the interaction of African Americans with members of other groups in the United States.

The historical importance of the differential treatment of African Americans, most blatantly through segregation and associated discrimination, ensures the continuing utility of whiteness as a politically consequential category. This is an important point. As Appiah remarks, "white people rarely think of anything in their culture as white: normal, no doubt, middle-class, maybe, and even, sometimes, American; but not white. Black Americans, by contrast, do think of much in their lives in racial terms."[67] Pursuing the implications of such a perspective, Ian Haney López calls for white identity to be "dismantled" because it expresses "a hierarchical fantasy that requires inferior minority identities . . . Whites should renounce their privileged racial status . . . because the edifice of Whiteness stands at the heart of racial inequality in America."[68] Appiah adds, "just as the European immigrants became white," so "Africans became blacks here."[69]

Appiah argues for a much greater attention to racial identities than to cultures in any consideration of the diversity constitutive of the United States polity, a sensible proposal.[70] Furthermore, he emphasizes how unsubtle and simplistic the conception of a group's culture is in the multicultural framework. The implication of this reasoning is significant: "African-American identity is centrally shaped by American society and institutions: it cannot be seen as constructed solely within African-American communities. African-American culture, if this means shared beliefs, values, practices, does not exist: what exists are African-American cultures, and though these are created and sustained in large measure by African-Americans, they cannot be understood without reference to the bearers of other American racial identities."[71] American society is composed of diverse identities, the very variety of which is sometimes paradoxically missed by multiculturalists.

A New Cultural Pluralism? Cosmopolitanism

In a widely cited article in 1915, Horace Kallen advanced the idea of "cultural pluralism" as a viable reading of the United States's history and composition, and a deliberate opposition to the melting-pot metaphor.[72] Kallen advocated a celebration of diversity in place of an emphasis on the creation of a single American identity—or rather that American identity should be recognized as composed of diverse elements. He welcomed a common sense of American national identity but was concerned that this should not be achieved at the cost of sacrificing individuals' ethnic traditions and values. Predating the entry of the United States into the First World War and the intensification of hostilities toward the hyphenated Americans, this view of diversity got lost in the animosities generated by the European inferno.

There are important differences between the cultural pluralism advocated in the 1910s and 1920s and multiculturalist arguments. The sorts of claims advanced by Kallen and others were, in practice, not especially open to nonwhite Americans, and indeed part of this cultural pluralism was prompted by white urban Americans' interest in exotic cultures, such as the burgeoning jazz culture and the Harlem Renaissance. Nor were cultural pluralists exercised by social and political inequalities, whereas such concerns have been a primary motive for multiculturalists.

This older cultural pluralism does have echoes of the arguments presented in favor of cosmopolitanism, such as those of Jeremy Waldron and David Hollinger. Waldron advocates a celebration of the cosmopolitan elements that most individuals enjoy in daily life, rather than an expectation that a common conception of a community should prevail. He writes that "we need cultural meanings, but we do not need homogenous cultural frameworks. We need to understand our choices in the contexts in which they make sense, but we do not need any single context to structure all our choices."[73] A direct challenge particularly to communitarians' use of community (and the assumption that identity requires explicit membership of a homogenous group), Waldron's cosmopolitanism does not provide obvious implications for addressing historic injustices experienced by individual members of groups discriminated against, despite the willingness fully to value groups' distinct cultural traditions. It is instead a rather more idealist argument. It also fails to explain why some versions of the values most apposite for a designated community become dominant. The call to pay greater attention to the multiple sources of individual identity and lifestyle presented by Waldron is, nonetheless, a corrective to the unduly oppressive presence of a particular definition of community. Hollinger's appeal—designed to counter the growth of ethnic- or group-based politics in the United States—is for greater respect of individualism and diversity, and a loosening of ethnicity as a category that individuals voluntarily assumed. He wants "each individual and collective unit to absorb as much varied experience as it can, while retaining its capacity to advance its aims effectively"; and he defines his "postethnic" perspective as one premised on the fact that "most individuals live in many circles simultaneously and that the actual living of any individual life entails a shifting division of labor between the several 'we's' of which the individual is a part."[74]

These are worthy agendas, but, nonetheless, cosmopolitanism seems unduly normative, overestimating both the extent to which people can slip in and out of identities voluntarily and the willingness of established social groups, exercising economic and political power, to accommodate new ones. Neither exponent seems fully cognizant of the levels of historical racism and discrimination against which multiculturalism and civil rights politics developed. It is doubtful that reviving an elite-based cultural pluralism provides a cogent framework for understanding deep-rooted group conflicts and political inequalities at the end of the twentieth century.

Conclusion

Both the articulation of new multiculturalist voices and the resurgence of ethnic loyalties expose limits of the melting-pot assimilation model of Americanization. Challenging the melting-pot assimilation model does not necessarily amount to a less individualistic conception of American identity, however. It simply means challenging the idea, as an empirical fact or as a normative theory, that all these cultures can "melt" into anything other than an Anglo white person. Analysis of the historical legacies from which a multiculturalist agenda emerges helps in understanding its appeal and resilience. The underlying need fully to acknowledge the United States's great diversity is the basis from which political debate and public policy can positively move beyond the multicultural debate. That diversity has been formed by inequalities as well as narratives based on success stories.

The development of a politics of group rights poses a fundamental challenge to liberal democracy. The latter is based on a notion of universalist citizenship, rooted in the rights and equality accruing to each individual member. Group rights proponents and theorists reject this universalism, however, arguing that it fails sufficiently to address the position of disadvantaged or marginalized groups. Western liberal democracies pride themselves on the creation of universal citizenship, in which equality of rights is bestowed on all members of the polity. This achievement is normally woven into teleological histories of these political systems that end in the relatively recent past. The stages by which new groups are incorporated into this final democratic state—such as the working class, women, minorities, or immigrants—is documented and delays explained in terms of historical and political contingencies.[75] The standard historical account is perfectly accurate as a description of the status quo and the way it was achieved. However, while the principle of equal membership is laudatory and legally guaranteed, the conventional historical account of the expansion of the rights of citizenship fails, in the case of the United States, sufficiently to analyze the legacies and causes of differential entry or to consider the extent to which previous exclusion or differential treatment creates distinct senses of group identity in the political system. It is precisely at this juncture that the rise of multiculturalism, in respect to historical inequalities or the continued choice of some European Americans to promote ethnic traditions after many generations in the United States, can be explained.

CHAPTER TEN

The Diverse Democracy

At the level of rhetoric and ideology, Americans project an image of the United States as open to diversity (that is, all nationalities and cultures); some celebrate this quality. Many Americans would concur, for instance, with President Truman's committee on immigration when it declared: "[T]he Commission believes that an outstanding characteristic of the United States is its great cultural diversity within an overriding national unity. The American story proves, if proof were needed, that such differences do not mean the existence of superior and inferior classes."[1] For many Americans the common description that "we are a nation of immigrants" has direct resonance, and this deep-seatedness constitutes a barrier to restrictionists. This is not to underestimate the force of the new restrictionist movement or the willingness of some of its numbers unashamedly to advocate a bias toward European and white immigrants,[2] but simply to note the powerful place of immigration in American political rhetoric and ideology. In this concluding chapter, I return to the themes introduced in Chapter 2 to the analysis of immigration in American political development, and then consider the implications of the preceding chapters for broadening the categories in which U. S. politics are analyzed.

Immigration and Americanization

National Origins as the Melting Pot

The immigration policy of the 1920s established a contradiction between the United States's self-image as a liberal polity open to all comers irrespective of 'race' or background and the reality of a racially based admissions procedure. The shift to a quota-based system of immigration from 1929, which used calculations about the national origins of the U.S. population, constituted a way of defining who constituted an "American." The definition biased such an identity toward a northwestern European view of America and toward whites to the exclusion of nonwhites. This bias converged with the views of the energetic Americanizers proselytizing among immigrants in the same decade. The quota-based reforms of the 1920s purposefully restricted the multicultural diversity of the nation and confirmed the statistical proportions of already underrepresented groups. The policy severely compromised the melting-pot rhetoric of immigration policy; concurrently, the aim of finding immigrants assimilable with the dominant tradition tarnished respect for members of the other national groups already present in the United States. Retrospectively, as one scholar comments, "one can take the melting pot seriously as the central process of American civilization only if one thinks that non-white groups are not really part of that civilization."[3] Failure to acknowledge these biases in the melting-pot model mars its utility. The influence of eugenic arguments among policy-makers further distorted the definition of U. S. identity, by limiting it to a particular conception of white, European-originating citizens.

In the decisions taken in the 1920s lies a significant part of the origin of multicultural debates (because the question of how should "America" and "Americans" be defined was answered in partial terms) and part of the reasons for the United States's slowness in granting full rights of citizenship to all members (because the decisions of the 1920s, combined with judicial rulings and existing policy, made membership of the polity problematic for nonwhites). The result of disregarding the Kallenian "cultural pluralism" option was a suppression of diversity to the altar of an Anglo-Saxon conformist conception of U. S. identity. To elite policy-makers, this treatment seemed the most appropriate way to build a nation. The fact that debates about identity and Americanization were solely about exclusion among Europeans underlies this conclusion. It is unremarkable that representatives of minority groups and cultures saw in the politics of multiculturalism an opportunity to advance their interests.

Immigration affects the identity of a nation. In the case of the United States, it has been fundamental to its identity, with successive groups of immigrants seemingly assimilated into the core values and beliefs of the United States. In practice, the apparently irresistible urge to daub the latest members of the polity "new immigrants," differentiated from those already present, has facilitated a group-orientated politics often at variance with the United States's individualist political ideology; it has also been overlaid by distinctions, often tortuously drawn, between nonwhites and whites. The national origins system implemented in the 1920s accentuated, and to some extent entrenched, these propensities. The consequences of these immigration policy choices have been increasingly in evidence and widely recognized by social scientists in the last two decades. The United States is a much more culturally and nationally diverse society than it was a hundred years ago, a characteristic consolidated in the immigration trends since the abolition of discrimination in 1965. A corollary of this transformation is a change in American identity, as Keith Fitzgerald observes: "After centuries of being predominantly white and Northern European, the United States is becoming darker skinned, African, Hispanic and Asian. These changes are more than skin deep . . . They are changes in American *identity,* and they necessitate the defining of a different 'we.'"[4] Immigration policy has played major roles in this transformation, through an ethnically restricted policy established in the 1920s, to the current policy of limiting numbers but not countries of origin. Without attention to the decisions taken in this earlier decade, combined with an appropriate broadening of the United States's history, there is a danger of retaining a partial account of the country's politics. Thus, Will Kymlicka chastizes scholars who fail sufficiently to acknowledge that the United States is constituted by both the minorities present before European settlers and the immigrants. Such scholars, he writes, are not simply making "a harmless over-simplification, confined to a few academic writings." Rather, their version "reflects and perpetuates a long history of denying the rights, even the very existence, of national minorities throughout North and South America on the grounds that these countries are 'immigrant countries.'"[5]

The Old Assimilation

The assimilationist model has robust defenders, recently spurred on by hostility to affirmative action and group politics. In his book *The End of Racism*, Dinesh D'Souza complains about what he calls the "new segregation" that these political developments have unleashed and praises the virtues of the conventional model of assimilation.[6] A modern defense of a traditional assimilationism has been mounted also by Peter Salins, who worries that Americans have forgotten the "magic of assimilation," exposing the United States to interethnic conflicts.[7] Eschewing and dismissing multiculturalist and related criticisms of traditional U. S. assimilation, Salins, an academic at Hunter College, advances an impassioned defense of this process as he understands it:

> Assimilation, American style set out a simple contract between the existing settlers and all newcomers. Immigrants would be welcome as full members of the American family if they agreed to abide by three simple precepts. First, they had to accept English as the national language. Second, they were expected to take pride in their American identity and believe in America's liberal democratic and egalitarian principles. Third, they were expected to live by what is commonly referred to as the Protestant ethic (to be self-reliant, hardworking, and morally upright).[8]

Salins overlooks how English was systematically made the dominant language as a result of lobbying and campaigning by assimilationists' groups and how many barriers were placed in front of immigrants wishing to assimilate.

An ardent believer in the United States's impressive ability to absorb and assimilate immigrants without sacrificing individuality—he firmly denies the identity between assimilation and acculturation— Salins looks on in horror at the revival of ethnic conflicts, aims of multiculturalists and advocates of separatism. Yet although Salins strives to differentiate assimilation from cultural conformity, he easily draws on a nationalism premised on homogeneity, declaring that "assimilation is about the expectations and attitudes of natives. It is about feeling unabashedly proud to be American."[9] This enthusiasm for traditional Americanization fails to appreciate either the new interest in fully acknowledging what political scientist Rogers Smith calls the United States's "multiple traditions"[10] or the real anxiety some opponents of assimilation have as a consequence of its narrowness in the 1920s.[11] Both of these issues are drawn more fully by an understanding of the debates of the first three decades of the twentieth century when many of the seeds of these subsequent concerns were planted.

A blinkered view of assimilation and American political development has scholarly examples. In his book *The First New Nation*, the eminent sociologist Seymour Martin Lipset proclaimed equality and achievement as the two "basic American values," which originated with the country's independence. As an example of equality, Lipset cites voting rights, noting that "the introduction of universal suffrage in America [came] long before it came in other nations."[12] Lipset's book contains also a discussion of how the United States's sense of national identity was forged. He writes that "the revolutionary, democratic values that thus became part of the national self-image, and the basis for its authority structure, gained legitimacy as they proved effective—that is, as the nation prospered."[13] Absent from this account is the role of ideas about who should belong to the political community and whose values define the national identity. Not only were African Americans excluded from membership and citizenship, but significant efforts from the late nineteenth century to determine who would be admitted to the country began. In his more recent book *American Exceptionalism*, Lipset gives fuller attention to the place of African Americans in the history of the United States, acknowledging their involuntary arrival and the effects of that circumstance (it is notable that these details were overlooked in his earlier volume). Assuming that other immigrants broadly conform to the assimilationist model, he writes of African Americans that "they are the great exception to the American Creed, to American ideological exceptionalism;"[14] this view not only reduces racial inequality to a problem of hypocrisy rather than a problem arising from identifiable historical processes of inclusion and exclusion in the construction of U.S. national identity but also neglects how central African Americans have been to American political development. Lipset dismisses issues of multiculturalism as concerns peculiar to the intellectual class only, with "little impact on mass behavior"; consequently, "the 'melting pot' remains as appropriate an image as ever."[15] This conclusion undercuts the implications of Lipset's own admission about the marginality constructed for African Americans within the assimilationist framework: that an exception has to be made exposes the analytical limits of the assumptions of a general American Creed.[16] Dismissing the post-1960s political agenda as of no interest to ordinary Americans runs the danger of privileging some purportedly neutral notion of "common sense," exactly the logic employed by the U.S. Supreme Court in 1923 to deny the Hindu petitioner Bhagat Singh Thind the right to naturalize.[17]

The New Americanization

Immigration remains a potent political issue in the United States. Although the 1990s began with a liberal immigration act that was passed in 1990, the decade quickly succumbed to alarm about illegal immigrants and the dangers of immigration to core American values, trends fostered by the Republican Party's revived electoral fortunes in the U. S. Congress and the work of the anti-immigration Federation for American Immigration Reform (FAIR, founded in 1979);[18] even legal immigrants have suffered diminution of their rights.[19] The reemergence of such issues, coupled with multiculturalism, demonstrates how the United States is a political system whose members self-consciously construct and contest the content of its core identity and values. This renewal is always part of the democratic process, though fuller appreciation of the choices taken in the 1920s and their consequences would enrich the contemporary debate, perhaps precluding the recurrence of earlier mistakes and a greater sensitivity among some of the participants.

The contradiction between the United States's willingness to absorb millions of immigrants decade after decade and its new harsh treatment of legal permanent residents is striking. Concurrently with these restrictions the development of new issues related to immigration can be observed. For instance, the question of having dual nationality has arisen in U. S. politics,[20] a policy that breaks significantly with the traditional assimilationist model. Dual nationality (that is, holding citizenship of the United States and one other country) is arguably an additional element in the multiculturalist approach, and indeed critics of multiculturalism have expressed a hostility to dual nationality precisely because they see such a connection. Americanization has resurfaced too, located intellectually at the vortex between immigration and multiculturalism, as a recent workshop based on *Becoming American/America Becoming* illustrates.[21] It appeared after the publication of the congressional-sponsored Commission on Immigration Reform report, chaired by Barbara Jordan. Both the Immigration Commission and the workshop project address the issue of how immigrants are integrated into the U. S. polity, a question that, as we saw in an earlier chapter, elicited the Americanization movement in the 1910s and 1920s.

Two points are worth making here. First, Americanization is in a new guise. Both the Commission on Immigration Reform and the workshop participants believe it is a defensible aspect of government policy toward immigrants but one that should be undertaken by American citizens and immigrants working in unison, rather than as an exercise in imposing one view on the other. Americanization is advocated as a necessary element in citizenship and the building of civic ideals and values. Its modern advocates are keen to distance themselves from the 1920s. Thus, the political scientist Noah Pickus, an advocate of Americanization, writes that "the naturalization process does not adequately incorporate newcomers, strengthen citizenship, or foster self-government." Therefore, Americans "need a process that generates a sense of mutual commitment among all Americans, naturalized and native-born alike."[22] Second, the rapid increase in the number of immigrants naturalizing as U. S. citizens is a source of concern to some existing citizens who believe that the standards of knowledge about the United States, required before naturalizing, should be increased rather than diluted, a belief again with echoes in the 1920s. Converging with the new interest in Americanization, this second issue is also one rooted fundamentally in a commitment to the notion of citizenship and the values necessary for it.

The historical parallels are striking. Ensuring that Americanization does not become oppressive will require vigilance. The treatment of legal aliens in the 1996 welfare reform act is a remainder of the potential for discriminatory policy toward immigrants. Plainly such treatment contradicts the aims of Jordan's Commission on Immigration Reform, whose members wish to foster a full sense of citizenship and not so blatantly to differentiate immigrants from citizens.

Writing for an audience ruminating on the commission's work, Charles Kesler finds a strong case in the United States for expecting immigrants and Americans to enter a process of "good citizenship" that lives "up to its own best principles." This process requires the "cultivation of a virtuous or responsible 'national spirit' and 'national character' . . . to live up to the universal principles animating that citizenship. . . American citizenship helps to form American culture; it is not just a by-product of a preexisting or somehow more fundamental culture."[23] Since the U.S. polity—its political institutions and culture—have got Americans to the historical point of recognizing that citizenship is a general set of rights from which no eligible person should be excluded (despite past perfidities), Kesler appears to maintain, it is plainly working as presently organized, and new immigrants should be "Americanized" into its intricacies without these latter being discarded in the interests of a multiculturalist alternative conception of citizenship. Since the principles and values of the U.S. polity—expressed, for instance, in the Constitution and its drafters' conception of rights—have historically permitted new groups of citizens to be included as equal members, there is no reason, Kesler suggests, why this access should diminish.[24] By implication, Americanization educates in the principles of U.S. citizenship, including the principles of self-government and patriotism—in the words of Kesler's essay title, "the promise of American citizenship"—that facilitate political development.

For critics of this view, it fails to restrain the powerful propensity toward assimilation often realized in Americanization and promoted by opponents of multiculturalism. It is this coercive tendency that the historian Gary Gerstle's analysis of Americanization unpacks. As he writes, in the process of becoming American, immigrants "invariably encountered structures of class, race, gender, and national power that constrained, and sometimes defeated their efforts to be free." As a consequence, "coercion, as much as liberty, has been intrinsic to our history and to the process of becoming American."[25] These coercive elements have not been confined to the treatment of voluntary immigrants, as we have seen.

Kesler's model is one that discounts the force of historical divisions associated with the kinds of distinctions imposed by policy-makers and judges in the 1920s. This traditional defense is severely criticized by law professor Juan Perea, who chides Kesler for disregarding the importance of race in U.S. history: "the course of racism in this country suggests either (and perhaps both) that it is difficult to live up to liberal republican principles or that these principles, not taking account of racism and a commitment to the maintenance of white supremacy, are not the full set of operative principles."[26] Perea furthermore argues that the appeal of any notion of Americanization is "dependent on one's race." He elaborates thus: "Whites can be most secure in their Americanization: It appears to be the least contingent and the least apt to fluctuate in value and social meaning." This is not true for other citizens: "[E]ven extraordinary efforts to Americanize on the part of peoples of color, and even the achievement of American citizenship, can be extremely contingent and of little protective value when opposed by the will of the majority. Accordingly, a very significant racial component is built into American citizenship, American identity, and Americanization itself."[27] The 1920s legislation contributed to this tendency in its emphasis on restrictive national origins quotas. Furthermore, Perea's concerns seem well-founded from the writings of populists such as Peter Brimelow, a naturalized American, who grimly reports that "the racial and ethnic balance of America is being radically altered through public policy. This can only have the most profound effects." He then asks, "*Is it what Americans want?*"[28] This description and accompanying question repeat so many of the errors about the sociological, legal, and historical construction of race and the history of the United States that the anxiety of writers such as Perea is vindicated. For instance, Perea argues that "the majoritarian will" has too often proved prowhite and that "even consummate assimilation does not guarantee acceptance by a hostile majority,"[29] propensities that imply an exclusionary core to American citizenship unacknowledged in Kesler's account. He gives examples of the treatment of Cherokee, Japanese Americans, and Mexican Americans at various points in the twentieth century and criticisms of the immigration legislation enacted as recently as 1986 and 1990.

Multiple Traditions and Whiteness

Multiple Traditions and Multiculturalism

The multiple traditions framework systematically attempts to incorporate the implications of acknowledging the United States's diversity into an account of American political culture and development. As developed by Rogers Smith, the framework is a response to the fact that through most of its history, "lawmakers pervasively and unapologetically structured U. S. citizenship in terms of illiberal and undemocratic racial, ethnic, and gender hierarchies, for reasons rooted in basic, enduring imperatives of political life."[30] The criteria for these restrictions were commonly inconsistent with the values imputed to the United States's political culture such as equality and individualism; instead, the criteria presented a United States that was white, Protestant, and "a nation in which true Americans were native-born men with Anglo-Saxon ancestors."[31] Smith found inegalitarian ascriptive traditions to be far more entrenched in American political culture than normally acknowledged, and certainly more salient than in conventional histories. He argues that citizenship laws illustrate the competing pressures—"civic ideologies that blend liberal, democratic republican, and inegalitarian ascriptive elements"—forming the multiple traditions framework. Citizenship laws are driven by political demands and imperatives that resulted in inequalities and hierarchies, a picture at variance with the egalitarian picture formulated by such observers as de Tocqueville. In fact, until the 1950s, ineligibility criteria based on "racial, ethnic, and gender restrictions" were "blatant, not latent," and "for these people, citizenship rules gave no weight to how liberal, republican, or faithful to other American values their political beliefs might be."[32]

In immigration policy, as earlier chapters have reported, consequential restrictions began in 1882 with the Chinese Exclusion Laws and culminated in the national origins system of 1929 and augmented as late as 1952. These restrictions were paralleled domestically by the dissemination of jim crow segregated race relations and the judicially legitimated, imposition of second-class citizenship on African Americans. It is crucial that the restrictions of the first type were new, whereas those of the latter form came after a brief post–Reconstruction era of political freedom. They both thus rest in purposeful political action. This inheritance of ascriptive inequalities has resulted in a set of multiple traditions, inadequately conceptualized by a dependence on a Tocquevillean egalitarian framework of American political culture (a view that Lipset, for instance, still seems to hold). Rogers Smith quite properly worries about this Tocquevillean inheritance (with variants from Hartz and Myrdal) because of its profound influence on subsequent accounts of U. S. development: "much scholarship today perpetuates the misleading features of these views of American political culture, for reasons similar to the ones motivating the original accounts."[33] A richer recognition of the inegalitarian aspects of U. S. history is required to understand the modern multicultural and group-based politics.

Analytically, the multiple traditions of which Rogers Smith eloquently writes does not mean just that the United States is composed of groups other than a dominant white-based elite but that those groups' distinctions and diverse traditions were fostered and formed in the very development of the polity and contributed to that polity's development. The two cannot be separated. Such group differences must be incorporated with the dominant ethos, as Smith advocates, since they "raise the possibility that novel intellectual, political, and legal systems reinforcing racial, ethnic, and gender inequalities might be rebuilt in America in the years ahead."[34] He retains a notion of a common culture in the United States: "most members of all groups have shared and often helped to shape all the ideologies and institutions that have structured American life, including ascriptive ones."[35] For instance, Americanism in the 1920s had ambivalent properties: orchestrated by Americanizers, committed to an Anglo-Saxon view of U.S. identity, it was a set of values that, as documented in earlier chapters, African Americans could also have claimed if policy-makers and administrators had chosen to include them.

Facing Whiteness

The importance of whiteness to the place of immigration in American political development was introduced in Chapter 2 and illustrated empirically in the ensuing chapters. There are two principal ways in which whiteness acquires analytical purchase.

The first way is as part of the narrative of U.S. history and political development. Not only did legislators construct an immigration regime that both assumed a white American society, an assumption powerfully reinforced by eugenists, but also their measures limited the numbers of blacks who immigrated. These priorities were strengthened domestically not only in the working assumptions of the Americanization campaign of the 1920s but also concretely in the Supreme Court's constitutional endorsement of segregated race relations (a practice introduced and sustained in the federal government) and in the Supreme Court's often convoluted interpretation of naturalization laws to prevent nonwhites naturalizing. The complexities of defining white and nonwhite—manifest not just judicially but in a host of administrative settings[36]—have rarely benefited the less privileged group.

Thus, there has been historically a convergence of factors (including the exclusion of blacks from the national origins scheme, the limited access enjoyed by African Americans to a working class that defined itself as white, and segregated race relations and residential segregation, collectively permitting the perception articulated by leading African American intellectuals that "American means white") that together determined that American political development followed a narrow rather than a broad path of ethnic and racial development.

Although whiteness has played this key role in American political development, both through its impact on immigration and more widely, analysis should not be a purely black-white binary one. The history of white Americans and nonwhite Americans has not unfolded on hermetically sealed trajectories; far from it. It is the interaction and the political uses of racial categories that have been fundamental. Here Claire Jean Kim's employment of a "racial triangulation" model with which to study the complex interrelationships among Asian Americans, whites, and African Americans is valuable. Kim identifies two concurrent processes: that of relative valorization, "whereby dominant group A (Whites) valorizes subordinate group B (Asian Americans) relative to subordinate group C (Blacks) on cultural and/or racial grounds in order to dominate both groups," and civic ostracism, "whereby dominant group A (Whites) constructs subordinate group B (Asian Americans) as immutably foreign and unassimilable with Whites on cultural and/or racial grounds"; through these processes the dominant group both marginalizes one group in respect to a third and ensures the unassimilability of the favored group.[37] Kim explicates this process historically, finding that a racial triangulation "of Asian Americans has persisted since its inception in the mid-1800s to the present."[38] In Chapter 5, we saw how this racial triangulation was used in Congress by proponents of the legislative initiative to exclude black immigrants entirely from the United States, as they were compared unfavorably with Asians who were themselves still characterized as unassimilable. Instead of mistakenly analyzing different groups as locked into distinct and autonomous historical trajectories, Kim's triangulation framework permits a richer study of how different experiences interact and how that interaction both defines general features of American political development and why triangulation endures. This framework also breaks with a black-white binary conception that not only exaggerates the rigidity of sociologically or judicially constructed distinctions but also removes the role of agency in their creation and transformation; however, as I have stressed in earlier chapters, for some African Americans, the historical legacy of inequality and the elevation of whiteness in U.S. society's dominant self-identity is too significant to permit any weakening of this key political dichotomy in analysis.

Second, whiteness matters as an impediment to the creation of a genuinely diverse democracy. Historically, whites have been confident about their identity and assumed that the United States should be constructed as a white, homogenous nation. This confidence and ambition both come through in the arguments advanced, for instance, by the eugenist Harry Laughlin (discussed in Chapter 5) in respect to how the "American race" should be defined and in the constitutional arguments for segregation; this presumption of whiteness is one that is often implicit among critics of post-1965 immigration policy. Ian Haney López concludes his analysis of how judicial decisions have constructed laws in favor of whites compared with nonwhites by arguing that "a self-deconstructive White race-consciousness is key to racial justice."[39] Because whiteness serves as the "linchpin for the systems of racial meaning in the United States . . . racial equality may well be impossible until Whiteness is disarmed." The imperative here is elemental, according to Haney López: "only the complete disassembly of Whiteness will allow the dismantlement of the racial systems of meaning that have grown up in our society over the past centuries and thus permit the end of racism and the emergence of a society in which race does not serve as a proxy for human worth."[40] To move toward an understanding of American diversity that pays richer attention to individuals, these modifications are apposite. One of the virtues of Haney López's analysis is to underline that the construction of identities and of political configurations does not happen without some agency and purposeful action. Individual choices matter.

It is certainly the case that the formulation of the national origins immigration regime in the 1920s was the work of policy-makers, soaked in racial hierarchy and eugenic arguments about various groups' relative "inferiority," "undesirability," or "superiority."

These were political choices, legitimized by reference to a biased de Crèvecoeurian concept of the melting pot. These purposeful decisions put in place a discriminatory immigration system that not only erected a wall of distinctions, based on judgments about relative worth, among hopeful immigrants but also consolidated racial distinctions already existing in U.S. society. It is these consequences that render examination of the interwar decades so important historically.

A challenge confronts students of immigration and American political development: it is not sufficient simply to recount the development of the American polity in terms of the story of the English settlers and their successors, later bringing in the experience of those groups already present (Native Americans) or brought there involuntarily (African Americans). Rather, a version that treats all these groups' narrative coequally is required. Constructing this narrative raises issues both about the relationship between acknowledging diversity and the need for political unity, and about the relationship between group rights and individuals in a polity that prides itself on privileging the latter in its political principles and institutional arrangements. The history of none of these groups was isolated: each contributed to the formation of others. It is here that the multiple traditions framework, with its ambition to give appropriate accord to all the groups constitutive of the U. S. political culture, is germane. Rogers Smith's broadening process implies integrating the values and preferences of previously excluded groups into the dominant political ethos of the United States in a way that recognizes that they are not isolated but, through interaction and shared experiences, have contributed to American political development. Assimilation, to be fair to previously excluded group, necessitates a widening of the dominant values to complement the inculcation of the new entrants with prevailing values. The United States's history suggests that such a project will succeed, and indeed, the recent attention to the idea of whiteness—as a source of identity whose carriers need self-consciously to consider its properties and consequences—constitutes such a reformulation. In the United States there is a strong national identity (although this been shared most enthusiastically by white groups who have benefited from it), with which many Americans wish to align themselves. The major problem concerns integration of the autonomous worlds and cultures of those groups that were politically marginalized historically as a consequence of intentional policy choices or unintended effects of legislation. Here the capacity of the United States creatively to harness individualism and to design political institutions that maximize individual freedom (and as a consequence, diversity) augur well for the future.

Appendix

Table A.1 Immigration into the United States, 1820–1986, by Decade

Year	Number of Persons
1820	8,385
1821–1830	143,439
1831–1840	599,125
1841–1850	1,713,251
1851–1860	2,598,214
1861–1870	2,314,824
1871–1880	2,812,191
1881–1890	5,246,613
1891–1900	3,687,564
1901–1910	8,795,386
1911–1920	5,735,811
1921–1930	4,107,209
1931–1940	528,431
1941–1950	1,035,039
1951–1960	2,515,479
1961–1970	3,321,677
1971–1980	4,493,314
1981–1986	2,864,406

Source: U. S. Immigration and Naturalization Service, 1976 *Annual Report,* p. 39.

Table A.2 Selected Immigration Legislation in the United States

Year	Legislation	Content
1783		George Washington declares an openness to all comers: "the bosom of America is open to receive not only the opulent and respectable stranger, but the oppressed and persecuted of all nations and religions, whom we shall welcome to a participation of all our rights and privileges."
1790	Naturalization Act	Only whites allowed to naturalize.
1819		The U. S. government starts to count the number of immigrants arriving annually.
1864		Importation of contract labor is made legal by Congress.
1875		Federal restrictions on immigration of convicts and prostitutes.
1882	Chinese Exclusion Act	Chinese laborers are excluded for a decade; renewed in 1892, 1902 (and made permanent in 1904; finally repealed in 1943). Law excluding idiots, lunatics, paupers (persons likely to become a public charge) and convicts also in 1882.
1885	Contract Labor Act	Employers were prohibited from recruiting labor in Europe and paying their passage to the United States.
1891	Immigration Act	Key piece of legislation that assigned responsibility for assessment of new immigrants to the federal government; Congress established Superintendent of Immigration in the Treasury Department to oversee this work in Ellis and Angel Islands. Main element was a medical evaluation.
1897	Literacy test	Literacy test for new immigrants passed by Congress but vetoed by President Grover Cleveland.

Table A.2 (continued)

Year	Legislation	Content
1903		Anarchists, epileptics, and beggars were added to list of proscribed immigrants.
1906	Naturalization Act	Knowledge of English became a requirement for a person to be naturalized.
1907	Immigration Act	This established the Dillingham Commission, which reported and published its massive 42-volume study in 1911. Head tax on immigrants was increased; both TB sufferers and those with mental or physical defects added to excluded list. Agreement ("Gentleman's agreement") between the United States and Japan restricts Japanese immigration.
1917	Literacy test	Literacy test was introduced (over President Woodrow Wilson's veto; also vetoed in 1913 and 1915); applicable to all immigrants over 16. Doubled the head tax on immigrants. Was significant achievement for the restrictionists. The Act itemized the eugenically excludable. It severely limited immigration from Asia.
1921	Emergency Quota Act	The law restricted European immigration through new quota system: limited immigration to 3 percent per annum of each European nationality already resident in the United States, taking the 1910 census as a baseline. Limited total number of immigrants to 350,000 a year, 55 percent from northwestern Europe, 45 percent from southeastern Europe. Renewed in 1922 to terminate on June 30 1924.

Table A.2 (continued)

Year	Legislation	Content
1924	Johnson-Reed Act	From 1927 immigration limited to a total of 150,000 annually from non–Western Hemisphere, of whom nationalities resident in the United States according to 1890 census could claim 2 percent each. Set up a commission to determine quota for a system based on national origins to be introduced in 1927. Empowered U.S. consular officers to conduct preliminary medical and "good character" tests of those seeking entry visas.
1927		Implementation of the national origins plan of 1924 act postponed.
1929		National origins quota formula came into effect after successive postponements in 1927 and 1928. It apportioned quotas on the basis of the estimated national origins distribution of the white population in the United States in the 1920 census. No quota for Mexico or Canada.
1940	Alien Registration Act	Act required the registration and fingerprinting of all aliens, and strengthened the law regarding immigrant admission and deportation.
1943		Chinese Exclusion Act repealed.
1952	Immigration and Nationality (McCarran-Walter) Act	Revised 1929 quotas but retained pro–Western European bias. Ended ban on whites only becoming naturalized. In detail: reaffirms the national origins framework giving each nation a quota equivalent to its proportion of the U. S. population in 1920; restricts immigration from Eastern Hemisphere to about 150,000, with no restrictions on Western Hemisphere; gives priority to skilled workers and relatives of U. S. citizens; and makes the screening tests and security more rigorous.

Table A.2 (continued)

Year	Legislation	Content
1965	Immigration and Nationality (Hart-Celler) Act	Finally abolished the national-origins systems and excised all references to race. In detail: abrogated national origins system; set an annual ceiling of 170,000 for the Eastern Hemisphere with a 20,000 country limit; created a seven-category preference ordering for distribution of visas; and set an annual ceiling of 120,000 for the Western Hemisphere with no preference system or per-country limit.
1978	Immigration and Nationality Act Amendments	Combined the ceilings for both Western and Eastern Hemisphere into a worldwide total of 290,000 with the same seven-category preference system and 20,000 per-country limit applied uniformly.
1986	Immigration Reform and Control Act	Provided for the legalization of seasonal agricultural workers who had been employed for at least 90 days in the year preceding May 1986 and undocumented aliens who had been in continuous residence since January 1, 1982. Close to three million illegal aliens gained amnesty. Outlawed the employment of undocumented workers but provided weak enforcement.
1990	Immigration Act	Increased immigration with special provisions for highly skilled immigrants.
1996	Illegal Immigration Reform and Immigrant Responsibility Act	Additional appropriations made to the INS for border controls. New deportation measures for illegal aliens. Restrictions placed on bringing in relatives according to income.

Notes

1. Introduction

1. This ambivalence continues, as Reimers reports from a review of opinion polls: "No poll after 1945 indicated a majority by those responding for an increase in immigration." D. M. Reimers, *Unwelcome Strangers: American Identity and the Turn Against Immigration* (New York: Columbia University Press, 1998), p. 29.
2. The standard scholarly historical study of immigration remains J. Higham, *Strangers in the Land: Patterns of American Nativism, 1860–1925* (New Brunswick, N.J.: Rutgers University Press, 1955; 2nd ed., 1988). For other valuable accounts, see, inter alia, T. J. Archdeacon, *Becoming American: An Ethnic History* (New York: Free Press, 1983); R. A. Divine, *American Immigration Policy, 1924–1952* (New Haven: Yale University Press, 1957); Reimers, *Unwelcome Strangers;* B. M. Solomon, *Ancestors and Immigrants* (Chicago: University of Chicago Press, 1956/1972); and R. Ueda, *Postwar Immigrant Policy: A Social History* (Boston: Bedford Books). For an important political science analysis, see K. Fitzgerald, *The Face of the Nation* (Stanford: Stanford University Press, 1996). For a documentary source, see E. P. Hutchinson, *Legislative History of American Immigration Policy, 1798–1965* (Philadelphia: University of Pennsylvania Press, 1981).
3. A term borrowed from R. M. Smith, "Beyond Tocqueville, Myrdal and Hartz: The Multiple Traditions in America," *American Political Science Review* 87 (1993): 549–566; and Smith, *Civic Ideals: Conflicting Visions of Citizenship in U. S. History* (New Haven: Yale University Press, 1997). For a conventional and comprehensive account of immigrants' integration into

the U.S. polity, see L. H. Fuchs, *The American Kaleidoscope* (Hanover: Wesleyan University Press, 1990).

4. For general accounts, see D. J. Kevles, *In the Name of Eugenics* (Harmondsworth: Penguin, 1986); M. Hawkins, *Social Darwinism in European and American Thought, 1860–1945* (Cambridge: Cambridge University Press, 1997); and G. E. Allen, "The Role of Experts in Scientific Controversy," in H. T. Englehardt, Jr., and A. L. Caplan, eds., *Scientific Controversies* (Cambridge: Cambridge University Press, 1987). For consideration of eugenics and immigration policy, see M. F. Jacobson, *Whiteness of a Different Color* (Cambridge, Mass.: Harvard University Press, 1998); K. Ludmerer, *Genetics and American Society* (Baltimore: Johns Hopkins University Press, 1972); and M. Haller, *Eugenics: Hereditarian Attitudes in American Thought* (New Brunswick, N.J.: Rutgers University Press, 1963).

5. On jim crow see C. V. Woodward, *The Strange Career of Jim Crow,* 3rd ed. (New York: Oxford University Press, 1974); L. F. Litwack, *Trouble in Mind* (New York: Knopf, 1998); R. D. G Kelley, *Race Rebels* (New York: Free Press, 1994); J. H. Shofner, "Florida's Black Codes," in L. Dinnerstein and K. T. Jackson, eds., *American Vistas,* 7th ed. (New York: Oxford University Press, 1995); and G. E. Hale, *Making Whiteness* (New York: Pantheon, 1998). On voting rights for African Americans, see E. Foner, "From Slavery to Citizenship: Blacks and the Right to Vote," in D. W. Rogers, ed., *Voting and the Spirit of American Democracy* (Urbana, Ill.: University of Illinois Press, 1992); J. M. Kousser, *The Shaping of Southern Politics: Suffrage Restriction and the Establishment of the One-Party South, 1880–1910* (New Haven: Yale University Press, 1974); and J. M. Kousser, "The Voting Rights Act and the Two Reconstructions," in B. Grofman and C. Davidson, eds., *Controversies in Minority Voting* (Washington, D. C.: Brookings, 1992). On white attitudes about African Americans, see G. M. Fredrickson, *The Black Image in the White Mind* (New York: Harper and Row, 1971; repr. Hanover, N.H.: Wesleyan University Press, 1987); G. M. Fredrickson, *White Supremacy* (New York: Oxford University Press, 1981); W. D. Jordan, *White Over Black* (Chapel Hill, N.C.: University of North Carolina Press, 1968); L. M. Newman, *White Women's Rights: The Racial Origins of Feminism in the United States* (New York: Oxford University Press, 1999); and G. B. Nash, *Red, White, and Black: The Peoples of Early America,* 2nd ed. (Englewood Cliffs, N.J.: Prentice-Hall, 1982). On racism, see B. J. Fields, "Slavery, Race and Ideology in the United States of America," *New Left Review* 181 (1990): 95–118; J. J. Fossett and J. A. Tucker, eds., *Race Consciousness* (New York: New York University Press, 1997); I. F. Haney López, *White by Law* (New York: New York University Press, 1996); R. Takaki, *Iron Cages: Race and Culture in 19th-Century America* (New York: Oxford University Press, 1990); and A. T. Vaughan, *Roots of American Racism* (New York: Oxford University Press, 1995). On "scientific racism," see E. Barkan, *The Retreat of Scientific Racism* (Cambridge: Cambridge

University Press, 1992); and T. F. Gossett, *Race: The History of an Idea in America* (New York: Oxford University Press, 1963; rev. ed., 1997). On the postwar racist order, see M. Goldfield, *The Color of Politics* (New York: New Press, 1997); T. J. Sugrue, "Crabgrass-Roots Politics: Race, Rights, and the Reaction against Liberalism in the Urban North, 1940–1964," *Journal of American History* 82 (1995): 551–578; and *The Origins of the Urban Crisis* (Princeton: Princeton University Press, 1996).

6. This conjecture concurs with Nathan Glazer's conclusion that multicultur-alism acquires "its force and vigor by our greatest domestic problem, the situation of African Americans." N. Glazer, *We Are All Multiculturalists Now* (Cambridge, Mass.: Harvard University Press, 1997), p. 10. Other scholars, notably O. Patterson, *The Ordeal of Integration* (Washington, D.C.: Civitas/Counterpoint, 1997), have underlined the danger of neglect-ing the heterogeneity of the African American population, significant num-bers of whom are successful members of the middle and working classes.

7. R. Takaki, *A Different Mirror: A History of Multicultural America* (New York: Little Brown, 1993), p. 204. In this context, see also A. Ancheta, *Race, Rights and the Asian American Experience* (New Brunswick, N.J.: Rutgers University Press, 1998); and R. Daniels, *Asian America: Chinese and Japanese in the United States since 1850* (Seattle: University of Wash-ington Press, 1988).

8. J. H. St. John de Crèvecoeur, *Letters from an American Farmer and Sketches of Eighteenth-Century America* (Harmondsworth: Penguin Clas-sics 1986/1782); and U. S. Commission on Immigration Reform, *Becoming an American: Immigration and Immigrant Policy,* A Report to Congress (Washington, D.C.: U.S. Commission on Immigration Reform, 1997).

9. On the way in which race and racial categories become objects of political choices and calculations that are reflected in institutional structures, see A. W. Marx, *Making Race and Nation* (New York: Cambridge University Press, 1998); and M. Omi and H. Winant, *Racial Formation in the United States* (New York: Routledge and Kegan Paul, 1986). Omi and Winant ad-vance the term "racial formation" to describe these processes: it refers to "the process by which social, economic and political forces determine the content and importance of racial categories, and by which they are in turn shaped by racial meanings. Crucial to this formulation is the treatment of race as a *central axis* of social relations which cannot be subsumed under or reduced to some broader category of conception" (pp. 61–62).

10. Smith, *Civic Ideals,* p. 448. And see J. Hochschild, *Facing Up to the Ameri-can Dream* (Princeton: Princeton University Press, 1995), ch. 13.

11. G. Gerstle, "Liberty, Coercion and the Making of Americans," *Journal of American History* 84 (1997): 524–558. See also D. A. Hollinger, "Reflections on the United States and Liberal Nationalism," *Journal of American History* 84 (1997): 559–569.

12. U.S. Commission on Immigration Reform (1997), *Executive Summary* 6.

13. Gerstle, "Liberty, Coercion and the Making of Americans."
14. On American political development, see K. Orren and S. Skowronek, "Regimes and Regime Building in American Government: A Review of the Literature on the 1940s," *Political Science Quarterly* 113 (1999): 689–702; I. Katznelson and B. Pietrykowski, "Rebuilding the American State: Evidence from the 1940s," *Studies in American Political Development* 5 (1991): 301–339; and R. Lieberman, *Shifting the Color Line* (Cambridge, Mass.: Harvard University Press, 1998).
15. G. Gerstle, "The Protean Character of American Liberalism," *American Historical Review* 99 (1994): 1043–1073. And see M. M. Ngai, "The Architecture of Race in American Immigration Law: A Reexamination of the Immigration Act of 1924," *Journal of American History* 86 (1999): 67–92. This important article was brought to my attention after I had completed *Making Americans*. I agree with the author's argument about the racial legacies of the 1924 Immigration Act and consider her thesis both intellectually important and empirically compellingly established.
16. T. W. Allen, *The Invention of the White Race* (London: Verso, 1997); and E. P. Kaufmann, *The Decline of Dominant Ethnicity in the United States: A Study in Cultural Modernization* (Ph.D. thesis, University of London, 1998).
17. N. Glazer, *We Are All Multiculturalists Now* (Cambridge, Mass.: Harvard University Press, 1997), p. 133.
18. J. R. Commons, *Races and Immigrants in America* (New York: Macmillan, 1907), cited in M. J. Anderson, *The American Census: A Social History* (New Haven: Yale University Press, 1988), pp. 143–144. On Commons's racism, see Smith, *Civic Ideals*, p. 416.

2. Immigration and American Political Development

1. See the valuable discussion in C. Sheridan, "Contested Citizenship: National Identity and the Mexican Immigration Debates of the 1920s," paper presented to the annual meeting of the American Political Science Association, 1998.
2. R. A. Divine, *American Immigration Policy, 1924–1952* (New Haven: Yale University Press, 1957), p. 18.
3. W. Cather, *Sapphira and the Slave Girl* (London: Virago, 1986, originally pub. 1940), p. 23.
4. I use the terms "Anglo-Saxon" and "Anglo-American" interchangeably throughout the text.
5. R. Horsman, *Race and Manifest Destiny: The Origins of American Racial Anglo-Saxonism* (Cambridge, Mass.: Harvard University Press, 1981), pp. 219–221.
6. A. de Tocqueville, *Democracy in America*, vol. 1 (New York: Vintage, 1945), p. 344.

7. F. K. Lane, "The Answer of the Foreign Born," 1918, p. 2, in National Archives (hereafter NA) Record Group (hereafter RG) 12 Records of the Office of Education, Records of the Office of the Commissioner, Historical Files 1870–1950, File 106, Entry 6, Box 7.

8. Report of the President's Commission on Immigration and Naturalization, *Whom We Shall Welcome* (Washington, D.C.: Government Printing Office, 1953), p. 23.

9. For a comprehensive history of U.S. immigration, see J. Higham, *Strangers in the Land* (New Brunswick, N.J.: Rutgers University Press, 1988).

10. M. J. Anderson, *The American Census: A Social History* (New Haven: Yale University Press, 1988), p. 149.

11. de Crèvecoeur, *Letters from an American Farmer* (Harmondsworth: Penguin, 1986/1782), pp. 68, 69–70.

12. I. Zangwill, *The Melting Pot: A Drama in Four Acts* (London: William Heinemann, 1914).

13. S. Bellow, *The Adventures of Augie March* (Harmondsworth: Penguin, 1966), p. 7.

14. J. Goebel, *Kampf um deutsche Kultur in Amerika*, published in 1914 and cited in R. E. Park, *Americanization Studies: The Immigrant Press and Its Control* (New York: Harper and Brother Publishers, 1922), pp. 61–62.

15. .W. Jordan, *White Over Black* (Chapel Hill: University of North Carolina Press, 1968), pp. 339–340.

16. W. Wilson, "The Meaning of Citizenship," address to newly naturalized citizens, Philadelphia, May 10, 1915, in W. Talbot, ed., *Americanization* (New York: H. W. Wilson, 1920), p. 78. Emphasis added.

17. For valuable overviews, see R. Daniels, *Coming to America: A History of Immigration and Ethnicity in American Life* (New York: Harper Collins, 1990); and L. Dinnerstein, R. L. Nichols, and D. M. Reimers, *Natives and Strangers: A Multicultural History of Americans* (New York: Oxford University Press, 1996).

18. Dinnerstein et al., *Natives and Strangers*, p. 4.

19. F. P. Prucha, ed., *Americanizing the American Indians* (Cambridge, Mass.: Harvard University Press, 1973), p. 8.

20. B. M. Solomon, *Ancestors and Immigrants* (Chicago: University of Chicago Press, 1972/1956), p. 59.

21. J. R. Pole, *The Pursuit of Equality in American History* (Berkeley: University of California Press, 1993, 2nd rev. ed.), p. 287.

22. Ibid.

23. Quoted in T. F. Gossett, *Race: The History of an Idea in America* (New York: Oxford University Press, 1963; rev. ed., 1997), p. 292.

24. P. D. Salins, *Assimilation, American Style* (New York: Basic, 1997), p. 4. And see the September 7, 1999, *USA Today* headline, "Blended races making a true melting pot."

25. Ibid., p. 107.

26. Continuing belief in a distinct American identity or civic culture, independent of any class or ethnic interests, is a claim advanced also by Diane Ravitch, though she eschews the term "race." Thus, she argues that "the civic culture is the heart of the American common culture. It is not grounded in race, ethnicity, gender, or anything else peculiar to a group or individual. It belongs to all Americans." This culture "promises freedom, opportunity, equality, and the right to be a self-governing member of a self-governing polity." D. Ravitch, "Our Pluralist Common Culture," in J. Higham, ed., *Civil Rights and Social Wrongs* (University Park: Pennsylvania State University Press, 1997), p. 138.

27. For a definition and discussion of the term's origin, see A. Aguirre and J. H. Turner, *American Ethnicity* (Boston: McGraw-Hill, 1998), ch. 3.

28. Solomon, *Ancestors and Immigrants,* pp. 207–208.

29. R. M. Smith, "American Conceptions of Citizenship and National Service," in A. Etzioni, ed., *New Communitarian Thinking* (Charlottesville: University Press of Virginia, 1995). Another version of the dominant group thesis is proposed by Eric Kaufmann regarding that part of the population represented in the American Revolution. He concludes that Americans differentiated themselves from surrounding populations: "[T]he Americans were considered to be *White,* in contrast to the Natives and the black slaves, they were *Protestant* and *English* (in speech and surname), unlike the 'papist' French and Spanish to the south and west, and they were *Liberal* democrats, in contrast to the British, both at home and in the colonies to the north." E. Kaufmann, "Ethnic or Civic Nation?: Theorizing the American Case," *Canadian Review of Studies in Nationalism* (1999 forthcoming), p. 9.

30. R. E. Park, *Americanization Studies: The Immigrant Press and Its Control* (New York: Harper and Brother Publishers, 1922), pp. 160–161.

31. *Ozawa v. United States,* 260 U. S. 178 (1922).

32. M. F. Jacobson, *Whiteness of a Different Color* (Cambridge, Mass.: Harvard University Press, 1998), p. 206.

33. See for example, J. A. Froude, "Romanism and the Irish Race in the United States," *North American Review* 277 (December 1879): 519–536, who reports that "the growth of the Irish element has, for some time, disturbed the minds of the Americans": 525.

34. Dinnerstein et al., *Natives and Strangers,* pp. 93–94.

35. R. A. Billington, *The Protestant Crusade, 1800–1860* (New York: Rinehart & Co., 1938), p. 327.

36. Ibid., p. 387.

37. Jacobson, *Whiteness of a Different Color,* p. 72.

38. See N. Ignatiev, *How the Irish Became White* (New York: Routledge, 1995).

39. O. Patterson, *The Ordeal of Integration: Progress and Resentment in America's "Racial" Crisis* (Washington, D.C.: Civitas/Counterpoint, 1997), p. 75. And see Jacobson, *Whiteness of a Different Color,* pp. 48–52.

40. Dinnerstein et al., *Natives and Strangers,* p. 170.

41. See the accounts in NAACP "Negro Wage Earners and Apprenticeship" (Washington, D.C.: NAACP, 1960), in Library of Congress (hereafter LC) Manuscript Division (MD), National Association for the Advancement of Colored People (NAACP) Papers Group III-A, Box A180; and P. Burstein, *Discrimination, Jobs and Policies* (Chicago: University of Chicago Press, 1985).

42. Patterson, *Ordeal of Integration,* p. 69.

43. Ibid.

44. Dinnerstein et al., *Natives and Strangers,* p. 191.

45. A. Saxton, *The Indispensable Enemy: Labor and the Anti-Chinese Movement in California* (Berkeley: University of California Press, 1971).

46. T. Almaguer, *Racial Fault Lines: The Historical Origins of White Supremacy in California* (Berkeley: University of California Press, 1994), p. 6.

47. Ibid., p. 154.

48. Ibid., p. 181. See also R. Takaki, *Iron Cages: Race and Culture in 19th-Century America* (New York: Oxford University Press, 1990) especially ch. 10.

49. Dinnerstein et al., *Natives and Strangers,* p. 211; and R. Takaki, ed., *From Different Shores* (Oxford: Oxford University Press, 1987).

50. For an account, see R. Drinnon, *Keeper of Concentration Camps: Dillon S. Myer and American Racism* (Berkeley: University of California Press, 1987); and D. S. Myer, *The Japanese Americans and the War Relocation Authority During World War II* (Tucson, Ariz.: University of Arizona Press, 1971).

51. R. Daniels, *The Politics of Prejudice* (Berkeley: University of California Press, 1977). For a commentary and trenchant criticism at the time, see C. McWilliams, *What About Our Japanese-Americans?* (Washington, D.C.: American Council Institute of Pacific Relations, 1944).

52. M. Omi and H. Winant, *Racial Formation in the United States* (New York: Routledge and Kegan Paul, 1986), p. 75.

53. In 1795, this period was extended to five years; and in 1798, as tensions mounted about aliens and traitors, the waiting period jumped to fourteen years, before returning to five years during the Jefferson administration. The Know-Nothing party later demanded further restrictions, which were not enacted. See P. McClain and J. Stewart, *Can We All Get Along? Racial and Ethnic Minorities in America* (Boulder: Westview Press, 1998), pp. 13–15.

54. Dinnerstein et al., *Natives and Strangers,* p. 224.

55. Almaguer, *Racial Fault Lines,* p. 9. And see Patterson, *Ordeal of Integration,* ch. 1.

56. I. F. Haney López, *White by Law: The Legal Construction of Race* (New York: New York University Press, 1996).

57. J. Strong, *Our Country* (New York: Baker and Taylor, 1885), pp. 43–44.

58. N. M. J. Pickus, "'Hearken Not to the Unnatural Voice': Publius and the Artifice of Attachment," in G. J. Jacobsohn and S. Dunn, eds., *Diversity and*

Citizenship: Rediscovering American Nationhood (New York: Rowman and Littlefield Publishers, 1996), p. 64.

59. U.S. Commission on Immigration Reform, *Becoming an American: Immigration and Immigrant Policy,* A Report to Congress (Washington, D.C.: U.S. Commission on Immigration Reform, 1997), p. 7.

60. Ibid., p. 1.

61. Ibid., p. 5.

62. Ibid., p. 6.

63. N. M.J. Pickus, *Becoming American/America Becoming: Final Report of the Duke University Workshop on Immigration and Citizenship* (Durham, N.C.: Terry Sanford Institute of Public Policy, Duke University, 1997), p. 8.

64. Smith, *Civic Ideals,* p. 429. And see Jacobson, *Whiteness of a Different Color,* ch. 7.

65. G. Gerstle, "The Protean Character of American Liberalism," *American Historical Review* 99 (1994): 1043–1073.

66. G. Gerstle, "Liberty, Coercion and the Making of Americans," *Journal of American History* 84 (1997): 524–558, 576.

67. H. Kallen, "Democracy Versus the Melting-Pot," Parts I and II, *The Nation,* February 18 and 25, 1915. And see also R. Bourne, "Trans-National America," *Atlantic Monthly* 118 (July 1916): 86–97.

68. Gerstle, "Protean Character of American Liberalism": 1051.

69. Kallen, "Democracy Versus the Melting-Pot": 219.

70. Ibid.: 219.

71. Gerstle, "Liberty, Coercion and the Making of Americans": 438.

72. Kallen, "Democracy Versus the Melting-Pot": 219.

73. Ibid.

74. Ibid.

75. J. R. Barrett, "Americanization from the Bottom Up: Immigration and the Remaking of the Working Class in the United States, 1880–1930," *Journal of American History* 79 (1992): 996–1020.

76. H. Kallen, *Cultural Pluralism and the American Idea* (Philadelphia: University of Pennsylvania Press, 1956), pp. 51–52.

77. Ibid., p. 99.

78. Cited in N. Glazer, *We Are All Multiculturalists Now* (Cambridge, Mass.: Harvard University Press, 1997), p. 86. And see A. Ryan, "Pragmatism, Social Identity, Patriotism and Self-Criticism," unpublished paper, Oxford, 1999.

79. H. Kallen, "Democracy Versus the Melting-Pot," *The Nation,* February 18, 1915: 193.

80. For a superb account, see D. L. Lewis, *When Harlem Was in Vogue* (New York: Oxford University Press, 1979).

81. Gerstle, "Protean Character of American Liberalism": 1055–1056.

82. Ibid.: 1056.

83. Ibid.: 1057.

84. For an outstanding discussion, see Gerstle, "Liberty, Coercion and the Making of Americans"; and see R. A. Kazal, "Revisiting Assimilation: The Rise, Fall, and Reappraisal of a Concept in American Ethnic History," *American Historical Review* 100 (1995): 437–471.
85. Kazal, "Revisiting Assimilation": 437.
86. Ibid.: 438.
87. Gerstle, "Liberty, Coercion and the Making of Americans."
88. For one important document, see American Association of Colleges of Teacher Education's Commission on Multicultural Education report, entitled *No One Model American* (1972).
89. D. T. Goldberg, ed., *Multiculturalism: A Critical Reader* (Cambridge, Mass.: Blackwell, 1994), p. 7. See also C. Taylor, *Multiculturalism and "the Politics of Recognition"* (Princeton: Princeton University Press, 1992).
90. A. M. Melzer, J. Weinberger, and M. R. Zinman, eds., *Multiculturalism and American Democracy* (Lawrence: University Press of Kansas, 1998), p. 4.
91. In June 1998, Californians voted on Proposition 227 to replace bilingual teaching with English immersion classes for immigrant children.
92. J. Higham, "Introduction," in J. Higham, ed., *Civil Rights & Social Wrongs* (University Park: Pennsylvania State University Press, 1997), p. 28.
93. N. Glazer, "Multiculturalism and a New America," in Higham, ed., *Civil Rights & Social Wrongs*, pp. 122–123.
94. Even among participants in the Million Man March in October 1995, relatively few were separatist, according to J. P. McCormick 2nd and S. Franklin's valuable paper, "Expressions of Racial Consciousness in the African-American Communities: Data from the Million Man March," paper presented to the annual meeting of the American Political Science Association, 1998. For the intellectual background, see R. Singh, *The Farrakhan Phenomenon* (Washington, D.C.: Georgetown University Press, 1997).
95. N. Glazer, *We Are All Multiculturalists Now* (Cambridge, Mass.: Harvard University Press, 1997), p. 10.
96. For conceptions of democracy, see S. Holmes, *The Anatomy of Anti-Liberalism* (Cambridge, Mass.: Harvard University Press, 1993).
97. Patterson, *Ordeal of Integration*, pp. 65–66.
98. R. Takaki, *A Different Mirror* (Boston: Little Brown, 1993), ch. 8.
99. I am grateful to Julie Suk for this example.
100. J. Ceaser, "Multiculturalism and American Liberal Democracy," in Melzer, Weinberger, and Zinman, eds., *Multiculturalism and American Democracy,* p. 147.
101. Patterson, *Ordeal of Integration*, pp. 65–66.
102. R. M. Smith, "Beyond Tocqueville, Myrdal and Hartz: The Multiple Traditions in America," *American Political Science* Review 87 (1993): 549–566; and R. M. Smith, Civic *Ideals* (New Haven: Yale University Press, 1997). See also J. Appleby, "Recovering America's Historic Diversity: Beyond

Exceptionalism," *Journal of American History* 79 (1992): 419–431, for a complementary discussion.

103. Smith, *Civic Ideals,* p. 1.
104. Ibid., p. 2.
105. Ibid., p. 3.
106. L. Hartz, *The Liberal Tradition in America* (New York: Harcourt, Brace & World, 1955); and A. de Tocqueville, *Democracy in America,* 2 vols. (New York: Vintage, 1945).
107. Smith, *Civic Ideals,* p. 15. And see Haney López, *White by Law,* for many complementary arguments and instances.
108. R. M. Smith, *The Policy Challenges of American Illiberalism* (Washington, D.C.: Carnegie Endowment for International Peace, International Immigration Policy Program Occasional Paper No. 2, 1998).
109. Almaguer, *Racial Fault Lines,* p. 17.
110. Smith, *Civic Ideals,* p. 471.
111. Smith, *Civic Ideals,* p. 480.
112. Smith, *Civic Ideals,* p. 497.
113. I. Berlin, *Four Essays on Liberty* (Oxford: Oxford University Press, 1969).
114. Smith, *Civic Ideals,* p. 489.
115. Smith, *Civic Ideals,* p. 504.
116. For an excellent recent analysis that makes "whiteness" the center of its explanation, see Jacobson's *Whiteness of a Different Color;* Jacobson's work builds on that of, in particular, D. Roediger, *The Wages of Whiteness* (London: Verso, 1991); Haney López, *White by Law;* and N. Ignatiev, *How the Irish Became White* (New York: Routledge, 1995). For other important contributions, see T. W. Allen, *The Invention of the White Race* (London: Verso, 1997); the essays in R. Frankenberg, ed., *Displacing Whiteness* (Durham, N. C.: Duke University Press, 1997), and in R. Delgado, ed., *Critical Race Theory: The Cutting Edge* (Philadelphia: Temple University Press, 1995); G. E. Hale, *Making Whiteness* (New York: Pantheon, 1998); C. Sheridan, "Contested Citizenship: National Identity and the Mexican Immigration Debates of the 1920s," paper presented at the annual meeting of the American Political Science Association, 1998; and R. Takaki, *Iron Cages: Race and Culture in 19th-Century America* (New York: Oxford University Press, 1990).
117. For example, see B. J. Fields, "Ideology and Race in American History," in J. M. Kousser and J. M. McPherson, eds., *Regions, Race and Reconstruction* (New York: Oxford University Press, 1992); or N. Stepan, *The Idea of Race in Science: Great Britain, 1800–1960* (London: Macmillan, 1982).
118. Jacobson, *Whiteness of a Different Color,* p. 9.
119. Haney López, *White by Law,* p. 106.
120. T. Morrison, *Playing in the Dark: Whiteness and the Literary Imagination* (Cambridge, Mass.: Harvard University Press, 1992), p. 9.
121. Ibid., p. 47.

122. I. De Reid, *The Negro Immigrant: His Background, Characteristics and Social Adjustment, 1899–1937* (New York: Columbia University Press, 1939), p. 41.

123. See, for example, S. M. Lipset, *The First New Nation* (New York: Anchor, 1967).

124. de Crèvecoeur, *Letters from an American Farmer,* p. 169.

125. For accounts, see L. Litwack, "Trouble in Mind: The Bicentennial and the Afro-American Experience," in L. Dinnerstein and K. T. Jackson, eds., *American Vistas,* 7th ed. (New York: Oxford University Press, 1995); L. F. Litwack, *Trouble in Mind* (New York: Knopf, 1998); R. D. G. Kelley, "'We Are Not What We Seem'": Re-thinking Black Working-Class Opposition in the Jim Crow South," *Journal of American History* 80 (1993): 75–112; J. W. Johnson, *The Autobiography of an Ex-Coloured Man* (New York: Vintage, 1989/1927); D. King, *Separate and Unequal: Black Americans and the U.S. Federal Government* (Oxford: Oxford University Press, 1995); D. King, "The Racial Bureaucracy: African Americans and the Federal Government in the Era of Segregated Race Relations," *Governance* 12 (1999): 345–377; and A. L. Higginbotham, Jr. *Shades of Freedom* (New York: Oxford University Press, 1996).

126. Interview, *The Sunday Times,* January 26 1997; at the time, Williams was delivering the BBC's Reith Lectures.

127. M. Storey, address to the Thirteenth Annual Conference of the National Association for the Advancement of Colored People, Detroit, June 18, 1922, p. 1, in LC MD NAACP I Papers Box B-5, Folder: Annual Conference, Speeches, 1922.

128. "The Economic Foundations of Race Prejudice," presented at NAACP annual conference 1929, in LC MD NAACP I Papers Box B-6, Folder: Annual Conference, Speeches, 1929.

129. Jacobson, *Whiteness of a Different Color,* p. 25. And see Haney López, *White by Law.*

130. T. G. Nutter, "The Negro and the Law," presented to the NAACP annual conference, 1922, p. 1, in LC MD NAACP I Papers Box B-5, Folder: Annual Conference, 1922.

131. For an excellent analysis of how the notion of white, as well as its shifting definition, has been constructed legally (and often required elaborate judicial exercises and reasoning), see Haney López, *White by Law.*

132. M. Rogin, *Blackface, White Noise* (Berkeley: University of California Press, 1996), pp. 5, 8. And see W. T. Lhamon Jr., *Raising Cain: Blackface Performance from Jim Crow to Hip Hop* (Cambridge, Mass.: Harvard University Press, 1998).

133. Rogin, *Blackface, White Noise,* p. 27.

134. Ibid., p. 17.

135. Ibid., p. 26.

136. Ibid., p. 44.

137. Rogin provides excellent discussions of these and other salient filmic examples. And see Hale, *Making Whiteness*, pp. 281–284.
138. M. W. Ovington, "Twenty Years of the N.A.A.C.P." address delivered to the NAACP annual conference, Cleveland 1929, p. 5, in LC MD NAACP I Papers, Box B-6, Folder: Annual Conference, Speeches, 1929.
139. Rogin, *Blackface, White Noise*, p. 56.
140. Roediger, *Wages of Whiteness;* Ignatiev *How the Irish Became White.*
141. Rogin, *Blackface, White Noise*, p. 57. For changing attitudes to the Irish in Boston in the 1890s and 1900s, see Solomon, *Ancestors and Immigrants*, pp. 153–155.
142. Solomon, *Ancestors and Immigrants*, p. 155.
143. Barrett, "Americanization from the Bottom Up": 1002.
144. J. Hochschild, *Facing Up to the American Dream* (Princeton: Princeton University Press, 1995), p. 243.
145. In *Shelley v. Kraemer.*
146. K. T. Jackson, "Race, Ethnicity and Real Estate Appraisal," in Dinnerstein and Jackson, eds., *American Vistas.*
147. For example, see T. J. Sugrue, *The Origins of the Urban Crisis* (Princeton: Princeton University Press, 1996).
148. Jacobson, *Whiteness of a Different Color*, ch. 7. And see Haney López, *White by Law.*
149. M. W. Ovington, *Half a Man: The Status of the Negro in New York* (New York: Longmans, Green and Co., 1911), p. 181.
150. See inter alia, E. Barkan, *The Retreat of Scientific Racism* (Cambridge: Cambridge University Press, 1992).
151. Haney López, *White by Law.*
152. Ibid, p. 9.
153. *Ozawa v. United States*, 260 U. S. 178 (1922); *United States v. Thind*, 261 U. S. 204 (1923). These cases are examined in Haney López, *White by Law*, ch. 4.
154. Haney López, *White by Law*, p. 19.
155. Haney López makes this point also in *White by Law* 103–106.
156. Hochschild, *Facing up to the American Dream*, p. 246.
157. N. Glazer, "White Noise," *The New Republic*, October 12, 1998: 43–46.
158. The phrase is from Haney López, *White by Law*, p. 31; I take this issue up in Chapter 10.
159. This term is borrowed from that school of political scientists who combine historical research with analysis of the development of the United States's political institutions.
160. Patterson, *Ordeal of Integration*, p. 66.
161. Gerstle, "Protean Character of American Liberalism": 1073.
162. Quoted by Senator Hiram Fong in *Congressional Record—Senate*, August 23, 1963, vol. 109, p. 15765. Emphasis added.
163. March 1, 1924.

164. E. R. Barkan, *And Still They Come* (Wheeling, Ill.: Harlan Davidson Inc., 1996), p. 11.

3. A Less Intelligent Class?

1. See H. C. Lodge, "The Restriction of Immigration," *North American Review* 152 (1891): 27–36.
2. U.S. Immigration Commission, vol. 1 (Washington, D.C.: General Printing Office [hereafter GPO], 1910), p. 13.
3. Quoted in B. M. Solomon, *Ancestors and Immigrants* (Chicago: University of Chicago Press, 1972, orig. pub 1956), pp. 118–119.
4. T. J. Archdeacon, *Becoming American: An Ethnic History* (New York: Free Press, 1983), p. 152.
5. W. Wilson, *A History of the American People* (New York: Harper & Brothers Publishers, 1902), vol. 5, pp. 212–213.
6. Lodge, "Restriction of Immigration," pp. 32, 35. See also W. L. Treadway, "Keeping the Alien Out of America," *Current History* 20 (1924): 913–920.
7. See papers of the League in Houghton Library, Harvard University; and papers of Franklin MacVeagh, Library of Congress (hereafter LC), Manuscript Division (hereafter MD). Active members included Samuel B. Capen, Thornton Cooke, Robert DeC. Ward, James Robert Dunbar, George Franklin Edmunds, Frank Boyd Gary, Madison Grant, Prescott F. Hall, Henry Holt, William Dewitt Hyde, Joseph Lee, Franklin MacVeagh, John F. Moors, Robert Treat Paine, Henry Parkman, James Horace Patten, James Bronson Reynolds, Charles Warren, and Owen Wister.
8. LC MD, Papers of Franklin MacVeagh, Box 31 Folder: Immigration Restriction League 1905–1928, Immigration Restriction League flyer, ca. 1923.
9. Solomon, *Ancestors and Immigrants*, p. viii.
10. LC MD, Papers of Franklin MacVeagh, Box 31 Folder: Immigration Restriction League 1905–1928, letter from John Moors, president, to MacVeagh, September 18, 1922.
11. Quoted in Solomon, *Ancestors and Immigrants,* p. 105.
12. Writing in 1897, quoted in Ibid., p. 111.
13. Lodge, "Restriction of Immigration"; and H. C. Lodge, "Lynch Law and Unrestricted Immigration," *North American Review,* 152 (1891): 602–612.
14. Solomon, *Ancestors and Immigrants*, p. 125.
15. Ibid., p. 135.
16. Ibid., pp. 193–194.
17. Ibid., p. 152.
18. See R. Hofstadter, *Social Darwinism in American Thought* (Boston: Beacon, 1955); and T. F. Gossett, *Race: The History of an Idea in America* (New York: Oxford University Press, 1963, new ed. 1997), ch. 7.
19. Archdeacon, *Becoming American,* p. 160.

20. See J. W. Trent, Jr., *Inventing the Feeble Mind* (Berkeley: University of California Press, 1994); K. M. Ludmerer, *Genetics and American Society: A Historical Appraisal* (Baltimore: Johns Hopkins University Press, 1972); and D. J. Kevles, *In the Name of Eugenics* (Harmondsworth: Penguin, 1986). For the comparative context, see N. L. Stepan, *The Hour of Eugenics* (Ithaca, N.Y.: Cornell University Press, 1991); P. M. H. Mazumder, *Eugenics, Human Genetics and Human Failings* (London: Routledge, 1992); and D. King and R. Hansen, "Experts at Work: State Autonomy, Social Learning and Eugenic Sterilization in 1930s Britain," *British Journal of Political Science* 29 (1999): 77–107.

21. Trent, *Inventing the Feeble Mind,* p. 138.

22. J. R. Pole, *The Pursuit of Equality in American History,* 2nd rev. ed. (Berkeley: University of California Press, 1993), p. 186.

23. R. E. Park, *Americanization Studies: The Immigrant Press and Its Control* (New York: Harper & Brothers Publishers, 1922), p. 214.

24. National Archives (hereafter NA) Record Group (hereafter RG) 233 Records of the US HR, 55th Congress, Committee on Immigration and Naturalization, Box 183, Folder: HR55A-H7.2, February 21, 1898, letter from President of the Circle to Congressman Daniel Ermentrout, February 14, 1898.

25. NA RG 233 Records of the US HR, 62d Congress, Committee on Immigration and Naturalization, Box 617, Folder: HR62A-H10.2, resolution of the American Purity Federation, October 21, 1909.

26. NA RG 233 Records of the US HR, 55th Congress, Committee on Immigration and Naturalization, Box 174, Folder: HR55A-H7.2, December 13, 1897–January 5, 1898, petition December 21, 1897. This is one example of hundreds of such submissions to the committee.

27. NA RG 233 Records of the US HR, 55th Congress, Committee on Immigration and Naturalization, Box 174, Folder: HR55A-H7.2, December 13, 1897–January 5, 1898, "Protest against any further Restriction of Immigrant" petition.

28. Petition from the North-American Turner Bund (Gymnastic Union) in Ibid.

29. Hundreds of this petition were mailed to the Committee: see NA RG 233 Records of the US HR, Committee on Immigration and Naturalization, Box 175, Folder: HR55A-J7.2. The German version was titled "Protest-Beschlusse aller dem Deutfchen Romitch Katholifchen Central Derein."

30. NA RG 233 Records of the US HR, 55th Congress, Committee on Immigration and Naturalization, Box 174, Folder: HR55A-H7.2, January 19–20, 1898, petition from the Deutsch-Amerikanifcher Central-Derein.

31. NA RG 233 Records of the US HR, 55th Congress, Committee on Immigration and Naturalization, Box 175, Folder: HR55A-H7.2, January 11–13, 1898, petition from the National Executive Committee of the UFCNA, St. Louis, December 1897. The petition was accompanied by a large number of signatures.

32. NA RG 233 Records of the US HR, 55th Congress, Committee on Immigration and Naturalization, Box 175, Folder: HR55A-H7.2, January 14–15, 1898, letter and petition from Edward Benneche, President of the Arion Society to the Committee. The group claimed 1,200 members.

33. NA RG 233 Records of the US HR, 55th Congress, Committee on Immigration and Naturalization, Box 176, Folder: HR55A-H7.2, January 25–27, 1898, Polish National Alliance of the United States of North America, January 20, 1898.

34. See the discussion in J. Higham, *Strangers in the Land* (New Brunswick, N.J.: Rutgers University Press, 1988 ed.), p. 141.

35. The other members were Senator Henry Cabot Lodge (Mass.); Senator Asbury C. Latimer (S.C.), replaced by Senator Anselm J. McLaurin (Miss.), replaced by Senator Le Roy Percy (Miss); Congressman Benjamin F. Howell (N.J.); Congressman William S. Bennet (N.Y.); Congressman John L. Burnett (Ala.); Mr. Charles P. Neill (from Washington, D.C.); Professor Jeremiah W. Jenks; Mr. William R. Wheeler; and three secretaries: W. W. Husband, C. S. Atkinson (who ceased working for the commission in June 1908), and Morton E. Crane (who was also disbursing officer). The chief statistician was Fred C. Croxton (U.S. Bureau of Labor). Both Husband and Croxton were well-known authorities on immigration policy, who continued to be active in its formation after the commission's work ended.

36. See M. J. Anderson, *The American Census: A Social History* (New Haven: Yale University Press, 1988).

37. U.S. Immigration Commission (created by section 38 of the immigration act of February 20, 1907), vols. 1, 12 (Washington, D.C.: GPO, 1910).

38. On the core English stock in Massachusetts, the self-named Brahmins, see Solomon, *Ancestors and Immigrants*. They provided a key intellectual framework of the restrictionist movement.

39. The Immigration Commission, vols. 1, 13 (Washington, D.C.: GPO, 1910). The term "native americans" refers to descendants of colonists, not to American Indians.

40. On those new immigrants who did settle in rural areas, see P. A. Speek, *Americanization Studies: A Stake in the Land* (New York: Harper and Brothers Publishers, 1921).

41. J. Daniels, *Americanization Studies: America via the Neighborhood* (New York: Harper and Brothers Publishers, 1920), pp. 89–90.

42. U.S. Immigration Commission, vol. 26, *Immigrants in Cities* (Washington, D.C.: GPO, 1910), p. 143.

43. W. M. Leiserson, *Americanization Studies: Adjusting Immigrant and Industry* (New York: Harper and Brothers Publishers, 1924).

44. Ibid., p. 249. And see Higham, *Strangers in the Land*, pp. 161–162.

45. M. R. Konvitz, *The Alien and the Asiatic in American Law* (Ithaca, N.Y.: Cornell University Press, 1946); and S. Lyman, *Chinese Americans* (New York: Random, 1974).

46. Leiserson, *Adjusting Immigrant and Industry*, p. 255.
47. U.S. Immigration Commission, vol. 1 (Washington, D.C.: GPO, 1910), p. 14.
48. Solomon, *Ancestors and Immigrants*, p. 163.
49. C. B. Davenport, *Heredity in Relation to Eugenics*, (New York: Henry Holt, 1911), p. 216, cited in Solomon, *Ancestors and Immigrants*, p. 173. And see comments by H. H. Laughlin, *Conquest by Immigration*, A Report of the Special Committee on Immigration and Naturalization (New York: Chamber of Commerce of the State of New York, 1939), pp. 20–21.
50. U.S. Immigration Commission, vol. 1 (Washington, D.C.: GPO, 1910), p. 38. For an extraordinarily rich portrait of immigration and employment, see U.S. Immigration Commission, vols. 6–25, *Immigrants in Industries* (Washington, D.C.: GPO, 1910).
51. Leiserson, *Adjusting Immigrant and Industry*, p. 178.
52. Solomon, *Ancestors and Immigrants*, p. 199.
53. "Relative to the Further Restriction of Immigration," Hearings before the Committee on Immigration and Naturalization, U.S. HR, 62d Congress, Second Session, Part I, 1912, p. 53.
54. See especially U.S. Immigration Commission, vol. 19, *Immigrants in Industries* (Washington, D.C.: GPO, 1911), ch. 7, "General Progress and Assimilation."
55. Ibid., p. 178.
56. Ibid., vol. 1 (Washington, D.C.: GPO, 1910), p. 42.
57. Ibid., vol. 5, *Dictionary of Races or Peoples* (Washington, D.C.: GPO, 1911), 150 pp.
58. "Europe as an Emigrant-Exporting Continent; the United States as an Immigrant-Receiving Nation," Hearings before the Committee on Immigration and Naturalization, U.S. HR, 68th Congress, First Session, March 8, 1924, p. 1307.
59. R. A. Carlson, *The Americanization Syndrome: A Quest for Conformity* (London: Croom Helm, 1987), p. 77.
60. Reports of the U.S. Immigration Commission, *Dictionary of Races or Peoples* (Washington, D.C.: GPO, 1911), p. 79.
61. Ibid.
62. M. F. Jacobson, *Whiteness of a Different Color* (Cambridge, Mass.: Harvard University Press, 1998).
63. These were African (black); Armenian; Bohemian and Moravian; Bulgarian, Servian, and Montenegrin; Chinese; Croatian and Slovenian; Cuban; Dalmatian, Bosnian, and Herzegovinian; Dutch and Flemish; East Indian; English; Finnish; French; German; Greek; Hebrew; Irish; Italian, North; Italian, South; Japanese; Korean; Lithuanian; Magyar; Mexican; Pacific Islander; Polish; Portuguese; Romanian; Russian; Ruthenian (Russniak); Scandinavian; Scotch; Slovak; Spanish; Spanish-American; Syrian; Turkish; Welsh; West Indian (except Cuban); all other peoples.

64. U.S. Immigration Commission, vol. 1 (Washington, D.C.: GPO, 1910), p. 17.

65. Boas's most influential work, *The Mind of Primitive Man,* was published in 1911.

66. U.S. Immigration Commission, vol. 38, *Changes in Bodily Form of Descendants of Immigrants* (Washington, D.C.: GPO, 1911).

67. See E. Barkan, *The Retreat of Scientific Racism* (Cambridge: Cambridge University Press, 1992), ch. 2.

68. See the useful discussion by K. Malik in his *The Meaning of Race* (London: Macmillan, 1996), pp. 150–160.

69. U.S. Immigration Commission, vol. 1 (Washington, D.C.: GPO, 1910), p. 44.

70. U.S. Immigration Commission, *Changes in Bodily Form of Descendants of Immigrants,* p. 1.

71. Ibid., p. 2.

72. Ibid., p. 7.

73. Though Omi and Winant write that Boas's work was "crucial in refuting the scientific racism of the early twentieth century by rejecting the connection between race and culture, and the assumption of a continuum of 'higher' and 'lower' cultural groups." M. Omi and H. Winant, *Racial Formation in the United States* (New York: Routledge and Kegan Paul, 1986), p. 60.

74. U.S. Immigration Commission, *Changes in Bodily Form of Descendants of Immigrants,* p. 27.

75. Ibid., p. 28.

76. Ibid., pp. 49–50.

77. Boas argued simply that children tended to reflect strongly the characteristics of one parent rather than a blend of both. U.S. Immigration Commission, *Changes in Bodily Form of Descendants of Immigrants,* pp. 54–55.

78. For example, see C. Aronovici, *Americanization* (St. Paul: Keller Publishing Co., 1919), pp. 10–11.

79. Gossett, *Race: The History of an Idea in America,* p. 23. And see Boas's own essays in *Race and Democratic Society* (New York: J. J. Augustin, 1945).

80. J. R. Pole, *The Pursuit of Equality in American History,* 2nd ed. (Berkeley: University of California Press, 1993), p. 297.

81. Pole, *Pursuit of Equality,* p. 298.

82. F. Boas, "Foreword," in M. W. Ovington, *Half a Man: The Status of the Negro in New York* (New York: Longmans, Green and Co., 1911), pp. vii–ix.

83. Gossett, *Race: The History of an Idea in America,* p. 424.

84. Letter from Prescott Hall to Charles Davenport, May 22, 1911, in Papers of the Immigration Restriction League, Box 1, Houghton Library, Harvard.

85. U.S. Immigration Commission, vols. 34 and 35, *Immigrants as Charity Seekers* (Washington, D.C.: GPO, 1911).

86. U.S. Immigration Commission, *Abstract of the Report on Immigration and Insanity* (Washington, D.C.: GOP, 1911), p. 7.
87. Ibid., p. 9.
88. Ibid., p. 22.
89. U.S. Immigration Commission, *Immigrants in Charity Hospitals* (Washington, D.C.: GPO, 1911), p. 40.
90. U.S. Immigration Commission, vol. 1 (Washington, D.C.: GPO, 1910), p. 33.
91. U.S. Immigration Commission, vol. 4, *Emigration Conditions in Europe* (Washington, D.C.: GPO, 1910), p. 209.
92. H. S. Nelli, "'An Italian Is a Dagi': Italian Immigrants in the United States," in L. Dinnerstein and K. T. Jackson, eds., *American Vistas* (New York: Oxford University Press, 1995), p. 95. And see the entry on Italians in U.S. Immigration Commission, *Dictionary of Races or Peoples,* pp. 81–85.
93. Dr. K. B. Davis, "The Delinquent Colored Woman," address to the NAACP annual conference 1914, p. 17, in LC MD NAACP I Papers Box B-1, Folder: Annual conference, 1914.
94. Archdeacon, *Becoming American,* pp. 163–164.
95. It was a dichotomy rehearsed until the end of 1920s: see, for example, the annual reports of the Committee of Immigration, 1921–1929, Allied Patriotic Societies, New York.
96. "Americanization of Adult Aliens," Hearings before a Subcommittee of the Committee on Immigration and Naturalization HR 69th Congress, 2d Session, February 17, 1927, p. 17.
97. "Europe as an Emigrant-Exporting Continent; the United States as an Immigrant-Receiving Nation," Hearings before the Committee on Immigration and Naturalization, HR 68th Congress, 1st Session, March 8, 1924, p. 1237.
98. K. Fitzgerald, *The Face of the Nation* (Stanford: Stanford University Press, 1996), p. 137.
99. I. R. Dowbiggin, *Keeping America Sane: Psychiatry and Eugenics in the United States and Canada, 1880–1940* (Ithaca, N.Y.: Cornell University Press, 1997), p. 209.
100. Letter from Charles Davenport to Prescott Hall, May 20, 1911, Papers of the Immigration Restriction League, Box 1. And see Hall's reply of May 22, ibid.
101. U.S. Immigration Commission, vol. 41, *Statements and Recommendations Submitted by Societies and Organizations Interested in the Subject of Immigration* (Washington, D.C.: GPO, 1911), p. 17.
102. Ibid., p. 16.
103. See records of meetings between Hall and Charles Davenport reported to the Immigration Restriction League, in Minutes (1894–April 1920), vol. 3, in Papers of the Immigration Restriction League, Houghton Library, Harvard.

104. U.S. Immigration Commission, vol. 41, *Statements and Recommendations Submitted by Societies and Organizations Interested in the Subject of Immigration,* p. 107.

105. Ibid.

106. See for instance, Hearings of the Committee on Immigration and Naturalization, HR 60th Congress, February 18, 1908, statement by Congressman John Burnett (Ala.) proposing a literacy test.

107. U.S. Immigration Commission, vol. 1 (Washington, D.C.: GPO, 1910), p. 47.

108. Solomon, *Ancestors and Immigrants,* p. 196.

109. Fitzgerald, *The Face of the Nation,* p. 128.

110. NA RG 85 Records of the INS, Records of the Central Office, Subject Correspondence 1906–1932, Box 45, Folder: 51632/13, Part II, letter from the National Liberal Immigration League to the Secretary of Commerce and Labor Charles Nagel, February 2, 1911, which refers to these efforts.

111. NA RG 85 Records of the Immigration and Naturalization Service (INS), Records of the Central Office, Subject Correspondence 1906–1932, Box 45, Folder: 51632/13, Part II, letter from the National Liberal Immigration League's President Charles Eliot to Secretary of Commerce and Labor Charles Nagel, January 10, 1911, p. 3.

112. Ibid., p. 4.

113. NA RG 85 Records of the INS, Records of the Central Office, Subject Correspondence, 1906–1932, Box 45, Folder: 51632/13, Part III, see letter from the league's president, Edward Lauterbach, to President Woodrow Wilson, December 7, 1912, opposing the Dillingham-Burnett Bill to introduce such a test: "it is as impracticable as it is immoral to slam the door in the faces of honest and healthy immigrants, when there is such a crying need for labor."

114. NA RG 85 Records of the INS, Records of the Central Office, Subject Correspondence, 1906–1932, Box 45, Folder: 51632/13, Part I, see letter from the league's president, January 26, 1907.

115. For a statement of labor's position in the year of the Johnson-Reed legislation, see N. P. Alifas, "The Immigration Bill Before Congress," *Labor Age,* 13(2), (February 1924): 1–7.

116. NA RG 233 Records of the US HR, 63d Congress, Committee on Immigration, Box 455 Folder: HR63A-H8.1, letter to Congressman H. H. Dale from Samuel Gompers, President AFL, January 22 1915.

117. NA RG 233 Records of the US HR, 62d Congress, Committee on Immigration, Box 618, Folder: HR62A-H10.2, petition from the Immigration Restriction League, May 24, 1912.

118. NA RG 85 Records of the INS, Central Office, Subject Correspondence, 1906–1932, Box 56, Folder: 51762/21, Immigration Restriction League, "The Reading Test," 1914, 6 pp., p. 6.

119. NA RG 85 Records of the INS, Central Office, Subject Correspondence,

1906–1932, Box 56, Folder: 51762/21, letter from Commissioner-General F. P. Sargent, to Prescott Hall, Secretary of the Immigration Restriction League, June 21, 1904.

120. The literacy test produced familiar divisions: native-born American groups and organized labor favored it, whereas representatives of northern European ethnic groups opposed it. See NA RG 233 Records of the US HR, 62d Congress, Committee on Immigration, Box 617, Folder: HR62A-H10.2, petitions from the Polish National Alliance, March 1912, opposing the test; and the Junior Order United American Mechanics, May 15, 1912, in favor.

121. Higham, *Strangers in the Land,* p. 190. Wilson proved equally dismissive of African Americans, permitting the introduction of systematic segregation in the federal civil service, having won their vote.

122. See NA RG 233 Records of the US HR, 62d Congress, Committee on Immigration, Box 617, Folder: HR62A-H10.2, various petitions and letters.

123. NA RG 233 Records of the US HR, 63d Congress, Committee on Immigration, Box 456, Folder: HR63A-H8.1: petitions from these and other labor organizations are included here.

124. R. A. Divine, *American Immigration Policy, 1924–1952* (New Haven: Yale University Press, 1957), p. 5.

125. NA RG 233 Records of the US HR, 69th Congress, Committee on Immigration, Correspondence, Box 342, Folder: HR69A-F20.1, letter from P. F. Snyder to Frank Mondell, July 14, 1926.

126. "The Old Stock and the New," editorial, *Outlook,* June 13, 1914, no. 107, reproduced in W. Talbot, ed., *Americanization* (New York: H. W. Wilson, 1920), p. 55.

127. Park, *The Immigrant Press and Its Control,* p. 67.

128. Ibid 67.

129. M. W. Ovington, *Half a Man: The Status of the Negro in New York* (New York: Longmans, Green and Co., 1911), p. 171.

4. *"The Fire of Patriotism"*

1. M. M. Gordon, *Assimilation in American Life: The Role of Race, Religion and National Origins* (New York: Oxford University Press, 1964). For a criticism of Gordon's concept of assimilation, see R. D. Alba, *Ethnic Identity: The Transformation of White America* (New Haven: Yale University Press, 1990), 310–311.

2. E. Kaufmann, "Ethnic or Civic Nation? Theorizing the American Case," *Canadian Review of Studies in Nationalism* (1999 forthcoming): 17–18.

3. This Anglo-American (or Anglo-Saxon) conception of U.S. identity implied differentiating and defending Protestantism from the new Catholic immigrants (by, for instance, establishing separate schools). In Eric Kaufmann's view, the United States's national composition has always privileged one group. He claims that "the case of the United States is exceptional in the an-

nals of ethnicity and nationalism studies because it has never had an ethnic component to its national identity." Instead, a unique notion of "American ethnicity" derived from an Anglo-Saxon "myth of descent whose boundaries were symbolically guarded by several key cultural markers had crystallized by 1820." Kaufmann, "Ethnic or Civic Nation,": 31.

4. See D. Brown, *Bury My Heart at Wounded Knee* (London: Vintage, 1991, orig. pub. 1970); C. A. Milner, "National Initiatives," in C. A. Milner, C. A. O'Connor, and M. A. Sandweiss, eds., *The Oxford History of the American West* (New York: Oxford University Press, 1990); F. P. Prucha, ed., *Americanizing the American Indians* (Cambridge, Mass.: Harvard University Press, 1973); R. Takaki, *Iron Cages: Race and Culture in 19th-Century America* (New York: Oxford University Press, 1990); and A. T. Vaughan, *Roots of American Racism* (New York: Oxford University Press, 1995).

5. Prucha, *Americanizing the American Indians,* p. 3. See also the fascinating discussion in L. M. Newman, *White Women's Rights: The Racial Origins of Feminism in the United States* (New York: Oxford University Press, 1999), ch. 5.

6. Prucha, *Americanizing the American Indians,* p. 7.

7. Ibid., p. 8. And see D. W. Adams, "Schooling the Hopi: Federal Indian Policy Writ Small, 1887–1917," in L. Dinnerstein and K. T. Jackson, eds., *American Vistas,* 7th ed. (New York: Oxford University Press, 7th ed. 1995).

8. *Tell Them Willie Boy Is Here* (Director: Abraham Polonsky, 1969).

9. See the chapter by Richard Pratt in Prucha, *Americanizing the American Indians.*

10. For stirrings of pre-1914 Americanization sentiment and organized activity, see E. G. Hartmann, *The Movement to Americanize the Immigrant* (New York: Columbia University Press, 1948), ch. 1. Hartmann's book is an excellent general study of Americanization.

11. Letter from Johnson to Dr. George Hinman, American Missionary Association, November 17, 1923, in NA RG, 85 Records of the Immigration and Naturalization Service (INS), Education and Americanization Files, 1914–1936, E18033-E17920, Entry 30, Box 265.

12. Letter from Raymond Crist, Commissioner for Naturalization, to Dr. George Hinman, Secretary, American Missionary Association, December 1, 1923, in NA RG 85 Records of the INS, Education and Americanization Files, 1914–1936, Entry 30, Box 265.

13. *Reports of the Department of Labor 1920,* Report of the Secretary of Labor and Reports of Bureaus (Washington, D.C.: GPO, 1921), Bureau of Naturalization, p. 195. The Bureau of Naturalization had a standard package of books that it sent to instructors, including *Federal Citizenship Textbook, Naturalization Information Forms, School Announcement Posters,* and *List of Periodicals Published by Students of Americanization Classes.* For details see the copious correspondence contained in NA RG 85 Records of

the INS, Education and Americanization Files, 1914–1936, E18033-E17970, Entry 30.

14. For an example, see the lecture outlines used in Los Angeles and sent to the Commissioner of Naturalization in Washington by the Chief Examiner in San Francisco: in NA RG 85 Records of the INS, Education and Americanization Files, 1914–1936, E18033-E17970, Entry 30, Box 265.

15. See Hartmann, *Movement to Americanize the Immigrant;* and also R. A. Carlson, *The Americanization Syndrome* (London: Croom Helm, 1987).

16. F. C. Butler, "Americanization: Its Purpose and Process," address to the Women's Federation of Wisconsin, Madison, 1919, 17 pp., p. 16, in NA RG 12 Records of the Office of Education, Records of the Office of the Commissioner, Historical Files, 1870–1950, File 106: Americanization, Entry 6, Box 11.

17. Letter from Secretary of Labor W. D. Wilson, to Raphael Herman, Diamond Power Speciality Co., Detroit, April 14, 1919, in NA RG 85 Records of the INS, Education and Americanization Files, 1914–1936, 27671/6942–27671/7093, Entry 30, Box 203. Herman had submitted a lengthy Americanization proposal to the Department of Labor, which Secretary Wilson greeted tactfully but about which he indicated that existing arrangements were sufficient.

18. M. R. Olneck, "Americanization and the Education of Immigrants, 1900–1925," *American Journal of Education* 97 (1989): 289, 398–423.

19. Letter from Alfred Zimmern to his Mother, October 20, 1911, in MS.Zimmern 8, letters to parents, 1911–1912, in Zimmern Papers, Bodleian Library, Oxford University.

20. For one account, see, for instance, *Uncle Sam's Magazine,* "published monthly in the interest of the United States of America," January 1920, copy in NA RG 12 Records of the Office of Education, Records of the Office of the Commissioner, Historical Files, 1870–1950, File 106: Americanization, Entry 6, Box 11.

21. J. Hochschild, *Facing Up to the American Dream* (Princeton: Princeton University Press, 1995), p. 233.

22. Nonpublic schools, that is, private or parochial ones, were also criticized. One Polish-American recalled the confusion of such an education in the first decade of the century: "after a child under twelve went through studying two languages the history of Poland in Polish, the history of the United States in English, the Bible in Polish, reading and writing in English and Polish, his mind was all confused and he left school just as ignorant as when he started." This citizen concluded with a modern message: "I think the system ought to be changed allowing no school to teach any child under ten years of age in no other language but the English."

Letter from Theodore Smith, Chicago, to Secretary of Labor, James Davis, September 4, 1921, in NA RG 85 Records of the INS, Education and Americanization Files, 1914–1936, 27671/15379–27671/15692, Entry 30,

Box 251. Smith enclosed his work of fiction "Currie Patch," a grim narrative of life in an immigrant neighborhood of a large American city.

23. W. Wilson, "Americanism," address to the Citizenship Convention, Washington, D.C., July 13, 1916, included in W. Talbot, ed., *Americanization* (New York: H. W. Wilson, 1920), 28–31.

24. N. H. Burroughs, "America—a Democracy with a Milestone About Its Neck," speech to the NAACP annual conference, 1929, p. 3, in NAACP I Papers Box B-6, Folder: Annual conference, Speeches 1929.

25. For a discussion of anti-German sentiment see D. M. Reimers, *Unwelcome Strangers: American Identity and the Turn Against Immigration* (New York: Columbia University Press, 1998), pp. 18–20.

26. Letter from Mr. Oscar Rohn, Director, National Park Service, Montana, to Secretary of the Interior Franklin Lane, April 25, 1918, enclosing memorandum on "Americanization," 10 pp., p. 9, in NA RG 12 Records of the Office of Education, Records of the Office of the Commissioner, Historical File, 1870–1950, File 106, Entry 6, Box 7, Folder: Americanization. And see reply to Rohn, May 14, 1918, in ibid.

27. Hartmann, *The Movement to Americanize the Immigrant*, p. 106.

28. H. H. Bierstadt, *Aspects of Americanization* (Cincinnati: Stewart Kidd Co., 1922), p. 21.

29. "It appeared to be to the interest of the Department to emphasize and even to aggravate the feeling against the immigrant, and it was fatally successful in its efforts." Bierstadt, *Aspects of Americanization*, p. 22.

30. For one intriguing example of its work, see the Department of the Interior, Bureau of Education, Americanization Division, "Racial Calendar for America," December 1918, 18 pp. In NA RG 12 Records of the Office of Education, Records of the Office of the Commissioner, Historical File, 1870–1950, File 106: Council of National Defense, 1917–1921, Entry 6, Box 12.

31. For an early description of the committee's work, see letter from Frances Kellor to Commissioner of Education P. P. Claxton, April 17, 1918, in NA RG 12 Records of the Office of Education, Records of the Office of the Commissioner, Historical File, 1870–1950, File 106, Entry 6, Box 7.

32. See Memorandum of Understanding Between the Secretary of the Interior and the National Americanization Committee for the Extension of the Work of the Division of Immigrant Education in the Bureau of Education, signed by Franklin Lane and Frank Trumbull, respective representatives of the two organizations. The memo began, "inasmuch as both the Department of the Interior through the Bureau of Education and the National Americanization Committee of New York desire to extend their work of education among the foreign born population of the United States in order to give the history and resources of the country, of our manners and customs, and of our social, civic, economic and political ideals, and through cooperation with loyal leaders of racial groups to win the full loyalty of these people

for the United States and their hearty cooperation in the war for freedom and democracy, the Department of the Interior accepts the cooperation of the National Americanization Committee for the extension of the work of the division of immigrant education which is now maintained in this Bureau through the cooperation of this Committee." Copy in NA RG 12 Records of the Office of Education, Records of the Office of the Commissioner, Historical File, 1870–1950, File 106, Entry 6, Box 7.

33. See letter from the Bureau's assistant secretary to Daniel Roper, U.S. Post Office, September 15, 1915, and Department of the Interior, Bureau of Education, "Americanization," both in NA RG 12 Records of the Office of Education, Records of the Office of the Commissioner, Historical File, 1870–1950, File 420: Immigrant Education Entry 6, Box 44, Folder: Americanization.

34. Compare, for example, "American First Campaign: What Women's Organizations Can Do," Bureau of Education, Division of Immigration Education Circular No. 10, with Bureau of Education "Syllabus of a Tentative Course in Elementary Civics for Immigrants," 4 pp., in NA RG 12 Records of the Office of Education, Records of the Office of the Commissioner, Historical File, 1870–1950, File 106, Americanization, Entry 6, Box 11.

35. National Committee of One Hundred, *"America First" Campaign*, August 1917, p. 1, enclosed with a letter from the Committee to Commissioner Claxton, in NA RG 12 Records of the Office of Education, Records of the Office of the Commissioner, Historical File, 1870–1950, File 106, Entry 6, Box 7.

36. He prepared a document on educating immigrants: H. H. Wheaton, *Standards and Methods in the Education of Immigrants*, Department of the Interior, Bureau of Education, Division of Immigrant Education, Washington, D.C., copy in NA RG 12 Records of the Office of Education, Records of the Office of the Commissioner, Historical File, 1870–1950, File 420: Immigrant Education Entry 6, Box 44, Folder: Americanization. Among the books recommended to instructors were H. P. Fairchild's *Immigration, a World Movement and Its American Significance* (New York: Macmillan, 1913); and Prescott Hall's *Immigration and Its Effects upon the United States* (New York: S. Holt and Co., 1908).

37. Letter from Frank Trumbull, chairman, National Americanization Committee, to Commissioner of Education P. Claxton, December 5, 1918, describing the work of this committee, in NA RG 12 Records of the Office of Education, Records of the Commissioner of Education, Historical Files, 1870–1950, File 106, Entry 6, Box 7.

38. P. P. Claxton, "What Is Americanization?" memo 1917, p. 1, in NA RG 12 Records of the Office of Education, Records of the Office of the Commissioner, Historical File, 1870–1950, File 106: Council of National Defense, 1917–1921, Entry 6, Box 12.

39. Ibid., p. 1.

40. Ibid., pp. 2–3.
41. For the lengthy list of individuals who contributed to the Americanization Committee in 1916–1917 and 1917–1918, see letter from Frances Kellor to Commissioner Claxton, April 25, 1918, in NA RG 12 Records of the Office of Education, Records of the Commissioner of Education, Historical Files, 1870–1950, File 106, Entry 6, Box 7. Frances Kellor herself offered to fund Americanization work "until such time as government funds can be secured for this work"; see letter from Kellor to Commissioner Claxton, April 10, 1918, in ibid.

    Commissioner Claxton passed the list on to the Secretary of the Interior, commenting, "I think you will be interested in the fact that these contributions come from a very large number of people from different parts of the country and are nearly all small contributions," letter from Claxton to Lane, April 30, 1918, in ibid.
42. And see memorandum of conference between Dr. P. P. Claxton, commissioner of education, and Miss Frances A. Kellor, Washington, D.C., April 30, 1918, in NA RG 12 Records of the Office of Education, Records of the Office of the Commissioner, Historical File, 1870–1950, File 106, Entry 6, Box 7, Folder: Americanization.
43. Letter from Frank Trumbull, chairman, National Americanization Committee, to Commissioner of Education P. Claxton, December 5, 1918, in ibid.
44. In fact, the National Americanization Committee "paid the salaries of specialists, assistants and clerks in the division of immigrant education"; letter from Secretary of the Interior Franklin Lane to Frank Trumbull, March 30, 1918, in NA RG 12 Records of the Office of Education, Records of the Office of the Commissioner, Historical File, 1870–1950, File 420: Immigrant Education Entry 6, Box 7, Folder: Americanization.
45. Letter from Claxton to Frances Kellor, July 17, 1917, in ibid.
46. Memorandum from Commissioner of Education P. P. Claxton to the Secretary of the Interior, August 10, 1916, pp. 1–2, in ibid.
47. Letter from Secretary of the Interior to Secretary of War, June 23, 1917, in ibid.
48. For the commissioner of education's justification of this role for his bureau, see letter from Commissioner Claxton to Senator Hoke Smith, April 23, 1918, and accompanying memoranda, in NA RG 12 Records of the Office of Education, Records of the Office of the Commissioner, Historical Files 1870–1950, File 106, Entry 6, Box 7.
49. See in particular, Division of Education Extension, Department of the Interior, "Suggestive outline of kinds of work that universities can do to promote Americanization," in NA RG 12 Records of the Office of Education, Records of the Office of the Commissioner, Historical File, 1870–1950, File 420: Immigrant Education Entry 6, Box 44, Folder: Americanization.
50. For an account of the separate responsibilities and their (often weak) coor-

dination, see Commissioner Claxton, memorandum on "conflict between federal agencies for Americanization," October 1918, 13 pp., in NA RG 12 Records of the Office of Education, Records of the Office of the Commissioner, Historical File, 1870–1950, File 106: Council of National Defense, 1917–1921, Entry 6, Box 12. The multiplicity of agencies involved was undoubtedly confusing, and Claxton concluded his memo by noting that "it is very important that the work of education which has come to be known as Americanization be centered in one agency." Ibid., p. 12.

51. See *Americanization as a War Measure: Program for Secretary Lane,* conference in the secretary's office, February 9, 1918, in NA RG 12 Records of the Office of Education, Records of the Office of the Commissioner, Historical Files, 1870–1950, File 106: Americanization Entry 6, Box 11. See also letter from Commissioner Claxton to the chairman of the New Hampshire Americanization Committee, September 10, 1918, in which Claxton reports that "there is at present no Federal funds that could be used for co-operation with the States." A bill was pending but failed. In NA RG 12 Records of the Office of Education, Records of the Office of the Commissioner, Historical Files, 1870–1950, File 106, Entry 6, Box 7.

52. See letter from Fred C. Butler, director of Americanization, to Commissioner of Education Claxton, March 5, 1919, in NA RG 12 Records of the Office of Education, Records of the Office of the Commissioner, Historical Files, 1870–1950, File 106: Americanization Entry 6, Box 11. Tougher measures in respect to aliens did succeed during the Second World War: the Alien Registration Act of 1940 required the registration and fingerprinting of aliens.

53. Letter from Franklin K. Lane to Congressman B. F. Welty (Ohio), May 15, 1918, in NA RG 12 Records of the Office of Education, Records of the Office of the Commissioner, Historical Files, 1870–1950, File 106, Entry 6, Box 7.

54. Kellor's involvement with immigrant assimilation began with her work for the New York Bureau of Immigration, established in 1910.

55. Letter from Frances Kellor to Commissioner Claxton, April 10, 1918, in NA RG 12 Records of the Office of Education, Records of the Commissioner of Education, Historical File, 1870–1950, File 106, Entry 6, Box 7.

56. Letter from Frances Kellor to Commissioner Claxton, March 1918, p. 1, in ibid.

57. See correspondence between Frances Kellor and Commissioner Claxton, May 14 and 28, 1918, in ibid.

58. Council of National Defense, Washington, D.C., Memorandum on the Alien Situation in the United States, January 1918, in ibid., Folder: Americanization.

59. Together with his specialist Wheaton: see Department of the Interior, Bureau of Education, H. H. Wheaton, *Establishing Fundamental Standards in the Education of Immigrants* (Washington, D.C.: GPO, 1916).

60. See "Plans for Americanization of the Department of the Interior," 5 pp., in NA RG 12 Records of the Office of Education, Records of the Office of the Commissioner, Historical Files 1870–1950, File 106: Americanization, Entry 6, Box 11. This memorandum systematically sets out the administrative means for Americanization policy.

61. See "Memorandum on Ways and Means" and "Requirements for the Americanization of immigrants," both by Frances Kellor, April 10, 1918, in NA RG 12 Records of the Office of Education, Records of the Office of the Commissioner, Historical Files, 1870–1950, File 106, Entry 6, Box 7.

62. Based in New York and founded in 1909. For details see letter from Frank Trumbell, chairman of the National Americanization Committee, to Commissioner of Education Claxton, April 1, 1919, in which he describes the committee's work thus: "[T]his committee has been a clearing house. It stimulated and helped other organizations engaged in immigration work or starting new work by furnishing them with information, literature, plans, standards, methods, experts and other assistance. It was a general consulting headquarters for immigration work throughout the country." In NA RG 12 Records of the Office of Education, Records of the Office of the Commissioner, Historical Files, 1870–1950, File 106: Americanization, Entry 6, Box 11.

63. Hartmann, *The Movement to Americanize the Immigrant,* p. 121.

64. Letter from Frank Trumbell, chairman of the National Americanization Committee, to Commissioner of Education Claxton, April 1, 1919, p. 2. In NA RG 12 Records of the Office of Education, Records of the Office of the Commissioner, Historical Files, 1870–1950, File 106: Americanization, Entry 6, Box 11.

65. For details, see letter from Frances Kellor to Education Commissioner Claxton, July 14, 1917, p. 2, in NA RG 12 Records of the Office of Education, Records of the Office of the Commissioner, Historical File, 1870–1950, File 420: Immigrant Education Entry 6, Box 44, Folder: Americanization.

66. Letter, together with a copy of the *Independence Day* 1918 statement, from Council of National Defense to state councils of defense, June 4, 1918, in NA RG 12 Records of the Office of Education, Records of the Office of the Commissioner, Historical Files, 1870–1950, File 106: Council of National Defense, 1917–1921, Entry 6, Box 12.

67. Letter from Frank Trumbell, chairman of the National Americanization Committee, to Commissioner of Education Claxton, April 1, 1919, p. 2. In NA RG 12 Records of the Office of Education, Records of the Office of the Commissioner, Historical Files, 1870–1950, File 106: Americanization, Entry 6, Box 11.

68. This was part of the Council of National Defense's war policy in place from October 1917.

69. Council of National Defense, *Bulletin No. 86 Americanization of Aliens,*

February 12, 1918, p. 1, in NA RG 12 Records of the Office of Education, Records of the Office of the Commissioner, Historical File, 1870–1950, File 106, Entry 6, Box 7.

70. See, for example, University of Minnesota, *The Goal of Americanization Training* (Minneapolis: University of Minnesota, January 1920), prepared by Albert Ernest Jenks, Director, Americanization Training Course, University of Minnesota. The document's definition of Americanization included "the combating of anti-American propaganda activities and schemes and the stamping out of sedition and disloyalty wherever found" and "the universal desire of all peoples in America to unite in a common citizenship under one flag." See also University of Colorado Extension Division, Bureau of Americanization, "Suggestions to Citizenship and English Class Instructors," in ibid.

71. For a summary, see letter from Commissioner Claxton to Secretary of the Interior, April 18, 1918, in NA RG 12 Records of the Office of Education, Records of the Office of the Commissioner, Historical File, 1870–1950, File 106, Entry 6, Box 7, Folder: Americanization.

72. For details and a general account of the state's work, see *Americanization: California's Answer,* Commission of Immigration and Housing in California (Sacramento: California State Printing Office, June 1, 1920).

73. Department of the Interior, Bureau of Education, *The Kindergarten and Americanization,* Kindergarten Circular No. 3, November 1918, p. 1, in NA RG 12 Records of the Office of Education, Records of the Office of the Commissioner, Historical File, 1870–1950, File 106, Entry 6, Box 7.

74. Department of the Interior, Bureau of Education "Immigrant Education Letter No. 2," 1, in NA RG 12 Records of the Office of Education, Records of the Office of the Commissioner, Historical File, 1870–1950, File 420: Immigrant Education Entry 6, Box 44, Folder: Americanization.

75. H. H. Wheaton, "Americanization," Department of the Interior, Bureau of Education 1918, p. 2, in ibid.

76. Department of the Interior, Bureau of Education and Council of National Defense, "Organization and Operation of Local War Information Service and Office for Immigrants," 1918, p. 1, in NA RG 12 Records of the Office of Education, Records of the Office of the Commissioner, Historical File, 1870–1950, File 106: Council of National Defense, 1917–1921, Entry 6, Box 12.

77. Council of National Defense, *Bulletin No. 8,* "Americanization," November 2, 1918, in ibid.

78. See, for example, Council of National Defense, "Americanization," July 11, 1918, in ibid.

79. See Committee on Public Information, Division of Four Minute Men, Bulletin No. 33, *The Meaning of America,* 16 pp. (Washington, D.C.: Committee on Public Information, June 1918).

80. Bureau of Education, Americanization Division, *Americanization* 2(3) (November 1919): 7, copy in NA RG 12 Records of the Office of Education,

Records of the Office of the Commissioner, Historical Files, 1870–1950, File 106: Americanization, Entry 6, Box 11.

81. Letter from Commissioner Claxton to Frances Kellor, June 13, 1918, in NA RG 12 Records of the Office of Education, Records of the Office of the Commissioner, Historical File, 1870–1950, File 106, Entry 6, Box 7.

82. Hartmann, *The Movement to Americanize the Immigrant*, p. 187.

83. G. Gerstle, "The Protean Character of American Liberalism," *American Historical Review* 99 (1994): 1043–1073.

84. C. Aronovici, *Americanization* (St. Paul: Keller Publishing Co., 1919), pp. 14–15.

85. Gerstle, "Protean Character of American Liberalism," p. 1053.

86. See letter and enclosure from J. F. Curtice, American Publishing Company, to Secretary of Labor James Davis, March 2, 1922, in NA RG 174 Records of the Department of Labor, General Records, 1907–1942, Chief Clerk's Files, 162/19–163/127, Box 164, Folder: 163/127 Americanization—Sundry Files, 1919–1922.

87. W. M. Leiserson, *Americanization Studies: Adjusting Immigrant and Industry* (New York: Harper and Brother Publishers, 1924), p. 65.

88. The study was directed by Allen Burns for the Carnegie Corporation, under the program "Study of Methods of Americanization." For details, see A. T. Burns, "American Ideals and Methods of Americanization," *Supplement to Community Leadership,* January 1, 1920, pp. 3–4, in NA RG 12 Records of the Office of Education, Records of the Office of the Commissioner, Historical Files, 1870–1950, File 106: Americanization, Entry 6 Box 11. And see letter from Frances Kellor to Commissioner Claxton, May 3, 1918, re the role of the Carnegie Corporation in ibid., Box 7. The Carnegie study was in cooperation with the Department of the Interior's Americanization division.

89. Leiserson, *Adjusting Immigrant and Industry,* pp. 80–81.

90. J. R. Barrett, "Americanization from the Bottom Up: Immigration and the Remaking of the Working Class in the United States, 1880–1930," *Journal of American History* 79 (1992): 996–1020.

91. Letter from Frank Trumbell, chairman of the National Americanization Committee, to Commissioner of Education Claxton, April 1, 1919, p. 2. In NA RG 12 Records of the Office of Education, Records of the Office of the Commissioner, Historical Files, 1870–1950, File 106: Americanization, Entry 6, Box 11.

92. Letter from Frank Trumbell, chairman of the National Americanization Committee, to Commissioner of Education Claxton, April 1, 1919, p. 4. In ibid.

93. *The Commonwealther,* "published every little while by the Commonwealth Fellowship Club for the benefits of the employees of the Commonwealth Steel Company, Granite, Illinois," (2), (May 1916): 127. In NA RG 85 Records of the INS, Education and Americanization Files, 1914–1916, 27671/44–27671/46/1 Entry 30, Box 15.

94. On the former, see letter from James Emery to Secretary of Labor James Da-

vis, December 23, 1921, in NA RG 174 Records of the Department of Labor, General Records, 1907–1942, Chief Clerk's Files, 162/19–163/127, Box 164, Folder: 163/127 Americanization, Sundry Files, 1919–1922.

95. Letter from President United Mine Workers of America to Secretary of Labor James David, July 22, 1921, in ibid.

96. See letter from Joe Bowers, International Benefit Secretary, to Davis, May 25, 1922. In ibid., Box 165.

97. Letter from Campbells to Secretary of Labor James Davis, April 12, 1922, in ibid.

98. Letter from Chas. Ogden to Secretary of Labor James Davis, September 22, 1922, in ibid.

99. Hartmann, *The Movement to Americanize the Immigrant*, p. 268.

100. Letter from Secretary of Labor James Davis to Mr. Earl Constantine, Secretary, National Industrial Council, February 9, 1922, in NA RG 174 Records of the Department of Labor, General Records, 1907–1942, Chief Clerk's Files, 162/19–163/127, Box 164, Folder: 163/127 Americanization, Sundry Files, 1919–1922. And see Constantine's letter to David, February 7, 1922, in ibid.

101. For examples, see ibid.

102. See his account in the letter from Davis to Senator Samuel Shortridge, May 4, 1922, pp. 1–2, in NA RG 174 Records of the Department of Labor, General Records, 1907–1942, Chief Clerk's Files, 163/127A–163/127D, Box 165, Folder: 163/127A Americanization, Sundry Files, 1922.

103. Letter from Davis to Mr. James McCreery, President, National Bank of Summers, Hinton, West Virginia, January 7, 1922, in NA RG 174 Records of the Department of Labor, General Records, 1907–1942, Chief Clerk's Files, 162/19–163/127, Box 164, Folder: 163/127 Americanization, Sundry Files, 1919–1922. In McCreery's letter to the Secretary of Labor, the banker warned that "two thirds of all the murders and robberies that are being committed is by the foreign element. This foreign element is filling all of our towns. Every town has from half a dozen to a dozen of these foreigners. The Government should stop the inflow of foreigners from every country for at least five years." In ibid.

104. Letter from Davis to Mr. J. W. White, Patriotic Order Sons of America, November 29, 1921, in reply to White's letter of November 26, in ibid.

105. J. R. Barrett, "Americanization from the Bottom Up: Immigration and the Remaking of the Working Class in the United States, 1880–1930," *Journal of American History* 79 (1992): 996–1020.

106. Letter from Secretary of Labor James Davis to Senator Samuel M. Shortridge, December 3, 1921, 11 pp., p. 2, in NA RG 174 Records of the Department of Labor, General Records, 1907–1942, Chief Clerk's Files, 162/19–163/127, Box 164, Folder: 163/127 Americanization, Sundry Files, 1919–1922.

107. Ibid., pp. 4, 6.

108. Ibid., p. 3.
109. Ibid., p. 9.
110. Letter from Davis to Robert Deming, Department of Americanization, State Board of Education, Hartford, Connecticut, May 22, 1923, in NA RG 174 Records of the Department of Labor, General Records, 1907–1942, Chief Clerk's Files, 163/127A–163/127D, Box 165, Folder: 163/127C Americanization—Sundry Files, 1922–1923.
111. Letter from Davis to Simon Wolf, Union of American Hebrew Congregations, March 5, 1923, p. 1, in ibid.
112. Ibid.
113. Letter from Raymond Crist to Stanley McMichael, Secretary, Cleveland Real Estate Board, June 6, 1918, in NA RG 85 Records of the INS, Education and Americanization Files, 1914–1936, 27671/4811–4849, Entry 30, Box 191.
114. Letter from Raymond Crist to Stanley McMichael, Secretary, Cleveland Real Estate Board, June 6, 1918, in ibid. Christ was then deputy commissioner in the U.S. Bureau of Naturalization and subsequently commissioner.
115. Lane wrote to Secretary of Labor William Wilson on May 19, 1919, proposing the conference: "I think it is advisable that we should have a conference with our Americanization work in order that your Department and mine may each know just what the other is doing and may harmonise our efforts along this line." In NA RG 174 Records of the Department of Labor, General Records, 1907–1942, Chief Clerk's Files, 162/19–163/127, Box 164, Folder: 163/127 Americanization, Sundry Files, 1919–1922.
116. For details, see material in NA RG 85 Records of the INS, Education and Americanization Files, 27671/4811–E4849, Entry 30, Box 191.
117. In ibid.
118. Conference on Methods of Americanization, held in the Interior Building, Washington, D.C., May 12–15, 1919. In ibid.
119. For example, see "Americanization Conference," Massachusetts Bureau of Immigration, State House, May 28, 1919. In ibid.
120. Letter from John Stewart, chairman, to Secretary of Labor James Davis, March 13, 1920, in NA RG 174 Records of the Department of Labor, General Records 1907–1942, Chief Clerk's Files, 162/19–163/127, Box 164, Folder: 163/127 Americanization, Sundry Files, 1919–1922.
121. For the program, Conference on Citizenship and Americanization, February 28–March 1, 1921, see copy in NA RG 12 Records of the Office of Education, Records of the Office of the Commissioner, Historical Files, 1870–1950, File 103, Entry 6, Box 13: Folder: Atlantic City Conference on Citizenship, February 1921.
122. See letter from Mrs. Fannie Farm Andrews to Commissioner Claxton, October 27, 1920, which also proposed the idea of such a conference, in ibid.
123. American School Citizenship League, *A Reconstruction Program* (1920), copy in ibid.

124. See correspondence between Secretaries of Interior and of Treasury, in NA GR 12 Records of the Office of Education, Records of the Office of the Commissioner, Historical Files, 1870–1950, File 106, Entry 6, Box 7. The program for the exposition, entitled *A New Word in Americanization,* by the Chicago Citizens' Committee, described it as an event "participated in by Americans, citizens of the United States, of as many as possible of the different national or racial strains that go to make up our national stock." It was intended to recognize the contributions of foreign-born citizens: "the object of this recognition is twofold: that of educating the unthinking native born as to the worth of our foreign born citizens, and that of giving to the foreign born a new object of pride: of substituting for his pride in the heroes of the land of his birth pride in the achievements of his blood-brothers in the land of their adoption."

125. E. R. Barkan, *And Still They Come* (Wheeling, Ill.: Harlan Davidson, 1996), p. 20. See also Olneck, "Americanization and the Education of Immigrants."

126. Carlson, *The Americanization Syndrome,* p. 64; and see A. F. Davis, *Spearheads for Reform* (New York: Oxford University Press, 1967) for a study of the settlement movement.

127. Fred C. Butler, "Americanization: Its Purpose and Process," address to the Women's Federation of Wisconsin, Madison, 1919, 17 pp., p. 4, in NA RG 12 Records of the Office of Education, Records of the Office of the Commissioner, Historical Files, 1870–1950, File 106: Americanization, Entry 6, Box 11.

128. Ibid., pp. 5–6.

129. Ibid., p. 10.

130. *Federal Council of Citizenship Training,* address before the American National Council by J. J. Tigert, U.S. Commissioner of Education, May 24, 1923, 10 pp. In ibid., Box 17.

131. Department of the Interior, Bureau of Education, *Community Score Card,* prepared by the Federal Council of Citizenship Training (Washington, D.C.: GPO, 1924), p. 1.

132. *Federal Council of Citizenship Training,* address before the American National Council by J. J. Tigert, U.S. Commissioner of Education, May 24, 1923, 10 pp., p. 3. In NA RG 12 Records of the Office of Education, Records of the Office of the Commissioner, Historical Files, 1870–1950, File 106: Americanization, Entry 6, Box 17.

133. Ibid., p. 5. This was one of five categories of targeted groups identified by the Federal Council. In ibid.

134. See, for instance, letter from Dr. J. M. Lloyd, Americanization Secretary, YMC PA, to Secretary of Labor James Davis, February 20, 1922, describing local Americanization program. In NA RG 174 Records of the Department of Labor, General Records, 1907–1942, Chief Clerk's Files, 162/19–163/127, Box 164, Folder: 163/127 Americanization, Sundry Files, 1919–1922.

135. Report of the Proceedings of the American Legion for the Year 1921, p. 4. In NA RG 233 Records of the U.S. House of Representatives, Committee Papers, Committee on the Judiciary, HR67A-F24.1, Box 404.

136. Ibid., p. 5.

137. Ibid., pp. 5–6.

138. Report of National Americanism Commission, 1920–1921, 26 pp., p. 11. In ibid.

139. Report of the Proceedings of the American Legion for the Year 1921, p. 6. In NA RG 233 Records of the U.S. House of Representatives, Committee Papers, Committee on the Judiciary, HR67A-F24.1, Box 404.

140. Letter from the Commissioner to Mrs. Benjamin Ostlind, December 4, 1923, and see her letter of November 24, 1923, both in NA RG 85 Records of the INS, Education and Americanization Files, 1914–1936, E18033-E17970, Entry 30, Box 265.

141. Included in a letter from Governor Ben W. Olcott to V. W. Tomlinson, Office of Examiner, August 24, 1921, in NA RG 85 Records of the INS, Education and Americanization Files, 1914–1936, 27671/15379–27671/15692, Entry 30, Box 251.

142. "Americanization Issue," *The Messenger* 6, (March 1919): 2. In NA RG 85 Records of the INS, Education and Americanization Files, 1914–1936, 27671/6942–27671/7093, Entry 30, Box 203.

143. See correspondence between W. F. Slade, Camp Educational Director, National War Work Council, YMCA and Bureau of Naturalization, December 1918, in NA RG 85 Records of the INS, Education and Americanization Files, 1914–1936, 27671/4811–E4849, Entry 30, Box 191.

144. At its third convention, in 1921, the legion resolved inter alia in "favor as a prerequisite to naturalization reasonable proficiency in the reading and writing of English and knowledge of civics and American history." Included in a letter from John Taylor, Vice-Chairman, American Legion's National Legislative Committee, to Secretary of Labor James Davis, November 17, 1921, in NA RG 174 Records of the Department of Labor, General Records, 1907–1942, Chief Clerk's Files, 162/19–163/127, Box 164, Folder: 163/127 Americanization, Sundry Files, 1919–1922.

145. Report of National Americanism Commission, 1920–1921, 26 pp., p. 2. In NA RG 233 Records of the U.S. House of Representatives, Committee Papers, Committee on the Judiciary, HR67A-F24.1, Box 404.

146. Barrett, "Americanization from the Bottom Up."

147. Report of National Americanism Commission—1920–21, 26 pp., p. 2. In NA RG 233 Records of the US House of Representatives, Committee Papers, Committee on the Judiciary, HR67A-F24.1 Box 404.

148. Carlson, *The Americanization Syndrome*, pp. 83–85.

149. G. Creel, "The Hopes of the Hyphenated," in *Century* (January 1916), reproduced in Talbot, *Americanization*, p. 172.

150. Hartmann, *The Movement to Americanize the Immigrant*, p. 96.

151. Cited in Olneck, "Americanization and the Education of the Immigrant," p. 412, from an issue of the *Bulletin* in March 1919.
152. *Outlook* 107 (June 13, 1914), "The Old Stock and the New," editorial, reproduced in Talbot, *Americanization*, p. 55. Emphasis added.
153. J. Daniels, *Americanization Studies: America via the Neighborhood* (New York: Harper and Brothers Publishers, 1920), p. 18.
154. For the best account of urban development and ethnic cleavages, see I. Katznelson, *City Trenches* (New York: Pantheon Books, 1981).
155. Letter from Ernest Carpenter, secretary to the Americanization Committee of New Haven to Secretary of Labor James Davis, March 15, 1922, in NA RG 174 Records of the Department of Labor, General Records, 1907–1942, Chief Clerk's Files, 163/127A–163/127D, Box 165, Folder: 163/127A Americanization, Sundry Files, 1922.
156. In letter from Secretary of Labor James Davis to Senator Samuel Shortridge, May 4, 1922, p. 2, in ibid.
157. See "100% American," *The Foreign Language Press* 1920, 24 pp., in NA RG 12 Records of the Office of Education, Records of the Office of the Commissioner, Historical Files 1870–1950, File 106: Council of National Defense, 1917–1921, Entry 6, Box 12.
158. Letter from Secretary of Labor James Davis to Senator Samuel M. Shortridge, December 3, 1921, 11 pp., p. 7, in NA RG 174 Records of the Department of Labor, General Records, 1907–1942, Chief Clerk's Files, 162/19–163/127, Box 164, Folder: 163/127 Americanization, Sundry Files, 1919–1922.
159. Frances Kellor played a central role in this work, as did the U.S. Bureau of Education's racial adviser. For relevant documents and letters about this work, see the material in NA RG 12 Records of the Office of Education, Records of the Office of the Commissioner, Historical Files 1870–1950, File 106, Entry 6, Box 7.
160. Hartmann, *The Movement to Americanize the Immigrant*, p. 237.
161. The Legion's lobbying helped the passage of state laws requiring the teaching of American history in Maine, Oklahoma, Iowa, Illinois, North Dakota, and Nevada. Report of the Proceedings of the American Legion for the Year 1921, p. 4. In NA RG 233 Records of the U.S. House of Representatives, Committee Papers, Committee on the Judiciary, HR67A-F24.1, Box 404.
162. N. McLean, *Behind the Mask of Chivalry* (New York: Oxford University Press, 1994).
163. Bierstadt, *Aspects of Americanization*, p. 26.
164. C. Cooper, "The Necessity for Changes in Americanization Methods," in *National Conference of Social Work*, Pamphlet no. 115, 1918, reproduced in Talbot, *Americanization*, p. 322.
165. *The Americanization Program of the United Neighborhood Houses of New*

York, 1919, p. 4, copy in NA RG 12 Records of the Office of Education, Records of the Office of the Commissioner, Historical Files, 1870–1950, File 106: Americanization, Entry 6, Box 11.

166. F. S. Kemesis, *Cooperation Among the Lithuanians in the United States of America*, Ph.D. thesis, Catholic University, 1924, p. 13.

167. Ibid., p. 33.

168. A. T. Burns, "American Ideals and Methods of Americanization," *Supplement to Community Leadership*, January 1, 1920, pp. 3–4, in NA RG 12 Records of the Office of Education, Records of the Office of the Commissioner, Historical Files, 1870–1950, File 106: Americanization, Entry 6, Box 11.

169. Letter from Frank Trumbell, chairman of the National Americanization Committee, to Commissioner of Education Claxton, April 1, 1919, p. 4. In ibid.

170. F. Kellor, *Neighborhood Americanization, A Discussion of the Alien in a New Country and of the Native American in His Home Country*, 1918, 27 pp., p. 10. Copy in ibid., Box 7.

171. Daniels, *America via the Neighborhood*, p. 100.

172. R. Putnam, *Making Democracy Work* (Princeton: Princeton University Press, 1993).

173. Daniels, *America via the Neighborhood*, p. 107.

174. Ibid., p. 152.

175. Ibid.

176. See, for instance, letter to Commissioner Claxton from his racial adviser, August 7, 1918, in NA RG 12 Records of the Office of Education, Records of the Office of the Commissioner, Historical Files 1870–1950, File 106, Entry 6, Box 7.

177. Daniels, *America via the Neighborhood*, p. 456.

178. M. F. Jacobson, *Whiteness of a Different Color* (Cambridge, Mass.: Harvard University Press, 1998), pp. 56, 58.

179. Daniels, *America via the Neighborhood*, p. 457.

180. Barrett, "Americanization from the Bottom Up," p. 998. And see R. Ueda, "Second-Generation Civic America: Education, Citizenship and the Children of Immigrants," *Journal of Interdisiplinary History* 29 (1999): 661–681.

181. Bureau of Education, Americanization Division, "What a Woman can Do in Americanization," 4 pp., p. 1, in NA RG 12 Records of the Office of Education, Records of the Office of the Commissioner, Historical Files, 1870–1950, File 106: Americanization, Entry 6, Box 11.

182. Bureau of Education, Americanization Division "Making America," 5 pp., pp. 3–4, in ibid.

183. Moorfield Storey, address to the NAACP annual conference, 1921, in De-

troit, p. 4, in NAACP I Papers Box B-5, Folder: Annual Conference, Speeches, 1921.

184. Ibid., pp. 4–5.
185. *Congressional Record—House,* vol. 52, part 2, January 7, 1915, p. 1133. Congressman Martin Madden speaking.
186. Fred C. Butler, "Americanization: Its Purpose and Process," address to the Women's Federation of Wisconsin, Madison, 1919, 17 pp., p. 2, in NA RG 12 Records of the Office of Education, Records of the Office of the Commissioner, Historical Files, 1870–1950, File 106: Americanization, Entry 6, Box 11.
187. On uses of this "child" metaphor, see Takaki, *Iron Cages,* pp. 112–115.
188. Fred C. Butler, "Americanization: Its Purpose and Process," address to the Women's Federation of Wisconsin, Madison, 1919, 17 pp., pp. 2–3, in NA RG 12 Records of the Office of Education, Records of the Office of the Commissioner, Historical Files, 1870–1950, File 106: Americanization, Entry 6, Box 11.
189. Ibid., p. i.
190. Ibid., p. 1.
191. Ibid., p. 10.
192. Butler R. Wilson, "The Growth of Prejudice in New England and How We Are Meeting It," address to NAACP annual conference, 1914, p. 2, in NAACP I Papers Box B-1, Folder: Annual Conference, 1914.
193. Butler, "Americanization: Its Purpose and Process," pp. 11–12.
194. Ibid., p. 12.
195. Barkan, *And Still They Come,* p. 107.
196. W. Wilson, "Message to Newly Naturalized Citizens," in NA RG 12 Records of the Office of Education, Records of the Office of the Commissioner, Historical Files, 1870–1950, File 106: Americanization, Entry 6, Box 11.
197. For instance, Olneck notes that a 1918 U.S. Bureau of Education bulletin declared that "'the government of the United States and the spirit of American democracy know no groups. They know only individuals . . . Not groups of any kind but free men, women and children make up the people of the United States.'" Cited in Olneck, "Americanization and the Education of the Immigrant," p. 402.
198. Ibid., p. 403.
199. U.S. Department of Labor, Naturalization Service, Office of Examiner, speech given by Judge Bledson to petitioners in Naturalization Court, September 22, 1922. In NA RG 85 Records of the INS, Education and Americanization Files, 1914–1936, E18033–E17970, Entry 30, Box 265.
200. Olneck, "Americanization and the Education of the Immigrant," p. 416.
201. Ibid.
202. G. G. Huebner, "The Americanization of the Immigrant," *Annals of the*

American Academy of Political and Social Science, May 1906, reproduced in Talbot, *Americanization,* p. 174.

203. Barrett, "Americanization from the Bottom Up."
204. Katznelson, *City Trenches.*
205. Barrett, "Americanization from the Bottom Up," p. 998.
206. Herman L. Collins, "What Americanization Means," Pennsylvania Council of National Defense, 1921, p. 1, in NA RG 12 Records of the Office of Education, Records of the Office of the Commissioner, Historical File 1870–1950, File 106: Council of National Defense, 1917–1921, Entry 6, Box 12.

5. *"Frequent Skimmings of the Dross"*

1. H. Kallen, "Democracy Versus the Melting-Pot," Part Two, *The Nation* (February 25, 1915), p. 219.
2. H. C. Lodge, "The Restriction of Immigration," *North American Review* 152 (1891), p. 32.
3. R. M. Smith, *Civic Ideals* (New Haven: Yale University Press, 1997), pp. 467–468.
4. The Commission's volumes included odd asides about African Americans. For instance, the Commission's examination of *Immigrants in Cities* revealed that the "proportion of clean homes is higher among the native-born whites than among the immigrants, and much higher among the white race as a whole than among the negro." The Immigration Commission, *Immigrants in Cities* (Washington, D.C.: GPO, 1911), p. 9.
5. M. F. Jacobson, *Whiteness of a Different Color* (Cambridge, Mass.: Harvard University Press, 1998), pp. 42–43.
6. On the court, see I. F. Haney López, *White by Law* (New York: New York University Press, 1996); and on the classifications used in the census, see S. M. Lee, "Racial Classifications in the US Census, 1890–1990," *Ethnic and Racial Studies* 16 (1993).
7. E. Schuster, "Methods and Results of the Galton Laboratory for National Eugenics," *Eugenics Review,* 3 (1), April 1911, pp. 10–24.
8. D. J. Kevles, *In the Name of Eugenics* (Harmondsworth: Penguin, 1986), p. 39.
9. W. Bateson, "Commonsense in Racial Problems," *Eugenics Review* 13 (1921): 325.
10. See H. H. Laughlin, "Eugenics in America," *Eugenics Review* 17 (1) (April 1925): 28–35.
11. See also L. Darwin, "First Steps Toward Eugenic Reform," *Eugenics Review* (4) 1 (April 1912): 38, who uses the terms "constructive eugenics" and "restrictive eugenics" to describe the same dichotomy.
12. Kevles, *In the Name of Eugenics,* p. 47.
13. J. W. Johnson, *The Autobiography of an Ex-Coloured Man* (New York: Vintage, 1989, orig. 1912), p. 161.

14. Dr. Harry H. Laughlin was a superintendent of the Eugenics Record Office from its organization on October 1, 1910, until January 1, 1921, and assistant director from 1921. He served as eugenics expert to the House of Representatives Committee on Immigration and Naturalization between 1921 and 1931.

15. "Europe as an Emigrant-Exporting Continent; the United States as an Immigrant-Receiving Nation," Hearings before the Committee on Immigration and Naturalization, HR, 68th Congress, 1st Session, March 8, 1924, p. 1293.

16. Letter from Goethe to Laughlin, January 15, 1925, in Laughlin Papers, Folder: Goethe Correspondence, C-4-1, Laughlin Papers, Truman State University, Kirksville, Missouri.

17. "Europe as an Emigrant-Exporting Continent," p. 1294.

18. H. H. Laughlin, *Conquest by Immigration,* A Report of the Special Committee on Immigration and Naturalization (New York: Chamber of Commerce of the State of New York, 1939), p. 7.

19. P. P. Claxton, "Racial Groups" memo, 1917, 4 pp. In NA RG 12 Records of the Office of Education, Records of the Office of the Commissioner, Historical Files, 1870–1950, File 106: Council of National Defense, 1917–1921, Entry 6, Box 12.

20. G. Myrdal, *An American Dilemma,* 2 vols. (New York: Harper and Row, 1944).

21. "Europe as an Emigrant-Exporting Continent: the United States as an Immigrant-Receiving Nation," Hearings before the Committee on Immigration and Naturalization, HR, 68th Congress, 1st Session, March 8, 1924, p. 1294.

22. "Immigration from Countries of the Western Hemisphere," hearings before the Committee on Immigration and Naturalization, HR, 70th Congress, 1st Session, February 21, 1928, p. 704.

23. Ibid., p. 705.

24. *Congressional Record—Senate,* vol. 52, part 1, December 31, 1914, p. 805. Senator Williams speaking. And see Congressman Joe Eagle's, Texas, proposals in *Congressional Record—House,* vol. 52, part 2, January 7, 1915, p. 1136.

25. "Europe as an Emigrant-Exporting Continent," pp. 1295–1296.

26. Letter from Fred Wilson, President, the Master Builders' Association of Boston, to Mr. Earl Constantine, National Industrial Council, New York (and copied to Secretary of Labor James Davis), January 7, 1922, in NA RG 174 Records of the U.S. Department of Labor, General Records, 1907–1942, Chief Clerk's Files, 162/19–163/127, Box 164, Folder: 163/127 Americanization—Sundry Files, pp. 1919–1922.

27. Material for Mr. Frank L. Babbott, Notes on Immigration in Relation to National Fortunes, 1927, pp. 3–4, in Laughlin Papers, Folder: Immigration Commission, C-4-2.

28. See, for example, letter from Irving Fisher to Professor H. S. Jennings, Johns

Hopkins University, September 22, 1924, in Laughlin Papers, Folder: Robert Ward, C-4-1.

29. C. Aronovici, *Americanization* (St. Paul: Keller Publishing Co., 1919), p. 9.
30. "Immigration from Countries of the Western Hemisphere," p. 709.
31. H. H. Laughlin, *Conquest by Immigration,* A Report of the Special Committee on Immigration and Naturalization (New York: Chamber of Commerce of the State of New York, 1939), p. 22.
32. NA RG 233 Records of the US HR, 69th Congress, Committee on Immigration, Committee Papers, Box 345, Folder: HR69A-F20.3, Immigration Restriction Conference, under the auspices of The Clergy Club of New York and Neighborhood, New York, April 21, 1924, proceedings, pp. 67–68.
33. Ibid., p. 68.
34. Ibid., p. 69. The chairman was Dr. Walter Laidlaw.
35. Notes for the Fourth Report of the Committee on Selective Immigration of the American Eugenics Society, nd, p. 1, in Laughlin Papers, Special Collections, University Archives, Truman State University.
36. Ibid., p. 2.
37. "Immigration from Countries of the Western Hemisphere," p. 717.
38. Laughlin, *Conquest by Immigration,* p. 31.
39. "Immigration from Countries of the Western Hemisphere," p. 706.
40. "Immigration from Countries of the Western Hemisphere," p. 708.
41. Laughlin, *Conquest by Immigration,* pp. 33–39.
42. Ibid., p. 36.
43. Ibid., p. 39.
44. W. E. B. Du Bois, *The Souls of Black Folk* (1903, Penguin edition, 1989), p. 5. For a useful discussion, see E. Allen, Jr., "On the Reading of Riddles," in L. R. Gordon, ed., *Existence in Black: An Anthology of Black Existential Philosophy* (New York: Routledge, 1997). For an excellent discussion of Du Bois's thought, see A. L. Reed, *W. E. B. Du Bois and American Political Thought* (New York: Oxford University Press, 1997).
45. J. P. Davis, *Let Us Build a National Negro Congress* (Washington, D.C.: National Negro Congress, 1935); and L. B. Granger, "The Negro Congress—Its Future," *Opportunity* 18 (June 1940).
46. K. Woodard, *A Nation within a Nation* (Chapel Hill: University of North Carolina Press, 1999), pp. 29–30.
47. R. D. G. Kelley, *Hammer and Hoe: Alabama Communists during the Great Depression* (Chapel Hill: University of North Carolina Press, 1990).
48. Kelley, *Hammer and Hoe,* p. 91.
49. J. W. Johnson, *The Autobiography of an Ex-Coloured Man* (New York: Vintage, 1989, orig. pub. 1912), p. 75.
50. R. D. G. Kelley, *Race Rebels* (New York: Free Press, 1994), p. 36.
51. See, for instance, K. Anthony Appiah and A. Gutmann, *Color Conscious: The Political Morality of Race* (Princeton: Princeton University Press, 1996); J. J. Fossett and J. A. Tucker, eds., *Race Consciousness: African-*

American Studies for the New Century (New York: New York University Press, 1997); Kelley, *Race Rebels;* W. Lubiano, ed., *The House That Race Built* (New York: Vintage, 1998).

52. D. L. Lewis, *When Harlem Was in Vogue* (New York: Oxford University Press, 1979).

53. W. James, *Holding Aloft the Banner of Ethiopia* (London: Verso, 1998).

54. As Robert Singh observes, "vehemently rejecting the racial integrationism of the fledgling NAACP, Garvey was the most influential early African-American exponent of a distinctive version of black separatism: Pan-African nationalism." R. Singh *The Farrakhan Phenomenon* (Washington, D.C.: Georgetown University Press, 1997), pp. 88–89. See A.-J. Garvey, ed., *Philosophy and Opinions of Marcus Garvey* (New York: Universal Publishing House, 1923); E. D. Cronon, *Black Moses: The Story of Marcus Garvey* (Madison: University of Wisconsin Press, 1955/1969); and T. G. Vincent, *Black Power and the Garvey Movement* (San Francisco: University of California Press, 1972).

55. Cronon, *Black Moses,* pp. 192–193.

56. For a good account, see M. W. Fitzgerald, "'We Have Found a Moses': Theodore Bilbo, Black Nationalism and the Greater Liberia Bill of 1939," *Journal of Southern History* 63 (1997): 293–320; and see M. Mitchell, "'To Inhabit a Free and Independent Country': African-Americans and the Politics of Emigration during the Late 19th Century," paper presented at the conference on "Race and American Political Development," University of Rochester, 1998.

57. K. Woodard, *A Nation within a Nation* (Chapel Hill: University of North Carolina Press, 1998), p. 10; Woodard provides an excellent analysis of this historical process.

58. See D. E. Bernstein, "Roots of the 'Underclass': The Decline of Laissez-Faire Jurisprudence and the Rise of Racist Labor Legislation," *The American University Law Review* 43 (1993): 85–138; D. King, *Separate and Unequal* (Oxford: Oxford University Press, 1995); D. King, "A Strong or Weak State? Race and the US Federal Government in the 1920s," *Ethnic and Racial Studies* 21 (1998): 21–47; G. Myrdal, *An American Dilemma,* 2 vols. (New York: Harper and Row, 1944); President's Committee on Civil Rights, *To Secure These Rights* (Washington, D.C.: GPO, 1947); and C. V. Woodward, *The Strange Career of Jim Crow* (New York: Oxford University Press, 3rd ed., 1974).

59. B. J. Fields, "Ideology and Race in American History," in J. M. Kousser and J. M. McPherson, eds., *Regions, Race and Reconstruction* (New York: Oxford University Press; 1992); and E. Foner, "Blacks and the US Constitution, 1789–1989," *New Left Review,* no. 183 (1990): 63–74.

60. For a good discussion, see L. M. Hershaw, "The Civil Service and the Colored Man," speech to the NAACP annual conference 1914, in NAACP I Papers Box B-1, Folder: Annual Conference, Speeches, 1914.

61. J. H. Franklin, *From Slavery to Freedom* (New York: Knopf, 1974, 4th ed.); D. King, "The Segregated State? Black Americans and the Federal Government," *Democratization* 3 (1996): 65–92; D. King, "The Racial Bureaucracy: African Americans and the Federal Government in the Era of Segregated Race Relations," *Governance* 12 (1999): 345–377; P. P. Van Riper, *The History of the United States Civil Service* (Evanston: Row, Peterson and Co, 1958); K. L. Wolgemuth, "Woodrow Wilson's Appointment Policy and the Negro," *Journal of Southern History* 24 (1958): 457–471; and N. J. Weiss, "The Negro and the New Freedom: Fighting Wilsonian Segregation," *Political Science Quarterly* 84 (1969): 61–79.

62. W. Wilson, *The Papers of Woodrow Wilson,* vol. 28 (Princeton: Princeton University Press, 1978), p. 65.

63. Letter to James Bennett, Director, U.S. Bureau of Prisons, September 1, 1942, in NA RG 129, Records of the Bureau of Prisons, Central Administrative File Box 41.

64. Letter to President Woodrow Wilson "On Federal Race Discrimination," by Moorfield Storey, President, W. E. Burghardt Du Bois, Director of Publicity, and Oswald Garrison Villard, Chairman of the Board, NAACP, August 15, 1913, in NAACP I Box G-34, Folder: DC Branch, 1913–1918.

65. Letter from Neval Thomas, DC, to Miss Mary White Ovington, Chairwoman, Board of Directors, NAACP, November 22, 1919, in Library of Congress Manuscript Collection, Papers of the NAACP I Box C-280, Folder: Discrimination, Restaurants, Supreme Court, 1919.

66. See letters from the chairmen in NAACP I Box C-280, Folder: Discrimination, 1919–1920.

67. Letter to President Woodrow Wilson "On Federal Race Discrimination," by Moorfield Storey, President, W. E. Burghardt Du Bois, Director of Publicity, and Oswald Garrison Villard, Chairman of the Board, NAACP, August 15, 1913, in NAACP I Box G-34, Folder: DC Branch, 1913–1918.

68. For one account, see King, *Separate and Unequal,* ch. 3. For some contemporary cases of discrimination, see Minutes of DC NAACP Branch meeting, November 13, 1918, in NAACP I Box G-34, Folder: DC Branch, 1913–1918.

69. Minutes of DC NAACP Branch meeting, January 17, 1919, in NAACP I Box G-34, Folder: DC Branch, January–April 1919.

70. Letter from Shelby Davidson, DC Branch, to Walter White, December 14, 1922, in NAACP I Box G-34, Folder: DC Branch, January–March 1923.

71. Letter from Walter White to Shelby J. Davidson, DC Branch, December 19, 1922, in ibid.

72. R. B. Sherman, "The Harding Administration and the Negro: An Opportunity Lost," *Journal of Negro History* 49 (1964): 151–168. And see King, "The Racial Bureaucracy."

73. Letter from James Johnson to George Christian, Harding's Secretary, Au-

gust 28, 1920, in NAACP I Box C-66, Folder: Special Correspondence, J. W. Johnson, 1917–1920.

74. Sherman, "The Harding Administration and the Negro," p. 165.

75. Letter from James Johnson to President Coolidge, September 25, 1923, in NAACP I Box C-66, Folder: Special Correspondence, March–December 1923.

76. See letter from James Weldon Johnson to President Coolidge, December 7, 1927, in NAACP I Box C-66, Folder: Special Correspondence, J. W. Johnson 1927. The letter itemized new segregation at the Department of the Interior and the General Land Office.

77. Sherman, "The Harding Administration and the Negro," p. 166.

78. Letter from Neval Thomas to President Calvin Coolidge, August 8, 1927, in NAACP I Box G-36, Folder: DC Branch July–October 1927.

79. Letter from Neval Thomas to President Calvin Coolidge, August 8, 1927, in ibid.

80. Quoted in a report in "NAACP Wins Fight Against Washington DC Segregation," The Negro Americans (November 1927).

81. Letter from Neval H. Thomas to James Weldon Johnson, Secretary NAACP, March 28, 1928, in NAACP I Box G-36, Folder: DC Branch, March–April 1928.

82. The War Department, in fact, was still segregating its employees in the 1940s, as a complaint about card-punch operators in the Machine Records Branch makes plain. NAACP Press Release "NAACP Condemns Jim Crow War Department Office," March 12, 1943, in NAACP II Box A237, Folder: Discrimination and Segregation: Government Agencies, 1941–1955.

83. Letter from Roy Wilkins to Walter White, March 2, 1942, in ibid.

84. Johnson, Autobiography of an Ex-Coloured Man, pp. 153–154.

85. Letter from Neval Thomas, DC, to Miss Mary White Ovington, chairwoman, Board of Directors, NAACP, November 22, 1919, in NAACP I Box C-280, Folder: Discrimination, Restaurants, Supreme Court, 1919.

86. Letter from Walter McCoy, Chief Justice, to John R Shillady, NAACP November 25, 1919, in ibid.

87. In respect to the restaurants, Ulysses S. Grant III—describing himself as "a very sincere friend of the colored race"—fell back on the conventional defense that they were not his responsibility, telling the NAACP that it was misinformed about segregation:

[T]he restaurants in the executive buildings are not Government institutions, as you seem to think, but are operated under concession agreements, and as far as I know the other departments in which restaurants are so operated, insists upon the same food and the same service and prices being made available to colored people as to white people. I do not believe there is any discrimination, nor any segregation which is in any way distressing or humiliating. In fact there is every reason to believe that the Government employees of your race who use these facilities are very well satisfied.

These restaurants or cafeterias, which are not supported by Government appropriations as you appear to think, must be permitted to operate under conditions which enable them to pay expenses. Wherever the service to colored people is separated in space, every effort is made to arrange this in such a way as not to hurt their feelings and it is not thought practicable to do away with the practice entirely under existing circumstances.

Letter from U. S. Grant 3d, Director, Public Buildings and Public Parks of the National Capital, to James Weldon Johnson, June 4, 1928, in NAACP I Box G-36, Folder: DC Branch, May–June 1928).

88. Letter from Neval Thomas to Justice Ashley Gould, December 1919, in NAACP I Box C-280, Folder: Discrimination, Restaurants, Supreme Court, 1919.

89. Letter from Morris Lewis to Walter White, January 25, 1934, in NAACP I Box C-280, Folder: Discrimination: January–February 1934.

90. Ibid.

91. Letter from Walter White to Senator Royal S. Copeland, March 20, 1934, in NAACP I Administrative File, Box C-280, Folder: Discrimination, March 1934.

92. Letter to Roy Wilkins, Assistant Secretary, NAACP, from Representative Sterling P. Strong, January 29, 1934, in NAACP I Administrative File, Box C-280, Folder: Discrimination, January–February 1934.

93. Letter from Roy Wilkins to Congressman Strong, 31 January 1934, in ibid.

94. On De Priest and other African American members of Congress, see R. Singh, *The Congressional Black Caucus* (D.Phil. thesis, University of Oxford, 1994).

95. Congressional Record, March 23, 1934.

96. Letter from Oscar De Priest to Walter White, February 17, 1934, in NAACP I Administrative File, Box C-280, Folder: Discrimination, January–February 1934.

97. 73d Congress, 2d Session H.Res. 236; it was introduced on January 24, 1934, but not voted on until April. The resolution stated "that a committee of five members of the House be appointed by the Speaker to investigate by what authority the Committee on Accounts controls and manages the conduct of the House Restaurant, and by what authority said committee or any members thereof issued and enforced rules or instructions whereby any citizen of the United States is discriminated against on account of race, color, or creed in said House restaurant, grill room, or other public appurtenances of facilities connected therewith under the supervision of the House of Representatives."

98. Declaration of the 13th Annual Conference, June 23, 1922, in NAACP I Papers Box B-5, Folder: Annual Conference, 1922.

99. Johnson, *Autobiography of an Ex-Coloured Man*, pp. 186–187. On the or-

ganization of the "Negro Silent Protest Parade," see memorandum to NAACP Branch secretaries, August 9, 1917, in NAACP I Papers Box C-334, Folder: Silent March, 1917.

100. J. W. Johnson, "The Dyer Anti-Lynching Bill," in NAACP I Box C-66, Folder: Special Correspondence, September–December 1922.

101. See "Sixty Lynchings in 1922," in NAACP I Box C-371, Folder: Lynchings—Studies, 1922–1923. The figure was later revised to 61.

102. Figures from NAACP I Box C-271, Folder: Lynching, Race Riots—studies 1935–1937.

103. For an excellent account, see R. L. Zangrando, *The NAACP Crusade Against Lynching, 1909–1950* (Philadelphia: Temple University Press, 1980).

104. Including "An American Lynching" (New York: NAACP, 1921). The association was encouraged by Woodrow Wilson's condemnation of lynching in July 1918.

105. "Why a Congressional Investigation of Lynching in the United States?" 3 pp., in NAACP I Box C-371, Folder: Lynching, 1919.

106. Since a commitment to such legislation was included in its 1920 platform.

107. For details of the committee's foundation and work, see reports in NAACP I Box C-205, Folder: Anti-Lynching Measures, 1919–1921, and Box C-206 Folder: Anti-Lynching Measures, November 1–30, 1922. It aimed systematically to propagate the outrages of lynching in the United States, to report all cases in detail, and to lobby Congress and the president for a federal response partly by stirring up public concern through newspaper advertisements and rallies.

108. "Federal Law Against Lynchings," speech by L. C. Dyer in the House of Representatives, May 7, 1918, 8 pp., p. 2, in NAACP I Box C-242, Folder Dyer Bill, August–September 1918.

109. Ibid., pp. 2, 4.

110. Letter from L. C. Dyer to John R. Shillady, NAACP, April 6, 1918, in NAACP I Box C-242, Folder: Dyer Bill, April–September 1918.

111. Letter from Dyer to John Shillady, Secretary NAACP, May 3, 1918, in ibid.

112. See Dyer's letter to Miss Nannie Burroughs, May 3, 1918, in ibid.

113. Letter from Shillady to Dyer, May 15, 1918, in ibid.

114. Letter from Moorfield Storey to George B. Christian (Harding's Secretary), August 20, 1920, in NAACP I Box C-66, Folder: Correspondence, Johnson, 1917–1920. The meeting was on August 9.

115. April 4, 1921, memorandum to Warren C. Harding, in NAACP I Box C-66, Folder: Correspondence, James Weldon Johnson, January–April 1921.

116. James Weldon Johnson, now secretary of the NAACP, thanked Harding for his support:

I hope that your recommendation regarding lynching will result in a strong and adequate bill making lynching a crime against the laws of the United

States. I believe it can be done because, as I said to you before, public sentiment, even in the South, is now ready to acquiesce in such legislation. There will, of course, arise some quibbling as to the constitutionality of such an act, but the thing before Congress is to take such action as it feels is necessary for the welfare of the country and leave the constitutionality of the act to the Supreme Court.

Letter from Johnson to President Warren G. Harding, April 20, 1921, in ibid.

117. Which Dyer considered significant as he told the NAACP, letter from Dyer, March 10, 1921, in NAACP I Box C-242, Folder: Dyer Bill, January–June 1921.

118. Letter from Johnson to President Warren G. Harding, July 6, 1921, in NAACP I Box C-66, Folder: Correspondence, James Weldon Johnson, January–April 1921.

119. Speech of Congressman Dyer on the Anti-Lynching Bill (HR 13), p. 6, to the NAACP thirteenth annual conference, June 22, 1922, in NAACP I Papers Box B-5, Folder: Annual Conference 1922.

120. Letter from Johnson to Storey, January 16, 1920, in NAACP I Box C-66, Folder: Correspondence, James Weldon Johnson, 1917–1920.

121. See Minutes of the House Judiciary Committee, June 18, 1921, in NA RG 233 Records of the House of Representatives, House Judiciary Committee, 67th Congress, HR67A-F241.

122. Minutes of the House Judiciary Committee, July 20, 1921, in ibid.

123. Zangrando, *NAACP Crusade Against Lynching,* p. 60. Receiving such endorsement was the strategic path advised in 1918 by Moorfield Storey, former president of the American Bar Association, to the NAACP. See letter, quoting from Storey, from John Shillady to L. C. Dyer, August 5, 1918, in NAACP I Box C-242, Folder: Dyer Bill, April–September 1918.

124. See the discussion in Minutes of the Committee on the Judiciary, May 5, 1921, and May 11, 1921, in NA RG233 Records of the House of Representatives, 67th Congress, HR67A-F24.1. It was shunted to a subcommittee and then back to the full committee.

125. Letter from Johnson to George Christian, Secretary to the President, November 4, 1921, in NAACP I Box C-66, Folder: Correspondence, James Weldon Johnson, May–December 1921.

126. Letter from Johnson to the President, November 28, 1921, in ibid.

127. Letter from NAACP Secretary, James Weldon Johnson, to members of Congress, January 2, 1922, in NAACP I Box C-66, Folder: Special Correspondence, J. W. Johnson, January–May 1922.

The same view had been articulated by Harvard lawyer Albert Pillsbury. As Johnson informed Pillsbury, Dyer's bill "is, I think, based very largely on the argument set forth by you in your article in the Harvard Law review," letter, December 20, 1919, in NAACP I Box C-242, Folder: Dyer Bill,

1919–1920. Pillsbury told Johnson in 1919 that "as the 14th Amendment makes all persons born within the jurisdiction citizens of the United States, and makes citizenship of the United States the primary thing and state citizenship derivative from it, exactly reversing the previous situation, and as the government has a direct interest in the lives of its citizens, the United States has the same power to protect them in their lives in the states that it has in all other parts of the world." This argument directly influenced Dyer's formulation.

128. Zangrando, *NAACP Crusade Against Lynching,* p. 65.
129. Given some of his writings, this was a turnabout: see, for example, H. C. Lodge, "Lynch Law and Unrestricted Immigration," *North American Review* 152 (1891): 602–612.
130. Zangrando, *NAACP Crusade Against Lynching,* p. 66.
131. Telegram to Harding from Johnson, August 22, 1922, in NAACP I Box C-66, Folder: Special Correspondence, J. W. Johnson, June–August 1922.
132. Letter from James Johnson to George Christian, September 9, 1922, in NAACP I Box C-66, Folder: Special Correspondence, J. W. Johnson, September–December 1922.
133. Letter from Johnson to J. E. Spingarn, December 15, 1922, in ibid.
134. Introductory Remarks of James Weldon Johnson, Twentieth Annual Conference of the NAACP, Cleveland, June 30, 1929, pp. 1–2, in NAACP I Papers Box B-6, Folder: Annual Conference, Speeches, 1929.
135. Letter from Johnson to George Christian, December 21, 1922, in NAACP I Box C-66, Folder: Special Correspondence, J. W. Johnson, September–December 1922.
136. See, for example, letters from James Johnson to President Calvin Coolidge, March 6, 1921, and June 3, 1925, in NAACP I Box C-66, Folder: Special Correspondence, J. W. Johnson, 1925.
137. Zangrando, *NAACP Crusade Against Lynching,* p. 63.
138. *Congressional Record—Senate,* vol. 52, part 1, December 31, 1914, p. 805.
139. Ibid.
140. See C. J. Kim, "The Racial Triangulation of Asian Americans," *Politics and Society* 27 (1999): 105–138.
141. *Congressional Record—Senate,* vol. 52, part 1, December 31, 1914, p. 805.
142. Ibid.
143. Ibid., p. 807.
144. *Congressional Record—House,* vol. 52, part 2, January 7, 1915, p. 1139.
145. One of his fellow congressmen, Texan Joe Eagle, characterized entering Madden's constituency as equivalent to "entering the heart of Africa. He has more voting negro constituents than any other member of Congress." Ibid., p. 1136.
146. Ibid., p. 1133.
147. Ibid.
148. Ibid., p. 1134. Congressman J. Hampton Moore, Pennsylvania, speaking.

149. Ibid., p. 1135, Congressman Neeley speaking.

150. Ibid., p. 1135.

151. Ibid., p. 1134. Congressman Quinn, a Mississippian, speaking.

152. Ibid., p. 1135. Congressman James Aswell, Louisiana, speaking.

153. See the account in *Crisis* 9 (February 1915): 185–190.

154. Ira Reid writes that "almost the entire body of Negro immigration to the United States comes from the Crown Colonies and the Dependencies of Great Britain and France, located in the West Indies." *The Negro Immigrant: His Background, Characteristics and Social Adjustment, 1899–1937* (New York: Columbia University Press, 1939), p. 45.

155. Reid, *Negro Immigrant*, p. 42; W. James, *Holding Aloft the Banner of Ethiopia* (London: Verso, 1997).

156. See "Jamaica Negro Influx Is Checked," *New York World* (July 7, 1924), in NAACP I Papers, Box C-373, Folder: Migration. The newspaper story reported that new regulations restricted significantly the number of Jamaicans able to emigrate to the United States. Marcus Garvey used the occasion to cite Liberia as the appropriate "goal of Negro emigrants."

157. James, *Holding Aloft the Banner of Ethiopia.*

158. Reid, *Negro Immigrant.* For the more recent experience, see P. Kasinitz, *Caribbean New York: Black Immigrants and the Politics of Race* (Ithaca: Cornell University Press, 1992).

159. *Congressional Record—Senate,* vol. 52, part 1, December 31, 1914, p. 806.

160. James, *Holding Aloft the Banner of Ethiopia,* p. 93.

161. Reid, *Negro Immigrant,* p. 190.

162. Ibid., p. 60.

163. Quoted in James, *Holding Aloft the Banner of Ethiopia,* p. 2.

164. In ibid., p. 50.

165. Reid, *Negro Immigrant,* p. 215. For an update, see M. Vickerman, *Crosscurrents: West Indian Immigrants and Race* (New York: Oxford University Press, 1999).

166. For African American attitudes toward other immigrants, see A. Shankman, *Ambivalent Friends: Afro-Americans View the Immigrant* (Westport, Conn.: Greenwood Press, 1982). Using newspaper and other primary sources, Shankman examines attitudes toward the Chinese, Japanese, Mexicans, Italians in the South, and Southern Jews. See also S. Lieberson, *A Piece of the Pie: Blacks and White Immigrants Since 1880* (Berkeley: University of California Press, 1980).

167. Statement by Walter F. White, July 17, 1923, pp. 2–3, in NAACP I Papers Box C-373, Folder: Migration, 1920–1923.

168. Reid, *Negro Immigrant,* p. 218.

169. See the excellent analysis in James, *Holding Aloft the Banner of Ethiopia,* ch. 6.

170. Ibid., p. 184.

171. Letter from Dr. C. Jackman, Secretary, Negro Foreign Born Citizens Alli-

ance, to Congressman Isaac Siegel, August 10, 1921, in NA RG 85 Records of the INS, Education and Americanization Files, 1914–1936, 27671/15379–27671/15692, Entry 30, Box 251.

172. Letter from Director to Alliance Secretary, August 17, 1921, in ibid.

173. Arthur Lazarus, Jr., "What the McCarran-Walter Immigration Bill (S. 2550; H. R. 5678) Means to Negroes," February 1952, 4 pp., pp. 1–2, in NAACP Washington Bureau Part I, Box I-107, Folder: Immigration 1952.

174. Letter from White to Mr. Albert G. Fraser, Travelers Aid Society, February 21, 1923, in NAACP I Papers Box C-373, Folder: Migration, 1920–1923. In another letter, White itemized in detail the push factors in the South and the attractions of the North: see letter to Mrs. Robert Bruers, The Survey, June 20, 1923, ibid.

175. Letter from Walter White to John Shillady, NAACP Secretary, October 26, 1918, in NAACP I Papers, Box C-417, Folder: Work or Fight, 1918.

176. See Reginald A. Johnson, "Population Trends and Migration," June 6, 1945, 4 pp., in National Urban League Papers, MD LC, Series 3, Box 18, Folder: Migrants.

177. Statement by Walter F. White, July 17, 1923, p. 2, in NAACP I Papers, Box C-373, Folder: Migration, 1920–1923.

178. "Migration Tide May Flow Back," New York World (December 8, 1918), in NAACP I Papers, Box C-372, Folder: Migration, 1917–1919.

179. Ibid.

180. Eugene Kinckle Jones, "The Negro in Labor and Industry," address to the NAACP annual conference, June 24, 1919, pp. 1–2, in NAACP I Papers, Box B-2, Folder: Annual Conference, 1919.

181. Congressman W. Mason, "Southerners for Return of Negroes," The Hartford Daily Times (September 4, 1919), in NAACP I Papers, Box C-372, Folder: Migration 1917–1919. And see "South Wants Its Negroes Back to Care for Crops," Chicago Post (August 19, 1919), in ibid.

182. "The Negro Migrant," talk by Phil Brown, Commissioner of Conciliation, U.S. Department of Labor, given before the International Association of Employment Services, Toronto, September 6, 1923, 8 pp., p. 4, in NAACP I Papers, Box C-373, Folder: Migration, 1920–1923.

183. Ibid., p. 5.

184. Ibid

185. Ibid., pp. 6–7.

186. Letter from Samuel Gompers to Jones, March 25, 1918, in NAACP I Papers, Box B-2, Folder: Annual conference, 1919.

187. "The Economic Foundations of Race Prejudice," presented at the NAACP annual conference, 1929, p. 3, in NAACP I Papers, Box B-6, Folder: Annual Conference Speeches, 1929. As noted in Chapter 2, Haney López's analysis of Supreme Court reasoning in its naturalization cases demonstrated just

how vacuous and poorly founded alleged legal arguments about race were at this time. I. F. Haney López, *White by Law: The Legal Construction of Race* (New York: New York University Press, 1996).

188. "The Economic Foundations of Race Prejudice," presented at the NAACP annual conference 1929, pp. 11–12, in NAACP I Papers, Box B-6, Folder: Annual Conference Speeches, 1929.

189. Nannie H. Burroughs, "America—a Democracy with a Milestone About Its Neck," speech to the NAACP annual conference 1929, p. 2, in NAACP I Papers, Box B-6, Folder: Annual conference, Speeches, 1929.

190. Ibid.

191. James, *Holding Aloft the Banner of Ethiopia*.

6. *"A Very Serious National Menace"*

1. L. Darwin "First Steps Toward Eugenic Reform," *Eugenics Review* 4 (1) (April 1912): 26. Also see his later statement: "Programme of Eugenic Reform," *Eugenics Review* 15 (3) (October 1923): 595–596.

2. G. E. Allen, "The Eugenics Record Office at Cold Spring Harbor, 1910–1940: An Essay in Institutional History," *Osiris* 2nd series 2 (1986): 225–264. For a contemporary account, see C. B. Davenport, "The Work of the Eugenics Record Office," *Eugenics Review* 15 (1) (April 1923). The philanthropist was Mrs. E. Harriman.

3. *Buck v. Bell*, 274 U. S. 200 (1927), p. 207. See P. A. Lomdardo, "Three Generations, No Imbeciles: New Light on *Buck v. Bell*," *New York University Law review* 60 (1985): 30–62.

4. As recounted in E. J. Larson's *Sex, Race, and Science: Eugenics in the Deep South* (Baltimore: Johns Hopkins University Press, 1995). See also A. C. Carey, "Gender and Compulsory Sterilization Programs in America: 1807–1950," *Journal of Historical Sociology* 11 (1998): 74–105; and P. R. Reilly, "The Surgical Solution: The Writings of Activist Physicians in the Early Years of Eugenical Sterilization," *Perspectives in Biology and Medicine* 26 (1983): 637–656.

5. D. J. Kevles, *In the Name of Eugenics* (Harmondsworth: Penguin, 1986), p. 52.

6. Ibid., p. 51.

7. S. Kuhl, *The Nazi Connection: Eugenics, American Racism, and German National Socialism* (New York: Oxford University Press, 1994), p. 87.

8. Kuhl, *The Nazi Connection*, p. 37.

9. D. J. Kevles, "Grounds for Breeding," *Times Literary Supplement* (January 2, 1998).

10. See, for example, L. Darwin, "How Should Our Society Now Strive to Advance?" *Eugenics Review* 13 (October 1921): 439–455.

11. F. Dikotter, "Race Culture: Recent Perspectives on the History of Eugenics," *American Historical Review* (1998): 467.
12. Dikotter, "Race Culture," p. 468.
13. T. F. Gossett, *Race: The History of an Idea in America* (New York: Oxford University Press, 1963, rev. ed. 1997), p. 145.
14. Ibid., p. 158.
15. Kevles, *In the Name of Eugenics*, p. 76.
16. I. R. Dowbiggin, *Keeping America Sane: Psychiatry and Eugenics in the United States and Canada, 1880–1940* (Ithaca, N.Y.: Cornell University Press, 1997), p. x.
17. Quoted in E. R. Barkan, *And Still They Come* (Wheeling, Ill.: Harlan Davidson, 1996), p. 12.
18. See Papers of the Immigration Restriction League, Box 1, Houghton Library, Harvard.
19. B. M. Solomon, *Ancestors and Immigrants* (Chicago: University of Chicago Press 1956/1972), p. 148.
20. Gossett, *Race: The History of an Idea in America*, p. 297.
21. Ibid., p. 364.
22. Ibid., p. 368.
23. Ibid., p. 369.
24. Ibid., p. 379.
25. NA RG 233 Records of the HR, 63d Congress, Committee on Immigration, Box 458, Folder: HR63A-H8.1, petitions from the New York and Massachusetts Medical Societies.
26. NA RG 233 Records of the HR, 69th Congress, Committee on Immigration, Committee Papers, Box 341, Folder: H69A-F20.1, letter from Frank L. Babbott, President, Eugenics Research Association, to Congressman Johnson, March 31, 1927.
27. Immigration Commission, *Abstract of the Report on Fecundity of Immigrant Women* (Washington, D.C.: GPO, 1911).
28. See J. Higham, *Strangers in the Land,* 2nd ed. (New Brunswick, N.J.: Rutgers University Press, 1988), pp. 151–157.
29. G. E. Allen, "The Role of Experts in Scientific Controversy," in H. T. Engelhardt, Jr., and A. L. Caplan, eds., *Scientific Controversies* (Cambridge: Cambridge University Press, 1987), p. 172.
30. "Amendment to Immigration Law," Hearings before the Committee on Immigration, U.S. Senate, 67th Congress, 4th Session, January 24, 1923, in evidence presented by W. W. Husband, Commissioner General of Immigration, p. 9.
31. Gossett, *Race: The History of an Idea in America*, p. 373.
32. On the eugenic principles influential with Laughlin, see the various memoranda in Laughlin Papers, Folder: Fundamental Biological Principles, C-4-4, Laughlin Papers, Truman State University.
33. See, for example, letter from the president of the Carnegie Institution of

Washington to Laughlin, December 1, 1925, in which the president, John C. Merriam, writes: "of course you know in advance my great interest in the whole question of immigration and my desire to see the Carnegie Institution make contribution toward solution of the problems involved through fundamental studies in eugenics." Laughlin Papers, Folder: Letters—Immigration 1923–1926, C-4-3.

34. See the curious "Memorandum and Outline of Tentative Working Agreement between the Carnegie Institution of Washington and the State Department of the Federal Government in reference to Collaboration in the Collection of First-Hand Data on Immigration at Its Sources," July 11, 1924 (prepared by Laughlin), and a letter from the Carnegie Institution's nonplussed administrative secretary to Laughlin, August 13, 1924, both in Laughlin Papers, Folder: Letters—Immigration 1923–1926, C-4-2.

35. NA RG 233 Records of the US HR, 69th Congress, Committee on Immigration, Correspondence, Box 342, Folder: HR69A-F20.1, letter from Johnson to F. A. Kinnicutt, April 27, 1926.

36. NA RG 233 Records of the US HR, 69th Congress, Committee on Immigration, Committee Papers, Box 341, Folder: H69A-F20.1, referred to in a letter from Madison Grant to Johnson, April 20, 1926; see also telegram from Laughlin to Johnson, April 15, 1926.

37. As Laughlin wrote to one correspondent in 1922: "Chairman Albert Johnson is much concerned with the new studies, and has recently designated me their agent with semi-official standing for the purpose of collecting and analysing data on the eugenical aspects of immigration." Letter from Laughlin to Frank Babbott, February 18, 1922, in Laughlin Papers, Folder: Letters, Frank Babbott, C-4-3.

38. NA RG 233 Records of the US HR, 70th Congress, Committee on Immigration, Committee Papers, Box 240, Folder: HR70A-F14.6, letter from Congressman Emanuel Celler to Harry Laughlin, January 23, 1928; the survey elicited information from the racial descent of American citizens about patents they registered in a three-month period. Laughlin wisely referred the letter to Johnson, who replied to Celler on February 6: "this study is but one of several statistical studies designed to show statistics—the nationality of the ancestry etc, of those active in public and other affairs." Celler was a liberal Democrat who consistently criticized restrictionist legislation, and as chairman of the House Judiciary Committee, he advanced legislation to assist displaced persons.

39. A study was also undertaken in 1927, for the House Committee on Immigration, by the Department of Labor, of the number of alien inmates in penal and public institutions in the United States. NA RG 233 Records of the US HR, 69th Congress, Committee on Immigration, Committee Papers, Box 345, Folder: HR69A-F20.3, letter from R. C. White, assistant secretary, to Congressman Albert Johnson, February 9, 1927. The study found a

total of 111,673 alien inmates of whom about 40 percent were considered likely to be eligible for deportation.

40. Letter from Laughlin to Frank Babbott, February 18, 1922, in Laughlin Papers, Folder: Letters, Frank Babbott, C-4–3. Babbott joined Laughlin's Eugenics Research Association and contributed funds to it.

41. On Laughlin's papers, see R. D. Bird and G. Allen, "The Papers of Harry Hamilton Laughlin, Eugenicist," *Journal of the History of Biology* 14 (2) (1981): 339–353. This provides an introduction to the collection at Truman State University (formerly Northeast Missouri State University) at Kirksville. And see the discussion in M. F. Jacobson, *Whiteness of a Different Color* (Cambridge, Mass.: Harvard University Press, 1998), pp. 82–87.

42. See, for example, his letter to W. W. Husband, Assistant Secretary of Labor, in 1930, congratulating him on a radio broadcast about immigration: letter from Laughlin to Husband, August 22, 1930, in Laughlin Papers, C-4–2.

43. For its pernicious international context, see M. Burleigh, *Death and Deliverance* (Cambridge: Cambridge University Press, 1994).

44. "Biological Aspects of Immigration," hearings before the Committee on Immigration and Naturalization, HR 66th Congress, 2d Session, April 16, 1920, p. 3.

45. In addition to the ones listed here, Laughlin identified 16 other topics for "scientific" investigation by his eugenics team: (1) deportation; (2) a study of the higher "racial" groups to complement the study of degenerates; (3) eugenic standards for admission; (4) the eugenic dimensions of a national registration policy; (5) special racial studies of Japanese and Chinese, Indians, and blacks; (6) the process of mate selection and racial mixing; (7) biology and interstate migration; (8) different rates of fecundity by race; (9) studies of oriental and occidental race mixes; (10) sex types and immigration; (11) emigration from foreign nations to evaluate relative worth; (12) "a study of the Jew as an immigrant with special reference to numbers and assimilation"; (13) naturalization records; (14) various racial aspects of assimilation; (15) eugenics of contract labor; and (16) study of "dumping" of undesirables. This chilling inventory struck Laughlin as "the most promising for scientific research." "Analysis of America's Modern Melting Pot," Hearings before the Committee on Immigration and Naturalization, HR 67th Congress, 3rd Session, November 21, 1922, p. 759.

46. See letter from Congressman John C. Box to Laughlin, February 16, 1928, in Laughlin Papers, Special Collections, University Archives, Truman State University.

47. He was appointed as "dollar-a-year" representative from the Department of Labor on one occasion. See letter from Laughlin to Madison Grant, July 23, 1930, suggesting a renewal of this arrangement, and a similar one with the State Department, in Laughlin Papers, Folder: C-4–1, Special Collections, University Archives, Truman State University.

48. Letter from Laughlin to Captain John B. Trevor, August 18, 1930, in ibid.

49. Letter from Laughlin to James J. Davis, Secretary of Labor, July 30, 1930, in ibid. He added, "if I could have an appointment from the Secretary of Labor as 'Immigration Investigator' or as 'US Immigration Agent or Representative' I could conduct this work under the most favorable auspices and could, I believe, produce a study which would throw some first hand light upon the particular problem. This would involve no financial obligations on the part of the Government."

50. Letter from C. Floyd Haviland to Professor Irving Fisher, January, 12 1924, in Laughlin Papers, Folder: Robert Ward, C-4–1. The state asked the federal government for $18 million to support them.

51. Hearings before the Committee on Immigration and Naturalization, HR, 69th Congress, 1st Session, March 25–26, 1926, p. 129.

52. Ibid., p. 130.

53. Dowbiggin, *Keeping America Sane*, p. 191.

54. "Admission of Mentally Defective Children," hearings before the Committee on Immigration and Naturalization, HR 67th Congress, 4th Session, December 5, 1922, and January 16, 1923; see especially testimony by W. W. Husband, pp. 203–216.

55. NA RG 233 Records of the US HR, 69th Congress, Committee on Immigration, Committee Papers, Box 341, Folder: H69A-F20.1; see letter from Henry Pratt Fairchild, January 15, 1927.

56. "Biological Aspects of Immigration," hearings before the Committee on Immigration and Naturalization, HR 66th Congress, 2d Session, April 17, 1920, p. 10.

57. Ibid., p. 11.

58. Dowbiggin, *Keeping America Sane*, p. 221.

59. "Biological Aspects of Immigration," hearings before the Committee on Immigration and Naturalization, HR 66th Congress, 2d Session, April 17, 1920, p. 120.

60. See Nicole Hahn Rafter, ed., *White Trash: The Eugenic Family Studies, 1877–1919* (Boston: Northeastern University Press, 1988).

61. Kenneth L. Roberts, "Lest We Forget," *Saturday Evening Post* (April 18, 1923): 160.

62. LC MD Papers of Calvin Coolidge, File 133 (Reel 78), Department of Labor, Memorandum "In the matter of cooperation between officers of States and Municipalities with officers of the United States in connection with the enforcement of the Immigration Laws," 14 pp., October 1923, p. 2.

63. LC MD Papers of Franklin MacVeagh, Box 31, Folder: Immigration Protection League, 1905–1928, Immigration Protection League Bulletin No. 28, February 1928, "Fake Economy."

64. See, for example, "Crime and Race Descent," October 1931, in Laughlin Papers, Special Collections, University Archives, Truman State University.

65. Letter from Laughlin to Frank L. Babbott, January 23, 1926, in Laughlin Papers, Folder: Letters to Babbott, C-4–3.

66. "Analysis of America's Modern Melting Pot," hearings before the Committee on Immigration and Naturalization, HR 67th Congress, 3rd Session, November 21, 1922, p. 731. Laughlin explained that the data compiled by him were designed to "gauge the relative soundness and stability of the different racial and nativity groups in the United States, which gauge, in turn, would constitute a measure of their relative long-term value to the Nation, especially when viewed in the light of the inborn quality of future generations."

67. "Biological Aspects of Immigration," hearings before the Committee on Immigration and Naturalization, HR 66th Congress, 2d Session, April 17, 1920, p. 13.

68. Ibid.

69. Dr. H. H. Goddard published the study of the Kallikak family in 1912 and was the author of an influential general study, *Feeble-mindedness: Its Causes and Consequences* (New York: Macmillan, 1914). He was a pioneer of I.Q. tests.

70. "Biological Aspects of Immigration," hearings before the Committee on Immigration and Naturalization, HR 66th Congress, 2d Session, April 16, 1920, p. 3.

71. Ibid., p. 4.

72. "Biological Aspects of Immigration," hearings before the Committee on Immigration and Naturalization, HR 66th Congress, 2d Session, April 17 1920, p. 17.

73. "Biological Aspects of Immigration," hearings before the Committee on Immigration and Naturalization, HR 66th Congress, 2d Session, April 16, 1920, p. 4.

74. Ibid., pp. 4–5. For one account and searing critique of the methodology deployed to study these families, see S. J. Gould, *The Mismeasure of Man* (Harmondsworth: Penguin, 1981), ch. 5; the limits of these cases are also discussed in ch. 10 on the British campaign for sterilization in the 1930s.

75. "The Eugenical Aspects of Deportation," hearings before the Committee on Immigration and Naturalization, HR 70th Congress, 1st Session, February 21, 1928, p. 35.

76. "Biological Aspects of Immigration," hearings before the Committee on Immigration and Naturalization, HR 66th Congress, 2d Session, April 17, 1920, p. 22.

77. Ibid., p. 23.

78. Ibid., p. 14. Emphasis added.

79. Ibid., p. 15.

80. "Analysis of America's Modern Melting Pot," hearings before the Committee on Immigration and Naturalization, HR 67th Congress, 3rd Session, November 21, 1922, p. 730.

81. Ibid., p. 731.

82. Ibid., p. 733.

83. Ibid., p. 755.

84. Ibid., p. 748.

85. "Europe as an Emigrant-Exporting Continent; the United States as an Immigrant-Receiving Nation," hearings before the Committee on Immigration and Naturalization, HR 68th Congress, 1st Session, March 8, 1924, p. 1317.

86. Jacobson, *Whiteness of a Different Color,* pp. 85–86.

87. Letter from Jennings to Professor Irving Fisher, September 27, 1924, in Laughlin Papers, Folder: Robert Ward, C-4–1. Jennings published his criticisms in *Science* 59 (March 24, 1924): 256–257.

88. Laughlin later addressed these criticisms before the congressional committee and rejected them: see his "Europe as an Emigrant Exporting Continent and the United States as an Immigrant Receiving Nation."

89. Letter from Fisher to Jennings, October 2, 1924, in Laughlin Papers, Folder: Robert Ward, C-4–1.

90. In a letter from Charles Davenport, Director of the Department of Genetics at the Carnegie Institution, to Laughlin, he writes that "a review of your sterilization book appeared in 'Nature' for September 15th. Dr Merriam [President of Carnegie] seems to take the criticisms involved somewhat seriously; tho he does not fail to recognize the excellence of the book." October 16, 1923. In Laughlin Papers, Folder: Field Workers, C-2–6.

91. Barkan, *And Still They Come,* p. 12.

92. Gossett, *Race: The History of an Idea in America,* p. 409.

93. Dikotter, "Race Culture," p. 471.

94. R. A. Nye, "The Rise and Fall of the Eugenics Empire: Recent Perspectives on the Impact of Biomedical Thought in Modern Society," *Historical Journal* 36 (1993), p. 696.

95. E. Barkan, *The Retreat of Scientific Racism* (Cambridge: Cambridge University Press, 1992); and Kevles, *In the Name of Eugenics.*

96. "Analysis of America's Modern Melting Pot," hearings before the Committee on Immigration and Naturalization, HR 67th Congress, 3rd Session, November 21, 1922, p. 757.

97. On the background to this study and Laughlin's preliminary findings from Europe, see his long letter, written in Brussels, to Charles Davenport, November 22, 1923, in Laughlin Papers, Folder: Field Workers, C-2–6.

98. "Europe as an Emigrant-Exporting Continent; the United States as an Immigrant-Receiving Nation," hearings before the Committee on Immigration and Naturalization, HR 68th Congress, 1st Session, March 8, 1924, p. 1237.

99. Ibid., p. 1238.

100. Ibid., p. 1307.

101. "The Eugenical Aspects of Deportation," hearings before the Committee on Immigration and Naturalization, HR 70th Congress, 1st Session, February 21, 1928, p. 23.

102. Ibid., pp. 20–21.
103. Ibid., p. 46.
104. Notes for the Fourth Report of the Committee on Selective Immigration of the American Eugenics Society, nd, p. 1, in Laughlin Papers, Special Collections, University Archives, Truman State University.
105. H. H. Laughlin, "The Control of Trends in the Racial Composition of the American People," ca. 1928, p. 3, in ibid.
106. In Britain, Laughlin also met the commissioners of immigration for British Dominions (Canada, Australia, New Zealand, and South Africa) whose "immigration problems are practically the same as those of the United States." "Europe as an Emigrant-Exporting Continent; the United States as an Immigrant-Receiving Nation," hearings before the Committee on Immigration and Naturalization, HR 68th Congress, 1st Session, March 8, 1924, p. 1233.
107. Ibid., p. 1269.
108. Ibid., p. 1316.
109. Ibid., p. 1273.
110. Ibid., pp. 1277–1278.
111. "The Eugenical Aspects of Deportation," hearings before the Committee on Immigration and Naturalization, HR 70th Congress, 1st Session, February 21, 1928, p. 3.
112. Ibid., p. 5.
113. Ibid., p. 6.
114. Ibid., p. 9.
115. Ibid., p. 23.
116. "Immigration from Countries of the Western Hemisphere," in ibid., pp. 712–714.
117. "Europe as an Emigrant-Exporting Continent; the United States as an Immigrant-Receiving Nation," hearings before the Committee on Immigration and Naturalization, HR 68th Congress, 1st Session, March 8, 1924, p. 1268.
118. "Biological Aspects of Immigration," hearings before the Committee on Immigration and Naturalization, HR 66th Congress, 2d Session, April 17, 1920, p. 7.
119. Ibid.
120. Ibid., p. 8.
121. NA RG 233 Records of the US HR, 69th Congress, Committee on Immigration, Committee Papers, Box 345, Folder: HR69A-20.3. Third report of the Subcommittee on Selective Immigration of the Eugenics Committee of the USA, "The examination of Immigrants Overseas, as an Additional Safeguard in the Processes of Enforcing American Immigration Policy," 1926, 12 pp., p. 2.

122. Ibid., p. 6.
123. Ibid.
124. Ibid., p. 8.
125. Ibid., p. 9.
126. "Researches on the Biological Aspects of Immigration," summary, 12 pp., May 1939, in Laughlin Papers, Folder: Reports 1938–1939, C-4-3.
127. See, for example, the correspondence between H. G. Dunlap, Immigrant Inspector, and Laughlin, contained in Laughlin Papers, Folder: Registration of Aliens, 1931, C-4-6. The folder includes Dunlap's memorandum on "Registration and Deportation of Aliens."
128. See "Shift in Responsibility for Inadequates," 1935, n.a., in Laughlin Papers, Folder: Immigration and Unemployment, 1935, C-4-4.
129. NA RG 233 Records of the US HR, 69th Congress, Committee on Immigration, Committee Papers, Box 341, Folder: H69A-F20.1, letter from Johnson to Kinnicutt, April 28, 1926.
130. J. Higham, *Strangers in the Land* (1988), p. 314.
131. See letter from Charles Davenport to Prescott Hall, May 1911, in Papers of the Immigration Restriction League, Box 1.
132. NA RG 46 Records of the US Senate, 71st Congress, Box 172, Folder: 71A-J32. Letter from Edward T. Clark to Senator R. S. Copeland, November 29, 1930, enclosing "Immigration Programme" Committee on Selective Immigration of the American Eugenics Society, November 11, 1930. The committee members who signed the programme were Madison Grant (chairman), Guy Irving Burch (Secretary), Charles W. Gould, Roswell H. Johnson, Francis H. Kinnicutt, H. H. Laughlin, John B. Trevor, Robert DeC. Ward, Roy L. Garis, and Henry Pratt Fairchild.
133. LC MD, Papers of Calvin Coolidge, File 133 (Reel 79), letter from Robert DeC. Ward to Coolidge, May 26, 1924.
134. NA RG 233 Records of the US HR, 70th Congress, Committee on Immigration, Committee Papers, Box 239, Folder: HR70A-F14.4, Edward R. Lewis, "National Origins and American Immigration," 30 pp.
135. NA RG 233 Records of the US HR, 69th Congress, Committee on Immigration, Correspondence, Box 342, Folder: HR69A-F20.1, letter from Johnson to Capt. John B. Trevor, February 21, 1927.
136. In ibid., letter from Stoddard to Johnson, January 14, 1927. The former was preparing his book *Re-Forging America*. Johnson replied obsequiously on January 18, reporting that "Captain Trevor and Francis H. Kinnicutt of New York, and J. H. Patten of Washington, are here and last night we held a conference at which I presented your letter."
137. Gossett, *Race: The History of an Idea in America,* p. 394.
138. NA RG 233 Records of the US HR, 69th Congress, Committee on Immigration, Correspondence, Box 342, Folder: HR69A-F20.1, letter from

Livermore to Johnson, March 4, 1927. Johnson replied, thanking Livermore for his views.

139. H. P. Fairchild, *The Melting-Pot Mistake* (Boston: Little Brown and Co., 1926).
140. Ibid.
141. Gossett, *Race: The History of an Idea in America*, p. 385.
142. NA RG 233 Records of the US HR, 69th Congress, Committee on Immigration, Committee Papers, Box 345, Folder: HR69A-F20.3, Immigration Restriction Conference, under the auspices of The Clergy Club of New York and Neighborhood, New York, April 21, 1924, proceedings, pp. 12–13.
143. Ibid., p. 18.
144. Ibid., p. 21.
145. NA RG 233 Records of the US HR, Committee on Immigration, Committee Papers, Box 239, Folder: F14.4, letter to Coolidge from Fairchild, January 15, 1927.
146. Fairchild, *The Melting-Pot Mistake* p. 206.
147. H. P. Fairchild, *Race and Nationality* (New York: Macmillan, 1947).
148. This mix of factors is recognized in the major monographs, though the eugenic dimension is often underplayed. For instance, Robert Divine argues of the 1921 legislation and the general shift to restriction that "fundamentally, it was the transformation in American economic and political development that set the stage for restriction." *American Immigration Policy, 1924–1952* (New Haven: Yale University Press, 1957), p. 9. Divine does discuss eugenic ideas in respect to the 1924 law, however, observing that "the effect of racial theory on the Congressional mind was easily discernible," p. 14.
149. K. Fitzgerald, *The Face of the Nation* (Stanford: Stanford University Press, 1996), pp. 143–144.
150. Dowbiggin, *Keeping America Sane,* p. 227.
151. Letter from Laughlin to Professor Robert DeC. Ward, November 22, 1924, in Laughlin Papers, Folder: Robert Ward, C-4-1. See also Laughlin's later letter to Ward, May 8, 1925, in ibid.
152. Jacobson, *Whiteness of a Different Color,* p. 87.

7. Enacting National Origins

1. See M. J. Anderson, *The American Census: A Social History* (New Haven: Yale University Press, 1988).
2. LC MD Papers of Calvin Coolidge, File 133 (Reel 78), letter from W. Sanders, Secretary, Immigration Restriction League, to Coolidge, February 14, 1924.
3. In ibid., letter from Congressman John L. Cable to Coolidge, October 22, 1923.
4. In ibid., Department of Labor, Memorandum "In the matter of cooperation

between officers of States and Municipalities with officers of the United States in connection with the enforcement of the Immigration Laws," 14 pp., October 1923, p. 3.

5. "Admission of Aliens in Excess of Percentage Quotas for June," hearings before the Committee on Immigration and Naturalization, HR 67th Congress, 1st Session, June 10, 1921.

6. For accounts, see R. Daniels, *The Politics of Prejudice* (Berkeley: University of California Press, 1977), p. I; P. Rose, *Tempest-Tost: Race, Immigration and the Dilemmas of Diversity* (New York: Oxford University Press, 1997), p. 3–27; A. Saxton, *The Indispensable Enemy: Labor and the Anti-Chinese Movement in California* (Berkeley: University of California Press, 1971); and R. Takaki, *Strangers from a Different Shore: A History of Asian Americans* New York: Penguin, 1990).

7. Rose, *Tempest-Tost,* p. 7.

8. T. F. Gossett, *Race: The History of an Idea in America* (New York: Oxford University Press, 1963; rev. ed. 1997), p. 290.

9. Daniels, *The Politics of Prejudice.* See also R. Ueda, *Postwar Immigrant America: A Social History* (Boston: Bedford Books, 1994); and R. M. Smith, *Civic Ideals* (New Haven: Yale University Press, 1997), p. 441.

10. Letter from Dr. George Hinman, American Missionary Association, San Francisco, to Congressman Johnson, November 19, 1923, in NA RG 85 Records of the INS, Education and Americanization Files, 1914–1936 E18033-E17920, Entry 30, Box 265.

11. On the end of the Chinese Exclusion Laws, see F. Riggs, *Pressures on Congress: A Study of the Repeal of Chinese Exclusion* (New York: King's Crown Press, 1950), which documents the work of the Citizen's Committee to Repeal Chinese Exclusion.

12. J. Higham, *Strangers in the Land: Patterns of American Nativism, 1860–1925* (New Brunswick, N.J.: Rutgers University Press, 1955, 1988), pp. 177–178.

13. Americanization of Adult Aliens, hearings before a Subcommittee on the Committee on Immigration and Naturalization, HR, 69th Congress 2d Session, February 17, 1927, p. 17.

14. See correspondence between Johnson and Prescott Hall, in Papers of the Immigration Restriction League, Box 2.

15. NA RG 233 Records of the US HR, 69th Congress, Committee on Immigration, Correspondence Box 342, Folder: HR69A-F20.1, letter from Johnson to Marvin H. Lewis, President General, National Society for the Sons of the American Revolution, May 19, 1926. Lewis chaired the SAR's Immigration Committee—see his letter to Johnson, May 4, 1926.

16. T. J. Archdeacon, *Becoming American: An Ethnic History* (New York: Free Press), pp. 171–172.

17. Published in *Scribner's* in September 1922; see Anderson, *American Census,* p. 144.

18. It was passed by 323 to 71 votes in the House and 62 to 6 in the Senate, with opposition concentrated in the Northeast states: R. A. Divine, *American Immigration Policy, 1924–1952* (New Haven: Yale University Press, 1957), p. 17.

19. NA RG 233 Records of the US HR, 69th Congress, Committee on Immigration, Committee Papers, Box 341, Folder: HR69A-F20.1, letter from Johnson to Frank Babbott, President, Eugenics Research Association, April 1, 1927.

20. LC MD, Papers of Calvin Coolidge, File 133 (Reel 79), letter from George Rittings to Coolidge, April 20, 1924.

21. In ibid., letter from Congressman Albert Johnson to Coolidge, May 13, 1924.

22. Divine, *American Immigration Policy*, p. 18.

23. LC MD, Papers of Calvin Coolidge, File 133 (Reel 79), letter from Congressman Samuel Dickstein to Coolidge, May 17, 1924.

24. In ibid., letter from Congressman Samuel Dickstein to C. B. Slemp, Secretary to President Coolidge, May 22, 1924.

25. In ibid., letter from Congressman A. J. Sabath to Coolidge, May 23, 1924.

26. Ibid.

27. In ibid., letter from James J. Davis to Coolidge, May 29, 1924.

28. "Amending the Immigration Laws," Report of the Hon. James J. Davis, Secretary of Labor, on S.3019, 70th Congress, 1st Session, Senate Committee on Immigration, March 24, 1928, 12 pp. See also Davis's letter to Congressman Albert Johnson, March 28, 1926, included in "Deportation of Alien Criminals, Gunmen, Narcotic Dealers, Defectives etc.," Hearings before the Committee on Immigration and Naturalization, HR 69th Congress, 1st session, March 25–26, 1926, pp. 94–95.

29. LC MD, Papers of Franklin MacVeagh, Box 31, Folder: Immigration Restriction League, 1905–1928, flyer from the League, June 14, 1924, p. 1.

30. The three secretaries delegated the work to a committee composed of R. W. Flourney and S. W. Boggs (for State), Joseph A. Hill and Leon R. Truesdell (for Commerce), and W. W. Husband and Ethelbert Stewart (for Labor). Husband was a key architect of U. S. immigration policy; Hill was the principal statistician.

31. US Senate 69th Congress, 2d Session, Document No. 190, "National Origins Provision of the Immigration Act of 1924," message from the president of the United States, January 7, 1927. Prepared by the three secretaries' committee.

32. Ibid., p. 2.

33. Ibid., p. 3.

34. "National Origins Provision Immigration Act of 1924," hearings before the Committee on Immigration and Naturalization, HR, 69th Congress, 2d Session, January 18, 1927, p. 9; Joseph Hill speaking.

35. Ibid., p. 11.

36. "National Origins Provision of Immigration Law," hearings before the Committee on Immigration, Senate, 70th Congress, 2d Session, February 4, 1929.

37. National Origins Provision Immigration Act of 1924, hearings before the Committee on Immigration and Naturalization, HR, 69th Congress, 2d Session, January 18, 1927, p. 13.

38. Ibid., p. 17.

39. Anderson, *American Census,* p. 147.

40. Divine, *American Immigration Policy,* p. 33.

41. Higham, *Strangers in the Land,* p. 319.

42. National Origins Provision Immigration Act of 1924, hearings before the Committee on Immigration and Naturalization, HR, 69th Congress, 2d Session, January 18, 1927, p. 38.

43. Ibid., January 19, 1927, p. 32.

44. Anderson, *American Census,* p. 148.

45. Higham, *Strangers in the Land,* p. 314.

46. National Origins Provision Immigration Act of 1924, Hearings before the Committee on Immigration and Naturalization, HR, 69th Congress, 2d Session, January 19, 1927, p. 32.

47. Ibid., p. 34.

48. Ibid., p. 33.

49. "Time to Put Up the Bars," *Saturday Evening Post* (November 24, 1928).

50. K. L. Roberts, *Why Europe Leaves Home: A True Account of the Reasons Which Cause Central Europeans to Overrun America* (London: T. Fisher Unwin, 1922).

51. NA RG 46 Records of the US Senate, 68th Congress, Committee on Immigration, Box 237, Folder: Sen 68A-J27; contains many petitions, with multiple signatures—for example, petition to Senator Arthur Capper from Paradise, Kansas, March 13, 1924. This collection contains many other examples, some sent to named senators, others just to members of Congress.

52. National Origins Provision Immigration Act of 1924, Hearings before the Committee on Immigration and Naturalization, HR, 69th Congress, 2d Session, January 18, 1927, memorial, p. 6.

53. US House of Representatives, 69th Congress, 2d Session, Report No. 2029, Repeal of "National Origins" Provisions of the Immigration Act of 1924, February 9, 1927, pp. 4–5.

54. National Origins Provision Immigration Act of 1924, Hearings before the Committee on Immigration and Naturalization, HR, 69th Congress, 2d Session, January 26, 1927, pp. 60–61.

55. Ibid., p. 61.

56. Ibid., p. 64.

57. Ibid.

58. NA RG 233 Records of the US HR, 70th Congress, Committee on Immigra-

tion, Committee Papers, Box 239, Folder: HR70A-F14.4, letter from Vanderveer Custis to Johnson, November 19, 1927.

59. In ibid., letter from Johnson to Vanderveer Custis, December 2, 1927.

60. In ibid., letter from Edward R. Lewis to Johnson, October 10, 1927, and see Johnson's reply, October 14.

61. NA RG 46 Records of the US Senate, 71st Congress, Box 172, Folder: 71A-J32; see petitions and letters from Swedish Methodist Episcopal Church, First Swedish Lutheran Church, Ancient Order of Hibernians (in Essex County, Massachusetts).

62. In ibid., telegram from Paul McNutt, National Commander, to Senator David Reed, May 20, 1929.

63. NA RG 46 Records of the US Senate, 70th Congress, Committee on Immigration, Box 179, Folder: Sen 70A-J17, resolution adopted by the American Legion departments in Illinois (September 11, 1928) and Texas (October 10, 1928), recommending continuance of restrictions on immigration.

64. The petitions typically stated, "We regard the National Origins system for the determination of quotas now embodied in the Act of 1924, as sound in principle, fair to all elements of the population, and the only basis by which just representation is given to the basic American stock, which evolved the institutions under which the nation has grown great," followed by many signatures.

65. NA RG 233 Records of the US HR, 69th Congress, Committee on Immigration, Correspondence, Box 342, Folder: HR69A-F20.1, report of the immigration committee of the SAR, May 1926, p. 1.

66. Ibid., p. 4.

67. NA RG 233 Records of the US HR, 70th Congress, Committee on Immigration, Committee Papers, Box 238, Folder: HR70A-F14.4, letter from Howard Rowley, National Society of the Sons of the American Revolution, to Albert Johnson, January 28, 1929.

68. NA RG 46 Records of the US Senate, 71st Congress, Box 172, Folder: 71A-J32, petition from the Junior Order of United American Mechanics, New Bern, North Carolina, April 5, 1929.

69. NA RG 233 Records of the US HR, 70th Congress, Committee on Immigration, Committee Papers, Box 238, contains multiple copies of such petitions.

70. NA RG 46 Records of the US Senate, 68th Congress, Committee on Immigration, Box 238, Folder: Sen 68A-J27, letter to Senator George McLean (Conn.) from Patriotic Order of the Sons of America, March 31, 1924.

71. NA RG 233 Records of the US HR, 71st Congress, Committee on Immigration, Box 322, Folder: HR71A-H5.2, petition from the National Camp, Patriotic Order of the Sons of America, March 5, 1930.

72. NA RG 46 Records of the US Senate, 67th Congress, Committee on Immigration, Box 212, Folder: Sen 57A-J29, for example, letter from Philadelphia Board of Trade.

73. LC MD Papers of Calvin Coolidge, File 133 (Reel 79), letter from C. M. Goethe, President, Immigration Study Commission, to Coolidge, May 26, 1924.

74. Ibid.

75. Such language and assumptions, of course, did not acquire their modern disapprobation until the 1940s. (See K. Malik, *The Meaning of Race* [London: Macmillan, 1996.]) Nonetheless, there were critics of such assumptions in the 1920s.

76. LC MD Papers of Calvin Coolidge, File 133 (Reel 79), letter from C. M. Goethe, President, Immigration Study Commission, to Coolidge, May 26, 1924. In fact, Australia did implement such a policy.

77. Gossett, *Race: The History of an Idea in America*, p. 354.

78. NA RG 233 Records of the HR, 70th Congress, Committee on Immigration, Box 322, Folder: HR70A-J3.4, letter from C. M. Goethe, President, Immigration Study Commission, to Congressman David J. O'Connell, December 10, 1928.

79. R. Ward, "Immigration," *Eugenics* (March 1929): 2.

80. NA RG 46 Records of the US Senate, 68th Congress, Committee on Immigration, Box 238, Folder: Sen 68A-J27, petition from Women's Zionist Organization to Senator Henrick K. Shipstead, February 5, 1924.

81. NA RG 233 Records of the HR, 69th Congress, Committee on Immigration, Box 404, Folder: HR69A-H3.1, letter from the Committee to Congressman James S. Gallivan, December 27, 1926.

82. NA RG 46 Records of the US Senate, 68th Congress, Committee on Immigration, Box 238, Folder: Sen 68A-J27, letter from the Citizen's Club of New Britain to Senator George McLean (Conn.), February 15, 1924,

83. NA RG 46 Records of the US Senate, 68th Congress, Committee on Immigration, Box 237, Folder: Sen 68A-J27, telegram to Senator George McLean from Sons of Italy, New Haven, Connecticut, January 28, 1924. These views were echoed by other Italian-American organizations throughout the country.

84. In ibid., letter and petition from St. Calogero Society, Thompsonville, Connecticut, to Senator George McLean, February 8, 1924.

85. In ibid., letter to Senator George McLean, February 5, 1924.

86. NA RG 233 Records of the HR, 70th Congress, Committee on Immigration, Box 322, Folder: HR70A-H3.4, petitions from Irish County Clubs of Massachusetts, December 11, 1927, and the United Irish-American Societies, December 15, 1927.

87. In ibid., petition from American Irish Historical Society, March 12, 1928.

88. MA RG 233 Records of the US HR, 70th Congress, Committee on Immigration, Committee Papers, Box 239, Folder: HR70A-F14.4, "Repeal the National Origins Clauses of the Immigration Act of 1924," American Irish Historical Society, March 12, 1928, 5 pp.

89. "National Origin Provision of the Immigration Act of 1924," *Senate Docu-*

ment No. 193, 69th Congress, 2d Session, 1927, p. 1 (cited in Divine, *American Immigration Policy,* p. 31).

90. Divine, *American Immigration Policy,* p. 31.
91. *The New York Times* (January 2, 1927), p. 1; (January 5, 1927), p. 1; (January 11, 1927), p. 21.
92. NA RG 233 Records of the US HR, 70th Congress, Committee on Immigration, Committee Papers, Box 239, Folder: HR70A-F14.4, letter from Congressman August Andresen to Johnson, February 4, 1928.
93. NA RG 46 Records of the US Senate, 70th Congress, Committee on Immigration, Box 180, Folder: Sen 70A-J19, letter from Sons of Norway (New London, Connecticut, branch) to Senator Hiram Bingham, January 31, 1928. Many other such petitions, in behalf of Scandinavians, were received by the Committee.
94. In ibid., petition from Vasa Orden af Amerika, Laramie, Wyoming, February 1, 1928; and from Danish Brotherhood of America, Bridgeport Connecticut, February 20, 1928.
95. NA RG 233 Records of the US HR, 71st Congress, Committee on Immigration, Box 322, Folder: HR71A-H5.3, petition to Congressman Richard Yates, February 26, 1929.
96. NA RG 46 Records of the US Senate, 71st Congress, Box 172, Folder: 71A-J32, letter from Swedish-American Republican Club of Waterbury, Connecticut, to Senator Hiram Bingham, May 9, 1929.
97. In ibid., petition of the German American Citizens League.
98. In ibid., letters from Council of Jewish Women, February 16, 1931, and Assembly of Hebrew Orthodox Rabbis of America and Canada, February 10, 1930. Each feared proposals that would completely stop immigration because they would divide families.
99. In ibid., letter from Ernest Trysell, Secretary of the Anti-National Origins Clause League, Michigan, to Senator Royal S. Copeland, April 30, 1929.
100. In ibid., petition to the Congress of the United States, organized by the Anti-National Origins Clause League.
101. In ibid., letter from Ernest Trysell, Secretary of the Anti-national Origins Clause League, Michigan, to Senator Royal S. Copeland, April 20, 1920.
102. NA RG 233 Records of the US HR, 70th Congress, Committee on Immigration, Committee Papers, Box 238, Folder: HR70A-F14.4, letter from F. Stuart Fitzpatrick, U.S. Chamber of Commerce, to Johnson, January 28, 1929.
103. Ibid. U.S. Chamber of Commerce to Johnson January 28, 1929. US Chamber of Commerce "National Immigration Policy" Report of the Immigration Committee, Chamber of Commerce, Washington, D.C., February 1929, 14 pp., p. 11.
104. In ibid., letter from F. Stuart Fitzpatrick, U.S. Chamber of Commerce, to Johnson, January 28, 1929. U.S. Chamber of Commerce "National Immigration Policy" Report of the Immigration Committee, Chamber of Commerce, Washington, D.C., February 1929, 14 pp., p. 12.

105. NA RG 46 Records of the US Senate, 71st Congress, Committee on Immigration, Box 171, Folder SEN71A/32, letter from Associated American Immigration Societies to Senator Felix Herbert, April 5, 1929, and resolution of the St. Brendan Society.

106. LC MD Papers of Calvin Coolidge, File 133, telegram from Johnson to President Coolidge, August 25, 1926.

107. *Congressional Record,* March 3, 1927, p. 5648.

108. NA RG 233 Records of the US HR, 70th Congress, Committee on Immigration, Committee Papers, Box 239, Folder: HR70A-F14.4, letter from Johnson to Arvid Rydstrom, March 24, 1928.

109. In ibid., letter from Johnson to Frederick Bausman, February 24, 1928. Frederick Bausman contributed to weekly magazines on this topic.

110. *Congressional Record,* March 3, 1927, p. 5785.

111. NA RG 233 Records of the US HR, 70th Congress, Committee on Immigration, Committee Papers, Box 239, Folder: HR70A-F14.6, letter from Johnson to C. L. Colburn, May 23, 1928.

112. See *Congressional Record,* February 14, 1929, p. 3482; March 2, 1929, pp. 5192–5197; June 5, 1929, pp. 2383–2394, and June 13, 1929, pp. 2777–2779.

113. For an initial response, see J. B. Trevor, *An Analysis of the American Immigration Act of 1924* (Washington, D.C.: Carnegie Endowment for International Peace, September 1924).

114. For a discussion of this clause, see Joint Statement by Sponsors of New Omnibus Immigration and Naturalization Bill, March 12, 1952, in NAACP Washington Bureau, Part I, Box I-107, Folder: Immigration 1952.

115. A. Lazarus, Jr., "What the McCarran-Walter Immigration Bill (S. 2550; H. R. 5678) Means to Negroes" (February 1952), 4 pp., p. 1, in NAACP Washington Bureau, Part I, Box I-107, Folder: Immigration 1952.

116. Department of Justice, Immigration, and Naturalization Service *Monthly Review* 4 (January 1947): 83, copy in Papers of Emanuel Celler, Manuscript Division, Library of Congress, Box 18.

117. Divine, *American Immigration Policy,* ch. 3.

118. This point is elegantly developed by N. Glazer in his *We Are All Multiculturalists Now* (Cambridge, Mass.: Harvard University Press, 1997), esp. ch. 6. And see M. M. Ngai, "The Architecture of Race in American Immigration Law: A Reexamination of the Immigration Act of 1924," *Journal of American History* 86 (1999): 67–92.

119. A theme of R. M. Smith's important essay, "Beyond Tocqueville, Myrdal and Hartz: The Multiple Traditions in America," *American Political Science Review* 87 (1993), pp. 549–566.

120. Report of the President's Commission on Immigration and Naturalization, *Whom We Shall Welcome* (Washington, D.C.: GPO, 1953), p. 14.

121. In ibid., p. 26.

122. In ibid., p. 87.

123. "Restriction of Immigration," HR House report No. 350, 68th Congress, 1st Session (Washington, D.C.: GPO, 1924), Part II, p. 4.

124. K. Fitzgerald, *The Face of the Nation* (Stanford: Stanford University Press, 1996), p. 132.

125. I. R. Dowbiggin, *Keeping America Sane* (Ithaca, N.Y.: Cornell University Press, 1997), p. 227. For an alternative view, see M. Snyderman and R. J. Hernstein, "Intelligence Tests and the Immigration Act of 1924," *American Psychologist* (1983): 986–995, who focus particularly on the use of intelligence testing in the immigration debate.

126. Fitzgerald, *The Face of the Nation,* p. 132.

127. NA RG 233 Records of the US HR, 69th Congress, Committee on Immigration, Box 341, Folder: H69A-F20.1, letter from Johnson to Mr. E. Barclay, State Council J. O. U. A. M., February 22, 1927.

128. NA RG 233 Records of the US HR, 69th Congress, Committee on Immigration, Box 341, Folder: H69A-F20.1, letter from Johnson to C. D. Bohannan, Vice Dean, College of Agricultural and Mechanic Arts, New Mexico, December 13, 1926.

129. NA RG 233 Records of the US HR, 69th Congress, Committee on Immigration, Box 341, Folder: H69A-F20.1, letter from President of the League to Johnson, June 24, 1924.

130. In ibid., letter from Knights of the Ku Klux Klan, Seattle, Washington, to Johnson, January 29, 1927; Johnson replied on February 18: "I appreciate the complimentary references, and beg to assure you that I shall do all that I can to make the laws still tighter, and to present only those amendments which will perfect the workings of the law with a view to the most limited immigration possible."

131. NA RG 233 Records of the US HR, 69th Congress, Committee on Immigration, Correspondence, Box 342, Folder: HR69A-F20.1, letter from Johnson to John B. Trevor, May 8, 1926

132. NA RG 233 Records of the US HR, 69th Congress, Committee on Immigration, Committee Papers, Box 341, Folder: H69A-F20.1, letter from P. Snyder to Miss Virginia Brown, American Consulate General, Ireland, November 17 1926.

133. NA RG 233 Records of the US HR, 70th Congress, Committee on Immigration, Committee Papers, Box 239, Folder: HR70A-F14.4, letter from Johnson to Leon F. Whitney, the secretary of the American Eugenics Society, February 23, 1927. Whitney, needless to say, urged Johnson to get President Hoover not to postpone the scheme.

134. In ibid., letter from Johnson to Edward R. Lewis, January 27, 1927.

135. NA RG 233 Records of the US HR, 70th Congress, Committee on Immigration, Committee Papers, Box 238, Folder: HR70A-F14.4, letter from Johnson to S. Chauncey Brewer, Boston, March 19, 1929, replying to Brewer's letter of March 5, which expressed mystification at the state representatives' voting: "On Sunday last the entire Massachusetts Republican delegation

voted for the retention of the 1890 quota clause (or what appears to me to be discriminatory legislation) for another year. This, as far as I know, is against the interests of the constituents of some of these Congressmen. I find it difficult to explain this action without assuming that there are powerful forces at work of which I, as a private citizen, am ignorant."

136. In ibid., letter from Albert Johnson to John D. Cirrues, March 6, 1929.

8. "A Slur on Our Citizenry"

1. R. Ueda, *Postwar Immigrant America: A Social History* (Boston: Bedford Books, 1994), p. 32.
2. In 1953 the Refugee Relief Act was enacted, providing for over 200,000 additional places for those escaping communism in central and eastern Europe. On this period generally, see K. Fitzgerald, *The Face of the Nation* (Stanford: Stanford University Press, 1996), ch. 6.
3. US Department of Labor Immigration and Naturalization Service, *Memorandum of Commissioner of Immigration and Naturalization* (April 1934), p. 1.
4. F. Riggs, *Pressures on Congress* (New York: King's Crown Press, 1950).
5. Coolidge's Secretary of State cited in R. A. Divine, *American Immigration Policy, 1924–1952* (New Haven: Yale University Press, 1957), pp. 52–66.
6. Divine, *American Immigration Policy,* p. 52.
7. US Commission on Civil Rights, *The Tarnished Golden Door: Civil Rights Issues in Immigration* (Washington, D.C.: GPO, September 1980), pp. 10–11.
8. Letter from L. M. Mans, Colonel, US Army, Retired, to Fred C. Butler, Director, Americanization Division, Department of the Interior, March 20, 1920, p. 1, in NA RG 12, Records of the Office of Education, Records of the Office of the Commissioner, Historical Files 1870–1950, File 106: Americanization, Entry 6, Box 11.
9. Ibid., pp. 1–2.
10. "Introduction," Chamber of Commerce of the State of New York, *Conquest by Immigration,* A Report of the Special Committee on Immigration and Naturalization by Harry H. Laughlin (New York: Chamber of Commerce, 1939), pp. 1–2.
11. Letter from L. M. Mans, Colonel, US Army, Retired, to Fred C. Butler, Director, Americanization Division, Department of the Interior, March 20, 1920, pp. 1–2, in NA RG 12 Records of the Office of Education, Records of the Office of the Commissioner, Historical Files, 1870–1950, File 106: Americanization, Entry 6, Box 11.
12. Ibid., p. 3.
13. Ibid.
14. Divine, *American Immigration Policy,* p. 54.
15. C. Sheridan, "Contested Citizenship: National Identity and the Mexican

Immigration Debates of the 1920s," paper presented to the annual meeting of the American Political Science Association, 1998, p. 1.

16. U. S. Senate, Judiciary Subcommittee on Immigration, Report 1515, *The Immigration and Naturalization System of the United States* (Washington, D.C.: GPO, 1950).

17. Cited in J. Vialet, *U. S. Immigration Law and Policy: 1952–1979* (Washington, D.C.: GPO, May 1979), p. 8. Formally titled "A Report Prepared at the Request of Senator Edward M. Kennedy, Chairman, Committee on the Judiciary, U. S. Senate, upon the formation of The Select Commission on Immigration and Refugee Policy." Prepared by the Congressional Research Service, Library of Congress, 96th Congress, First Session, May 1979 (Washington, D.C.: GPO, 1979), cited in US Senate, Committee on the Judiciary, 96th Congress, First Session, May 1979.

18. Fitzgerald, *The Face of the Nation,* p. 200.

19. This aggregate was removed by Congress in 1961. Re the 1952 law, see "Memorandum on Proposed Immigration Bill," in NAACP Washington Bureau, Part I, Box I-107, Folder: Immigration, 1950–1951.

20. US Senate, Committee on the Judiciary, 96th Congress, First Session, May 1979, *U. S. Immigration Law and Policy: 1952–1979,* J. Vialet, p. 8.

21. NAACP, "Statement on McCarran Bill," September 16, 1952, p. 1, in NAACP Washington Bureau, Part I, Box I-107, Folder: Immigration, 1952.

22. See Memorandum on "Immigration," 3 pp., March 1952, in ibid.

23. Statement by Senators Hubert Humphrey, Herbert Lehman, William Benton, and Blair Moody, May 17, 1952, p. 5, in ibid.

24. Report of the President's Commission on Immigration and Naturalization, *Whom We Shall Welcome* (Washington, D.C.: GPO, 1953), p. 88.

25. See M. L. Dudziak, "Desegregation as a Cold War Imperative," *Stanford Law Review* 41 (1988), pp. 61–120.

26. Quoted in US Senate, Committee on the Judiciary, 96th Congress, First Session, May 1979, *U. S. Immigration Law and Policy: 1952–1979,* J. Vialet, p. 5.

27. Ibid., p. 6.

28. A fourth preference gave 50 percent of any remaining places to brothers, sisters, and married children of U. S. citizens.

29. Statement by Senators Lehman, Humphrey, and Benton on the Presidential Veto of the McCarran-Walter Immigration Bill, June 25, 1952, p. 1, copy in National Urban League Papers, LC MD, Series III, Box 17, Folder: Immigration.

30. Report of the President's Commission on Immigration and Naturalization, *Whom We Shall Welcome,* p. 263.

31. Ibid., p. 263.

32. Letter from Congressman Adam Clayton Powell, Jr., to his congressional colleagues, March 10, 1952, in NAACP Washington Bureau, Part I, Box I-107, Folder: Immigration 1952. And see P. M. Von Eschen, *Race Against*

Empire: Black Americans and Anticolonialism, 1937–1957 (Ithaca: Cornell University Press, 1997); and C. Fraser, "Understanding American Policy Towards the Decolonization of European Empires, 1945–64, *Diplomacy and Statecraft* 3 (1992): 105–125.

33. It granted 214,000 visas, not mortgaged against the future of quotas of the areas from which the refugees originated.

34. The Act of September 11, 1957.

35. *Congressional Record—Senate,* August 21, 1957, p. 14124.

36. Ibid., February 7, 1963, vol. 109, p. 2022.

37. Ibid.

38. "National Quotas for Immigration to End," *Congressional Quarterly Almanac,* 89th Congress, 1st Session, 1965 (Washington, D.C.: Congressional Quarterly Press, 1965), p. 463.

39. P. Gay, *My German Question* (New Haven: Yale University Press, 1998), p. 140.

40. "The President's Veto Message," June 25, 1952, in Report of the President's Commission on Immigration and Naturalization, *Whom We Shall Welcome,* p. 277.

41. Ibid., p. 278.

42. See D. King, "'The Longest Road to Equality': The Politics of Institutional Desegregation under Truman," *Journal of Historical Sociology* 6 (1993): 119–163.

43. Ueda, *Postwar Immigrant America,* p. 43.

44. Cited in Vialet, *U. S. Immigration Law and Policy,* p. 52; from H. Rept. No 745, 89th Congress, 1st Session, August 6, 1965, p. 11.

45. E. R. Barkan, *And Still They Come* (Wheeling, Ill.: Harlan Davidson, 1996), p. 81.

46. *Congressional Record—Senate,* vol. 111, February 2, 1965, p. 1809; Senator Douglas speaking.

47. See King, "'Longest Road to Equality.'"

48. In a similar vein, Matthew Jacobson notes that "mid-century civil rights agitation on the part of African-Americans—and particularly the protests against segregation in the military and discrimination in the defense industries around World War II—nationalized Jim Crow as *the* racial issue of American political discourse." M. F. Jacobson, *Whiteness of a Different Color* (Cambridge, Mass.: Harvard University Press, 1998), p. 95. And see D. Kryder, *Divided Arsenal* (New York: Cambridge University Press, 2000).

49. K. Malik, *The Meaning of Race* (London: Macmillan, 1996).

50. Jacobson, *Whiteness of a Different Color,* pp. 110–111.

51. Quoted in Vialet, *U. S. Immigration Law and Policy,* p. 48. Kennedy was speaking on July 23, 1963, to the 88th Congress when his immigration reforms were submitted.

52. Quoted in "National Quotas for Immigration to End," *Congressional*

Quarterly Almanac, 89th Congress, First Session (Washington, D.C.: Congressional Quarterly Publications, 1965), p. 467.

53. Vialet, *U. S. Immigration Law and Policy,* p. 52.
54. *Congressional Record—Senate,* August 23, 1963, vol. 109, p. 15765.
55. Ibid., p. 15766.
56. Ibid., p. 15767.
57. *Congressional Record—House,* September 10, 1964, vol. 110, p. 21877.
58. *Congressional Record—Senate,* August 23, 1963, vol. 109, p. 15768.
59. Ibid., p. 15769.
60. Ibid.
61. Ibid., p. 15781.
62. *Congressional Record—Senate,* February 2, 1965, vol. 111, p. 1808.
63. Ibid., p. 1809.
64. Quoted in D. Reimers, *Still the Golden Gate: The Third World Comes to America* (New York: Columbia University Press, 1985), p. 71.
65. Kennedy issued these words in the preface to a report that he commissioned, as chairman of the Senate Judiciary Committee, in 1979 preliminary to further reforms. J. Vialet, *U. S. Immigration Law and Policy,* p. 1.
66. E. M. Kennedy, "The Immigration Act of 1965," *Annals of the American Academy of Political and Social Science* (September 1966) 367: 137–149. For an excellent analysis of the 1965 Act's enactment, see A. O. Law, "Shifting Ethnic Alliances—The Politics of American Immigration Reform," paper presented to the annual meeting of the American Political Science Association, 1999.
67. "National Quotas for Immigration to End," p. 463.
68. See ibid., p. 469.
69. Seven preferences and one nonpreference were established: (1) unmarried adult children of U. S. citizens (54,000, 20 percent); (2) spouses and unmarried adult children of permanent resident aliens (70,000, 26 percent and any unused preference one places); (3) members of professions and scientists or artists of exceptional ability (27,000, 10 percent); (4) married children of U. S. citizens (27,000, 10 percent); (5) brothers and sisters of U. S. citizens aged over 21 (64,000, 24 percent); (6) skilled and unskilled workers for occupations where the U. S. had a labor shortage (27,000, 10 percent); and (7) political refugees from communism or from the Middle East (6 percent). The nonpreference referred to applicants not entitled under any of the preceding seven categories.
70. See statement of Mrs. Olive Whitman Parsons, Immigration Committee, American Coalition of Patriotic Societies, *Immigration: Hearings Before the Subcommittee on Immigration and Naturalization of the Committee on the Judiciary,* US Senate, 89th Congress, First Session, on S.500, Part 2.
71. *Congressional Record—Senate,* March 4, 1965, vol. 111, pp. 4143–4146.
72. Ibid., p. 4145.
73. *Congressional Record—House,* April 6, 1965, vol. 111, p. 7194.

74. *Congressional Record—House,* May 20, 1965, vol. 111, p. 11183.
75. *Congressional Record—House,* June 1, 1965, vol. 111, p. 12104. Congressman Benjamin Rosenthal (D-N.Y.) speaking. And see R. M. Smith, *Civic Ideals* (New Haven: Yale University Press, 1997).
76. The survey was by Gallup and appeared in *The Washington Post* (July 1965). For the views of the groups supporting the new law, see the copious correspondence in Folder: Legislative Background of Immigration Law 1965, Box 1, Lyndon Baines Johnson Library.
77. E. P. Hutchinson, *Legislative History of American Immigration Policy, 1798–1965* (Philadelphia: University of Pennsylvania Press, 1981), pp. 377–378.
78. Cited in V. Briggs, Jr., *Immigration Policy and the American Labor Force* (Baltimore: Johns Hopkins University Press, 1984), p. 69.
79. Hutchinson, *Legislative History of American Immigration Policy,* p. 379.
80. For example, P. Brimelow, *Alien Nation* (New York: Random House, 1995) p. 1.
81. For a characteristically astute analysis of this xenophobia, see M. Rogin, "Christian v. Cannibal," *London Review of Books* 1 (April 1999): 18–20.
82. Hutchinson, *Legislative History of American Immigration Policy,* p. 379.
83. See N. Bowles, *The White House and Capitol Hill* (Oxford: Clarendon Press, 1987).
84. Vialet, *U. S. Immigration Law and Policy,* p. 63.
85. Barkan, *And Still They Come,* p. 116.
86. The bracero program, a U. S.-Mexican agreement, operated from 1942 until 1964. It was set up to address wartime labor shortages.
87. US Senate, Committee on the Judiciary, 96th Congress, First Session, May 1979, *U. S. Immigration Law and Policy: 1952–1979,* J. Vialet, p. 26.

9. After Americanization

1. For one account, see R. D. Alba, *Ethnic Identity: The Transformation of White America* (New Haven: Yale University Press, 199).
2. J. T. Rhea, *Race Pride and the American Identity* (Cambridge, Mass.: Harvard University Press, 1997).
3. R. Ueda, *Postwar Immigrant America: A Social History* (Boston: Bedford Books, 1994), p. 83.
4. P. D. McClain and J. Stewart, Jr., *"Can We All Get Along?" Racial and Ethnic Minorities in America* (Boulder: Westview Press, 1995).
5. E. R. Barkan, *And Still They Come* (Wheeling, Ill.: Harlan Davidson, 1996), p. 147.
6. O. Handlin, *The Uprooted* (Boston: Little Brown, 1951), p. 166.
7. For a helpful discussion, see R. A. Kazal, "Revisiting Assimilation: The Rise, Fall, and Reappraisal of a Concept in American Ethnic History," *American Historical Review* 100 (1995): 437–471.

8. Alba, *Ethnic Identity,* p. 293.

9. N. Glazer and D. P. Moynihan, *Beyond the Melting Pot* (Cambridge, Mass.: Harvard University Press, 1963; rev. ed., 1970).

10. Ibid., p. xxiii.

11. Ibid., p. xxxiii.

12. M. Novak, *The Rise of Unmeltable Ethnics* (New York: Macmillan, 1972).

13. J. R. Pole, *The Pursuit of Equality in American History,* 2nd Rev. Ed. (Berkeley: University of California Press, 1993), p. 440.

14. See, for example, P. Brimelow, *Alien Nation: Common Sense about America's Immigration Disaster* (New York: Random House, 1995), whose book begins, "there is a sense in which current immigration policy is Adolph Hitler's posthumous revenge on America"; p. xv.

15. Alba, *Ethnic Identity,* p. 290.

16. Ibid., pp. 292–293.

17. M. C. Waters, *Ethnic Options: Choosing Identities in America* (Berkeley: University of California Press, 1990), p. 147.

18. Ibid., p. 157.

19. S. Steinberg, *The Ethnic Myth* (New York: Atheneum, 1981), p. 51.

20. Ibid., p. 53.

21. Alba, *Ethnic Identity,* p. 306.

22. Kazal, "Revisiting Assimilation": 467–469.

23. The activities of homeowners' associations in midwestern and northeastern cities that organized, from the 1940s, to keep out African American residents is probably a germane example too. See T. J. Sugrue, *The Origins of the Urban Crisis* (Princeton: Princeton University Press, 1996). More generally, see B. Nelson, "The 'New' Labor History Meets the 'Wages of Whiteness,'" *International Review of Social History* 41 (1996): 351–374.

24. On separatist tendencies, see J. H. Wilkinson, *One Nation Indivisible: How Ethnic Separatism Threatens America* (Reading, Mass.: Addison-Wesley, 1997), chs. 4–8.

25. A. M. Schlesinger, Jr., *The Disuniting of America* (New York: W. W. Norton, 1992), p. 43.

26. I. F. Haney López, *White by Law: The Legal Construction of Race* (New York: New York University Press, 1996), p. 171.

27. For this context, see, for instance, M. C. Dawson, *Behind the Mule* (Princeton: Princeton University Press, 1994); P. Sniderman and T. Piazza, *The Scar of Race* (Cambridge, Mass.: Harvard University Press, 1993); E. G. Carmines and J. A. Stimson, *Issue Evolution* (Princeton: Princeton University Press, 1989); G. Ezorsky, *Racism and Justice* (Ithaca, N.Y.: Cornell University Press, 1991); M. Gilens, "'Race Coding' and White Opposition to Welfare," *American Political Science Review* 90 (1996): 593–604; M. Gilens, *Why Americans Hate Welfare* (Chicago: University of Chicago Press, 1999); P. Sniderman and E. G. Carmines, *Reaching Beyond Race* (Cambridge, Mass.: Harvard University Press, 1997); and S. Thernstrom

and A. Thernstrom, *America in Black and White* (New York: Simon & Schuster, 1997).

28. M. F. Jacobson, *Whiteness of a Different Color* (Cambridge, Mass.: Harvard University Press, 1998), pp. 246–247.

29. R. Delgado and J. Stefancic, "The Social Construction of *Brown v. Board of Education*," in N. Devins and D. M. Douglas, eds., *Redefining Equality* (New York: Oxford University Press, 1998), p. 161.

30. Haney López, *White by Law,* p. 170.

31. M. Gilens, P. M. Sniderman, and J. H. Kuklinski, "Affirmative Action and the Politics of Realignment," *British Journal of Political Science* 28 (1998): 159–183.

32. L. K. Kerber, "The Meaning of Citizenship," *Journal of American History* 84 (1997): 833–854.

33. Under Title V of the Education Amendments of 1972 (PL 92–318). Congress authorized expenditure of $15 million and also established a National Advisory Council on Ethnic Heritage Studies.

34. The speaker was Professor William T. Liu; quoted in "Ethnic Studies Center" (February 16), *Congressional Quarterly Almanac 1970* (Washington, D.C.: Congressional Quarterly Press, 1970), p. 722.

35. Merrill F. Hartshorn, quoted in "Ethnic Studies Center" (February 17), in ibid., p. 722.

36. Rudolph J. Vecoli, University of Minnesota, quoted in "Ethnic Studies Center" (February 18), in ibid., p. 722.

37. A. Stille, "The Betrayal of History," *New York Review of Books* (June 11, 1998), p. 15. Comparatively see E. Bleich, "From International Ideas to Domestic Policies," *Comparative Politics* 31 (1998): 81–100.

38. N. Glazer, *We Are All Multiculturalists Now* (Cambridge, Mass.: Harvard University Press, 1997), p. 71.

39. Ibid., p. 28.

40. See A. Levine, *When Hope and Fear Collide* (Chicago: Jossey-Bass, 1998); and B. Clark, "The Next Move Is Mine," *The Financial Times* (December 6, 1997).

41. For the most influential statement, see C. Taylor, *Multiculturalism and "the Politics of Recognition"* (Princeton: Princeton University Press, 1992).

42. J. N. Shklar, *Redeeming American Political Thought,* S. Hoffmann and D. F. Thompson, eds. (Chicago: University of Chicago Press, 1998). And see S. Benhabib, ed., *Democracy and Difference* (Princeton: Princeton University Press, 1996).

43. And internationally, see R. Grillo, *Pluralism and the Politics of Difference* (Oxford: Oxford University Press, 1998).

44. For the historical background, see inter alia, T. Branch, *Parting the Waters* (New York: Touchstone, 1988); H. Brogan, *The Pelican History of the United States* (Harmondsworth: Penguin, 1985); D. Chong, *Collective Action and the Civil Rights Movement* (Chicago: University of Chicago Press,

1991); J. Egerton, *Speak Now Against the Day* (Chapel Hill: University of North Carolina Press, 1994); M. Goldfield, *The Color of Politics* (New York: New Press, 1997); D. King, *Separate and Unequal: Black Americans and the Federal Government* (New York: Oxford University Press, 1995); R. Lieberman, *Shifting the Color Line* (Cambridge, Mass.: Harvard University Press, 1998); and D. S. Massey and N. A. Denton, *American Apartheid* (Cambridge, Mass.: Harvard University Press, 1993).

45. As one scholar notes: "the school desegregation policy, and its assimilationist implementation, was a direct result of the belief that a 'Western' education was superior because white culture was superior and other cultures had no value"; the same writer warns against simply replacing this approach with an "Afrocentrism that attempts to make African culture superior," however. L. B. Inniss, "The Legacy of the School Desegregation Pioneers," in M. P. Smith and J. R. Feagin, eds., *The Bubbling Cauldron* (Minneapolis: University of Minnesota Press, 1995), p. 161.

46. See J. Rabkin, "Racial Divisions and Judicial Obstructions," in N. Devins and D. M. Douglas, eds., *Redefining Equality* (New York: Oxford University Press, 1998); and W. A. Drake and R. D. Holsworth, *Affirmative Action and the Stalled Quest for Black Progress* (Chicago: University of Illinois Press, 1996).

47. Glazer, *We Are All Multiculturalists Now*, p. 94.

48. J. P. McCormick 2nd and S. Franklin, "Expressions of Racial Consciousness in the African-American Communities: Data from the Million Man March," paper presented to the annual meeting of the American Political Science Association, 1998.

49. Glazer, *We Are All Multiculturalists Now*, p. 95.

50. L. F. Litwack, "Trouble in Mind: The Bicentennial and the Afro-American Experience," in L. Dinnerstein and K. T. Jackson, eds., *American Vistas* (New York: Oxford University Press, 7th ed., 1995), p. 14.

51. A. M. Schlesinger, Jr., *The Disuniting of America* (New York: Norton, 1992), p. 13.

52. Ibid., p. 53.

53. On this tendency, see Wilkinson, *One Nation Indivisible*.

54. Schlesinger, *The Disuniting of America*, p. 104.

55. M. Rogin, *Blackface, White Noise* (Berkeley: University of California Press, 1996), p. 28.

56. J. W. Ceaser, *Reconstructing America: The Symbol of America in Modern Thought* (New Haven: Yale University Press, 1997), pp. 124–135.

57. Ibid., p. 132.

58. Ibid., p. 126.

59. Ibid., p. 127.

60. Ibid., p. 133.

61. For a valuable study, see R. Tatalovich, *Nativism Reborn? The Official Eng-*

lish Language Movement and the American States (Lexington: University Press of Kentucky, 1995).

62. Schlesinger, *The Disuniting of America,* p. 108.
63. P. D. Salins, *Assimilation, American Style* (New York: Basic Books, 1997), pp. 77–78.
64. Ibid., pp. 81–82.
65. *Regents of the University of California v. Bakke,* 438 U. S. 265 (1978), extracted in A. L. Davis and B. L. Graham, *The Supreme Court, Race, and Civil Rights* (Thousand Oaks, Calif.: Sage, 1995), pp. 316–317.
66. K. Anthony Appiah, "The Multiculturalist Misunderstanding," *New York Review of Books* (October 9, 1997): 30.
67. Ibid., p. 30.
68. Haney López, *White by Law,* p. 31.
69. Appiah, "Multiculturalist Misunderstanding," p. 30.
70. K. Anthony Appiah, "Race, Culture, Identity: Misunderstood Connections," in K. Anthony Appiah and Amy Gutmann, *Color Conscious* (Princeton: Princeton University Press, 1996).
71. Ibid., pp. 95–96.
72. H. Kallen, "Democracy versus the Melting Pot," *The Nation* (February 18, 1915: 190–194; and February 25, 1915: 217–220); and see H. Kallen, *Culture and Democracy in the United States* (New York: Boni and Liveright, 1924).
73. J. Waldron, "Minority Cultures and the Cosmopolitan Alternative," in W. Kymlicka, ed., *The Rights of Minority Cultures* (Oxford: Oxford University Press, 1995), p. 108.
74. D. A. Hollinger, *Postethnic America: Beyond Multiculturalism* (New York: Basic Books, 1995), pp. 84, 106. See also D. A. Hollinger, "How Wide the Circle of We? American Intellectuals and the Problem of the Ethnos Since World War II," *American Historical Review* 98 (1993): 317–337.
75. J. S. Dryzek, "Political Inclusion and the Dynamics of Democratization," *American Political Science Review* 90 (1996): 475–487.

10. *The Diverse Democracy*

1. Report of the President's Commission on Immigration and Naturalization, *Whom We Shall Welcome* (Washington, D.C.: GPO, 1953), p. xiv.
2. For a review of this new tendency, see D. M. Reimers, *Unwelcome Strangers: American Identity and the Turn Against Immigration* (New York: Columbia University Press, 1998).
3. J. Isbister, *The Immigration Debate* (West Hartford: Kumarian Press, 1996), p. 186.
4. K. Fitzgerald, *The Face of the Nation* (Stanford: Stanford University Press, 1996), p. 8.

5. W. Kymlicka, *Multicultural Citizenship* (Oxford: Clarendon Press, 1995), p. 21.
6. D. D'Souza, *The End of Racism* (New York: The Free Press, 1995). See the discussion in D. T. Goldberg, *Racial Subjects* (New York: Routledge, 1997), ch. 10.
7. P. D. Salins, *Assimilation, American Style* (New York: Basic, 1997).
8. Ibid., p. 6.
9. Ibid., p. 18.
10. R. Smith, *Civic Ideals* (New Haven: Yale University Press, 1997).
11. G. Gerstle, "Liberty, Coercion and the Making of Americans," *Journal of American History* 84 (1997): 524–558.
12. S. M. Lipset, *The First New Nation* (New York: Anchor, 1967), p. 2.
13. Ibid., p. 103.
14. S. M. Lipset, *American Exceptionalism* (New York: Norton, 1996), p. 113.
15. Ibid., p. 250.
16. Of the sort presented by Gunnar Myrdal in *An American Dilemma: The Negro Problem and American Democracy,* 2 vols. (New York: Harper and Row, 1944).
17. *United States v. Thind,* 261 U. S. 204 (1923).
18. For the intellectual context, see P. Brimelow, *Alien Nation* (New York: Random House, 1995); and J. O'Sullivan, "America's Identity Crisis," *National Review* 21 (November 1994). For a review of the new restrictionist organizations, see Reimers, *Unwelcome Strangers,* chs. 2 and 6.
19. For instance, the Personal Responsibility and Work Opportunity Act of 1996 and the Illegal Immigration and Immigrant Responsibility Act of 1996 both significantly reduced the rights of legal immigrants compared with those of citizens (with whom few formal differences had previously existed). Some of the new restrictions were subsequently modified, but the general propensity to impose regulations on legal immigrants was established. For California's Proposition 187, see A. J. Wroe, *Why Proposition 187 Won: Explaining the Success of California's 1994 Illegal-Immigration Initiative* (Department of Government, University of Essex, 1999). Proposition 187 was followed by Proposition 206, negating the state's affirmative action policy, and by Proposition 227, abrogating the state's bilingual education. Proposition 187 has in fact been trammeled by legal challenges since its passage in 1994 and has never become law. No further legal appeals are planned, so it is effectively defunct.
20. See T. A. Aleinikoff, *Between Principles and Politics: The Direction of U. S. Citizenship Policy* (Washington, D.C.: Carnegie Endowment for International Peace, 1998); W. R. Brubaker, ed., *Immigration and the Politics of Citizenship in Europe and North America* (New York: University Press of America, 1989); M. Jones-Correa, *Between Two Nations: The Political Predicament of Latinos in New York City* (Ithaca, N.Y.: Cornell University Press, 1998); P. Schuck, "The Re-Evaluation of American Citizenship,"

Georgetown Immigration Law Journal 12 (1997): 1–34; P. Schuck and R. M. Smith, *Citizenship Without Consent: Illegal Aliens in the American Polity* (New Haven: Yale University Press, 1985); Y. Soysal, *Limits of Citizenship: Migration and Postnational Membership in Europe* (Chicago: University of Chicago Press, 1994); and P. J. Spiro, "Dual Nationality and the Meaning of Citizenship," *Emory Law Journal* 46 (1997).

21. N. M. J. Pickus, *Becoming American/America Becoming,* Final Report of the Duke University Workshop on Immigration and Citizenship (Durham, N.C.: Terry Sanford Institute of Public Policy, Duke University, 1997).

22. N. M. J. Pickus, "To Make Natural: Creating Citizens for the Twenty-First Century," in Pickus, ed., *Immigration and Citizenship in the Twenty-First Century* (New York: Rowman & Littlefield Publishers, 1998), p. 108.

23. C. R. Kesler, "The Promise of American Citizenship," in Pickus, ed., *Immigration and Citizenship,* p. 22.

24. For a similar philosophy, see R. Ueda, *Postwar Immigrant America: A Social History* (Boston: Bedford Books, 1995), ch. 5.

25. G. Gerstle, "Liberty, Coercion and the Making of Americas," *Journal of American History* 84 (1997): 558.

26. J. F. Perea, "'Am I an American or Not?'" in Pickus, ed., *Immigration and Citizenship,* p. 51.

27. Ibid., p. 52. And see M. M. Ngai, "The Architecture of Race in American Immigration Law: A Reexamination of the Immigration Act of 1924," *Journal of American History* 86 (1999): 67–92, who concludes of the 1920s that "immigration policy and its specific constructions of race enabled the state to demarcate and police both the external boundaries and the internal spaces of the nation"; and that "the Immigration Act of 1924 contributed to the racialization of immigrant groups around notions of whiteness, permanent foreignness, and illegality—categories of difference that have outlived the racial categories created by eugenics and post–World War I nativism" (p. 92).

28. Brimelow, *Alien Nation,* p. 17, and see pp. 9–11.

29. Perea, p. 62.

30. R. M. Smith, *Civic Ideals: Conflicting Visions of Citizenship in American History* (New Haven: Yale University Press, 1997), p. 1.

31. Ibid., p. 3.

32. Ibid., p. 15. On alarming trends, see R. Smith's recent *The Policy Challenges of American Illiberalism* (Washington, D.C.: Carnegie Endowment for International Policy, 1998).

33. Smith, *Civic Ideals,* p. 26.

34. R. M. Smith, "Beyond Tocqueville, Myrdal and Hartz: The Multiple Traditions in America," *American Political Science Review* 87 (1993): 549–566, p. 550. See also his book *Civic Ideals.*

35. Smith, "Beyond Tocqueville, Myrdal and Hartz": 558.

36. In respect to classification in the segregated U.S. Armed Services, see, for ex-

ample, the account in D. King, "'The Longest Road to Equality': The Politics of Institutional Desegregation under Truman," *Journal of Historical Sociology* 6 (1993): 119–163.

37. C. J. Kim, "The Racial Triangulation of Asian Americans," *Politics and Society* 27 (1999): 105–138.
38. Ibid.
39. I. F. Haney López, *White by Law: The Legal Construction of Race* (New York: New York University Press, 1996).
40. Ibid., pp. 187–188.

Index

Abbott, Grace, 63–64
Addams, Jane, 63, 106
Affirmative Action, 264–266
African, 17, 229
African-American: and discrimination, 2, 141–152, 274; and segregation, 3, 139–140, 264; and restriction of immigration, 12; and restrictions, 12; and melting pot, 16–17, 274; and Irish, 22; and trade union, 22; and assimilation, 22, 81, 127, 128, 132, 140, 161, 268–269, 274; and naturalization, 24; and cultural pluralism, 30, 35, 115; and multiculturalism, 33, 34, 268–269; and immigrants, 40–42; and whiteness, 46, 288–290; and diversity, 48; and Boas, 70; and Dillingham Commission, 80, 128; and Americanization, 89–90, 120–123, 124, 125, 126; and education, 89–90, 120, 269; and American race, 127; and eugenics, 130–131; and Laughlin, 132, 137; and Anglo-Saxon Americanism, 138–152; and politics, 139, 282; and U.S. government, 141–152; and immigration, 152–163, 171; and Caribbeans, 156; and migration, 159–162, 242; and national origins, 162–163, 164; and dependency, 182; and Johnson-Reed Act (1924), 224, 225–226; as ethnic group, 260; and history, 269; and Schlesinger, 270, 271; and cultures, 275; and U.S. identity, 282
Alabama, 139
Alba, Richard, 260, 261, 262–263
Alcoholism, 72
Alien, registration of, 101, 189, 217
All-American Exposition, 105
Allen, Garland, 171
Almaguer, Tomás, 23, 38
Amateur Athletic Union, 116–117
America First, 91
American Eugenics Society, 191, 202, 214, 218
American Federation of Labor, 78
American Indian. *See* Native American
American Irish Historical Society, 219–220
American-Irish Republican League, 214
Americanism Commission, 109
Americanization: as unifying concept, 2; factors affecting, 3–4; and values, 18; and U.S. identity, 19–27, 85–126; and Abbott, 63; and old vs. new immigration, 80; and naturalization, 87–88, 105–106, 284; origins of, 87–100; and cultural pluralism, 97; and registration, 189; new, 283–286; and assimilation, 285; and racism, 285–286. *See also* Assimilation

of, 61; and Dillingham Commission, 64; and education, 87; and Americanization, 87–88, 105–106, 284; and work, 98, 99; and language, 109; frequency of, 123; and black immigrants, 158; and registration, 189
Naturalization Act (1790), 21, 24
Naturalization Bureau, 158
Natural selection, 168
Nazism, 70, 167, 168
Neapolitan, 67
Negro Foreign Born Citizens Alliance, 158
Neighborhood. *See* Community, ethnic
Nelli, Humbert, 73
Netherlands, 135
New Deal, 48
New England, 18, 61–62
Newspaper, 55–56, 90, 105, 110–115
New York, 96, 175
New York Times, 49
Nordic stock, 133, 171
North, 159, 160, 161
North American Civic League for Immigrants, 109–110
Northern European, 128
Northwestern European: preference for, 12; shift from, 50–51; as old immigrant, 59; and assimilation, 64; and Dillingham Commission, 74, 79–80; and Laughlin, 134; and eugenics, 135, 200; and quotas, 210, 279; and national origins, 212, 229–230; and Johnson-Reed Act (1924), 225
Novak, Michael: *The Rise of Unmeltable Ethnics,* 260, 262
Nye, Robert, 184

O'Connor, Daniel J., 249
Office of Education, 88, 90
Olcott, Ben W., 108
Olneck, Michael, 89, 125
Omi, M., 24
"One hundred percent American" campaign, 97, 98
"On Federal Race Discrimination," 142
Order of United American Mechanics, 217
Oregon, 108
Oregon State Federation of Women's Clubs, 108
Osborn, Henry Fairfield, 70
Outlook, 80

Ovington, Mary White, 45, 81
Ozawa v. United States, 20, 45–46

Pan-Americanism, 233, 235
Park, Robert, 20, 56, 80
Patriotic Order of the Sons of America, 101, 217
Patterson, Orlando, 22, 23, 34, 36, 48
Pearson, Karl, 129
Pennsylvania, 108–109, 126, 214–215
Pension Office, 144
Perea, Juan, 285
Pickus, Noah, 25, 284
Pittsburgh Provision & Packing Company, 100
Plessy v. Ferguson, 141, 142, 164, 225, 265
Pole, 67, 218–219, 262
Pole, J. R., 18, 54, 69, 127
Polish National Alliance, 57
Politics: and eugenics, 1, 186; and multiculturalism, 32, 35, 267–268; and multiple traditions, 37; and race, 39–47, 133–134, 282, 289–290; and whiteness, 39–47, 274–275; radical, 54, 55–56; and Americanization, 100–115; and African-Americans, 139, 282; and lynching, 147–152; and Caribbeans, 156, 157–158; and Jennings, 183; and science, 189; and Johnson-Reed Act (1924), 214–216; and national origins, 222–223, 227–228; and ethnicity, 259–266; and individual vs. group, 263, 277, 280
Polonsky, Abraham: *Tell Them Willie Boy Is Here,* 86
Populism, 74, 81
Poverty, 122, 130, 168
Powell, Adam Clayton, 239
Progressive, 3, 48, 98, 168, 169
Proposition 227, 272
Protestant, 17, 21, 37, 56, 85, 86
Prucha, Francis, 17–18, 86
Putnam, Robert, 117

Quota: development of, 11–12; institution of, 50; and Dillingham Commission, 76; and work, 79; and Laughlin, 135, 136; and social inadequacy, 176; and eugenics, 184, 187, 194; and Fairchild, 193; 1921 legislation for, 199, 200; and Johnson, 201; and census, 203, 204–205; and